THE HOLLOW MEN

THE HOLLOW MEN

A study in the politics of deception

Nicky Hager

CRAIG
POTTON
PUBLISHING

First published in 2006 by Craig Potton Publishing
98 Vickerman Street, PO Box 555, Nelson, New Zealand
www.craigpotton.co.nz

© Nicky Hager

ISBN 10: 1-877333-62-X
ISBN 13: 978-1-877333-62-0

Printed by Astra Print, Wellington, New Zealand

*Dedicated to the principled conservatives
in the New Zealand National Party*

CONTENTS

FOREWORD

In April 2006 someone inside the caucus of the Hungarian Socialist Party recorded Prime Minister Ferenc Gyurcsany at a closed sitting of his party. This is what he said: 'You cannot quote any significant government measure we can be proud of, other than at the end we managed to bring the government back from the brink. Nothing. If we have to give account to the country about what we did for four years, then what do we say? We lied in the morning; we lied in the evening.' Someone inside this caucus, like those National Party people who leaked material to Nicky Hager, wished for 'more principled and democratic behaviour' within the Socialist Party. Nicky is not alone in having had access to private communications, and making the choice to disclose.

The resulting book is extraordinarily comprehensive in its coverage of the topic. This is assisted by the range of correspondence and key informant information Nicky has amassed in the past three years. To my knowledge, there has been no New Zealand politics thesis containing this amount of detail. Nicky would never, though, have been able to enrol in a New Zealand university to write this as a thesis: because of the extraordinary access he has had to private and personal communications he would never have received ethics approval. And even if his enrolment were permitted, the thesis would have been buried alive and not made available to the public.

Nicky deals with this in his preface, and there should be concern about these extraordinary breaches of privacy. While none of the detail was surprising, the extent of the leaks was shocking to me.

But this must be balanced with the choices that faced those who possessed the material. Before emails, I was a sophisticated leaker, and I was also good at getting others to leak to me. Documents 'fell off trucks' and were 'left on photocopiers'. I believed I did this in the public interest. As a student of politics myself I studied *The Pentagon Papers* thanks to Daniel Ellsberg, and *All the President's Men*. Carl Bernstein and Bob Woodward were much lauded for their work in these leaks with former FBI official W. Mark Felt, and Woodward continues such disclosure in respect of the Iraq War. The Blair Cabinet leaks. Robert Noval leaked the identity of CIA agent Valerie Plame.

Nicky's approach is thorough. He generally assembles the subject matter in each 'case study' chronologically, so we can trace the emails, any other correspondence, the diary entries and the newspaper coverage, point by point. In the social sciences we call this 'sophisticated rigour' and Nicky would mark very highly in this respect. And *The Hollow Men* is a damn good read. Nicky writes well. The book is always accessible, never turgid. He handles a great deal of material very competently, and each chapter has its point and purpose.

In an effort to undermine and distract from the contents of *The Hollow Men*, Nicky will undoubtedly be criticised and called some lefty names. Some will try to find offence in the commentary he makes. There will be accusations that he has committed any number of breaches. There will be witch hunts and blaming and name calling. But this work meets some high academic standards. I also believe, as Nicky states in his preface, that this is a story about democracy, and the public of New Zealand deserve to know what they have when they speak of such an ideal. I would expect to see much of the evidence set out in the book reported to the Electoral Commission, Parliamentary Services, the police and the Auditor-General.

There is *nothing* in this book that surprises me. But I think only a few hundred people in New Zealand would be in this camp. My own history and my current work mean that I pay attention to this aspect of the world, and how democracy does or doesn't work. I would expect the content of *The Hollow Men* to be very shocking to a serious number of those in the current National caucus, people who ran in the election believing the 'inoculated' versions of policies, and were then advised that they 'owed' their marginal or party list win to Brash, which meant he couldn't be changed or challenged. (I'm not naïve enough to believe that there weren't also those who worked out exactly what was going down and liked it.) The book will also shock the good, genuine party people I remember from my own campaigning days, and those I know now – at my country golf club, for example – who support the National Party.

In some ways not a lot of the principles raised are new. There has always been church engagement in politics. The Catholic church was a big player in my years in Parliament. That tight cabal of Robert Muldoon, Wellington lawyer and SPUC president Des Dalgety and *Tablet* editor John Kennedy worked very closely together: the *Tablet* was at times a

Muldoon mouthpiece. Muldoon frequently pushed the *Tablet* position, on private schools for example, in caucus, so there's nothing new there. I always had a bill in my drawer ready for introduction to remove the tax-deductible status of their 'education' campaigns if they drove me too crazy. Dalgety was also very helpful to the government in the aftermath of the *Erebus* disaster as Muldoon had appointed him to the Board of Air New Zealand. There are a lot of untold stories there.

Those who paid attention could work out who the National Party's larger funders were. We were reminded about the brewery contribution every time a conscience bill came to the House on the drinking age or similar. The viticultural industry was cleverly even-handed in a party political sense, but a number of protected manufacturers were very close to Muldoon.

Nicky Hager describes the different person Don Brash has chosen to become. Politics can drive people to become 'other'. In *Three Masquerades* I wrote about this process happening to me and the self-contempt I developed figured largely in my own decision to leave politics – though the need to 'seize the moment' precipitated this departure a little earlier than I had presumed. Many women politicians have spoken and written about the pressure to become what you aren't, but generally they have meant a change in character, not a consciously contrived change in what they believed in and stood for, which was an invitation to lie constantly.

Politicians have been trained in dealing with the media for years, since the advent of television. 'Ignore the question and say the same thing over and over again' is not a new trick. I used to think that was all right, because I trusted the New Zealand public had enough information to see through the trick and into the shallow content. But with the popularity of talkback radio and the absence of good *journalism* as opposed to columnists, I now despair of that happening.

There's nothing new, either, about political parties going to an election with no intention of legislating for the policies they espouse. Sometimes this is also a consequence of their choosing ignorance. We find this every election in the human rights field, where there is always a raft of policies, especially from minor parties who are untroubled by such ethics, that contravene New Zealand's fundamental human rights obligations. The policy on criminal liability for children of twelve, to which Brash's wife Je Lan objected (see Chapter 7), is in this camp. And it will yet be demonstrated, as the Supreme Court found in Canada, that New Zealand's second-class Civil Union right is a breach of these fundamental principles.

These memories demonstrate why Nicky's book is so important. I can recall these events and patterns, but no one has ever held them up to the light, and it is time that this happened, so that New Zealanders can decide the nature of the democracy they want.

Of course, many of the events and communications recorded in *The Hollow Men* were legitimate, written by people going about their lawful business. We mightn't like their ideologies, but they would profess as genuine a love and concern for this country as I do. We just see it in a completely different way. But I don't have their business interests. (There's not too much conspiracy in some of the letters quoted from old politicians. I once wrote to John Banks agreeing with something he had said, but I certainly wouldn't want anything to be inferred about my political ideology from that!). There will undoubtedly be a lot of commentary of that nature, but Nicky has undertaken an excellent systems analysis. You cannot take isolated and separate instances away from the whole, and still make sense of the analysis. The constant build-up of data and texture means the book must be examined as a whole. I hope the reviewers will see that.

I must admit to a sense of anticipated despair about the treatment *The Hollow Men* might receive. Most of the people I know (and a number of them sit in parliamentary seats) are disgusted with the sandpit the House has become – and it was certainly this bad when I was an MP. We are desperate for a government and an opposition with policies that have content. We are desperate for intelligent debate about the wrinkles around the shades of grey that are the real choices. There's tremendous impatience from many of us with the present simplistic black/white approach. We feel ashamed that a country with such a basically decent and principled population can be so manipulated.

There's a real chance that both politicians and the media, and especially the talkback hosts, will see this book as more grist to the sensationalist mill. The focus may be on looking for and condemning the leakers, as opposed to scrutinising an appallingly mendacious political campaign. This is not the outcome Nicky intends. I am sure, as he notes, that there are unpleasant little stories in the emails of other political parties. They may be best to stay well away from the task that now lies in front of National. There have always been people of integrity, intelligence and liberal disposition in the National Party, and they have often been spurned for the cheap sensation of the poll-driven leader. But the country may now like the look of such a refreshingly different group of people: I always prefer the honesty of politicians who agonise in the grey areas.

In March 1984 I wrote a piece for the *New Zealand Listener* on 'Leaving Parliament'. Early in the essay I quoted from Adrienne Rich's writing in

Women and Honour: Some Notes on Lying: 'We assume that politicians are without honour. We read their statements trying to crack the code. The scandal of their politics. Not that men in high places lie, only that they do so with such indifference, so endlessly, still expecting to be believed. We are accustomed to the contempt inherent in the political life.'

It is my hope that the ultimate effect of *The Hollow Men* will be the return of honour and honesty to our democracy. I thank Nicky Hager for his courage and extraordinary hard work.

Marilyn Waring
1 November 2006

PREFACE

In September 2005, National Party leader Don Brash came within a hair's breadth of becoming New Zealand's prime minister and the National Party of controlling the government. News reports and commentators said National had run a good campaign, achieving the outstanding result of nearly doubling the party's electoral support. Some said Don Brash might have gone a bit far with policies that appeared anti-Maori, but overall his campaign had been remarkably successful.

Behind the scenes, however, some people in the National Party were profoundly unhappy with how some of this 'success' had been achieved. They believed that some of this 'good' campaigning had been so unprincipled and even unlawful that the country was lucky they had lost the election.

It is not uncommon for there to be conflicting views and even fierce differences within a political party, but in this case these people were willing to back up their allegations with proof. Over two years they fronted up with evidence – internal reports, emails, travel itineraries and meeting minutes – documenting the inside story of Don Brash's rise to leadership and many details of how National went about trying to gain power.

Collected together, these inside papers give an unprecedented look at the workings of a political party, the tactics it used to try to win power and the identities and influence of the financial backers whose money nearly won the election. It is apparent why the people were prepared to leak internal party business. The story that emerges is an extraordinary case study of unprincipled and anti-democratic politics: repeated cases of deceiving the public, hidden agendas, dodgy election finance issues and, underlying it all, a deeply cynical approach to winning the votes of those whom Brash described as the 'punters out in punterland'.

It is not that the activities and themes described in this book have never happened before: such cynicism is found to varying degrees in most eras and parties. But this study of the National Party covers a period of

extremely cynical political behaviour. And what is unique is the opportunity it offers to observe politics up close and in the politicians' own
words. *The Hollow Men* covers the term of one National Party leader,
from his rise to power until what appears (at the time of writing) to be
his approaching demise. But though the story is about the politicians and
political staff at a particular point in New Zealand history – from 2003 to
2006 – the themes and insights into techniques and strategies are relevant
to all modern politics, in New Zealand and beyond.

Some important issues arise concerning the use of leaked materials.
The first is checking the motives of those who provide it. After spending
many hours with these people, in series of meetings, I am confident that
their primary motivation for releasing the information to me was a wish
for more principled and democratic behaviour in the National Party. The
sources were approached separately and were acting independently. They
considered providing documentary evidence only when we had built up
trust and talked through the reasons for writing the book.

Second, there is the question of the legitimacy of using leaked material.
Among the documents I received was incidental personal information.
Some of this would perhaps have been picked out first by some news
organisations, but I believe that the people concerned have an overriding
right to privacy in these matters and it has not been included. I believe
that leaking information to the public can be justified only when there
is a strong public interest. Readers will be amazed at the level of detail
and some will wonder whether such secret party business should be made
public. The intrusion is permissible because of the scale of dishonesty and
unprincipled behaviour it reveals. There is no other way that the public
and electoral authorities could ever get to learn about these things.

Moreover, the activities brought to light involve public figures, all of
whom enjoy high salaries paid by the public and who wanted the ultimate privilege of being entrusted with control of the entire government.
Many of these people will run for office again. In government, they would
control the nation's public assets and services, have wide powers to make
laws and send people to war and generally shape the country we live in.
Informing the public about their beliefs, attitudes and actions is not only
desirable but necessary.

The origin of this book can be pinpointed exactly to Tuesday, 27 January 2004. When the news was broadcast of Don Brash's controversial but
poll-lifting 'Nationhood' speech at the Orewa Rotary Club, I was curious
about the political calculations that seemed to lie behind its claims about
'race-based privilege'. My first impressions of Brash as National Party

leader had been of a principled right-wing politician. But here he was, a millionaire belonging to the social group that enjoys most privilege, in his first major speech as leader, subtly attacking many of the poorest people in New Zealand. What was going on? My interest grew. I wanted to understand National – what they believed in, who had influence on the party and their methods of trying to gain power. But at the beginning I simply decided that, if I could somehow find the necessary sources, I would make it a priority to research Don Brash and the National Party.

It was some months before I heard about and met the first potential National Party sources. Since then, by separate routes, I have had extensive contact with others. Over time they provided the many documents quoted in this book.

I gave some of this information to other journalists before the 2005 election. The sources agreed that, since this present book was then far from completion, I could pass their information on so that the public might know more about Don Brash before they voted. The documents included emails and faxes showing that Brash, who was being presented to the electorate as a mild centrist politician, had been helped into the party leadership by a surprising network of people from the ACT Party and the New Zealand Business Roundtable – that is, the far right of New Zealand politics. These 'leaked National Party emails' were in the news in late August and early September 2005.

Following those news stories, there were some separate leaks of National Party material, to media organisations and to an MP, in which I was not involved. To avoid unnecessary speculation, I should say that none of my sources provided information to achieve any kind of personal political advantage.

The leaked papers came from the highest levels of the National Party hierarchy, centred on the leader Don Brash. He was an almost obsessive email writer, often spending hours each day writing and replying to correspondence. Many of these emails were leaked, as were numerous other types of documents produced by his staff. And the closer those staff were to Brash, the more documentation there was about them and their communications.

The underlying theme of the book is the conduct of politicians and others in politics – how their strategies, expediencies and the games they play to advance themselves can harm the whole political system. Short-term political necessities get in the way of the long-term good of the country. The chapters that follow show how easy it is to spin and manipulate and how our defences as a society (news media, electoral laws and so on) are inadequate to protect the public. This in turn creates the situation where many people 'don't like politics' and leave it to the politicians – and if anything is clear from this story it is that politics should not be left to the politicians. The story is, in essence, about democracy – that ideal everyone in politics applauds and few respect.

This book is about the New Zealand National Party, but if you could look inside Labour and other parties, many of the same themes would apply. It also raises fundamental questions about private influence and power in New Zealand. Revealed in these pages are the identities and motives of the main National Party donors – none of whom are ever declared publicly. Their money is one of the means by which these radical right reformers of the 1980s and 1990s – the key figures behind the privatisation, deregulation and cuts of social services – retain influence within the National Party and, through it, over New Zealand politics.

Those 'reforms' allowed foreign companies to buy up most major New Zealand businesses, lowered income and job security for many people by reducing employment protections, left the public health system in crisis, introduced youth pay rates and university fees and, in these and many other ways, scuttled hopes for an egalitarian society. The rift between richer and poorer New Zealanders has been widening ever since.

The book's title comes from the T.S. Eliot poem of that name. It was published in 1925, not long after the First World War, when he was feeling disillusioned with contemporary society and politicians. Early in the 21st century many in New Zealand and elsewhere feel the same.

Philosophy and ideology have helped to create a type of politics that disappoints and repels many ordinary people. But this book is not about the inevitability of expedient and unprincipled politics. Understanding what is wrong means things do not have to remain that way.

While reading the following chapters, be aware of how rare it is to see the way politicians behave when they confidently believe that they are acting in secret. The public is usually fed an unnutritious diet of scripted media statements, clever advertisements and practised denials. This is a chance, thanks to the National Party sources, to see and judge for yourself some of what really goes on.

ACKNOWLEDGMENTS

This book has been a group effort, contributed to by an outstanding variety of people. First there were those in and near the National Party. Six people in particular provided most of the information and trusted me with telling the story. I hope the book lives up to what I told them I was trying to achieve.

Many others made it a much better book than it would otherwise have been, including those who commented on the drafts and who responded generously to my requests for information. In particular I am blessed with an exceptional publishing team: Steven Price for legal advice, Anna Rogers as editor, Peter Dorn and the staff at Astra Print, and Craig Potton, Tina Delceg, Gwen Redshaw, Arnott Potter and Phillippa Duffy at Craig Potton Publishing. I am especially grateful to Robbie Burton, Managing Director and Publisher at Craig Potton Publishing, for his support over many years.

Thanks, finally, to the friends who helped to support me financially and in other ways during two years' work on the book, to my three remarkable sisters – Debbie Hager, Mandy Hager and Belinda Hager – and to Julia Wells for her daily encouragement and good humour.

CHAPTER 1

THE PATH OF PRINCIPLE
National and the Exclusive Brethren

On the evening of Monday 7 August 2006 the leader of the New Zealand National Party, Don Brash, gave a strong speech about the difference between his party and the Labour government. 'In our quest for victory, we choose the harder path, the path of principle and persuasion over the path of bribery and corruption,' he told his Christchurch audience. 'Corruption is not a word you use outside Parliament without being very sure of your ground. But I feel very safe, if rather sad, in pointing out that Helen Clark's Labour government is quite simply the most corrupt government in New Zealand history.'[1]

These were lines he was soon repeating in Parliament, as National MPs launched increasingly loud attacks on the government's integrity. Prime Minister Helen Clark had 'misappropriate[d] half a million dollars of taxpayers' money to fund her campaign'. His colleagues, following an obviously pre-arranged plan, chanted, 'Pay the money back! Pay the money back!' Brash went on: 'Helen Clark stole the election.... She should pay the money back.... She should then resign, go to the country and have a fair election.'[2] The scandal revealed 'a degree of corruption and dishonesty never before seen in New Zealand politics'.[3]

Labour deserved to be attacked over the use of its Parliamentary Services budget for electioneering (its election pledge card). It had stretched the rules beyond credibility, and was later forced to pay back hundreds of thousands of dollars. But what made the National Party attacks remarkable – in fact, breathtakingly audacious – was that these politicians had guilty election secrets of their own. The senior members of the National Party obviously believed that their own unprincipled and unlawful actions, and their dishonesty, would never come back to haunt them.

The story begins at the most dramatic moment of New Zealand's 2005 election, when Brash was forced to admit that his party knew in advance about a controversial Exclusive Brethren-funded election advertising campaign. He had spent the week denying any knowledge of this or any links to it but by late morning on the Thursday, strained and exasperated, he admitted to journalists that he had known about it after all. He insisted that he was 'not a liar' and said he had only been told about the plans in a brief meeting with Exclusive Brethren representatives a few weeks earlier. But that was not true and nor were the statements made by his colleagues. The way politicians and political staff respond to a sudden crisis and unwelcome publicity tells us much about whether they follow the path of principle.

The first hint of interaction between National and the Exclusive Brethren was an obscure item on the agenda of National's Campaign Strategy Meeting on Tuesday, 5 April 2005. Held in the National Party's 'War Room', on the second floor of the old Parliament Building, the meeting began with more internal polling results showing National still stuck behind Labour. The campaign team, which consisted of five middle-aged men, faced the perennial problem that, if only men voted, they would be neck and neck with Labour. If only middle-aged men voted, they would be set to win that year's election resoundingly. But once women voters were added, National was well behind.

The five campaign strategists who gathered that afternoon are central to the story. Murray McCully, assistant to the leader, had long before gained control of the party's strategy and was deferred to by everyone on matters of tactics and spin. Gerry Brownlee, deputy leader, was a bull of a man who was relied upon to play the attack role in Parliament. Steven Joyce, the campaign manager, was a millionaire businessman turned party official who oversaw fundraising and all campaign activities. Richard Long, chief of staff, was in charge of media management and Peter Keenan was chief strategist and speechwriter for Brash.

One of the items on the agenda that Tuesday was the bland-sounding 'Outside Groups – Defence and Education', which referred to quiet contact between National and various seemingly independent 'outside groups' that supported the party and were willing to provide support to its election campaign. The 'education' part referred to relationships between National and the private schools lobby, the New Zealand Business Roundtable's Education Forum and the Auckland-based thinktank Maxim.[4] National had produced policies promising, once it was in government, to shift money from public to private schools; these lobby groups were planning actions to help National win the election.

But what was the 'Defence' part?

Unbeknown to the rest of New Zealand, a large anonymously funded advertising campaign was scheduled to begin at the end of that week – early April 2005 – stridently attacking Labour's defence and anti-nuclear policies. The ads would be saying things that many senior National Party people privately believed, but which they could not say openly without losing public support. Only the National Party campaign strategy team (and possibly the right-wing ACT Party) had received prior warning of the advertising and knew who was behind it.

The campaign involved delivery of about a million pamphlets to homes around the country and large advertisements in major newspapers. Headed 'Wake-up call for all New Zealanders', they called for repeal of the 'illogical, impractical and totally unrealistic' nuclear ship ban, said the Iraq War was a case of the United States using its military power 'for the good of mankind' and urged closer alliance with the United States, 'bastion of the free world'. They accused the Prime Minister (incorrectly) of reducing the country's defence spending and said that 'as a result New Zealand is practically defenceless'.[5] The only contact on the pamphlets and advertisements was 'A. Smith' at an Auckland post office box address, giving no way to identify or reach anyone involved.[6]

The $350,000 for this anti-Labour government campaign came from such a strange and unlikely source that no one even guessed: the small Exclusive Brethren church, whose members do not vote and who, for much of their history, have stayed away from involvement in worldly politics.[7]

On the morning of the strategy meeting, chief of staff Richard Long had sent an email to Don Brash, Gerry Brownlee and other senior MPs: 'It might pay the caucus to know that the Brethren advertising campaign to repair defence links (bring back the ships) will start this Friday'. Long said the Brethren had 'agreed today to publicly take ownership of the campaign, to avoid conspiracy theories and to prevent the finger being pointed at us'. National was trying hard to avoid being questioned about its nuclear policy views during an election year.

Long, a former editor of Wellington's *Dominion* newspaper, had arranged with the Brethren that they would have a consistent line in the event of media questions about National's prior knowledge of the advertising. He wrote to Brash and Brownlee: 'To other questions, on whether they consulted us, the [Brethren] have agreed to say that they have advised all political parties'. It is hard to believe that National really thought the Exclusive Brethren had told Labour about the campaign. Long advised on what MPs should say if questioned on links to the advertisements. 'I suggest we and our MPs should say simply that it is a church campaign, National is certainly not sponsoring it. We did know in advance it was going ahead as we were advised along with, as we understand it, all political parties.'[8]

Later that week Long wrote again, reminding Brash of the agreed line over prior knowledge of the advertisements: 'Don, just a reminder that the Brethren adverts start tomorrow (in the *NZ Herald*) in case you get questions. Suggestion: I understand this is a campaign by members of the Brethren Church. My staff and other political parties were, I understand, informed in advance that it was planned.'[9]

Long's lines were not required. The Brethren's involvement remained anonymous and secret. The National Party people kept their knowledge of the anti-Labour campaign to themselves. The Exclusive Brethren and National's campaign committee now knew it was possible to have hundreds of thousands of dollars of third-party political advertising without having to reveal to the public who was behind it.[10]

The sudden rise in Exclusive Brethren political activism can be traced to the world head of the church – known as the Elect Vessel and the Lord's Representative on Earth – Bruce Hales, who took control when his father died in 2002. The Exclusive Brethren are strictly hierarchical and no major decisions are made without Hales's approval or direction. Ex-members have described how, some years ago, the Elect Vessel ordered that all Exclusive Brethren leave South Africa, and they did. In New Zealand they were similarly instructed to leave the suburb of Miramar and move to the northern Wellington suburbs, which they also obediently did.

Soon after Hales took control, anonymous Brethren political advertising started to appear in different countries simultaneously. In the weeks before the Australian election of October 2004, anonymous brochures and newspaper advertisements appeared in various parts of Australia backing Liberal leader and Prime Minister John Howard and attacking the Labor and Green Parties. No one realised at the time that they were from the Exclusive Brethren. In the United States the Brethren's Thanksgiving 2004 Committee spent hundreds of thousands of dollars on newspaper advertisements supporting George Bush and a Republican Senate candidate from Florida, Mel Martinez.[11] At the same time as the New Zealand 'Wake-up call' campaign, leaflets and newspaper advertisements throughout Canada attacked MPs who supported same-sex marriage legislation. This vigorous campaign was sponsored by an untraceable group called Concerned Canadian Parents, using a post office box in a Toronto Seven-Eleven convenience store.[12] Only many months later was the Brethren link uncovered. Campaigns in other countries followed and there are probably more such campaigns in countries with Exclusive Brethren communities that have not yet been linked to the church.[13] Each of the known campaigns cost in the vicinity of a million dollars, none mentioned the Exclusive Brethren and, at least for a while, they succeeded in remaining anonymous.

It was no coincidence that the New Zealand Exclusive Brethren started the same kind of anonymous campaigning at the same time. The first example of this was during 2004, when the church joined a range of other fundamentalist Christian groups opposing the Labour government's Civil Union Bill. Now law, this provided for a new legal form of marriage (without using that word) for de facto and same-sex couples.

Exclusive Brethren advertising appeared in December 2004, urging all MPs 'to recognise the Supremacy of God' and not 'institutionalise immorality' by voting for the bill.[14] We know from internal National Party communications that Don Brash and his staff had contact with the Exclusive Brethren by then and were tipped off about the anti-Civil Union Bill advertising. When an advertisement appeared in the Wellington newspaper on 9 December 2004, Brash's assistant Bryan Sinclair wrote: 'full page ad in today's Dom Post is your Brethren friends'.[15] Brash dropped his support for the bill just before the final vote in Parliament (see Chapter 4).

As with the later campaign, this advertisement gave no hint of the Brethren involvement. It was 'authorised' by ten named husbands and wives and included the post office box number of an Auckland office furniture company.[16] Several of those named people were prominent Brethren whose identities emerged during the election campaign but at that stage no one appeared to have recognised the Exclusive Brethren involvement.

Contacts between the Brethren and National became increasingly frequent after Brash's change of heart about the Civil Union Bill. At noon on Monday 14 February 2005 he agreed to meet Doug Watt and 'his colleagues from the Brethren Church' in his parliamentary office. At that point, however, some National Party staff were sceptical about the worth of contact with the Brethren. While discussing the planned meeting, appointments secretary Anne Small wrote to Don Brash: 'Personally,

I question the wisdom of devoting time to a group of people who don't vote and who won't contribute financially'. She suggested they be inflexible about the meeting date offered and only give the Brethren 45 minutes. She appeared to have organised meetings with them before as she noted her wish 'to restrict their time (give them an inch, they take a mile!)'.[17] Chief of staff Richard Long questioned Don Brash's openness to the Brethren later in February. 'Anne turned down the repeat visit from the Brethren, but you responded positively to a direct approach. Complete waste of time.'[18] But discussions were soon occurring on the Brethren's election advertising campaign and the contact between National and the church accelerated over the last six months before the election.

The next contacts were between National Party staff and the Brethren about the 'Wake-up call' campaign in April 2005 and then, two weeks after that, Brash met them again to receive 'a package' during a visit to South Auckland, which is one of the Exclusive Brethren strongholds, particularly around Mangere Bridge. National's Manurewa candidate, Fepulea'i Ulua'ipou-O-Malo Aiono, contacted Brash's parliamentary office to pass on the request for the meeting.

Ms Aiono, herself a member of the Mount Zion Assembly of God and a volunteer for the Otahuhu Salvation Army Corps,[19] wrote to Bryan Sinclair on 21 April 2005 saying she had 'just received a phone call from the Closed Brethren in South Auckland. They would like three minutes with Dr Brash on Saturday at some point in private and to deliver a package.' Sinclair replied: 'On the Brethren, not sure where they can do this. There is not really any private meeting place at Otara markets.... Can they please make themselves known to me/you at the markets? I am sure we can find a spot away from the crowd where he could receive their package (as long as it is nothing bad!!!) at, say, 11am just before he departs. They are welcome to call me on the day.'[20]

This became the pattern for a series of meetings over the following months, when Exclusive Brethren representatives and Brash would snatch opportunities for meetings as he was travelling and electioneering. He met Doug Watt and Ron Hickmott at a Chamber of Commerce breakfast address at Christchurch's Millennium Hotel on 24 May, Andy Smith (the 'A. Smith' of the advertisements and pamphlets) at a Napier Chamber of Commerce luncheon on the Mission Estate the following day and, later, senior Brethren in the Koru Club Lounge at Wellington Airport.

There is no record of what was in the package handed over at the Otara Markets but from this time on discussions were under way about the Brethren's planned election activities – particularly their advertising campaign that would dwarf the previous Civil Union and 'Wake-up call' activities and create the greatest controversy of the 2005 election.

At the same time, Exclusive Brethren communities throughout the country began offering other forms of campaign support to National. Electorate by electorate, small delegations of church members approached the local National MP or candidate. According to National Party insiders, many MPs and candidates accepted financial contributions from the Brethren for their personal election campaign funds. This was centrally directed by the Brethren hierarchy. Because candidate donations of $1,000 or less do not have to be declared it is unlikely that a single one of these donations had to be made visible to the public. The only MPs known to have refused the offer of money were Katherine Rich, Maurice Williamson and Simon Power, who later told TV3 that he had 'politely declined' the Exclusive Brethren donations, telling them he already had enough money.[21]

Brethren-owned companies displayed National Party hoardings on their land and gave candidates free and cheap services. Church members provided a supply of committed volunteers nationwide to help with National Party telephone canvassing, delivering party literature and erecting election hoardings. All this assistance added up to a huge contribution to National's election campaign.

A few National Party MPs and candidates had misgivings about the Exclusive Brethren support. The subject was discussed by the caucus at least once but, with the leadership and most MPs behind it, there was no chance that the party would turn down all this money and free help. Most MPs and candidates were simply pleased to get the donations, hoarding sites and volunteers. The assumption was that as long as the public did not know about the Exclusive Brethren links they could not hurt National.

During May 2005 Exclusive Brethren representatives had a series of discussions with National over the planned election advertising. Don Brash met Exclusive Brethren representatives in Christchurch on 24 May and Napier on 25 May and, in the week of 16–20 May, campaign manager Steven Joyce had a formal meeting with the Brethren who were organising the advertising campaign.[22]

As will be seen later in the book, Joyce met quietly with other pro-National lobby organisations at this time to suggest how they could most effectively direct their assistance. His two crucial messages were that they should emphasise the party vote and that they use the phrase 'Change the government'. If 'independent' advertising said 'Change the government', National could then say 'and the only way to change the government is to party vote National', which it proceeded to do on every possible occasion. In this way third-party campaigns could effectively boost the National Party advertising budget and get more votes for National while keeping a sufficient distance to avoid declaration as part of the party's campaign spending. It seems likely that Joyce gave the same advice to the Exclusive Brethren and those are the words that were used in their advertisements.

Shortly after the meeting with Joyce, on 24 May the Exclusive Brethren recorded their plans in writing and sent copies to Don Brash and finance spokesman John Key. (Brash forwarded it to Steven Joyce.) Headed 'Urgent, Important and Strictly Confidential', the letter began: 'Good afternoon Don and John, Doug Watt and myself enjoyed your presentation this morning at Millennium Hotel'. They reminded them that they were 'backers of the recent "Wake Up NZ" campaign', which they said had cost $350,000, and said it was important that they met Brash and Key soon to talk about their next project: 'a very extensive election campaign ($1,000,000) with the sole goal of "Getting Party Votes for National"'. They noted this meeting would follow on from one with Steven Joyce the previous week.

> Basically, we believe marketing is the name of the game. Whilst the meeting this morning was excellent it would not have got one extra vote for National. (Everyone there is going to vote National anyway). Getting the message out and to a younger age bracket is paramount.
>
> We believe time is of the essence. Our campaign (a total of seven nationally distributed flyers) is direct and simple:–
>
> It creates and demonstrates MISTRUST in the current Government.
>
> It builds TRUST in a DON BRASH led National Government.

The letter ended by repeating that the Brethren wanted a meeting with Brash and Key 'at your earliest convenience anywhere in New Zealand'. The writer, Rangiora Brethren Ron Hickmott, provided phone numbers where he could be contacted and told them he was essentially working on what he called 'our/your election campaign' full-time.[23]

The letter appears to have been the culmination of three sets of National Party–Exclusive Brethren discussions. In addition to separate meetings with Brash and Joyce, the Brethren had also had contact with John Key.

A meeting between Key and two Exclusive Brethren was caught on film shortly before the letter, in early May, when a TVNZ current affairs team was following Key for the day. TVNZ identified the men as Exclusive Brethren but they were unhappy about the presence of the cameras and were shown arranging to return when the filming was over. The programme showed them with their faces pixilated and they were identified only as Andrew and Nick.[24] One of them, however, appeared to be senior Brethren member Andrew Simmons, one of the main organisers of the election advertising campaign and joint owner of the company that had provided the address for the anti-Civil Union Bill advertising.

Brash was well aware what the Brethren were offering and the legal issues surrounding third-party advertising. On the same day that the Brethren letter arrived, Brash happened to be writing about another plan for third-party advertising involving his friend Diane Foreman, businesswoman and deputy chair of the New Zealand Business Roundtable, with whom he was later alleged to have had an affair. He said he had checked out 'whether people could fund "parallel campaigns" outside the scope of the limit on electoral expenses and I understand that that is feasible, provided that the funding and control are clearly not directed by the National Party (which would mean we would need to be careful to be "arms length")'. He said: 'I guess the stuff which the Exclusive Brethren are doing is one example'.[25]

The Electoral Act 1993 specifically says that no person can publish – or cause or permit to be published – newspaper advertisements or pamphlets which encourage or appear to encourage voters to vote for a political party unless the advertising is authorised by the secretary of the party. One of the points of this law is to ensure that parties cannot exceed their election spending limits by having others advertise for them. Election spending limits have an important democratic function, which is to try to avoid elections being won and lost according to who has the biggest advertising budget. The various possible breaches of the electoral laws arising from the Exclusive Brethren advertising campaign are looked at in Chapter 15.

National was aware not only of the plans, but of the potential legal problems. It appears they raised these issues with the Brethren after receiving the formal letter in late May. In early June the author of the Brethren letter, Ron Hickmott, phoned Chief Electoral Officer David Henry to arrange a meeting. He explained in a follow-up email that he was one of a group of 'Christian businessmen' planning a $1.2 million election programme with the goal of getting party votes for National: 'we write seeking clarification and direction re the election funding issue, specifically that anything we do does not compromise National's funding position'.[26]

Hickmott asked, 'does it compromise National's position if we communicate to MPs and candidates our strategy?', knowing of course that they already had. He also wanted to know: 'does it compromise National's position if we show them draft publications before they are published?' At that stage the Brethren were planning to have pamphlets with Don Brash's photograph and also asked if they could do this without compromising National's funding position.[27] David Henry organised a meeting with Hickmott and three colleagues for 14 June 2005. He commented to his Electoral Office colleagues in a letter that it was 'clear that on the basis of their current proposal the advertising will have to be authorised by National and will form part of National's election expenses'.[28] The conclusion of that meeting is not known.

The Exclusive Brethren letter to Brash and Key arrived nearly four months before the election. After that the Brethren were working on the designs and wording of their seven pamphlets and the newspaper advertisements. During June they regularly discussed their plans with the National Party.

These meetings were conducted very confidentially, but some hints of what was going on are evident in internal National Party communications to Brash's assistant, Bryan Sinclair. In June, National's Napier electorate campaign manager, Simon Lusk, wrote to Sinclair, passing on various pieces of news about conversations between National Party MPs and the Exclusive Brethren. 'Bryan, make sure you talk to Don/[Northland MP] John Carter about the discussion John had today in Napier – some very interesting stuff to do with defence and the guy you met up here.'[29]

It becomes clear in following emails that 'the guy you met up here' refers to an Exclusive Brethren member, which means it was Andy Smith. The 'interesting stuff to do with defence' referred to an Exclusive Brethren-funded opinion poll that supposedly found public support for dropping the nuclear-free policy. The Brethren offered the poll to National but Richard Long told his colleagues it looked 'dodgy'. The ACT Party subsequently released the poll to the *Herald on Sunday*, saying it was from 'a group of concerned New Zealanders'.[30]

Lusk then wrote: 'Bryan, make sure you find out about what they are going to do with the Greens'. The Brethren 'dusted up the Greens in Tasmania, did a good job there', and so were 'considering... going after the Greens' in New Zealand as well. This shows that by early June National

MPs had been told about the Brethren's proposed anti-Green Party advertising and confirms the link with anti-Green leaflets that were distributed
anonymously in Tasmania the year before. The September 2005 New
Zealand and October 2004 Tasmanian anti-Green Exclusive Brethren
pamphlets were almost identical. Lusk went on to express concern about
anti-Green campaigning because he was counting on Green voters to split
the vote in Napier and help his National candidate win. 'They could hurt
our chances in Napier if they go after the Greens,' he wrote, 'we need as
many Greens votes as possible to win the electorate race.'[31]

Two weeks later, another Lusk email reveals that actual copies of the
Exclusive Brethren election advertisements were being shown to National
Party MPs. 'Bryan some of the ads we were discussing in Napier were
shown to a selection of MPs yesterday. Apparently there were some very
nervous people after hearing them.'[32] The reason for the nervousness was
not explained.

These documents confirm that, months before the election campaign,
National Party MPs and staff – who would later earnestly deny any knowledge – were fully aware of the Exclusive Brethren advertising campaign
plans and that at least some MPs had seen the draft publications. They
or at least Bryan Sinclair were bound to have shared this with the party
leadership. The emails also suggest that the advertisements were discussed
face-to-face with Brash and Sinclair when they visited Napier on 25 May
2005, the day after they received Ron Hickmott's letter.

Each of the Exclusive Brethren pamphlets was very focused on that 'sole
goal of Getting Party Votes for National'. They showed voting ticks in
boxes in blue and ended with the slogan 'Use your party vote to change
the government' or equivalent words.[33] Some pamphlets attacked the
Labour government, the Green Party or the Progressive MP Jim Anderton
and said it was time for a 'new and responsible government'. Others were
entirely promoting a change of government.

One of the pamphlets, which was delivered over the final weekend
before the election, was headed 'Claim your seat to watch the ALL BLACK
action!' and pictured a crowded rugby ground. It suggested that, with tax
cuts, 'you could fly to Aussie and watch the ALL BLACKS every time!'
Inside was a list of other things voters could buy from a tax cut – a new
car, new clothes, a Caribbean cruise – if they 'use [their] party vote to
change the government'.[34] The main party campaigning on the promise
of tax cuts was, of course, National.

Another pamphlet was headed 'A NEW LEADER with integrity is
urgently needed if New Zealand is to move forward and prosper'. The
content of this one is indistinguishable from official National Party election publications. Its list of six key issues is the same as National's and
uses the same kinds of words as National election publications. 'Social
engineering and political correctness' in education 'has to go'. 'Choose
a new leadership team that has the courage to spend roading money on
roads.' Lower taxes 'will return money to hard-working kiwi battlers
where it belongs.'[35]

These advertisements were unlike anything the Exclusive Brethren
had done before or have produced since. Their other publications spoke
of the 'Supremacy of God' and the sanctity of marriage.[36] Then suddenly
the church was saying that tax cuts could help voters fly to see the All
Blacks in Aussie. This does not sound like Exclusive Brethren. They are not
allowed to attend large sports events and do not believe in self-gratifying
consumerism. They are not big spenders on clothes. This was an appeal to
the Supremacy of Mammon, not the Supremacy of God – an expedient
exercise in buying the votes of some floating voters. It seems highly likely
they had received outside help.

Did the National Party have input into the Brethren advertisements?
The internal documents provide no answer but some good guesses can be
made. Since we know that the Exclusive Brethren met the National Party
campaign manager, Steven Joyce, and were showing the draft pamphlets
and advertisements to other MPs, it is highly likely that National had at
least some input and may have had a lot. The National Party people were
all highly focused on anything that could enhance or detract from their
election chances. It seems highly likely that they would have taken an
opportunity, if offered, to make the Brethren materials more helpful for
their campaign.

About two months before the election, a senior National Party source
gave an intriguing, and worried, hint. 'There is something I cannot tell
you about, but it's our biggest risk in the campaign. If it comes out, we're
sunk.' When the Exclusive Brethren's pro-National advertising hit the
news ten days before the election, the person said wryly, 'Remember that
thing I mentioned? Well, this is it.'[37]

The effectiveness of the Exclusive Brethren campaign was based on
being able to keep their role and contacts with National completely secret.
Until then they had got away with anonymous political advertising both

overseas and in New Zealand. They hoped and expected to do so again, and very nearly did.

The campaign for the Australian election served as the model for the New Zealand activities. Australian Exclusive Brethren advertisements and pamphlets were 'authorised' by unknown individuals at obscure or incorrect addresses. No organisations were named. The advertisements arrived without warning shortly before the election and the election had passed before anyone managed to track some of the advertisements back to the church.[38]

In New Zealand two pamphlets were authorised by a man using his middle rather than first name and no street number.[39] Another two used an address where no such person was known.[40] One was supposedly from a group called New Zealand Advocates for Timely Healthcare, which does not appear to have any existence outside the pamphlet. Another attacking Labour's coalition partner, Progressive MP Jim Anderton, was delivered to his Wigram electorate the day before the election, bearing the address of an empty shop a few doors from Anderton's home.[41] And so on. The Brethren had formed a front company called Strategic Information Services Limited to hide the financial backers of the campaign.[42] The obvious intention was that no one would trace the advertising back to the church, at least until the election was safely over.

But the news did get out. There are no people more aware and critical of Exclusive Brethren church activities than former members. Once the first anonymous leaflets appeared prominently in the news media, ex-Exclusive Brethren started to recognise names. Some of them decided to tip off Television New Zealand and TV3 reporters and the Green Party, providing a copy of the April 2003 Exclusive Brethren 'New Zealand Address Book', which included the names on the brochures. Only three days after the first pamphlet appeared, five people named on the brochures were publicly identified as being Exclusive Brethren and it quickly became the biggest controversy of the election.

After all the months of preparation, the first pamphlet arrived in letterboxes on Saturday, 3 September 2005. Headed 'Beware!', it warned that the Green Party was 'economically unsustainable', 'socially destructive' and 'downright dangerous'. Radio New Zealand reported Green Party co-leader Jeanette Fitzsimons recalling anti-Green leaflets produced by National in the previous election and 'challeng[ing] the National leader Don Brash to state categorically the party had nothing to do with the pamphlet'.[43]

National's first reaction was the typical one used by politicians when they believe their opponents and the media have no proof of an allegation: they confidently denied involvement. When approached by reporters on the Monday, Don Brash said they 'totally had nothing to do with' the pamphlets.[44]

As usual, the issue was monitored and responses were co-ordinated by the National Party media staff. On Saturday afternoon media officer Anita Ferguson sent an email to the leader's staff: 'TVNZ is chasing a story about a brochure put out bagging the Greens.... Jeanette Fitzsimmons has called on all party leaders and especially Don to come clean and categorically say they have nothing to do with it'. She said, 'TV wanted Don but couldn't have him. I passed them on to Steven [Joyce] who has basically said as far as he's aware [the person named on the pamphlet, Stephen Win] isn't a National Party guy and it certainly isn't a National-funded campaign because if it was it would have to be authorised by him. From Don I have said that it has absolutely nothing to do with National and as far as he (Don) is aware he has never met Stephen Win.'

At this stage the staff were relaxed. The assumption was that, like previous Brethren advertising, this would remain anonymous and the media would lose interest. Ferguson concluded: 'there is a chance this will be pursued tomorrow.... I wanted Don to say "If you want to talk dirty politics you have come to the wrong political party" but he wasn't keen. Maybe he could lead in with that if asked tomorrow. Just wanted to let you know what has been said.'[45]

When questioned by reporters on the Monday, Brash used the suggested line: 'If you're interested in talking about dirty tricks, you've come to the wrong party'.[46] And his denials were categorical. He told TV3: 'The National Party has had nothing to do with the pamphlets or the pamphlet drop at all'. When the reporter asked, 'Do you know who's responsible for it?', Brash replied, 'No, I do not'.[47]

During that day the two main National election strategists, Steven Joyce and Murray McCully, began to feel nervous about the possibility of trouble over the pamphlets. Brash's denials were based on the assumption that the secrecy surrounding the planning and preparation of the pamphlets would hold. As a precaution, they cancelled a long-planned meeting between Brash and church leaders of several denominations scheduled for later that week in case it ended up being exactly the wrong background for some unwelcome media stories.[48]

The following day, Tuesday 6 September, thanks to the former church members, the strange fact that the Exclusive Brethren were behind the smear campaign hit the news. That evening, Richard Long wrote to his media staff warning that reporters 'will be pushing [Don] tomorrow on when and who he met and what they talked about. TV1 even wanted to provide a list of names of people for Don to say whether he had met.'

These were Long's instructions for handling the issue: 'It's best to be open and frank and someone else, eg Gerry or Steven, should divert the debate into Labour's links and funding with the unions and should Labour explain and release their email traffic with the unions, and their misinformation etc. National was NOT involved with this, but Labour IS involved with the mass union disinformation campaign. Can you please onpass to Murray/Steven/Gerry.'[49]

As the head of 'spin' for the National Party leader's office, one of Long's main jobs was scripting the words used by the politicians when talking to journalists. Long always referred to these as 'lines', a term borrowed appropriately from the world of theatre and fiction. The Exclusive Brethren lines his staff prepared for Brash that evening were as follows.

Q. Exclusive Brethren have been involved with phone canvassing for the National Party?

A. We have lots of different people from all denominations and all walks of life working on our campaign. We are a broad church party with wide spread appeal in mainstream New Zealand.

Q. Have John Key and Don Brash met with members of the Exclusive Brethren at campaign meetings? What influence has the church had on the campaign?

A. Dr Brash has met with the leaders of most church groups in the past few months. He has listened to their concerns and to the concerns of many different groups of New Zealanders.

Q. Did anyone in the National Party have any knowledge of these pamphlets?

A. Well, I can't speak for the tens of thousands of party members all around the country but I can assure you that the party's governing body had absolutely no knowledge of the material you describe, and neither did the leader or any other member of the caucus.[50]

Brash and his colleagues stuck to these lines the next day – Wednesday 7 September – even after the Exclusive Brethren held a press conference acknowledging their backing of the campaign and mentioning that they had met Brash during the previous month. After the Brethren said they had met him, Brash confirmed having an August meeting but said they had offered only 'prayerful support'. (When the on-line news service NewsRoom reported his admission about the meeting, Brash's chief press secretary, Jason Ede, forwarded the story to his colleagues and campaign manager Steven Joyce with a one-word comment, 'Hmmmm'.[51]) The news report said that when Brash was pressed on the subject of whether he had been told about the pamphlets he 'walked away'.[52]

Meanwhile, deputy leader Gerry Brownlee had told Radio New Zealand that morning, 'We were not aware they were coming out and have had nothing to do with it.'[53] A day later McCully 'was still maintaining National knew nothing about the pamphlets'.[54] He also continued to 'divert the debate into Labour's links and funding', as Long had advised, with a long press release titled 'Look left for conspiracies'.[55] John Key, whose filmed meeting with the two Exclusive Brethren men in May was replayed on the TVNZ news, told Radio New Zealand he had 'met several members of Exclusive Brethren in the past but they did not tell him about any publicity campaigns they had planned'. He said the May meeting had been to discuss relieving the 'family tax burden'. Though 'not necessarily National supporters', the church 'loathes the direction the Labour government is taking the country'.[56]

Brash obviously could not dodge the questions for long and it was straining credibility to suggest he had met the Brethren but heard nothing about their election plans. So that night, Richard Long wrote a new set of lines, conceding some vague knowledge of the campaign as a way of not having to admit more and, he hoped, stopping the damaging questioning from going on for days.

Q. Did the Brethren tell you of their plans when you met them?

A. They mentioned they wanted to change the Government as they were so concerned about Labour's policies. They intended to distribute pamphlets attacking the Government.

Q. Were you shown the pamphlets?

A. I certainly don't recall seeing any and I certainly didn't read any. And I have been assured by the campaign director that National did not have anything to do with the funding, printing or distribution of the pamphlets.

Long then scripted how Brash should try to dodge further questions by feigning irritation.

Then, time to get mildly irritated:
Look, this is nothing but a great diversion, which you have been banging on about for three days. The Brethren have admitted they were behind the pamphlets. Labour and the Greens were wrong in pointing the finger at National. You should point out that Labour were wrong....

If it continues, even more irritable:
This is getting absurd. First Labour said National was in the hands of the Americans. Then we were in the hands of the Australians, then in the hands of the Business Round Table and Act, now we are supposed to be in the hands of the Brethren. And to top it all off Helen Clark says National would bring a disaster of the proportions of the New Orleans catastrophe. It is time to get back to the real issues that mainstream New Zealanders are concerned about: a fair tax system that returns incentives for hard work, a stop to this march down the road to separate development....[57]

The next morning, Thursday 8 September, people assumed that Brash had made a huge slip when he suddenly went back on his previous denials during an 8.35am interview on the student radio station 95bFM and admitted the Exclusive Brethren had told him in advance about the pamphlet campaign. But, as we can see, he was still simply following the lines prepared for him by his staff. Here is Brash with 95bFM's Noelle McCarthy:

Noelle McCarthy: Now, is it true that two weeks ago you met with members of the Exclusive Brethren who are behind this anti-Government leaflet campaign?

Don Brash: Oh yes, I have met with them; I've made that quite clear.... They told me they were utterly fed up with the government and I agreed with them....

34

Noelle McCarthy: Apart from indicating that they were going to pray for you, was anything else of a campaigning nature discussed?

Brash: Oh, yes. They indicated they were going to campaign against the government. They were going to issue some pamphlets, but I did not read those pamphlets and have had absolutely no part in reading them, writing them, funding them or distributing them, and it's high time that the media pointed that out. Labour and the Greens have been arguing that the National Party was behind those pamphlets, and we were not. The people who have been behind it have now said who they are.

And later in the interview, when McCarthy kept pushing him, Brash even used the feigned irritation:

Noelle McCarthy: So why was Gerry Brownlee at such pains to distance National from the Exclusive Brethren?

Don Brash: Because Labour and the Greens have been trying to portray this as a National Party plot, and it is a lie. Frankly, I'm getting fed up with it. In the last month, Noelle, we've been accused of being in the pockets of the Americans, then of the Australians, then of the Business Roundtable, then of ACT, then of Exclusive Brethren. Yesterday, I think Helen Clark suggested we'd be responsible for a Katrina-type catastrophe if we were in government. This has gone far enough.[58]

This 'admission' was calculated damage control. It was designed to divert attention from the extent of National's involvement and in particular to end damaging media probing and scepticism as quickly as possible, so that National could enter the last week of the election campaign with the issue behind it. As a tactic, it succeeded in both of those objectives. However, though National could manoeuvre to minimise the damage, they could not avoid it completely.

Later that morning Brash was launching National's 'First Ten Things' pamphlet at a netball centre on Auckland's North Shore. But the journalists present were naturally interested only in the Exclusive Brethren controversy, and especially in why he and other National Party people had kept saying they knew nothing about the pamphlet campaign. The TV3 reporter asked: 'Why didn't you say a few days ago that you knew it would be coming out? Or that you knew about it?'[59] Brash replied: 'I wasn't asked if I knew about it'. That evening TV3 contrasted that reply with Brash's answer three days earlier, when he was asked if he knew who was responsible and he had said, 'No, I do not'.[60]

After the North Shore interviews Brash's minders made a strategic decision that they had to get him on television, before that evening's televised leadership debate, so he could try to talk his way out of the crisis. They changed his schedule and accepted an interview with Susan Wood on TVNZ's *Close Up* programme at 7pm.

Wood began the interview by asking bluntly, 'Why didn't you tell the truth from the beginning?' What followed had the look and feel of a child not very convincingly making up stories to avoid getting in trouble. The rationale was clearly that, though Brash's explanations would not be believed by many people, they were necessary to reassure other voters to stay with National.

Don Brash: Oh, I did. I'd never seen that pamphlet until Monday this week when Rod Donald waved it in front of my face in Rotorua.... And when asked on Tuesday if the Brethren were behind the pamphlet I said, 'I don't know. I know it's not National Party.' And what I did know is that the Brethren had spoken to me sometime in the last month, I can't give you an exact date, to say that they were going to put out some anti-government pamphlets. Did I know that was the pamphlet? No, I didn't.

Susan Wood: Why didn't you know? How many other people have come to you and said they're putting out anti-government literature?

Don Brash: Not too many, I'm bound to say. I didn't know that leaflet was the one the Brethren were talking about. The Brethren were talking about doing something against the government. This was against the Green Party....

Susan Wood: What I want to talk about is your credibility.

Don Brash: I'm very happy to do that.

Susan Wood: And I know you're here tonight only because you're very concerned about what's being said.

Don Brash: Well, I don't like being called a liar, to be frank. Helen Clark has called me a liar and I can assure the New Zealand people I am not a liar.

Susan Wood: Dr Brash, on Tuesday you said to Paul Holmes, when he asked you who was doing the nasty pamphlets, 'I don't know, Paul. One thing I know is it's not the National Party.'

Don Brash: That's right.

Susan Wood: Today you tell us you knew they were going to issue pamphlets attacking the government.

Don Brash: And both those statements are absolutely consistent. I did not know the pamphlet I was shown by Rod Donald on Monday was put out by the Brethren.

Susan Wood: Why didn't you work it out?

Don Brash: I knew it could have been, sure.

Susan Wood: Well, why didn't you say so?

Don Brash: It's not my position to dob in the Brethren. The Brethren only yesterday said, 'Hey, this was us.' I said, 'Great, now I've connected the two – the meeting I had back in August and the distribution of the pamphlet and that's fine, that's the Brethren.' ....

Susan Wood: It absolutely is [your responsibility to say what you know about who's behind the pamphlets]. Because you're putting out statements saying you don't know and this is the situation you find yourself in tonight, in that you're being accused of lying. It makes you look dishonest.

Don Brash: Well, there is nothing I said on Tuesday, Wednesday or Thursday that I resile from in any way.... Why is it, Susan, that this campaign by the Brethren is being regarded as a nasty, dirty smear campaign and when the PPTA, the teachers' union, spend $373,000 attacking the National Party's policies, unfairly, that's all clean?

Susan Wood: Because it's done above board and these pamphlets were not done above board. That's the fundamental issue.... Gerry Brownlee actually said, 'We were not aware they were coming out and had nothing to do with it'.

Don Brash: Well, Gerry Brownlee did have no knowledge of it.

Susan Wood: So you didn't talk to him about the meetings?

Don Brash: No. I have meetings with people all the time, Susan. This was after Parliament finished for the year. Gerry Brownlee was not in Wellington. The meeting was in Wellington. It was a 20-minute meeting at 5.40pm in the evening....

Susan Wood: Are you going to apologise to the people of New Zealand?

Don Brash: No, I'm not. I said nothing that was untrue.[61]

There is no doubt that, if the smear campaign had remained anonymous, as was intended, National would have continued to deny all knowledge. Brash would have continued to say the party 'totally had nothing to do with' it. Brownlee and McCully would also have been unaware and known nothing. Key would not have had to say he had met them several times but that 'they did not tell him about any publicity campaigns'. If the Exclusive Brethren had not mentioned meeting Brash at their Wednesday press conference, he would have continued obfuscating with some line about having met with the leaders of most church groups in the past few months. What little 'truth' came from National appeared only after the information had already become public anyway. Everything else was kept secret, thereby allowing scope for denials and untruths.

Brash and other National Party MPs and staff had had numerous meetings with Exclusive Brethren about its election campaign, for months before the one August meeting to which Brash was forced to admit. National MPs had been told about the anti-Green pamphlets, not just the anti-government ones, as Brash suggested to Susan Wood. The Brethren put their plans in writing to Brash and Key four months before the election. Drafts of the brochures had been shown to at least one group of MPs long before the election. And National had been actively encouraging this sort of third-party campaign support during 2005 so that it could, in effect, boost its advertising while getting around the legal spending limit.

Once some of the denials are exposed, others cease to be credible. Brownlee's claims that he knew nothing were perhaps faintly credible when Brash had only heard about the pamphlets shortly before the election and after his deputy had left Wellington. But it defies belief that senior MPs working together on the election campaign over several months did not discuss the million-dollar Brethren plans. The same is true of John Key. He would continue strenuously to deny any knowledge of the plans. But it is not credible that he was somehow left in the dark for months when other senior MPs were discussing and even nervous about the plans; that he missed the 24 May 2005 email from Ron Hickmott; and that while Brethren members were meeting other MPs and telling them about the pamphlet campaign, he was apparently visited by one of the main organisers of the pamphlets and they talked only about reducing the family tax burden.

Susan Wood summed up the issue: 'A lot of your appeal, Dr Brash, is that you're not a politician, that you don't play loose and fast with the facts. You have damaged your reputation because people will be thinking, well, I don't know if he's telling the truth.' For two years Brash's advisers had promoted the idea that he wasn't like other politicians; that he was the non-politician politician who could be relied on to tell the truth. But this had just been more spin. When Don Brash said 'I am not a liar' on national television at the end of that week, the ghost of Richard I-am-not-a-crook Nixon must have been looking on approvingly.

CHAPTER 2

BACKING BRASH
The coup makers

On Tuesday, 28 October 2003, Don Brash was elected leader of the National Party in a secret ballot of National MPs. He had gone into caucus with three prepared speeches. The first was for his caucus colleagues, in which he replied to concerns that he lacked experience to be leader, was 'too old' and 'too right wing'.[1]

Brash also listed 'what, positively, I would bring to the table as leader'. He mentioned his personal experience as a CEO and in public policy, then emphasised that having him as leader was vital for collecting sufficient corporate election donations. 'I have good connections in the business community,' he said. 'The business community can't give us enough votes to win, but... [they] can provide us with money. As you and I both know, the Party is currently very short of money, with no obvious willingness on the part of those who could do so to write out big cheques. We need money badly. Indeed, without a substantial injection of funds in the near future, we are in big trouble. I believe that attracting that money would be substantially easier with me as leader.'[2]

The other two speeches he arrived with that morning were a concession speech to read to the press if he lost the vote and the victory speech he read as new leader of the party. This said: 'The public in their hearts support us. We have to earn their trust. And we do that by speaking clearly and truthfully.'[3] He also made the usual promises about taking notice of the party membership. 'I need to earn the trust and support of the membership,' he said. 'I want to meet the membership face-to-face, listen to them, and involve them in our plans.'[4]

But already, in those first days, Brash was hiding much more about himself and his plans than he was revealing. Nothing demonstrates this more clearly than an inside view of who rallied behind and assisted Brash in his bid to become leader. If his National Party colleagues, and the public, had known then who was behind the challenge – and what that implied about what would follow – it is doubtful he would have won the vote.

Those people helping Brash's leadership campaign – planning his lobbying, writing for him and rallying support – included the 1980s Labour Cabinet ministers Roger Douglas and Michael Bassett, key past and present members of the New Zealand Business Roundtable (some of whom were the big cheque writers who had withheld donations to pressure for a change of leadership) and a collection of political activists including Brian Nicolle and Catherine Judd, who were associated with the ACT Party and the Wellington public relations firm Awaroa Partners. These are not the people that the 21st-century National Party membership would have expected or, in many cases, wanted, to be involved in deciding their leader.

National Party people also helped with Brash's leadership challenge – but not very many. Since he lacked a strong support base in the party, Brash relied instead on this informal network of people from the right of New Zealand politics, people who saw him as a golden opportunity to gain renewed dominance for their beliefs.

Attempts to move Don Brash into the leadership had begun only eight months after he became an MP. Despite denials, it is likely that this had been the plan of at least some people since then party president Michelle Boag first approached Brash to be a candidate in April 2002. In April 2003 a Brash supporter arranged a highly contrived splash across six pages of the *National Business Review*, headed 'Brash on target to topple English'. The newspaper had a two-page spread of photographs showing a possible Brash-led shadow cabinet and an editorial headed 'English must go – and quickly'.[5] It was more like a political advertising supplement than journalism, but it showed that Brash's supporters were on the move.

NBR ran an article the following week quoting unnamed National Party business donors who had 'turned off the funding tap until Bill English quits the leadership'.[6] Don Brash was quoted that week saying that 'As the duly elected leader of the National Party, Bill English has my full support', which, as the *Dominion Post* noted, 'pledge[d] exactly nothing to his leader'.[7] But the *NBR*'s overenthusiastic help for Brash did not impress various influential National MPs and that first coup attempt was abandoned.

Six months later Brash tried again, in the week of 20–24 October 2003, after leader Bill English had made some widely criticised comments about inviting a United States warship to New Zealand. The *New Zealand Herald* reported that Brash was 'under increasing pressure... from Auckland business interests' to become leader.[8] The plans nearly unravelled again when MP Simon Power declined an invitation to be Brash's deputy in a leadership challenge. By the Saturday the *Herald* headlines declared: 'Brash's clumsy coup bid puts National in turmoil'.[9] Brash's backers outside the party realised it might be now or never to get their man into the National Party leadership.

Brash publicly declared his challenge on the Saturday, 25 October 2003. Suddenly there were only five days until the presumed Thursday vote and that time shortened when English moved the vote forward to the Tuesday. Brash was woefully unprepared for the challenge and – just as important – if he won. He urgently needed help.

The first person Brash brought in to help him was a National Party-aligned PR consultant named Matthew Hooton,[10] who had been assisting Brash on and off during the preceding months. He arranged the Saturday afternoon press conference where Brash announced his challenge and it was he who drafted Brash's three caucus vote speeches. His approach to politics can be seen in the thinking behind the victory speech.

In this, Brash explained (using Hooton's words) that he had 'taken the Leadership' because he believed 'the Labour/Anderton/Green Government is slowly but surely destroying New Zealand. It is destroying the New Zealand in which we grew up. It is destroying the New Zealand which we still love today. And – most importantly – it is destroying the New Zealand that, with leadership, we could be.'[11]

Hooton wrote these words when the Labour-led government was high in the polls and most New Zealanders were saying they were reasonably happy with the direction of the country. He later explained his use of the 'destroying New Zealand' line. The idea was that Brash should stick to repeating two simple messages in his first weeks as leader: 'National stands for the BEST and Labour is destroying New Zealand'. This, he explained, was following the example of Ronald Reagan, who spoke 'with big ideas direct to the voter'. Only 'bigness and boldness' works, because 'you usually have to communicate through a cynical or even hostile press gallery [and] that demands constant strong messages to keep them busy'. The key was constant repetition of the main ideas. 'The perception the [journalists] have of you will quickly be how the public also perceives you: the perception becomes the reality.'

Hooton ended the email by saying: 'We are going to be an outstanding success. I just hope you... don't think I am a populist. I'm not. I'm a right wing academic neocon [neo-conservative] ultra. I just believe in winning too.'[12] Hooton had worked as an assistant to National Cabinet minister Lockwood Smith in the 1990s, where he had developed strong pro-American views and links with neo-conservatives in the United States. In July that year, as a delegate at the National Party annual conference, he had pushed for a vote to amend or dump the country's nuclear-free legislation.

At the same time he was working as a private PR consultant to try to stop tobacco control policies. It is not known who was paying him, but it was presumably either the tobacco or the hospitality industry. In this work he vigorously probed government grants to anti-smoking groups using the Official Information Act. The results of his research then appear to have been passed to ACT MP Rodney Hide, who used the information to attack and try to stall anti-smoking legislation that was being debated in the House in October 2003.[13]

Son-in-law of former National Party president Sue Wood, Hooton was clearly aligned to the National Party. So too was Nicola Young, PR consultant and daughter of former National Cabinet minister Bill Young, who helped to co-ordinate some caucus lobbying during the leadership challenge and advised on the first month's 'plan of action' after Brash won.[14] But most assistance came from people with no connection to the party.

Brash's next close supporter was Michael Bassett, whose personal website modestly describes him as 'probably New Zealand's best known political historian'.[15] Bassett was a Labour Party MP from 1972 to 1990 and a minister in the 1984–90 Labour government, in which he was a staunch supporter of the post-1984 free market reforms. Since then he had become a newspaper columnist, been a Waitangi Tribunal member (1994–2004) and a commissioned biographer to two leading free market advocates, Roderick (Rod) Deane and Douglas (Doug) Myers.

Bassett presented himself as an independent writer and commentator. On the day of the leadership vote, his column in the Wellington newspaper was entitled 'Time to stand aside, Bill', which sounded as if he had weighed up the issues in a dispassionate way before concluding that 'Dr Brash is [National's] only credible option'. He wrote that 'new and politically inexperienced Mr Brash might be, but he could provide hope to the legions of potential centre-right voters currently at the edge of despair.... Surely he's worth trying?'[16]

But Bassett was not at all independent. Straight after Brash announced his challenge on that Saturday, he rang Bassett, who wrote him a five-page campaign plan on how to arrange his lobbying, select a deputy, manage the caucus after a victory and choose a shadow cabinet – each section ending with a cheery 'Good Luck'. Then he wrote his pro-Brash newspaper column, sending it to Brash the night before publication with a note wishing him luck in caucus the next morning.[17]

Bassett's campaign plan argued that 'For Bill English and the brat pack [the 1990 intake of National MPs] this is a fight to the finish for their political careers, so they'll use every trick in the book, clean or dirty'. He advised Brash to tell wavering MPs he was willing to discuss which port-folios they wanted. The plan included a full list of National MPs ordered according to how Bassett thought they would vote, with comments like 'Leaning to English: Pansy Wong (but could come your way fairly easily)', 'For English: Gerry Brownlee (but with a high degree of bile in his craw)' and 'Leaning to Brash: Murray McCully (his hissy fit will pass)'.[18]

Bassett gave specific political advice on how to manage individual MPs. Regarding Simon Power he wrote: 'Don, following our discussion, and a later discussion with a caucus member, I am convinced that SP has his eyes fixed on spilling English after he loses the 2005 election – that is the only rational reason why he won't accept the deputy position [offered by Brash] now. He fears you will stay on as Leader and he will miss his chance as PM. If so, you must allay these fears and say he is more likely to become a viable leader under you, than English.'[19]

He suggested that, if elected leader, Brash create teams of MPs for policy development: 'Let me know if you would like more work on this'. He even gave advice on MP seating positions. 'The positioning in terms of ranking is important. I would not put Nick Smith on the front bench, but high up on the second bench, with a clear message from you he has to earn his way back to the FB with loyalty and work. English should be mid rank on the second bench (seat him with one of your strong support-ers). Sowry and Ryall onto the back benches, well separated. Ensure the allocation of offices is such that the brat pack MPs are floors apart from each other and each is next door to one of your strong supporters.'[20]

Thus Bassett had plotted in detail with Brash to help him secure the leadership and then, without declaring any personal involvement, gave Brash a further boost through his newspaper column in the role of impartial commentator. Later Bassett was closely involved in helping to write some of Brash's most extreme speeches and then made comments on those issues, as if from a distance, in the media.

The day after Brash won the leadership, Bassett wrote again giving 'hearty congratulations'. He said that 'the next three weeks will be incred-ibly important.... My inclination would be for a few more smiles and a rehearsed joke or two.' Then he advised that 'At least one speech needs to sock it to the Government HARD.... Happy to be of help if you think I can be.'[21] Bassett's newspaper column the day before had called for a 'new authoritative face' for National, one willing to take 'hard decisions' like confronting the 'Treaty industry' and 'racial separatism'. A few weeks later Bassett would be closely involved in writing Brash's first big speech, his January 2004 Orewa 'Nationhood' address on race.

Also giving advice to Brash during those crucial days before the caucus leadership vote was 1980s Labour finance minister Sir Roger Douglas, who led Labour's programme of deregulation, corporatisation and privatisation and later worked as an 'international consultant on privatisation and structural reform in countries as various as Russia, Brazil [and] Mexico'.[22] In 1993 he published the book *Unfinished Business*, which urged continued reforms, was a founder of the ACT Party and became its first leader. He was a close friend of Michael Bassett, with whom he went on holiday each year.

Douglas's assistance to Brash is seen in three pieces of writing he sent in the days before and after the leadership vote. In the first, sent to Brash on the Sunday, Douglas drafted words Brash might use to explain 'Why I want to be Prime Minister'. There was no hint of the policies in which both he and Brash believed. He proposed unexceptional lines like 'I joined the National Party because these are the things I believe it stands for: Equal opportunity for all New Zealanders, not just the favoured few'.[23]

The next missive was sent the following day with a copy to New Zealand Business Roundtable head Roger Kerr, a sign of the collaboration between the backers of the challenge. Douglas wrote: 'Campaign appears to be going well. My only concern is that National Party MPs will see you as narrowing the party's appeal, not widening it'. His suggestion was an attached paper that 'you might send to MPs to overcome this problem. You will need to add your own touches to it if you like what you see.'

The accompanying paper said the 'key issues for the coming election' would be 'race, crime, health, education, housing, unemployment and the economy'. He proposed an overarching theme of National providing 'real sustainable gains in living standards of all New Zealanders, particularly the hard-working low income earners and disadvantaged' and argued that 'The approach suggested would enable us to move into Labour, United Future and NZ first territory.... No other approach has the power to hurt Labour where they believe they are strongest.'[24]

A few days after Brash became leader Douglas was in contact again, via a phone call to his assistant Bryan Sinclair who passed on in an email

'Words of advice from Sir Roger Douglas', offered 'as someone who has been through this sort of thing before'. Sinclair said Douglas had 'suggested as follows (and asked me to note down for you)':

> Leadership change leaves a bit of a strategic vacuum for a while, during staff changes, portfolio changes etc....
> Make a 'major change' of some description within 10 days – stamp your mark on the party and the leadership.
> Don't get painted 'hard Right' including how you present yourself....
> Diagnose what thousands of NZers lack as a result of the Government (usually money) and how it leads to a lack of power. Present the National Party solution....
> [Use] language that average people can understand [and] associate words such as 'fake remedies' and 'phoney panacea' with Labour.[25]

Of course being offered advice is not the same as taking it, but in the case of the next person helping Brash – ACT Party campaign manager Brian Nicolle – he definitely did follow the suggestions with which he was presented.

The most organised supporters of the Brash coup were Nicolle and others from the ACT Party and Awaroa PR company, where Nicolle and ACT president Catherine Judd worked. They leapt into action and provided Brash with the most concrete, practical support during the crucial three days before the vote. Nicolle happened to be in Timaru on the Saturday when Brash announced the challenge. He received a phone call from Judd suggesting he assist Brash and by 6.30pm that day he had sent a handwritten strategy plan to Brash's home fax machine in Auckland.

Brian Nicolle is perhaps the most experienced right-wing campaigner in New Zealand.[26] His biographical notes say he worked for 'legendary finance minister, Sir Roger Douglas' in 1989 and 1990,[27] a time when the latter was leader of Labour's right-wing Backbone Club. In 1993 Nicolle teamed up with businessman Peter Shirtcliffe to run a campaign against the introduction of mixed member proportional representation (MMP) in New Zealand, spending well over a million dollars from anonymous donors on weeks of saturation advertising.[28] A year later, he and Roger Douglas set up ACT and, using the MMP system they had opposed and spending more on the election campaign than any other party ($1.65 million), their fledgling free market party managed to get eight MPs into Parliament. Since then Nicolle had worked as ACT campaign manager and also as campaign manager for the ACT Party-linked Auckland mayor

John Banks. During Banks's 2004 mayoral campaign Nicolle was criticised for arranging anonymous printing and distribution of *National Business Review* articles smearing Banks's main opponent, Dick Hubbard.

Nicolle's fax to Brash contained plans for frantic organising over the following days. 'I am still thinking about D Day [the leadership vote] and of course the month following which will be crucial,' he wrote. 'All in all I see everything from now on as a campaign.' The 'desired outcomes' were 'Don Brash leader of the National Party by the end of this week', 'media writeup in the weekend media is generally positive' and then an encouraging poll result. He said Brash should immediately write to 'selected financial supporters' to seek their 'support and funds' for the coming days.[29]

His 'Tactical Plans' included purchasing full-page advertisements in the main cities on the (presumed) day before the vote, headed 'An Open Letter to all New Zealanders' and 'Why I want to be Leader of the National Party' – subtitled 'For the Future Not the Past, For the Many Not the Few'. 'I think that radio media can be harnessed on each of the 3–4 days next week.... We need to target key talkback hosts in ZB and Pacific – there are plenty sympathetic – and we could produce some common lines that become the "mantra" on your journey to become leader of National and the country.' He also proposed public endorsements of Brash, 'women especially', and suggested Diane Foreman for this role. Some of these plans were overtaken by events when the early caucus meeting left no time for placing advertisements and articles.

In Nicolle's 'Statement of Positioning' – how they wanted Brash to be perceived – he said, 'He is a new kind of politician – he is not part of the club.' The next line said 'one of the architects of our strong economy', but Nicolle crossed these words out, perhaps because they risked reminding people of the 1980s and 1990s free market reforms. Staying right away from his part in these, Nicolle continued: 'Brash is honest, sincere and energetic. He has a vision of a New Zealand that is rooted in the future... not the past.'[30]

He proposed as an overriding theme for publicity: 'For the many, not the few – National is a party for all New Zealanders, unlike Labour which is a party of special interests'. This is ironical coming from Nicolle, who had developed a style of campaigning that relied not on broad support but on large sums of money from a few rich supporters. Nicolle had worked repeatedly with the same small set of political collaborators, many of whom turned up to help Brash over those days.

One of them was Peter Shirtcliffe, the public face of the 1993 anti-

MMP campaign and then chair of the recently privatised Telecom corporation. As one of the National Party donors who had been unhappy with Bill English, Shirtcliffe sent a message of support to Brash on the Sunday morning before the vote to use in lobbying wavering MPs. 'Don. If the National Party is to regain relevance, and avoid the risk of oblivion, it is vital that your caucus colleagues support your leadership aspirations. You have the integrity, intellectual grunt, dignity and administrative experience that are sorely needed. Share this e-mail with anyone if it would be helpful. Warmest good wishes, Peter.'[31]

Shirtcliffe's political activities epitomise corporate activism in New Zealand. Besides his anti-MMP work with Nicolle in 1993 (and a second anti-MMP campaign in 2001), Shirtcliffe was one of the main financial backers of a 2000 campaign called One Voice, which aimed to stop the Labour-led government from reversing the previous government's privatisation of the Accident Compensation Commission. The campaign included full-page newspaper advertisements and the 'campaign organiser' was Catherine Judd of the PR company JM Communications, which later became Awaroa.[32] Shirtcliffe was a driving force behind the privately funded New Zealand Enterprise Trust and Enterprise Education Foundation, which aims to teach market ideas and entrepreneurial skills to school students; and he was part of an unpublicised 'school choice' campaign, promoting private schools and fronted by the Auckland right-wing thinktank Maxim Institute.[33] He was joined in this by Michael Friedlander, one of the anonymous donors to the ACT Party,[34] and by a young marketing man called Richard Poole,[35] the 'patriotic young New Zealander' who in October 2000 organised a supposedly personal anti-Labour campaign called 'A Generation Lost?', which turned out to have been supported by the Business Roundtable and, once again, Catherine Judd's PR company.[36]

In the days before the leadership challenge, the message coming from donors like Shirtcliffe was, bluntly, 'No Brash, No money'. Multi-millionaire businesswoman Diane Foreman used exactly those words when she wrote to Brash on the same day as Shirtcliffe:

Hi Don,
I am currently overseas but have been phoned by a mutual friend who suggests that you may be in need of help....

Could you contact all your friends in the business community and ask them to lobby their MP's for you ie no Brash no money?

I understand that you must be frantic and that advice must be coming from everywhere but if there is anything I or my friends can do to help please let me know.

Kindest regards

Diane...[37]

In an email the day after the coup, she said: 'I have been speaking to [Business Roundtable head] Roger Kerr so know that the message got given!!!'[38]

There is a relatively small number of people, but plenty of money, at the heart of radical right activism in this country. Kerr, Judd, Nicolle, their young protégés and old business funders appear repeatedly in different guises. Besides its close links to the ACT Party, Awaroa Partners was also the PR company to the New Zealand Business Roundtable (which paid the firm 'around $400,000 a year for communications services and advice'),[39] part of the pro-Transmission Gully road lobby in Wellington and an adviser to unnamed 'energy advocacy groups, and business, education and enterprise lobby groups'.[40] Common features are undisclosed financial backers, with undisclosed vested interests, and paid campaigners who arrange sympathetic news coverage, plan advertising and co-ordinate lobbying.

In a postscript to his fax to Brash, Nicolle said, 'A couple of articles appearing in the papers being ghost written for you could be helpful. I think that could be arranged.' This was the point where another important player came into the story. The fax did not say who would write them, but the day after Nicolle made this offer two draft speeches arrived written by Wellington economist Peter Keenan, each trimmed neatly to about 1000 words for publication. 'Don, A couple of draft articles attached.... Hope they are of some use, and good luck in the days ahead. Let me know if there is anything more I can do.'[41] Brash replied: 'Very many thanks Peter. I'll thank you more adequately when I have time to draw breath – which will be tomorrow evening if I lose, and next weekend (I hope!) if I win! Don.'[42]

Keenan wrote again the day before the leadership vote, giving the first signs of the kind of pragmatic advice that would become his hallmark:

Don, Just a quick thought... if you do win tomorrow, in the interviews that follow I feel you should:

a. Be the opposite of what Labour will brand you (ie narrowly focused on the economy, just wanting to cut taxes for the wealthy, and a clone of ACT).

b. instead focus on three social policy issues... declining education standards, ... law and order, and... the welfare trap that Labour have laid for the least well off in society, and which is particularly responsible for the demoralisation of Maori (here emphasising the carrot rather than the stick – assistance in retraining etc).

You will of course be asked about taxes. Say the most immediate concern is to unwind the increase in taxes that all taxpayers have experienced (ie fiscal drag, but don't use the term), and medium term (when conditions are right etc etc, 'who knows what the future may hold') to bring rates down more generally – the key is not to let that seem your immediate priority.

And then, more general issues of dealing with NZ incomes falling behind the world, but always bringing the issues back to the 'softer' social policy concerns. No need to commit to anything. And if bloody Kim Hill asks a leading/loaded question, attack the nature of the question.

Fundamentally in politics, you (ie the centre right parties) have to convince more than 50% of the electorate that you are on their side.

Good luck,

Peter[43]

A few days later Keenan wrote again, congratulating Brash on 'the outstanding results of the past week or two' and saying he would be interested in working for him full time. Brash also received an email from Business Roundtable head Roger Kerr enthusiastically supporting Keenan being given a job in the leader's office. Keenan could not resist the urge to give a bit more advice as well.

'From observing the media over the past week,' he wrote, 'my quick thoughts on required political strategy are: Firstly, the tax cut story should be heavily de-emphasised – leave that largely to ACT.... The story should be [that] Labour is making everybody relatively poorer... the causes are the many aspects of regulation and govt fiddling, together with our tax system (but note that National should reduce the focus on the tax issue, making it just one of many points in relation to relative decline, ie why it is so hard to make a living, and so forth – even though in fact it is much more important).... And get all the caucus singing from the same song sheet.'[44] A few weeks later Keenan was appointed and moved into the new leader's office as chief strategist and speech writer.

Brian Nicolle's biggest single contribution in the rush before the leadership vote was finding a personal assistant/adviser for Brash. Nicolle had started thinking about what Brash would need on Saturday afternoon, sent him the campaign plan fax in the early evening and that evening tracked down, in Sydney, Bryan Sinclair, with whom he had worked on John Banks's successful 2001 Auckland mayoral campaign. He persuaded Sinclair to drop everything and fly to New Zealand to assist Brash in the challenge and for the weeks that would follow.

Later that evening, after being briefed by Nicolle, Sinclair spoke with Brash by phone. Brash agreed to hire him on Nicolle's recommendation and Sinclair flew to join Brash the next morning – the day after Brash had announced the leadership challenge.[45] Sinclair was appointed full time to the leader's staff a couple of weeks later.[46] Thus both of Brash's main advisers, Keenan and Sinclair, appear to have been shoulder tapped to help him by Nicolle in Brash's hour of need.

Sinclair sent his first advice to Brash by email that night. 'Thanks for your call earlier. It seems to me that we are pretty quickly going to need an "engine room" for your bid and to manage the transition period. We need to have you supported and surrounded wherever you go and we need to get a firm hand on your media, image and communications from day one.... I think between us we can probably organise some discreet shoulder-tapping to ensure we have the funds to pull this all together quickly.'

Brash's 'personal packaging/appearance' was 'already okay' but 'the whole look, the packaging, the appearance must be carefully refined at the edges wherever necessary and not left to chance'. The goal was to 'create momentum wherever [Brash] goes 24/7. Senior National MPs to travel together more often – team, sparkle, charm, stability, always supported, united. Have appearances cleverly organised in a way that is not apparent, strong, powerful, presidential, build a bit of celeb appeal while still having the absolutely common touch.'[47]

Bryan Sinclair was one of a group of young right-wing activists who had been cultivated by Roger Kerr over the preceding years. Kerr had nurtured (and financially supported) Student Choice, a campaign against compulsory student union membership centred on Waikato University. The student politicians from that university, buoyed by their success in that campaign, ended their university years encouraged to continue in radical right-wing politics.[48] Sinclair's links with right-wing politics had been cemented in July 1999 when Roger Kerr arranged for him to attend a Liberty and Society course at the Sydney-based thinktank, Centre for Independent Studies.[49] Sinclair, who had embarked on a career in marketing, had just attended the advanced Liberty and Society course in October

2003, together with Ruth Richardson and another Awaroa staff member, Todd Stephenson, when he got the phone call from Brian Nicolle.

Although of different ages, personalities and backgrounds, Nicolle, Keenan and Sinclair were linked through their political beliefs. None was naturally a National Party supporter: instead they had in common their membership of the Centre for Independent Studies.[50] The CIS, which has its New Zealand base in the Awaroa PR company offices, is the meeting point for the radical right in New Zealand. The thinktank promotes a simple programme: privatisation, removing environmental controls, favouring private hospitals and education over public ones, cutting tax for the rich and generally leaving most society-shaping decisions to the market. Its 21 November 2005 Tax Forum in Wellington had speakers from the United States Heritage Foundation, Cato Institute and Centre for Peace and Prosperity thinktanks, all representing the far right of American politics. Brash was also a member of the CIS, regularly attending its functions and maintaining contact with its head and founder, Greg Lindsay.

In practice CIS-type beliefs attract only limited public support, which is why, from the start, Brash's supporters like Keenan and Douglas were urging him to 'heavily de-emphasise' such policies and avoid being 'painted hard right'. That is also why political strategists like Nicolle and Keenan essentially believe in political progress by stealth – whether it be by hiding their real agenda and manipulating the 'punters', as seen in the next chapter, or setting up well-funded 'community' lobby groups where the backers are not revealed.

The membership of the radical right in New Zealand is well demonstrated by the guest list for a CIS breakfast held in Auckland on 6 August 2004. The occasion was a visit by University of Chicago academic Richard Epstein, author of numerous publications for the New Zealand Business Roundtable, with titles such as *The Case for a Flat Tax* (2004) and *MMP: The Right Decision?* (1999). Regular events like this maintain contact within this small but influential network.

About 25 guests had gathered from around New Zealand for the breakfast meeting, held at the home of Diane Foreman, in St Stephens Avenue, Parnell. The guest list included Ruth Richardson, Roger Kerr, Catherine Judd, two ACT MPs, Rodney Hide and Stephen Franks, Auckland mayor John Banks, Business Roundtable chair Rob McLeod, Jenny Gibbs, well-known right-wing donor Michael Friedlander, various heads of large companies and *Independent* newspaper editor, Jenni McManus.[51] But notice who was not present: the National Party. The only National MP present was Don Brash, escorted by Bryan Sinclair. This was Brash's political peer group, including people who helped him to power, but they were all politically to the right of the National Party.

Diane Foreman and Ruth Richardson were friends and supporters of Brash; Roger Kerr and Catherine Judd liaised regularly with him; Rodney Hide was a close family friend; Michael Friedlander was also a friend, whose birthday Brash made time to attend during the 2005 election campaign; Rob McLeod would help him with fundraising during the election year; and Jenny Gibbs gave her home for a Brash fundraising evening two weeks after he became leader.

These friendships and connections did not fit the public 'positioning' of Brash as a straightforward, centrist politician. So as soon as Brash became National Party leader he had secrets to keep about the people who had helped him to power and who remained his close political allies. A week after his election Brash was asked by the *New Zealand Herald* who he would count as his close friends. Here was a man who went on family holidays with Rodney Hide, who was good friends with people like Michael Bassett and Ruth Richardson and whose old mates had just rallied to his aid during the leadership challenge. He replied:

> It's funny. I have found in recent years that I have allowed my close friendships to atrophy just for lack of time. I used to be a very close friend of John Hinchcliffe, for example, at [Auckland University of Technology]. We've known each other for years and years and years. A guy who was my campaign manager back in 1981, a guy called Malcolm Bailey, in Auckland, has been a very close friend. But I haven't set eyes on them for quite a while. I don't have as many close friends as I used to have.[52]

The night before the leadership vote, Bill English's supporters had retired to the Backbencher Pub across the road from Parliament to celebrate their victory. But the numbers were not as certain as they believed. Notably, the MP John Key had visited English at his Wellington residence that evening and, after asking what advancement was available to him with English as leader, pledged to give him his vote. The next day he instead voted for Brash,[53] who won the leadership by one vote (insiders calculated that one less vote for Brash would have created a draw). Leadership change with such a narrow margin had not happened before in National. Brash had not followed the long-standing convention of challengers collecting a 'super majority' of supporters' signatures to present to the leader – providing a transparent process and decisive majority – and pushed instead for a secret ballot.

It is impossible from the outside to know how much influence the 'No Brash, no money' argument had on individual National MPs, since it would have had its effect at the level of one-to-one lobbying. But it was probably substantial. Certainly Bill English stated publicly that he believed this.

Congratulations poured in for Brash, a lot by email. Many were from rank and file National Party members who primarily hoped Brash could improve the party's political fortunes. Some were from wise older politicians who understood the obstacles ahead, like former National deputy prime minister and party leader Jim McLay who wrote: 'Congratulations. A great achievement.... Welcome to the Worst Job You Will Ever Have! No power to do anything and all the blame for not doing it.'[54]

The congratulations showed who was most pleased about Brash winning the leadership. There were ACT Party and CIS supporters such as *NBR* owner Barry Colman, Trevor Farmer, Peter Shirtcliffe and CIS director Greg Lindsay. There were also right-wing lobbyists such as Bruce Logan of the Maxim Institute ('[I] really like the bit about National returning to its traditional fundamental values. Anything we can do to help please let us know')[55] and Norman LaRocque, the Business Roundtable's private education lobbyist: 'Congrats and all the best. As usual, always happy to help in any way I can!'[56]

Brash's rise was also welcomed by some wealthy property developers. One from Auckland wrote to Brash: 'you have a massive amount of support out there – just go and DO IT! ... If there is anything either myself or my network of friends can do to get the Party back in power then just let me know.'[57] A Bay of Plenty property developer was an example of the people to whom National's Resource Management Act (RMA), welfare and race policies appealed. He wrote to Brash:

> Congratulations.... I will once again vote for National rather than having to hide my face in shame from the Bolger, Shipley, Bill English years....
>
> National needs well sold strong policy to roll back RMA stupidity and all those many costs and hindrances (welfare dependency, DPB, Teachers and Unions bullshit, lack of individual responsibility, the Nanny State, the 'System Failed' mantra etc, etc) that are dragging New Zealand down to third world status.
>
> As employer of 83 staff I am well aware that Labour's policies are deeply damaging to success and economic growth as well as divisive. Reverse apartheid in fact. The Treaty of Waitangi must be removed from Legislation. You and your team have a huge job. Best wishes and all success.[58]

Not everyone in National was pleased. A member of National's Bluegreens environmental wing wrote to Brash, other MPs and party officials: 'Please accept my resignation forthwith from the National Party. While my past loyalties will not allow me to join another party... I cannot in conscience remain identified as a member of a party which has turned its back on its history and traditions and sold its soul.'[59]

Some of Brash's warmest support came from the members of the 1980s Labour government who had pushed through the free market policies. Messages arrived from Roger Douglas, Richard Prebble, Michael Bassett and the less prominent but as strongly right-wing Margaret Austin. Writing the day before the vote, Austin encouraged Brash to get on with some unfinished business. 'Good luck for tomorrow. If ever there was a time for clear heads and forward thinking it is now and as you know with the economy ticking along it is time to tackle social welfare.... I hope that sense will prevail and that you will find the support you need to establish yourself as a force to be reckoned with. Warm regards, Margaret Austin.'[60]

Douglas's successor as Labour finance minister, David Caygill, wrote the most interesting letter of congratulation:

> Congratulations.... You always knew that politics would be exciting, but I guess that neither of us thought that it would get quite this exciting quite so soon.
>
> Don, I wish you all the very best. I am confident of your capacity to lead National and ultimately the country. And I have no doubt that the country needs the kind of clear, radical leadership that I am sure you are keen to bring.
>
> I'm less certain that the country yet appreciates that need. The task now is to build the case for change without either alienating the electorate or so compromising your manifesto that the mandate you ultimately secure isn't worth having. This is by no means an easy and certainly not a quick task.... Kindest regards always, David C.[61]

Unlike those others, Caygill had maintained his links to the Labour Party and Labour-led government, despite being encouraged to retire from Parliament in the 1990s owing to his free market reputation. (He had, for example, pushed through the Reserve Bank Act that established Brash as the independent Reserve Bank governor.) Indeed, he ran a secret trust fund for the Labour Party at his Buddle Findlay law firm during the 1999 and 2002 elections to receive corporate donations gathered by party officials and then forward them to be recorded as 'anonymous' on the party's election donation declarations (this was legal under pre-2003 rules). But he was excited by the prospect of having 'radical leadership' of the country again.

Winning the National Party leadership was just one step in this. The people who had rushed to help Brash win the leadership were not doing it to replace one centrist National Party leader with another. What had gone on was not so much a leadership coup as a political coup, in which a group of ACT Party and others from the radical right succeeded in gaining control of the National leadership. It showed how vulnerable a political party can be to a takeover, especially when it is at as low an ebb as National then was. This coup set the stage for a two-year fight in which Brash and his backers from the 1980s and 1990s tried to regain control of the government. The following chapters show how that fight, which was nearly successful, was fought.

VOL. 2

Irish Party

The Sean O'Neill Band

100 ALL TIME FAVOURITES

FORTY SHADES OF GREEN
IF YO'URE IRISH COME
INTO THE PARLOUR
WHISKEY IN THE JAR
THE IRISH ROVER
McNAMARA'S BAND
THESE ARE MY MOUNTAINS

COLLECT THESE GREAT MUSIC WORLD COMPACT DISCS!

MWCD-255	HOOKED ON BIG BAND SWING
MWCD-256	GOLDEN PLAYS the HITS OF ELTON JOHN
MWCD-257	ALL THE BEST FROM THE MAORIS OF NEW ZEALAND
MWCD-258	ANOTHER AUSSIE SINGALONG PARTY - The Wayfarers
MWCD-259	HOOKED ON HAMMOND - 40 Fabulous Favourites
MWCD-260	REVERIES -20 Golden Pan Flute Favourites
MWCD-261	ALL THE BEST OF AMERICA'S MARCHING BANDS
MWCD-262	CLASSICS FOR LOVERS
MWCD-263	FAIR DINKUM! 20 AUSSIE COUNTRY SONGS
MWCD-264	FRIENDS FOR LIFE - 20 Favourites From Spain
MWCD-265	HOOKED ON CLASSICS 2 -34 Non-Stop Favourites
MWCD-266	HOOKED ON CLASSICS 3 -38 Non-Stop Favourites
MWCD-267	HOOKED ON CLASSICS 4 -32 Non-Stop Favourites
MWCD-268	TANGO - Strictly Dancing
MWCD-269	MAMBO - Strictly Dancing
MWCD-270	SAMBA - Strictly Dancing
MWCD-271	SWING - Strictly Dancing
MWCD-272	CHA CHA - Strictly Dancing
MWCD-273	FOXTROT - Strictly Dancing
MWCD-274	RHUMBA - Strictly Dancing
MWCD-275	WALTZ - Strictly Dancing
MWCD-276	LATIN - Strictly Dancing
MWCD-277	BALLROOM FAVOURITES- Strictly Dancing
MWCD-278	UNFORGETTABLE - 40 Singalong,Dancealong Hits
MWCD-279	YODELLING DOWN UNDER

CHAPTER 3

THE GRAND PLAN
The return of the radical right

There have always been both principled and unprincipled people in politics, and many politicians are a bit of both. In recent decades, however, there seems to have been a growth in a shamelessly expedient style of politics. There has been a proliferation of well-paid, unelected political advisers – media managers, PR advisers, speechwriters and strategists – who pride themselves on their Machiavellian prowess. The internal National Party papers give an unprecedented look at the variety of political operators surrounding the leader, people who appear to believe genuinely and without concern that manipulation and deception are justified in the pursuit of political success.

The political advisers in Brash's new leader's office included media controller Richard Long, personal assistant Bryan Sinclair and, as a free-lance adviser, Matthew Hooton. But the cleverest of the National leader's advisers was strategist Peter Keenan, who started work for National four weeks after helping during the coup.

Keenan brought to the job his fascination with American and British political strategists, by whom he was strongly influenced, and years as a supporter and publicist for the free market reforms. He had an impeccable free market curriculum vitae. He was a Treasury official from 1980 to 1984, economist for stockbrokers Jarden & Co. (later CS First Boston) from 1986 to 2000, a friend of Business Roundtable head Roger Kerr and a member of the Centre for Independent Studies.

In the 1990s, while research director at CS First Boston, he wrote numerous articles praising the free market reforms. One of these, written in December 1995, by which time public sympathy for the Roger Douglas/Ruth Richardson policies had largely run out, said, 'Children should be marching in celebration in the streets, chanting the praises of the great helmsman, and carrying placards reverentially displaying the faces of Douglas, Richardson and Birch.'[1]

An example of Keenan's advice is a paper he wrote on election strategy in August 2004. He sent it to Brash with the warning that they needed 'to be careful that these thoughts are kept to a very tight group, because the whole election strategy hangs on it.... I will send these notes to just you and Murray',[2] acknowledging McCully's dominance in most strategy matters by that time. 'I have been reading quite a bit about US elections.... The best man and the best policies don't win – the best campaign does.... A winning election campaign requires that: we set and control the agenda; there must be a significant element of surprise; we must be on the attack, not defending; and we must have themes which resonate with the necessary constituencies. In my view there are any number of ways to lose from here, and not many ways to win.'[3]

His main advice was that National must stop making 'major' policy releases, as they were leaving little to use in election year and, besides, such announcements were getting less and less attention. 'It matters not one bit whether we are 3% ahead or 3% behind from now until the election,' he said. 'As all past elections have shown, the campaign will deliver significant shifts in support – how well we campaign will be crucial, and we need to prepare some major hits for that campaign.'

Next Keenan discussed how to manage public opinion to favour National. 'Politics is a battle,' he wrote, 'and we must choose the terrain that suits us best to fight it on.' The three elements to consider were what would make National look good, getting the public's mind off issues that made National look bad and repeating a series of attacks on the Labour government over and over to build the idea that it was not up to the job. As he said in a later email, 'please everybody, we are talking about the electorate's perceptions here, not the reality (unfortunately, they vote on the former)'.[4]

The issues that were good for National were 'The Treaty, Law and Order, Welfare... but on these issues we have already fired our best shots.... The other potentially winning area for us is: Tax and benefits.' But while emphasising these issues, National had to get other 'losing issues' out of the public's minds: 'Apart from thinking about our winning issues, we need to put some thought into how we go about inoculating our losing issues'. National's strategy term for techniques of hiding and closing down politically unhelpful issues was 'inoculation'. 'Some of those [losing issues to inoculate] are: privatisation, nuke ships (plus the possibility that we may ourselves get nuked a day or two out from the election by further releases regarding alleged comments made to the US Senators), the notion of secret agendas, tax cuts for the rich, and so forth. We also need to soften National's image, thereby removing reasons to not vote National. In my view this is extremely important.'

Keenan explained the anti-Labour government perception building as follows. 'The major job of the caucus through until the election is an attack job. Key ministers must be tied up in defending themselves.' He emphasised: 'Unless we create a public perception that this Government is not up to the job, <u>we will not win</u>'. 'Our senior MPs must each have a target on the other side of the House, and their job is to have them tied up defending their position. That should be their performance require-ment, the base hurdle for access to Cabinet.'[5] This is why opposition MPs seem to spend so much time in the House hectoring and attacking, wearing away with criticisms that seem to have little merit or substance: as Keenan plainly states, it is an obvious but effective tactic for trying to build negative public perceptions of their opponents.

Keenan's closeness to Brash is clear in the way they talked openly about problems. An August 2004 paper Keenan sent Brash contained 'stuff other people won't tell you'. National's parliamentary performances were 'hope-less' and Brash and others' annual conference speeches were 'lacklustre'. He had 'attempt[ed] to set up a standing ovation at the conference' for Brash's speech but it failed because 'when a few of us jumped to our feet to clap, most in the crowd looked a bit bewildered as to why'. The answer was to have 'everybody going through presentation skills courses' so that they could pull off 'sincerity'. 'The secret of success is sincerity and conviction,' he quoted. 'Once you can fake that you have got it made.'[6]

The most revealing strategy discussions between Keenan and Brash came later in 2004, eleven months before the election. On 29 October, Keenan sent a four-page strategy paper to Brash in preparation for a discus-sion at the next week's strategy meeting. The paper was headed 'Strategy Issues: Speech and Policy Releases', but it covered much wider issues about what it would take for National to win the election. Some of Keenan's election-winning pragmatism was too much for Brash, who balked at the policy compromises suggested. The resulting email debate between these two tells us a lot about their underlying beliefs and strategies.

Keenan began the strategy paper uncontroversially by referring to widespread concerns in the party about poll results. 'There is a strong feeling that we need to do "something" dramatic before the end of the year to give our poll rating a nudge up. The question is – what do we do? One view is that we need another big policy release, perhaps Welfare – a hot button policy issue that will go down well with our constituency, and perhaps have wider appeal.'

'What evidence could we provide to support that view?' he asked. 'One might be that many of our core supporters are urging us do this. In my view that is worthless as evidence for what to do (except when we are in danger of losing our core vote). People are simply asking us to do what they want to hear. Core supporters are the wrong people to listen to. We should be listening to uncommitted centrist voters, wavering Labour, NZF [New Zealand First Party] and UF [United Future Party] voters, and women.'

He argued that 'The party faithful are looking for another Orewa. But we know that there is no such thing available – there never will be another Orewa. In my view we have spent the last nine months shoring up our core constituency. I think by now we have won that 35% vote about three times. I don't see the point of shoring it up once again. That would give us a better election defeat than last time, but a solid defeat none the less.'[7]

Keenan then made a very interesting comment, considering he was National's main policy and strategy adviser. 'I am a core supporter,' he said, but 'if Don said all the things I personally like to hear, Don would be unelectable.' 'In my view the problem is not lack of new policy, especially tough policy stances, but rather public perception of what National and Don Brash stand for – ie perceptions of existing policy, many of which are significant negatives... that will stop people voting... for us.'

These negatives included 'a worry that National under Don Brash means a return to the days of major reform, with privatisation, welfare cuts, spending cuts on core services, and another round of employment law reforms that will drive wages down'. He wrote, 'I suspect there is a more general sense amongst voters that National/Brash would cause upheavals in a number of areas, via reforms of some unspecified sort – ie secret agendas.'[8]

Keenan sent this paper off on a Friday afternoon and at 10.35am on the Sunday morning Don Brash responded. 'First, you say that "core supporters are the wrong people to listen to". I understand what you are saying, but I am not at all sure that I agree with you. Bill [English] ignored National's core supporters with disastrous results, both in the polls and in terms of financial support.'

The thing Brash objected to most was the suggestion that the policies he believed in might have to be watered down to win the election. 'I'm not at all sure that what you are suggesting – agreeing with most of the undesirable things that Labour is proposing (four weeks annual leave, total opposition to asset sales, total opposition to flattening the tax scale, etc), in other words trying to be "Helen Lite" – will get us there.'

Keenan had struck a raw nerve. 'I'm also left wondering what it is that I will actually achieve by winning the election – maintaining a whole lot of dopey Labour policies, not granting choice in education because it would scare the horses, not doing anything useful to improve the tax system, not doing anything much to improve the growth rate, etc. I don't have much interest in being just another "me too" Prime Minister. Indeed, I'd much prefer to go and do something enjoyable, and more lucrative, than being a Prime Minister of a status quo Government.'[9]

Keenan replied the next day with 'a few responses to Don's comment, before our meeting, by way of clearing up any misunderstandings'.[10] He set about giving a lesson in election-winning expediency.

'First, re core supporters, I am not suggesting they be ignored in any general sense – if we can't hold their support there is no hope.... But the policies that National/Brash stand for are not widely enough shared in the community to win an election, and most core supporters will understand that (just as core Labour supporters know that Clark has to counter you on the Treaty and Law and Order by saying things that her core supporters disapprove of – but they trust her not to follow through in government).'

In other words, Keenan was aware that most New Zealanders would not support the kind of free market beliefs that took Brash into politics and that most of his wealthy financial backers wanted to see put into practice. The solution was to tell the public what they wanted to hear but not necessarily to reveal plans with which they would not agree. Brash had to face the reality that 'an uncompromising freemarket liberal stance results in ACT level support'.

'So, be "bold, strong, visionary",' Keenan wrote, 'as those [core] supporters suggest – but there is no need to re-enact the charge of the light brigade.' He repeated the advice of United States Republican strategist David Horowitz: 'politics is war, and you have to choose the terrain that suits you. eg Privatisation is hostile terrain; you will get ambushed and wiped out.'[11]

This is both frank and illuminating. Keenan was acknowledging that a pure free market stance, which he believed in, would result in 'ACT level support', which at the time he was writing meant only about 4 per cent of voters.[12] Most people did not want a return to those policies. This observation echoes Horowitz, often quoted by Keenan, who argued in his *How* to *Beat the Democrats and other subversive essays* that 'there is no natural conservative majority'. But according to Horowitz, the art of 'political war' does not involve changing your policies to those the public agrees with, but sticking to your policies and creating a majority by 'political strategy'.[13] Keenan saw his and Brash's job in the same way. He believed strongly that National and Brash were the vehicle to introduce free market policies. His proposed strategy was not to drop those publicly unpopular policies – as an alarmed Brash had assumed from his paper – but instead to play them down and hide them until after an election win, then proceed with them when or as political circumstances allowed.

For instance, on the subject of privatisation he reassured Brash: 'I am not suggesting a blanket opposition to asset sales. I think the line should be that we will always reconsider the structure of the public sector balance sheet from time to time, but privatisation is not a pressing issue.... In Government you would need to painstakingly build public understanding re privatisation, perhaps moving faster in that area in a second term.' He was not talking about what they should *do* in government, merely what they should not *say* during an election campaign: 'While the public are hostile to the idea, it doesn't make any sense to make a big issue of it – unless you think you can win the argument in 5 second soundbites (which you can't!)'.[14]

Keenan and Brash also debated other issues. On superannuation Keenan argued that 'Our stance on raising the age of eligibility of superannuation (however honest that might be) is a huge political negative for us – we simply have to neutralise the political damage as best we can'.[15]

Brash was unhappy about backing down on this issue. His reply says a lot about his character. 'You suggest that one of the "negatives" is an incomplete stance on superannuation, and in particular you are concerned about our stance on raising the age of eligibility ("however honest that may be"),' he wrote. 'I am more than happy to debate that, and in particular whether it would be better to lie!'[16]

Keenan replied: 'I am not concerned about the stance on superannuation, just the fact of it being deeply unpopular'. There was no need to be blatantly untruthful. 'I am not suggesting a need to lie.... We just need a more nuanced way of talking about super issues.' He proposed that National make some statements on short-term issues to reassure the 'elderly constituency' while keeping open long term options.

Likewise, on tax he reassured Brash that he was 'not suggesting anything remotely like total, or any, opposition to flattening the tax scale. Only that we don't put all the emphasis on knocking the top rate down in one shot, that we emphasise a gradual reduction at the top end.' On education, his advice was to play down their policy during the election. 'Of course we should be granting choice in education' – encouraging competition and supporting private schools – 'it is just a question of whether we want to make it one of the election issues. I am still in two minds about how much of an issue we should make of this and how radical we should be in terms of an election campaign, but can certainly see the case for doing so, as Murray [McCully] argues. It is debateable. I am in no doubt that shifting to full portability of funding [allowing state funding for private schools] is the appropriate thing to do – only in doubt about whether to run hard on it in a campaign.'

And, on Labour's four weeks of annual leave policy, he hammered home his overriding point. 'Would it help if I put it this way,' he said, 'is it worth losing an election over? If we decide not, then we need to do our flip-flop before Xmas, and look to ways that could reduce the impact.'

Keenan concluded: 'So is this just Helen-lite? Treaty reform, Law and Order reform, Welfare reform, reversing the latest employment law reform package, RMA reform, tax and benefit reform, the beginning of a two-term tax cutting package, providing greater choice in education (pace yet to be determined) etc. Doesn't look like Helen-lite to me. Don,... if we could do that lot half well it would be a remarkable achievement.'

Essentially he was reminding Brash that their priority must be whatever was needed to win power, and that once there they could get on with their agendas. He reassured Brash that, despite the necessary election expediency, they still had the same ultimate goals. Keenan ended the discussion by saying that they could 'Sort out privatisation in the second term!'[17]

Keenan had pointed out some other problem areas too, to which Brash did not reply at that stage. These included 'a feeling that National/Brash means cuddling up to Uncle Sam and the removal of our no-nukes policy'; 'A sense that Brash is cut off from the concerns of ordinary New Zealanders... that big business have his ear, and nobody else'; and 'a feeling that National has no concern for the environment, and will just follow whatever the US/Australia does on Kyoto'.[18]

One other area where Keenan and Brash disagreed was on race policies. Keenan suggested there was 'a sense that we are failing the political hygiene test on Maori issues'.[19] He argued that National was being seen as 'always on the negative side of things, with no indication at all that we are actively engaged with Maori. Evidence: our polling re "best on race relations", showing National almost -30%.'[20]

Brash, who had made great political gains from attacking Maori 'special privilege', was reluctant to accept this. He reacted to the percentage, saying, 'I find it impossible to believe that that number is telling us what you imply. You might be correct, but I don't think so!'[21] Keenan replied: 'The absolute number doesn't tell us anything, but the decline from approximate balance to -30% I think does. And I continue to get feedback from people concerned that National seems to be always on the Maori-bashing end of the spectrum.'[22] Keenan got his way on most of the election-winning necessities he raised at this time, but on the continuation of negative attacks on Maori, Brash would prevail.

Some of Keenan's advice was simply the reasonable frustration of practical people in political parties who are faced with unhelpful advice from the membership. For instance, he ended his comments about the relevance of core supporters' views by saying: 'I might add that some core supporters, in my humble view, are almost barking mad when it comes to choosing a package of measures that enough people might vote for – i.e. I am thinking of those who think that slashing the top tax rate and reinstating the strike wing of the airforce should do the trick.'[23]

Keenan concluded his strategy paper with the following 'to do' list. '1. Deal with our negatives, inoculate them.... 2. Get serious about building key constituencies, [notably] the elderly and women. 3. Try and change the perception of National as a club for older white male business people... and 4. do [something] about Don's image (he needs to be seen out of a suit, be seen around women and children and working people).... We can't start doing this two months out from the election – it will look fake and unconvincing.'[24]

The underlying philosophy seems to be that politicians should not change their plans in response to public opinion any more than absolutely necessary: as Don Brash said, he did not go into politics just to go along with dopey Labour policies. Instead a political party will hide its unpopular objectives or distract people from them, emphasise a small number of issues that attract its target voter groups, essentially as camouflage and whether or not they are representative of the party's overall plans, and use a wide range of tools to manufacture positive impressions of its side and negative ones of the other. Then, if they win the election, any policies they did not specifically promise not to do are fair game. The assumption is that it is normal and legitimate for politicians to seek and exercise power in pursuit of their preferred policies *despite* what the public wants and hopes for.

When he was pitching for the job in Brash's office in the week after the latter won the National Party leadership, Keenan quoted Horowitz on this subject. 'Politics is a War of Emotions,' he wrote. 'For the great mass of the public, casting a vote is not an intellectual choice, but a gut decision, based on impressions that may be superficial and premises that could be misguided. Political war is about evoking emotions that favour one's goals. It is the ability to manipulate the public's feelings in support of your agenda, while mobilising passions of fear and resentment against your opponent.'[25]

In a similar vein, Keenan wrote disparagingly about public attention to 'policy detail'. 'We can deal with [that] nearer to election time,' he advised, 'when the average voter is at least paying some transitory attention to them.'[26] In his view, it was better to try to appeal to the public at a 'subliminal' level. As he told Brash, 'I have become... enthused about the approach that [United States President Ronald] Reagan's team had – as described [to Brash in secret meeting with Reagan's former adviser] by Dick Allen. And what he described – a list of five words with a generally soft message, to counterbalance what Reagan's political opponents were saying about him – strikes me as what we should do as well.

'When we have you speaking on platforms, such as you will have at the regional conferences, we would have a huge blue banner across the stage behind you, with the words: Family, Security, Work, Community, Freedom. Then we have to make sure that in all your speeches, you hit those "buttons" – ie refer to those issues/messages so that they become part of the subliminal view of National and Don Brash.'[27]

This idea was carried out, and thereafter pictures of Brash speaking showed a blue banner with these words repeated over and over in the background. As Keenan explained, 'then when Cullen/Clark paint you as an extremist, giving tax cuts to the rich, taking NZ back to the horror and despair of the 90s etc etc blah blah, it will jar with the image of you that people keep seeing'.

'The other reason for painting this soft image,' he continued, 'is that, as the NBR [*National Business Review*] poll shows today, we are dominating the male vote and there is no way Clark will pull that back – but we are behind with females. If we can get back to parity on the female vote, we are home free!'[28]

Brash's other closest adviser, Bryan Sinclair, had an equally cynical view. 'The vast majority of punters,' he wrote to a National Party supporter, 'simply want their emotional levers pulled. Hopefully we're doing a bit of that at the moment.'[29] Sinclair believed that the way to get to the 'hearts and minds of the average news-averse punter'[30] was marketing. He wrote to Brash: 'To me, the art of successful politics is not the great mystery that some make it out to be. At its core, politics is the art of persuasion.... It's largely the same as selling a product. I look it at very simply, along these lines... 1. Analyse the market and the competition (research your voters, their needs, their hotzones) 2. Design your product/service.... 3. Consistently package (using simple policy and "kitchen table" language) and.... 4. Always ensure there is an emotive "gut" reaction to your product/service... button pushers and lever pullers.'[31]

Later chapters will show how sophisticated focus group research was used to identify the most politically useful lines, but the basic idea, as with Keenan, was to develop what they called a 'mantra' of simple, emotive statements and then repeat them endlessly until sooner or later the 'punters' would start to believe and respond to them. During the 2005 election campaign, 'rewarding hard-working New Zealanders', 'the drift to racial separatism', 'Labour's waste' and 'political correctness' and 'tackling the issues of mainstream New Zealanders' stand out as phrases that had obviously been selected for this endless repetition.[32]

The expression 'punters', as used in the internal discussions, is inherently contemptuous of the supposedly ill-informed, uninterested, irrational and easily influenced masses. Brash, as we have seen, referred to them as 'the punters out in punter land'. It is as if they are a different and inferior species.[33]

In contrast to the 'punters', there were others who were taken very seriously by the National Party leadership. One of the people Brash respected greatly and regularly took guidance from was the 1990s National politician Ruth Richardson. She symbolises the small and private grouping of far right political identities who supported and advised Brash throughout his leadership of the party.

The presence of Richardson had great significance. She was the embodiment of what Keenan sarcastically called 'the horror and despair of the 90s'. She had led the 'privatisation, welfare cuts, spending cuts on core services and... employment law reforms that... drove wages down'. She was removed from the National Cabinet after only three years and switched to the ACT Party. She continued the crusade, including arguing for all public schools to be sold off.

Brash and Richardson were close political allies from the free market years – he as Reserve Bank governor and she as finance minister from 1990 to 1993. She had probably the greatest influence on his decision to go into parliamentary politics. In early 2002 there had been a very private meeting at the late Sir Peter Elworthy's South Canterbury farm, Craigmore, where Richardson and other old friends had persuaded Brash to become a National candidate in that year's election. A year later she had pushed from the background for him to become party leader. Three weeks before his leadership coup, in early October 2003, she was guest speaker at the Centre for Independent Studies in Sydney, talking about 'Repositioning New Zealand's political spectrum'. Brash, she believed, was the way to achieve this.

Once Brash became leader, Richardson continued to advise him but they met only very quietly: at Centre for Independent Studies get-togethers or in private meetings away from Parliament. To ensure that such meetings remained secret her name was never written in Brash's diary. For instance, when Brash was worrying about how to improve the party's fortunes in late 2004,[34] he arranged to meet Richardson in Christchurch at 11.15am on Tuesday 9 November 2004 to get her advice. The entry in his official diary was simply 'Private Appt in Chch – refer Anne' (his appointments secretary).[35]

This meeting is mentioned in email correspondence between Richardson and Brash's ever-present helper, Bryan Sinclair. Sinclair had a dinner date with Richardson coming up, about which she had written 'you choose the venue and I will set the agenda!' On the agenda was the recurring concerns of Brash's closest supporters about the inadequacy of his National Party campaign advisers. Sinclair wrote: 'Hi Ruth, very keen for a frank discussion on Monday.... Your support for The Grand Plan would be highly valued. Diane F [Foreman] will be contacting you shortly, if she has not done so already. I am pretty confident you will be on exactly the same wavelength as me on this stuff. DB has huge respect for you, and he needs to accept that he has a real big problem right around the corner, if he leaves things as they are at the moment. There is no second chance, and B grade will simply not cut it.'[36] The Grand Plan will be introduced shortly.

Richardson replied, referring to American President George W. Bush's 2004 election win: 'If ever there was a vindication of being your own man of principle and making sure the architecture of the campaign to win/retain office is of the highest quality, this week's electoral tour de force of Dubya is it! I am seeing Dr D on Tuesday as you probably know.... Don seems to be in the thrall of people not fit to tie his shoelaces let alone wash his smalls! ... Look forward to Monday ... Ciao, Ruth.'[37]

Another email from Ruth Richardson to Sinclair and Brash in the midst of the 2005 election campaign triumphantly predicted that Brash would soon be prime minister. 'I have long held the unfashionable view that Don would be very competitive and that he could get the centre/right over the line. I am a patient man,' she wrote (a curious typo for a woman), 'as the polls finally catch up with my prediction!' She ended this June 2005 email with a piece of advice that sums up the morality of power. 'Stick to your guns,' she said, 'being in government is worth everything.'[38] Sinclair forwarded Richardson's enthusiastic message to Brash with the note, 'And your biggest fan...!'[39] Brash replied: 'She is GREAT!'[40]

The National Party staff and politicians also had close relationships with the small circle of big donors to the party. The public is normally told that fundraising is handled by the party officials and that the politicians have no idea who is putting up the money for their election campaigns. Certainly for National, and probably all other parties, that was not correct. New Zealand is mostly free of the blatant forms of corruption seen in some parts of the world, but this has made the public complacent about the possible compromising of politicians and politics that can occur. What politicians want most – more than gifts of cash or free overseas trips – is to gain power, to win elections, and winning elections requires lots of money. This need, coupled with ineffectual political donation laws written by the same politicians who need the election funds, opens the way for all sorts of undeclared relationships involving money.

As the coming pages will reveal, many of National's main donors were also important political allies and advisers of the party leadership, a situation that created blurred, informal lines of mutual interest. These donors included millionaire leading figures in the Business Roundtable, industry lobbyists and other wealthy individuals who wanted to help ensure election of a Brash-led National government. The Exclusive Brethren link was just one of many relationships the National Party used to help it attain power.

Among these major donors was Diane Foreman. The closeness of the political relationship was illustrated by a July 2005 email from Foreman to Sinclair in which Foreman, taking a close interest in National's internal politics, expressed similar misgivings to Ruth Richardson about some of Brash's advisers. 'I am kind of stunned that the polls look as good as they do, and still maintain that it's got nothing to do with the "dark side".'[41] In other emails from Foreman, the 'dark side' is a recurring reference to Murray McCully and other advisers who were competing for Brash's ear. 'Of course I am sure your boss has other thoughts,' she said, 'but let's hope "they" don't get too much power after the election. I will be very interested to see the front bench!'

Sinclair agreed. 'We still have a helluva campaign to come from Labour,' he wrote, 'and even with a win, the dark side will still be there and, I'd wager, even more dominant as a consequence.' Outsiders might imagine that National staff and supporters would use a term like the 'dark side' to describe the Labour Party, or trade unions or maybe New Zealand First. But they were equally concerned about who had influence within their own party and so what kind of National Party would become the government.

Neither Sinclair nor Foreman was a long-term National supporter and having National win the election was not their primary goal. They had a bigger plan in mind, which centred on Brash being prime minister. Sinclair was referring to this when he explained his presence in the National leader's office in an email to Peter Keenan. 'It is worth mentioning,' he wrote, 'that I did not step off a plane from Sydney at Don's front door ... entirely by accident, nor did I need a job, especially one as a glorified secretary and travel arranger, like I think some of our other colleagues might presume. There is a far bigger picture here....'[42]

The bigger picture was what Brash, Sinclair, Foreman and other closest Brash supporters referred to privately as the 'Grand Plan'. The phrase appeared in such communications as the following email from Sinclair to Brash in September 2004. 'Don, I would like to have a private, sit down chat with you about a couple of things before Thursday, when we both return to Wellington,' Sinclair wrote. 'Firstly ACT. I met with [ACT Party president] Catherine [Judd] today to work out where the "centre right" land lies and to refocus on The Grand Plan.... I remain confident that there is light at the end of our long tunnel to the ninth floor, Don (!!).'[43] Brash replied that he was 'happy to have a chat'.

Although the Grand Plan term was obviously slightly facetious, it referred to a very serious political purpose. For ten years, from 1993 to 2003, the principal supporters of free market reform had watched with frustration as public opinion hardened against their vision of privatisation and smaller government and, in their view, the country drifted. According to insiders, the Grand Plan meant a concerted effort to move New Zealand politics back to the right, renewing the economic and social reform that occurred in the 1980s under Labour Finance Minister Roger Douglas and in the early 1990s under Ruth Richardson.

The key to this plan was having Don Brash as National Party leader and then prime minister. Most of the people who backed him in this, including the financial backers who put up the millions that nearly carried National to power, shared this goal. Mainly men in their 60s and 70s, they had been leading supporters and financial beneficiaries of the Roger Douglas/Ruth Richardson reforms. They were the ones who, for three elections, had funded the ACT Party to keep the flame alive. Chapter 14 discusses each of these donors and their pasts.

In early 2005 the National Party campaign manager Steven Joyce wrote to electorate campaign committees saying that 'in this election National is planning to go close to its legal limit for Party Vote campaign expenditure [meaning $2,240,000]. This has not happened previously.'[44] After some years of financial problems, a dozen or so big donors had begun supporting National again. When the official donation declarations were delivered to the Electoral Commission a few months after election day, not a single one of their names was there. Their donations had gone to National via the legal channel of lawyers' trust accounts and other special anonymising trusts that ensured secrecy. The political influence of these big donors, and a wider circle of medium-level donors, on the National Party and the country is one of the important untold stories of New Zealand politics.[45]

Donors including Foreman, ideological allies including Richardson and strategy advisers including Keenan and Sinclair were Brash's three main supports as leader. Most of them knew, as Keenan had stated bluntly to Brash, that if National openly espoused all their personal beliefs, it would be unelectable. Hence the slightly distasteful but necessary job of pulling levers, pressing buttons, evoking emotions and exploiting fears so that the punters would cast their votes the right way.

As is obvious in much modern politics, to do this politicians do not particularly need the party membership, except to supplement fundraising efforts. They do not particularly need the rest of caucus either. Other MPs often just cause problems. The main things needed are one or more politician frontpeople, a small group of hired advisers, focus group researchers, advertising people, direct mail experts, web designers, media managers, PR advisers, speechwriters and strategists – plus lots of money from the big donors. Whatever it takes. Because, as Richardson said, being in government is worth everything.

CHAPTER 4

REPACKAGING THE LEADER
Making a man of spin

The first task for Brash's new staff in the weeks following the leadership coup was marketing the leader himself, a job referred to privately as 'repackaging'. Bryan Sinclair took charge of this. He approached Australian speech coach Neil Flett a month after the coup, explaining that 'our initial emphasis has been on reinforcing Dr Brash's perceived credibility, integrity and leadership abilities'.[1] Flett visited New Zealand to help Brash with presentation skills (paid for privately by *NBR*'s Barry Colman),[2] including advice on television interviews that read 'What NOT to do: Answer questions'.[3]

Sinclair also escorted Brash while he bought new clothes to fit the leader image. He wrote to former National Party president Sue Wood, now in PR, saying the new clothes would be 'Fashionable, chic but in a very understated, classic, gentlemanly kind of way. Well dressed conservative. Crisp, credible.' As with Flett's bill, he preferred to approach wealthy business supporters to pay: 'it will probably be $5K ballpark on all this'. He was looking for someone who would 'like to contribute in some way to this side of things' by 'picking up the bill'.[4]

It was not hard to promote the credibility and integrity image. Initial stories about Brash had already described him as 'probably the most honest man in politics', possessing 'honesty, intelligence, frankness, personal likeability [and] gravitas' and 'super ethical'.[5] This is the familiar but curious phenomenon whereby new political leaders tend to be presented in a thoroughly uncritical way by the media when they first appear – more or less just repeating the version of the politician that he or she chooses to present. This changes when their inevitable flaws and weaknesses become obvious, but not usually until much later.

There was, however, one large and immediate negative to overcome in selling Brash. The same newspaper editorial that praised his 'honesty, intelligence' etc summed up the problem: Brash, it said, 'is annoyed by the "Act MP" tag but it has much truth in it. Brash would fit better into Act than National. If Brash tries to turn National into a far-right party, one that would mirror his own principles, he will kill it as a significant political force. The public simply will not go for the policies that caused so much grief in the 1980s and 1990s.'[6]

Don Brash was one of New Zealand's early and leading free market advocates. When he headed the merchant bank Broadbank in 1981 he personally arranged a tour of the country by Milton Friedman, the foremost new right thinker in the world and adviser, a generation ago, to British Prime Minister Margaret Thatcher and to Ronald Reagan.[7] Brash hosted Friedman again during an unpublicised private visit in January 2005, as National Party leader at the beginning of election year.

In the early 1980s, Brash stood twice for the National Party in the East Coast Bays electorate and was one of a small number of renegade free market believers on the right of the party who challenged the leader Robert Muldoon's policies. Brash's biography quotes the 'likeminded young new MP' Ruth Richardson, writing to him after he narrowly missed becoming an MP in the 1981 election. 'At times,' she said, 'democracy really does have no taste.'[8] The 'non-politician' Brash had been a politician since at least the early 1980s.

When Roger Douglas and Richard Prebble took control of economic policy in 1984, they used Brash to chair review committees in 1985, 1986 and 1987 advising on the reforms; and in 1988 they chose him to be Reserve Bank governor, overseeing the deregulated monetary system, under finance ministers Douglas, David Caygill and later Ruth Richardson. Brash's biography says he 'had been introduced to Roger Douglas by his friend Michael Bassett in the early 1970s' and 'found much to admire in what Douglas was saying about the need for economic reform'.[9]

When public opinion turned against the free market revolution in the 1990s, Brash became increasingly outspoken in defence of continuing the reforms. In February 1996 he threatened to resign if a finance minister wanted him to use monetary policy to improve growth or employment.[10] Later that year he received the far-right honour of giving the Fifth Hayek Memorial Lecture in London, where he praised New Zealand's foreign ownership, labour and health sector reforms and said the country should continue with further reforms including privatising New Zealand Post, ACC and the Electricity Corporation.[11] Over the following seven years he became more and more political, publicly proposing scrapping the minimum wage, limiting benefits and cutting tax for the highest earners.[12]

All of this helped to explain why, when Brash was guest speaker at the ACT Party Upper South Regional Conference four weeks before becoming National Party leader, the ACT president Catherine Judd introduced him warmly as the 'ninth ACT MP'.[13]

It was this same Don Brash whom we saw balking at the need for short-term political compromise in discussion with Peter Keenan in November 2004, complaining petulantly that he was 'left wondering what it is that I will actually achieve by winning the election.... I'd much prefer to go and do something enjoyable, and more lucrative, than being a Prime Minister of a status quo Government.'[14] According to his biography, only a month after becoming an MP in 2002 he had read political scientist Tim Bale commenting that European centre-right parties only returned to power after they renounced their pasts and moved to the centre. In his diary Brash had written 'yuck' beside Bale's comments.[15]

His staff and supporters were well aware that for Brash to succeed it was essential to take attention off his well-documented political beliefs. It took them only a short while to get Brash 'on message'. In interviews around the time of the leadership coup he had restated his long-held views on the importance of cutting tax rates for the wealthiest earners and resuming privatisation of state enterprises, including Television New Zealand.[16] There were a few news articles at that time recalling his staunchly free market beliefs, with titles like 'Fundamentally Right'. But his staff soon closed around him to ensure he said as little as possible that would clash with their repackaging of him as a centrist politician.

For example, when Brash considered making a comment about an ACT Party report on Radio New Zealand, Sinclair warned him that 'it would probably be unwise for you to lead the criticism of National Radio because they will paint you as Don Brash the Privatisation Man'.[17] Roger Kerr of the Business Roundtable wrote to congratulate him on his success in deflecting questions about his political beliefs. 'Don, You've been handling the criticisms of your alleged "extreme", "right-wing" views very well. Your views are totally mainstream.' He then wrote: 'Next there will be talk about "having views like the Business Roundtable". Someone may even discover you were a member. I won't be helping them – we've been lying low, as you may have noticed.'[18]

In the same way that politicians can manufacture an image by talking about 'family', or 'security', Brash's staff simply repeated the idea that he was centrist until it started to seem true. Here is Richard Long on the job. 'Can we please book in New Zealand Press Association editor Peter Wilson and staffer Kevin Norquay for 11–11.30 Wednesday March 10 for a private off the record chat with Don,' he wrote to Brash's secretary. 'This will be for them to get an idea from him on where things are going, what Don's plans are and for Don to set the record straight with them on Labour's spin mechanisms: tax cuts for the rich... and all the rest. National will be centre of the road etc. NZPA is the basic news service going to ALL newspapers so is of huge importance to us.'[19]

And after a while this worked. Brash's staff wrote his speeches and prepared his media 'lines' with care to 'de-emphasise' his more extreme views, and deliberately steered him away from situations that might contradict the repackaged image. In between, as we saw in Chapter 3, close advisers like Peter Keenan counselled him to bide his time on policy until he was in government.

Quite soon the new image was, if not actively believed, at least being passively relayed by most news media. After National reversed its policies on four weeks' annual leave and superannuation in December 2004 – moves described internally as 'very hard ideological compromise' necessary for vote winning[20] – these were reported in the media as evidence of the new more centrist Brash. The silence on privatisation was taken as a softening of his beliefs. Despite his history – which showed that Brash was no more a centrist than if a repackaged Ruth Richardson had returned to head National – the far-right record was being quietly left behind.

For instance, when National's broadcasting spokesperson, Georgina Te Heuheu, talked about privatising TVNZ and Radio New Zealand at a regional party conference in 2004, 'National Party sources' were 'quick to play down the prospect'. Brash stuck to bland prepared lines – 'I haven't seen exactly what Georgina said... but there has certainly been no discussion on the sale of any assets at all' – and the reporter said, 'Dr Brash went into the leadership with a reputation as an economic hardliner, but since his appointment he has indicated a more centrist path.'[21]

By election year, the whole subject of Don Brash's political beliefs had largely disappeared from the news, showing a strange lack of interest in the difference between what politicians say about themselves and what they really believe. The news media should serve as a kind of public memory, but when most political news simply reports politicians speaking their lines – quotation journalism – they can fail in this role.

One of the casualties in all this was Brash himself – the supposedly super-ethical, honest non-politician. At heart, he was most comfortable when he was being open about his strongly held beliefs. The trouble was that what he believed would, as Keenan put it, 'result in ACT level support'.[22] The more they succeeded in repackaging him, the less was he the straight-talking man of integrity. National's spin doctors were in effect making a man of spin. They stripped him of the things that made him a political liability, but also of the things that made him authentic. There were now too many hidden political dealings and less-than-forthright policy positions for straight talking. Even for the party there were drawbacks, because the disparity between the image and reality left Brash vulnerable should the real person inadvertently be revealed. This is exactly what happened in the midst of the election campaign.

The sales pitch was, in Brian Nicolle's words, that Brash was 'a new kind of politician' who was 'honest, sincere and energetic'. The staff planted the idea that he might sometimes be politically clumsy, but this was merely evidence of his being a 'non-politician', free of the usual political game playing. But behind the scenes they were open about their doubts.

'Can we stop Don from giving speeches?' Sinclair wrote to Keenan two months before the election. 'Today's speech delivery is about as exciting as watching paint dry. The speech delivery is too long, monotonous, slow paced, and he is having far too many stumbles.'[23] Keenan believed Brash looked good on television, where he could follow his lines, but worried frequently about his poor performance elsewhere. Privately, he said, 'I would not be so confident about his main strength being as a "non-conventional politician". It is only true to an extent. Equally you could argue that the more the electorate has got to know him the less they like what they see: somebody who cannot foot it in Parliament, who often seems to lack energy and charisma in interviews.'[24]

An important element of the Brash public image was that he was a man of principle. This is the part that could and should have been true. The repackaging advice from Brash's freelance adviser Nicola Young had been for him to say that his leadership was 'not a swing to the right' because 'I am a liberal conservative, that's why I am in National, not ACT'.[25] Colin James described him as a 'classical liberal with a social conscience'.[26] The socially liberal side of the man was not as strong as the economically liberal side, but it was genuine.

Brash was one of a small group of high donors to Amnesty International, brought together by lawyer (and later National MP) Christopher (Chris) Finlayson. After becoming an MP, but before becoming leader, Brash and National MP Katherine Rich had arranged a petition calling for a royal commission inquiry into the 1993 conviction of Christchurch crèche worker Peter Ellis, also a politically principled act. In the same period he voted for the Prostitution Reform Bill. Once he became National Party leader, however, there was less and less sign of the principles carrying through into action.

On the case of the wrongfully imprisoned refugee Ahmed Zaoui, for instance, Brash wrote to his colleagues: 'Guys, I have to say that, after reading some of the stuff on this case today (for the first time, sitting on umpteen aircraft flights), I am absolutely appalled at the way it has been handled. I think the evidence that Zaoui is a security risk is extremely flimsy.' He thought the issue should be reviewed by the Intelligence and Security Committee of which he was a member.[27]

But there was no petition or action this time. Long advised him neither to follow it up on the committee nor appear on a scheduled current affairs programme about the issue. Long got his way and sent round an email about the television appearance: 'Don's not going on this and nor should any of our people. It's one the Government should take the rap for, not us.'[28]

The biggest test of Brash's liberal views was the Civil Union Bill. In February 2004 he wrote to his advisers, passing on an email about the bill he had received from his gay friend Michael Coote. He noted that Coote had been an ACT Party candidate the year before and 'if Bryan had not joined the team, I would have thought seriously about hiring him'. Coote had argued that National's 'One law for all New Zealanders' should lead to the party letting gay people be married and get on with their lives like anyone else. Brash asked the team for 'Any views on how we play the matters that he raises?'[29]

Peter Keenan and Bryan Sinclair responded that they agreed with Coote and that being liberal on this issue was worth votes to National in the cities. Brash replied: 'I certainly know of a number of people who are not gay, but who have gay friends, who would be quite offended if we adopted an aggressively anti-gay position, and I have no inclination to adopt such a position myself in any case'.[30] He announced his intention to support the bill. Various of Brash's closest political allies – staff, MPs and outside Parliament – were gay men and appreciated his stand.

In early April Coote organised the first meeting of a new National gay and lesbian chapter in Auckland and Stephen Rainbow proposed setting up a group in Wellington. Brash received positive news coverage on the subject and was interviewed in the gay magazine *Express*. Press officer Jason Ede circulated lines explaining Brash's position. 'Don is offering conditional support to the Civil Unions Bill, subject to seeing the fine print,' he wrote. 'He has no problem if consenting adults want to commit to each other in a contract. But when it comes to "gay marriage" he says there is a connotation of that being between a man and woman and he doesn't support use of the word "marriage" for same sex couples.'[31]

A few days later Brash wrote to all National MPs saying he knew there were a 'wide range of views' on the Civil Union Bill in the caucus. He encouraged them to read two articles from the *Economist* magazine Coote had sent him, which put the case for the Conservatives supporting gay marriage and explained the electoral benefits to be gained. 'I am not proposing to make a big thing of my support for the Civil Union Bill (subject to seeing the fine print) and will be emphasising the fact that this will be a conscience vote for the National Party.'[32] By mid-year, when he was being deluged with mail for and against the bill, the standard written reply was that Brash was 'comfortable with two individuals (irrespective of sexual preference) finding a way to more formally commit to one another, however he is not on record as favouring gay "marriage". After considering a large amount of public feedback... Dr Brash remains unconvinced that the legislation devalues traditional marriage between a man and a woman.'[33]

The next four months, from July to October, were the period of sinking poll support and growing worries in the campaign team. As a result of that, and faced with anti-civil union lobbying from conservative Christians, Brash seems to have lost his nerve. On 7 November 2004, at the time of the big strategy review, he forwarded to the strategy team an article from the British *Telegraph* newspaper, saying, 'I think this article is highly relevant to us in New Zealand.'[34] The article argued that George W. Bush's 2004 election win had been brought about by 'values' issues, such as Bush's opposition to gay marriage. It pointed to growing numbers of 'values voters' and ran through a range of reasons why they might feel uncomfortable about gay marriage. Its conclusion was that 'George W. Bush minutely studies the anxieties of such people and tries to attend to them. That is why he won.' The British Tories do not, 'and that is why they lose, and lose, and lose'.[35]

The Christian right thinktank the Maxim Institute had argued the same way, telling Brash in a confidential lobbying letter to 'appreciate the huge political mileage you can make out of this'. Maxim director Bruce Logan said that 'by supporting [the Civil Union Bill] National will gain a few votes. By rejecting it you will get thousands.'[36]

Four weeks after he circulated the 'highly relevant' values voters article, Brash suddenly dropped his year-long support for the Civil Union Bill.

Peter Keenan confided to Bryan Sinclair that he was 'dismayed' by Brash 'caving in on the CUB – the simple politics of it. I don't much care what his personal view is. He seems to have been convinced by core Nats that a change would do him some political good, whereas all I could see was a striking parallel with [US presidential candidate John] Kerry.... Arrrg-ghhh.'[37]

Brash explained his decision in Parliament on 2 December 2004. 'This Bill is seen by many New Zealanders as an attack on the institution of marriage.... More generally, the Bill is seen as part of a broader Government agenda to change our moral and social institutions, and that makes a great many New Zealanders very uneasy indeed. Well, Mr Speaker, I don't think that this Parliament should be lending its support to this agenda.'[38]

He had let down his urban liberal supporters but from that time on his relationship developed with groups like the Exclusive Brethren – whose members had sat in the parliamentary gallery looking down on the MPs through each stage of the bill – evangelical churches and the Maxim Institute. The non-politician had been politely pushed aside by the politician.

A small amount of literal rewriting of the Don Brash sales pitch was required. A few weeks before the Civil Union Bill vote, Brash's biographer, Paul Goldsmith, had sent him the latest version of the nearly completed manuscript. The chapter on Brash as National Party leader included this sentence: 'On traditional conscience issues, as we have seen, Brash has been prepared to let people decide matters of sexual morality for themselves'.[39] In the version sent to the publishers a few weeks later, the sentence had been discreetly removed.

On the evening of the Civil Union Bill final vote, Brash's long-time right-wing friend, gay broadcaster Lindsay Perigo, sent him an email with the one-word heading 'Integrity'.

> The reason I didn't go to the Nats party last night is that I couldn't have coped with socialising with such horrible, unprincipled homophobes. Your caucus is despicable, and your own recent conduct – a disgrace to your late father – is little better. You have succumbed to McCullyism, and there is nothing more despicable in politics than that. Plus ca change. You'll all go down, which is what you all deserve.
>
> In sorrow and anger ...
> Your former friend, Linz.[40]

CHAPTER 5

THE 'BIG SPLASH' AT OREWA
The strategies behind the speech

Brash and his advisers decided that his first major speech as leader, timed for 27 January 2004 at the Orewa Rotary Club, would be about 'racial separatism'. It was not a cautious address. It presented a highly negative version of Maori history, questioned the very idea of being Maori and characterised political consultation with Maori as a 'deeply corrupt' process that 'allows people to invent or rediscover beliefs for pecuniary gain'. Most powerfully, he aroused feelings of resentment and envy by describing a greedy 'grievance industry' in which 'the minority has a birthright to the upper hand', and vowed to put an end to 'special privilege' for Maori.

The speech is now remembered not so much for its content as for the extraordinary effect it had on National's poll results. After a long period stuck in the low 20s, the party's support leapt to about 45 per cent. The wave of emotion that drove up the polls lasted only a few months, but that one speech put Brash and National in a position where they were seriously challenging the Labour-led government and within reach of winning the 2005 election.

Brash was immediately branded as a racist by his opponents and likened to Australian Pauline Hanson and her One Nation party. But Brash was not driven by racsim. The speech marks his descent into unprincipled politics because of the motives and political calculation that lay behind the decision to make that sort of speech at that time.

Publicly, Brash claimed to have noble motives. 'In many ways,' he said, 'I am deeply saddened to have to make a speech about issues of race.' But 'I believe in plain speaking' and the risk of 'disaster' had required him to be 'blunt'.[1] Was it a courageous speech, as Brash's supporters claimed, or was he just cynically playing the race card to capture voters off other parties, as his detractors argued? That question can now be answered. The internal National Party communications before and after the speech give a clear picture of what was in the minds of the people responsible.

It was no surprise that Maori rights were on the agenda in early 2004. Controversy was still raging over the foreshore and seabed issue, which had been sparked by a Court of Appeal decision allowing Maori organisations to make claims over coastal waters and shorelines and continued when the government introduced and passed legislation restricting those rights. Brash became National Party leader when the topic was hot. Much of his initial advice on this subject came from freelance speech writer and strategist Matthew Hooton.

A few days after the leadership vote, Hooton sent Brash a five-page communications strategy plan entitled 'Internal vs External Audiences'. He began by noting that 'One prominent right-wing MP described the situation to me as "the best week for the right" in his lifetime'. Hooton argued that people who identify themselves as left or right 'are the most interesting people to share dinner with, but they are not important to us politically, because they vote one way or the other. The people who count would be described by a political scientist as "centre".' The paper, which described how Brash could appeal to these centre voters, is an excellent example of the thought process of a Beehive spin doctor. Hooton summarised his plan as:

* Keep the [right-wing] base happy, but do this below the threshold, with nods and winks, and private functions – plus the odd staunch statement to the NBR etc.
* In association with the wider base, unify the party at all costs.
* Use the highest-possible quality research to identify potential groups (eg, superannuitants) who could switch votes, what they think about you, and what they want to see from you.
* When developing strategy, appointing an office, communicating – in everything you do – be informed by the need to reach across the divide and touch base with the audiences identified from research.
* Be surprising but not confusing.
* Buy some light-blue shirts![2]

A couple of days later Hooton elaborated on the 'be surprising' part. His paper had used the example of George W. Bush inviting Muslim clerics to the White House, noting that no one thought Bush had gone soft on

Muslims but that it seemed intriguing and attracted media attention. He suggested that Brash could do something similar by engaging constructively with Maori.

According to Hooton's plan, which was very different from the subsequent aggressive strategy behind the Orewa speech, 'the surprise comes from Constitutional/Treaty/Maori issues'. The idea was to surprise and interest the public by National responding sympathetically to Maori concerns about the foreshore and seabed. 'If we can surprise everyone on these issues,' Hooton argued, 'we will:

Eliminate perceptions Don is only about economics
Eliminate perceptions Don is hard right
Surprise urban liberals and make them consider us
Pick up conservative Maori votes, and
MOST IMPORTANTLY put the shits up Labour and force them into a more radical 'pro' Maori position and pick up red neck votes as well.[3]

Hooton's advice was born of political manoeuvring more than strong principle – how to use the issue to Brash and National's advantage – but it was also much more in accord with the traditional National Party approach to Maori matters than the final Orewa speech would be. Later that week Hooton spelt out the case against a more confrontational approach, unknowingly anticipating some of the flaws in the Orewa speech. 'Be very careful with the use of "separatism". What does it mean? Are you really against Maori communities in the Far North from being able to run the local school based on Maori culture? No? What about health clinics in Kaeo? No? What about a Maori ONLY private boarding school getting vouchers? Maybe. But it seems to me you can't be for devolved delivery of social services and community autonomy and against "separatism", whatever that means in a modern context.'[4]

He presented a 'recommended political plan for Maori issues':

1. Appeal to more conservative Maori leaders on property rights (article two issues)
2. Appeal to sensible liberal 'urban' Maori on vouchers for schools, health etc (article three issues)
3. In doing so, take enough support away from Labour to give NZ First a chance of winning the Maori seats again
4. In doing so, push Labour into taking a more radical 'pro-Maori' stance, and pick up redneck working class votes too.

He offered to discuss these ideas with Brash in more detail, 'perhaps in the new year'. 'But it is all dependent on getting rid of the Pauline Hanson-style "One Nation" rhetoric.'[5]

At that stage, only a week after the leadership challenge, the idea of a strident attack on 'separatism' and rhetoric about 'special privilege' had not arisen. Hooton was writing Brash's speeches and the tone on Maori issues was generally positive and conciliatory. This was not a radical position, considering that the Business Roundtable was openly backing a grouping of major iwi called the Treaty Tribes Coalition, which was urging the government to allow the seabed and foreshore dispute to be heard in the courts. But over the following weeks a very different plan emerged.

In late November 2003 Hooton gave Brash another piece of advice that was highly relevant to the decisions that followed. After Brash became leader National's opinion poll results had risen, then sunk again in the following weeks during messy struggles over the deputy leader position. Hooton had some undeniably sound advice for Brash on the link between poll results and his ability to control the caucus and thus National Party strategy. 'In response to concerns about the management of your caucus colleagues, the answer is that you can do anything you like if you keep going up in the polls. And if you make big bold moves based clearly on leadership preference [i.e. Brash making the calls], you will go up in the polls. So it is a virtuous cycle situation.'[6]

'On the other hand,' he said, 'if you don't take big bold moves based on leadership preference, you'll go down in the polls and won't be able to take any initiatives in future. You'll become a prisoner of the caucus. I figure you have the next few weeks to establish which one it will be.' The Orewa speech, which Keenan began work on shortly after, would be a perfect example of a big, bold move that would establish Brash's control over the leadership and party.[7]

Sinclair wrote to Brash and Keenan, who had just arrived in the office, saying he agreed with Hooton. 'From a purely political standpoint, there is considerable value in [Hooton's] bit about the potential for [Brash] to become a prisoner of the caucus.... We need to have him on the front foot showing strong leadership on something in the next few weeks.'[8] Keenan replied that he could draft a 'good speech' and 'have it delivered at whatever opportunity is the highest profile'.[9] Brash responded: 'Thanks guys. We need to review communications strategy soon, perhaps on Monday morning.'[10]

At this stage, early December 2003, there was still no hint of plans for a confrontational stand on Maori issues. This is clear from a Brash email on 5 December, where he reacted to New Zealand First leader Winston Peters circulating a leaflet critical of Asian immigrants. Earlier that day Richard Long had emailed Brash about Maori television, urging him to be more aggressive: 'You need to get a little more populist on some of these issues, even controllably angry. If we make our policies too bland... we are not going to get traction.' But that evening Brash emailed his closest staff and several National MPs about Peters exploiting racism for political gain, exclaiming 'Peters is a totally cynical politician of the worst kind'. They should find arguments to attack Peters and 'expose his total cynicism'. 'Might it cost us votes? Possibly, but I don't want the votes of the totally bigoted... that is what Peters is trying to attract.'[11]

In mid-November the *National Business Review* had reported 'Brash lifts National's hopes with strong party-vote poll'.[12] *NBR* owner Barry Colman had sent the poll results to Brash the day before with a note saying, 'This is the shot in the arm we've all been praying for'.[13] But the following month's *NBR* poll showed National dropping again while Winston Peters's New Zealand First went up. This is the news that Brash and his staff faced on Friday 12 December 2003:

Poll bashes Brash

The Don Brash honeymoon is over.... The new National Business Review-Phillips Fox poll shows the small gain by National following its coup in installing Dr Brash for Bill English has evaporated.

Political scientists are warning that, although it is only one poll result, it is indicative of real electoral trouble for National.

Auckland university political scientist Raymond Miller said, 'If that is the honeymoon, it was pretty short and not very sweet. There are danger signs there.'

Most of National's lost support seems to have gone to New Zealand First.... [Political scientist] Barry Gustafson said Mr Peters was cannibalising National's vote....

As for National, Dr Miller said its leader had to deliver in the next few months or supporters would question whether dumping Mr English was sensible.[14]

That morning Peter Keenan sent a briefing note to Brash about the poll. 'What is the message from the NBR Poll?' he wrote. 'Basically the Peters immigration stunt.' This, he said, 'has worked to boost NZF, taking support from National' and such a move was 'Very deliberate from [Peters's] point of view, trying to damp the National resurgence – and successful'.

Keenan argued, however, that the shift would 'not [be] enduring if we react appropriately'.[15]

This note contained the first suggestion that they might use the Orewa speech to counter Peters. Referring to the New Zealand First leader's successful exploitation of the immigration issue, Keenan said, 'There is no quick fix on this; we will always be vulnerable to Peters on these issues until we can credibly position National as being aware of and concerned about these issues. We can include some of this in the Orewa speech.'[16]

Bryan Sinclair replied to Keenan's note agreeing with 'the analysis of the NBR story' but stressing 'the other key message, and one that concerns me more... that Don Brash is invisible and is failing to make an impact as leader'.

> The party's prospects are very much linked to Don Brash. The vote is won on the stage not in the backroom. That's what moves public perception. It's like New Zealand First – that issue was a Peters-based issue. No issue National is plugging at the moment is a Brash-based issue.... Don is being painted as lack lustre and unfortunately this is the feedback that he's getting from those close to him outside of this place. This public perception will concern him greatly, particularly when its even started coming from our 'friends'.[17]

Keenan emailed back to Sinclair: 'Well, I sort of agree with much of that'. But, he said, 'More fundamentally, our problem is our product. The only big easily understood messages floating in the public consciousness about Don's version of National is a cut in the tax rate to 30%, and the age of super eligibility moving up to 68. Even my bloody TV repairman has the latter in his mind, and he doesn't like it. We have a major repositioning required in the New Year.'[18]

Keenan continued: 'I think we will do Don a disservice if he is led to believe that he just needs to get himself on TV more and find some big populist issue to push. We will need to do that some time next year, but we will need to do a hell of lot more.' But the idea of a 'big populist issue' had taken root. 'It would be great to have a big issue', Keenan mused, or to 'manufacture one like Peters', and he concluded that 'the only real prospect is the Foreshore issue'.[19]

The next day, 13 December, a Saturday, Keenan wrote a long email to Brash on the subject, headed 'Some thoughts re a speech on the foreshore'. 'Don,' it began, 'I know all sorts of people are pressuring you to get up and make some strong statements on the foreshore, or any other issue, to keep some profile, maintain momentum etc etc. Sometimes I feel we are surrounded by panic merchants. They need to get a grip.'

He pointed out that the fortnight before Christmas was a hopeless time for Brash to gain public attention. 'Labour are releasing all these policies right now for the very good reason that it is a period when nobody but the chattering classes are focusing on politics – everybody else is thinking of xmas and the summer holidays. Most want some merciful release from politics, if they ever think much about it.' [20] He presented his plan:

So, thinking about the time to make a speech that would make a big splash, the Orewa one is probably the best time. It will come after a summer with demonstrations on beaches, so that should set it up well. To be done well, this sort of speech needs some serious time to work on – it needs to have an elevated tone, not day-to-day politics. If we knocked up something in the next few days it would not be very good, and would be lost in the noise of politics and xmas in any case.

'What I have in mind,' he concluded, 'is a major speech on race relations in this country, dealing also with the immigration issues that Peters has manipulated, delivered at Orewa.' [21] Since Brash's election as leader, his staff had been identifying the need to target the approximately 15 per cent of centre-right parliamentary seats held by the New Zealand First and United Future parties. [22] This had become more urgent with support moving in the other direction.

Brash deferred to Keenan's advice on timing. 'Peter, thanks for that sober reflection. Certainly there are a number of my colleagues urging that we "MUST" raise National's/DTB's [Brash's initials] profile before everybody heads off to their barbeques. And I have some sympathy with that view. But you may well be right. Let's work on the assumption that we will not do a big speech on race issues pre Christmas.' [23] Keenan began work on the 'major speech on race relations' for delivery in January.

The 'elevated' tone Keenan planned for Orewa might not sound much like what eventuated, a speech that National Party historian Barry Gustafson would describe tactfully as 'oversimplifying and polarising the issue of the Treaty and the place of Maori'. [24] But remember that Keenan had a particularly cynical attitude to the public. This is the man who quoted with approval United States Republican strategist David Horowitz: 'Political war is about evoking emotions that favour one's goals. It is the ability to manipulate the public's feelings in support of your agenda.' In this war, he argued, 'the most potent weapons' were anger, fear and resentment.

'Remember that swing voters are not partisans, do not relate to politics as a political war and can barely tell the difference between the parties.'[25]

The change from Hooton to Keenan advice on race issues is evident shortly after the big-splash email, when Hooton contacted Brash with his latest strategy idea on 15 December 2003 after public criticism of the government's foreshore and seabed plans that morning by the 'powerful iwi Nga Puhi and Ngai Tahu'. He proposed a Brash media statement attacking Deputy Prime Minister Michael Cullen's 'mishandling of the issue', including the message that 'You don't tell iwi leaders that their most cherished beliefs are worthless, as Dr Cullen is reported to have done'.

Hooton suggested that Brash note that 'National's experience with aboriginal rights and Treaty issues under Prime Minister Jim Bolger and Treaty Minister Sir Douglas Graham in the 1990s had taught it the importance of maintaining an open mind and treating all involved with respect. The goal had to be to find innovative solutions that met the expectations of all New Zealanders, Maori and non-Maori.' He proposed that Brash say, 'There is no room for smugness and poll-driven politics on an issue that is about our history and our future.'[26]

Until now Brash had been reasonably receptive to similar advice from Hooton. But things had changed. When Hooton wrote this draft press release it was just three days since the *NBR* poll that had shown National Party support dropping. Poll-driven politics was at the front of their minds. Brash politely declined Hooton's suggestions, explaining that notions of an 'open mind' and 'respect' might not go down well with some National Party supporters. 'As I mentioned on the phone last night,' Brash said in an email, 'I don't see how we can exploit the divisions in the Labour Caucus without running a big risk of offending our traditional non-Maori supporters.'[27] (For Hooton, politics often seemed to be a game. Two days after Labour announced its foreshore policy he wrote to Sinclair: 'The government's foreshore and seabed package is the most cynical propaganda exercise I have ever seen. I almost admire them.')[28]

In a follow-up email to Brash on 13 December, Keenan cemented his strategy dominance. He gave qualified support to Sinclair: 'I have a lot of respect for Bryan. I like him, and he has made a major contribution (probably more than I am aware) but he is a young guy who gets a bit overly focused on today's publicity issues.' He was scathing, however, about Hooton. 'By the way, frankly, I think Matthew Hooton is an idiot. I had a long chat with him and his wife (she seemed much more sensible) and Bryan. Matthew is totally full of himself, and not half as good as his own self-image. He tries hard to impress, with over-the-top enthusiasm

– an actor. He would be massively disruptive around here.'[29] For months Hooton had been writing Brash's speeches and advising him almost daily on media and tactics. But these comments appear to have been the end of his prospects of getting a full-time job in the leader's office, and also the end of the less aggressive approach to Maori issues.

From this point on, a small group of close Brash allies worked on the Orewa speech. The change of direction over race relations was not shared with the wider caucus until just before delivery. Keenan prepared the first draft, which was more strident than the final speech. Then he passed it to Brash's friend Michael Bassett, who had long held bitter and angry views about Maori history and treaty issues, which he wove into the speech. MP Murray McCully, another with strong opinions about Maori issues, also reportedly had input.[30] Brash would later name other people as being involved, but they were consulted at the last minute, and were not architects of the speech.

Back in 2002 when Brash was campaigning for Parliament he had made some populist public statements about Maori issues, using the ACT Party's language about a treaty 'gravy train'.[31] But as he pursued the party leadership he had adopted a much softer line. When he had spoken to the ACT regional conference in September 2003, his Hooton-written speech had pointed out the small scale of treaty claims. The ACT speech started with the same 'Labour destroying New Zealand' line Brash had used after winning the leadership, but he questioned why there should be a 'fierce argument over the $1 billion for Treaty settlements which, in the context of the overall size of our economy, is almost irrelevant – about what we spend on social welfare benefits and New Zealand Superannuation every month'.[32] Four months later in the Orewa speech the treaty claims would be exaggerated.

In his first speech as leader, Brash had said that National was proud of its record in Maori development. 'In the 1990s, we promoted Maori self-management in education, health and social policy, just as we encouraged other communities to have more say in their schools, and their health and other services.'[33] In the Orewa speech only weeks later Brash would attack these Maori services as being 'separatist' and 'special privileges' and declare 'there can be no basis for government funding based on race'.[34]

A Wellington PR company client newsletter written in November 2003 by television producer Richard Harmanz had discussed precisely the tactics that the Orewa speech would employ. Under the title 'Dog Whistling, a handy tool for aspiring leaders', it advised: 'Dr Brash's tactics must be to win as much of the Winston Peters vote as he can without doing a Bill English and losing National's core vote in the process. This is where some "dog whistling" could come in handy.'[35] Dog whistle politics is the term associated with Australian prime minister John Howard and his appeal to so-called blue-collar voters on anti-immigration and race issues. It refers to political actions and rhetoric that, while superficially appearing reasonable, contain language, claims and racial stereotypes designed to excite the prejudices of certain target audiences, in the same way that dogs will react to a high-pitched whistle that humans cannot hear.

Brash's advisers had decided that he needed to be seen 'on the front foot showing strong leadership on something in the next few weeks' so they made very sure that the Orewa speech would have maximum impact. National's media staff talked up the speech in the weeks before delivery, promising a 'stinging attack' on the government's policies, 'more trenchant' in its criticism than Bill English had ever been.[36] Deputy leader Gerry Brownlee would say later that a key reason for the speech's success had been 'conditioning work' to fire up the media in advance. 'Orewa was a huge success,' he wrote to Brash, 'because of the topic but also because the work was done over a three week period to prime the media up into a state that forced them to write positively about the topic.'[37] As a result there was a large crowd of journalists present on the day to hear the most explosive speech in New Zealand's recent political history.

The initial media reaction to the speech was cautious, almost shocked, with headlines like 'Brash's risky Maori strategy'[38] and editorials questioning its divisive style. But the dog whistle had worked. Within days the headlines changed to 'Readers back Brash speech' and 'Strong support for Brash's race relations speech'.[39] The greatest impact was exactly where they had been aiming: low- to medium-income men and the elderly. After years trailing Labour badly in the polls, this one speech catapulted National into the lead.

The speech had been skilfully worded to evoke the Horowitz feelings of anger, fear and resentment. Anger was encouraged by painting Maori as 'mischievous minds' who interpreted the Treaty of Waitangi to 'suit their financial purposes' and 'invent or rediscover beliefs for pecuniary gain'. Fear was evoked using a negative picture of 'conflict', 'corruption', 'stand-over tactics' and 'tragedy' – and by promoting a sense that 'non-Maori' New Zealanders were somehow becoming second-class citizens in their own land. Resentment was fanned by talk of a privileged minority with 'a birthright to the upper hand', who had 'greater civil, political [and] democratic rights... than any other New Zealander' and 'power to veto' development projects 'which could provide us all with jobs'. 'Non-Maori' who supported 'the Maori cause' were a treacherous 'fifth column'.

It is not hard to see how these words could raise feelings of injustice and envy in people who were not wealthy and powerful themselves. Although the 5000-word speech covered many issues, the part that resonated with the most people and was remembered longest was the idea that Maori were enjoying special race-based privileges – an idea that grates in a society that sees itself as egalitarian. Because the message was coming from the respectable Dr Brash, it was easy for people to forget, at least temporarily, all the competing evidence telling them that privilege and wealth are located elsewhere in our society. But in the carefully concocted heat of the moment there was something satisfying about seeing a mainstream politician on his high horse about someone else's unearned advantage. It was a classic exercise in manipulating the feelings of the 'political middle ground'.[40]

To avoid going too far or leaving Brash open to accusations of racism, Keenan and Bassett peppered the speech with a few uplifting statements and legitimate challenges to conventional thinking: 'The indigenous culture of New Zealand will always have a special place in our emerging culture and will be cherished for that reason' and the 'outstanding performance of Maori in fishing and other primary industries and in a range of entrepreneurial business, sporting and cultural activities'.[41] But each positive comment was like a drawing of breath before the next attack.

Keenan had explained the thinking behind this style in an email to Richard Long. 'I think it is essential that every time we talk tough on [Maori] issues, we also run hard with a compassionate line – otherwise we fail the political hygiene test.'[42] This concept came from a British Conservative politician, Robert Darwell, whose writing on this subject had been sent to Don Brash by Ruth Richardson shortly before.[43] Darwell argued that the way to stop the public feeling uncomfortable with radical policies that might harm disadvantaged people was to 'over-compensate' by sounding concerned and wanting the best for those people.[44] The positive elements provide political cover; the negative bits are what most listeners remember.

And the speech was overwhelmingly negative. Business journalist Rod Oram took issue with the argument that there were 'widespread [Treaty] abuses starting to destroy the country' and concluded that Brash's view was wrong on four counts.

First, the [abuses] are exceptions, not the rule; second, they are not confined to Maori (Pakeha are just as capable, for example, of exploiting the

Resource Management Act to extract compensation from their neighbours or to stop a competitor's project); third, junking the Treaty, as he advocates, once historic grievances are settled, would make a mockery of the settlement process. Fourth, the view of Maori – as expressed in his speech – was disparaging about Maori behaviour and values. Literally, only one sentence in a 10-page speech had anything positive to say about recent Maori economic, cultural, social and political progress.

The gulf between this rhetoric and reality is enormous, both positively and negatively. On the plus side, Maori have taken big economic strides.... Among highlights, the Maori economy is more profitable than the general economy, has a higher savings rate and is a net lender to the general economy; it has grown faster than the general economy since 1997. Maori households are not a drain on the national budget: while they received $2.3bn a year in fiscal transfers, they pay taxes totalling $2.4bn. On the negative side, there are still many ways in which Maori are seriously disadvantaged, most obviously with life expectancy some 10 years shorter than Pakeha.[45]

The speech gave a sole concrete example of Maori privilege. This was the Nelson-Tasman Public Health Organisation (PHO), which, it said, 'is required to have half of the community representatives on its board representing local iwi, even though the number of people actually belonging to those local iwi is a tiny fraction of the population covered by that PHO'.[46]

The interesting thing about this example is that the staff in the National Party leader's office knew that the Nelson PHO was not typical.[47] They discussed the risks resulting from this one 'good example' in fact being an exception. But it still went into the speech and no effort was made to explain that most PHOs are different and that their structures are decided by local GPs and other representatives, not by government requirement.

Having generated public reaction and outrage from the subject of race-based privilege, Brash's staff found themselves being asked by journalists for evidence and examples of the supposed widespread abuses. You might imagine that the staff would be eager to hammer home the most powerful allegations in the speech. Instead, the internal communications show them urgently trying to bat the enquiries away. The power of the speech had come from emotional lever pulling and button pushing, not factual accuracy. As soon as the media started asking about the facts, the staff started dodging and ducking.

For instance, a couple of weeks after the speech, Brash's media staff received an email from *New Zealand Herald* reporter Ruth Berry who was writing a backgrounder on 'race-based funding'. She asked National to say what it meant by this term and to name the top ten examples of race-based funding which it would prevent. Instead of being pleased, Richard Long was immediately defensive. He forwarded her email to Peter Keenan and Murray McCully saying, 'Can you confer? We need to come up with a credible holding answer for these, that will avoid "National gone to ground and can't answer" type articles. The DomPost is doing similar, as you are aware.'

Long proposed that they say the information was not yet ready or available – 'Something along the lines of this week we commissioned the first in what could be a series of professional reviews of legislation to judge the full extent of the infiltration and what needs to be done to remove/correct etc. This will not be hurried and we are not prepared to address this in a piecemeal fashion.'[48]

Media assistant Phil Rennie chipped in that they needed to talk the media out of expecting that major examples of race-based funding existed. 'Isn't the point though not the amount of money,' he added in an email, 'but the principle, and the resentment that this racial differentiation creates? We need to dampen down media expectations that we are going to uncover big monetary figures.'[49]

The next day press officer Jason Ede drafted a reply to Berry saying that it was hard to 'disentangle' race-based from needs-based funding and it would take a National government its 'first year or two' to do so. Ede also tried to shift onto more defensible ground: 'there are areas where race-based funding might be acceptable', such as Maori teacher training. This directly contradicted Brash's black and white stand in the Orewa speech: 'There can be no basis for special privileges for any race, no basis for government funding based on race'. Ede said, 'The reality is that there are examples all along the spectrum: from clearly unjustified, through the merely debatable, to those that are justified and effective programmes.'

He then criticised the journalist for following up the part of the speech that was being most discussed. 'Your question line appears to trivialise the issue by imagining clear distinctions where there are none, by suggesting such programmes do not matter because the funding amounts may not be large... and by distracting from the major points of the Orewa speech.' He accused the Labour government of being behind 'the enthusiasm of some commentators to focus on this relatively minor part of the Orewa speech'.[50]

Murray McCully subsequently took over, writing to Berry: 'Ruth, No,

I can't provide detailed responses on the issues you have raised. Two weeks ago, Don Brash made a speech which will shape the direction of our policy for the next election. But being very thorough people, it is normally our practice to spend more than two weeks going through a consultative and deliberative process before announcing policy.'[51] Richard Long, pleased with McCully's response, sent it to all Brash's staff to use. 'Attached is a reasonable response we can make to the nitpickers demanding instant detailed policy answers from us,' he wrote.[52]

After the staff had wriggled out of that one, Brash was broadcast on TV One that very evening trying to throw more fuel on the race-based privilege fire. His example this time was universities providing access quotas for Maori medical and law students, which, he suggested, resulted in their being not properly qualified and competent for these jobs. Like the other claims, this sounded initially convincing. Then the universities replied that quotas are common – for instance for mature and rural students – and that all Maori students had to pass exactly the same exams as other students from entry to graduation. The standard of Maori degrees was exactly the same as others.

Rather than back down, the National media staff came up with a clever answer to deal with media calls the next day. 'Don's comments on TV One,' Jason Ede wrote as a guide, 'were related to perception.' The Maori quota had 'the potential to leave the perception among non-Maori that Maori students have favourable treatment and may be less qualified'.[53] Ede seemed to have forgotten his own statement days earlier that some race-based programmes were 'justified and effective', for instance where Maori teachers were needed – which sounds very like the point of quotas for Maori doctors and lawyers.

When commentator Colin James, in an article otherwise complimentary of Brash and his Orewa successes, wrote that Brash had been forced to backtrack on his 'devaluation' of Maori degrees, Ede told him that 'Dr Brash has never devalued Maori degrees'. He said Brash was speaking only of 'perception while discussing entry level quota for Maori students'.[54] James replied that 'by averring a perception, he thereby devalued the [Maori degrees]. If he had added that he personally rejected the perception, which I have not heard or seen him do, your point would be valid.'[55] Ede sent the correspondence to Long and Keenan, admitting that Brash's latest Maori privilege example was not very convincing: 'I accept we are not on strong ground on the complaint about degrees'.[56]

Long had written to Brash advising him how to handle the Maori quota subject in future. 'When questioned, as you will be, about the education comment,' he said, 'you should explain that you were basically talking about perceptions.' It might be 'a good idea... to slip into example/anecdote mode... that came across well in the NZ Herald today.... You need to step from the specific detail of policy into broad brush when they attempt to nail you from now on.'[57] Brash replied: 'Excellent stuff thanks Richard. Very helpful.'[58] He could be seen following this advice in subsequent interviews, often using the same anecdote over and over and, when challenged about inciting prejudice, claiming he was discussing only perceptions.[59]

This ignored the obvious point that Brash himself was helping to create the perceptions by repeatedly raising the issues and by choosing unrepresentative and inflammatory anecdotes. The idea of Maori having special privileges had always been at best exaggerated and at worst malicious.

Having written the Orewa speech, created the big splash and reaped the poll rise, Keenan confided during the election year that 'I hate the "race based privilege" line'. National was still milking the 'end race-based privilege' slogan, which was one of six main election messages selected for endless repetition. But Keenan told Sinclair he thought this was 'ludicrous when Maori are largely at the bottom of the heap'.[60]

Keenan seems to have been admitting that, when all the 'elevated' rhetoric was stripped away, the speech he drafted was based in part on an unpleasant lie. Brash had told his well-heeled Orewa audience that much of the 'non-Maori' tolerance for the treaty settlement process was based on a 'perception of relative Maori poverty'. In other words, he was denying that many Maori were at the 'bottom of the heap'. He used 'much publicised' research by 'sociologist Simon Chapple' (actually, an economist) to claim that 'Maori income distribution is not very different from Pakeha income distribution'. Chapple later said he was 'less than happy' with the way his research had been used.[61] The 'much publicised' referred to earlier misuse of the research by the ACT Party, which is presumably what had attracted Brash's staff to Chapple's paper.

There was no shortage of research to inform Brash and Keenan of the facts. For instance, three studies by the University of Otago's Wellington School of Medicine and Health Sciences plotted how differences between Maori and Pakeha health and life expectancy diverged dramatically from the early 1980s. The 'clear and disturbing' results showed that at the end of two decades of diverging incomes there was a ten-year difference in life expectancy, whereas in the 1960s and 1970s they had been getting closer.[62]

The Orewa argument about Maori poverty – coming from Keenan,

Bassett and Brash – was particularly distasteful because this poverty increased dramatically in the 1980s and 1990s as a result of the free market reforms championed by them and their colleagues. Employment levels for Maori men had dropped sharply. As the free marketeers amassed personal fortunes and enjoyed genuine special privilege, the University of Otago research found that unemployment, poor housing, lack of access to services and discouragement that 'coincided with [the] major social and economic changes starting in the early 1980s' were quietly killing large numbers of people of Maori descent before their time.

To add injury to insult, the speech had real effects when funding for Maori support organisations, dealing with such issues as health and violence, was subsequently reduced or stopped. Panicked by the public reaction to the Orewa speech, the Labour government turned off the 'race-based' funding and in some cases there was nothing to replace it.

The morning after delivering the Orewa speech, Brash was interviewed for a television documentary. The programme recorded his discomfort about whether he had written the speech himself. 'I don't have any regret at all about the content of the speech,' he said. 'I looked at it very carefully. I read it, of course. Wrote it.'[63] The missing 'I' was telling.

Once the Orewa speech's claims about race-based privilege were firmly planted in the public mind, Brash was willing to admit that this potent argument did not actually amount to much financial benefit for Maori. He told *Mana News* reporter Carol Archie: 'I don't think the financial benefits to Maori from having funding formula based on race, not need, are enormous at all. And I never suggested they were. I just think they are very damaging, indeed, to race relations in New Zealand.'[64]

By then Brash was riding high and, at least for the audiences he was targeting, he had already won the point. The *Sunday Star-Times* described him speaking to another Rotary club in Newmarket three weeks later. He mixed jokes with warnings about 'time running out' on race relations, exuding the 'relaxed triumphalism of a master surfer riding a monster wave'.[65] Now the polls had gone up, National mostly got away with acting as if this was a lucky but unintentional consequence of a principled speech, rather than the very point of the speech in the first place.

Brash had spoken of being 'deeply saddened' at having to speak about 'issues of race', but now his mood was more one of elation. He wrote to Matthew Hooton two days after Orewa: 'The speech got a fantastic reception – better than I dared hope'.[66] He told another correspondent that informal polls seemed to be running 76–90 per cent in his favour,[67] and later joked to Hooton about how well it was all going. 'As Hirohito

[Japanese emperor during the Second World war] might have said, the war is not going quite as well for Labour as the PM might have hoped!'[68]

Columnist Jane Clifton described other National MPs strutting in Parliament, 'engorged' by the high poll ratings. Deputy leader Gerry Brownlee got carried away and called one Maori MP a 'black fella'. Brash's staff used facetious kia oras to each other in their emails and after a protester hit Brash with mud during the February Waitangi Day celebrations Bryan Sinclair joked, 'Hahaha, I was in disguise'.[69] The then National Party senior whip, John Carter, was captured on a television documentary telling Brash that the mud-throwing incident should be worth a good three or four points in the polls.[70] National staff and MPs appeared far more interested in their political achievement than in the supposedly grave and pressing issues that had required the painful but necessary 'plain speaking'.

It is useful to consider how different things might have been if the speech had never been delivered. Quite likely Brash and National would have begun the year 2004 mired in the mid-to-late 20s in the polls and Brash may have been finished as a leader before he began. Without the prominence and confidence provided by the Orewa success, he could have been written off as his predecessor had been. The race issue had been a convenient stepping stone to establish Brash as a serious contender for the general election and he continued to use it up to election day whenever he wanted more of the Orewa magic.

Is a poll rise always a sign of political success? It is hard for politicians not to see it that way, given that they often see politics as a game of win and lose and that the polls directly affect their personal prospects. But political journalists and the public should be equally interested in why the polls move, since politics is also about reality, where the words and actions affect people's lives, hopes and – in the case of race relations – self-respect.

After the election the Orewa policies were challenged from within the National Party. Only two weeks after the votes were counted, MP Bill English gave a speech at Auckland University about 'Treatyology' that advocated a 'more constructive way ahead' than one constrained by rigid 'ideological advocacy'. The language of blame, debt, separation and guilt, he said, needed to be replaced by a new language built on the foundation of justice. No one doubted he was talking about Brash's Orewa speech.

At the same time a group was formed called Nationals for the Treaty. The spokesperson, National's Waitakere branch treasurer Michael Kidd, said many National members were concerned about the party's stance on the treaty, the Maori seats and its plans to abolish a number of key

Maori agencies. The group aimed to return to the party's roots of working co-operatively with Maori.[71] National Party historian Barry Gustafson, commenting on the new group, said that National's race policies during the 2005 election campaign had been the work of the 'radical right'. 'From time to time, the more free market ideologically driven radical right manages to seize control' of the National Party, and this had been one of those times.[72] By then, for most New Zealanders, the Orewa themes that had seemed so urgent and important in January 2004 now seemed extreme and negative. The fever had passed.

CHAPTER 6

OVER HERE
The American neoconservative connection

In Brash's first speech as leader of the National Party, he told a Chamber of Commerce conference: 'I don't want us to be afraid of the electorate by watering down our message... I want us to have the utmost integrity. We are going to develop policy. We are going to say what it is. And we are going to be proud of it.'[1]

As National rose in the polls, Matthew Hooton continued to offer strategy advice to Brash. Although the Orewa speech had gone against his more conciliatory suggestions, he wrote congratulating Brash on the public reaction: 'Well, you can't argue with success'. He offered Brash 'congratulations for taking a bold move against the advice of your friends. I'm still not happy with elements of the means, but I know I'm sure going to like the polling outcome!' He then presented 'an idea about how to keep the momentum going on the Treaty'.[2]

He proposed to Brash that 'If you can now be seen to empathise with Maori (without changing policy at all) you will avoid any potential charge of being "divisive".' Hooton was quite open about the thinking behind his idea. 'You call a Hui Taumata (summit) to which you ask each iwi and UMA [urban Maori authority] to send a representative (not necessarily their leader), along with a wide range of academics and other Maori leaders (including [Business Roundtable chair] Rob McLeod).... The reason for the hui is because you want to explain your views and vision for New Zealand face to face with Maori leaders and also because you want to "hear their concerns".'

He believed that National would benefit whether the Maori representatives agreed to come or not. 'If the Maori leadership etc refuses you,' he wrote, 'you express your "disappointment" while setting the dogs (Gerry Brownlee, McCully et al) on them, saying that Maori need new leadership if the existing leadership won't even meet with and engage with the "next Prime Minister of New Zealand" about their concerns.'

'If however the leadership does send representatives, we have the po-whiri-to-end-all-powhiris on the steps of parliament, with you welcoming the attendees one by one with a well-practiced hongi etc.... Then we move inside, and you give exactly the same policy speech as [at Orewa] (with if anything a stronger message) but "through Maori eyes".... This may even win some over, but that is not so important. You then spend the rest of the day (and it would be the rest of the day!) "listening". You then change nothing about the policy but can forever say you have "engaged" Maori and that you have taken their views on board.'

Note the use of quotation marks – 'hear their concerns', 'disappoint-ment', 'listening', 'engaged' – to make absolutely clear that he is talking about a political stunt. He suggested they get onto it reasonably quickly: 'You don't want this to either look too cynical or too much like an after-thought'.[3] Brash replied: 'your idea of announcing a big hui at Parliament sounds like a great idea to me, and I'll discuss with some of my close colleagues over the next few days'.[4]

A few weeks later Hooton was in touch again with more advice: 'It looks to me like the time to move onto the next issue is now rapidly approaching'. He suggested it was 'time for a date, venue and topic to be chosen for the next major speech, and for your inner circle to start talking the next speech up to draw attention to it, as they did so successfully last time'. When choosing the next topic, he said, 'the objective should be to solidify the additional support you have picked up – which is probably best characterised as socially-conservative working-class voters – perhaps "Mike Moore people" is the best shorthand'.[5]

Hooton suggested that the best option for the next speech was welfare, followed by law and order, then education, but definitely not economic or nuclear issues. 'Economy and nukes, I would think, would turn the target demographic back to Labour at this stage. These are issues for when voters have heard and loved you on a range of other topics, and are prepared to trust you on positions they don't agree with.'[6] In other words, National's economic and foreign policy plans needed to be downplayed or hidden until the time was right.

We now know that in early 2004, while Brash was in the first flush of post-Orewa confidence and promoting himself far and wide as the honest, straight-talking non-politician, he had begun a series of secret contacts with

United States government people, including discussion about changing or dropping New Zealand's nuclear-free policy.

On 19 February 2004, as the Orewa speech dominated the news, Hooton emailed Brash with important news. This was the same day the National Party staff were fobbing off journalist Ruth Berry for wanting examples of race-based privilege and Brash was making his television claim that Maori university degrees were of lower value. Hooton explained that he had been in contact with one of National's old American connections, who was interested in helping Brash become prime minister.

'Don, I've received this email from Dick Allen, who worked in the Nixon White House and was Reagan's first National Security Advisor, and had a leading role in their successful campaigns in 1972 and 1980,' Hooton wrote. He explained that Allen 'now serves in a number of roles in the States, most prominently as a member of the Defence Policy Board at the Pentagon, advising [Secretary of Defence Donald] Rumsfeld on strategy, and in various neo-con ultra roles'.

Allen was one of the wealthy foreigners who had used New Zealand's deregulated land laws to buy a summer home here: a vineyard and large home in Gibbston Valley near Queenstown, where he stayed for three months each year.[7] Hooton explained that after the Orewa speech Allen was 'enthused by the prospect of the right getting back in in New Zealand'. He had written an email of several pages of 'thoughts on political strategy etc' that he thought might assist Brash. Hooton forwarded Allen's advice to Brash and Peter Keenan. He suggested they take the trouble of sending him a 'thank you' message: 'For possible donations, he's loaded, and he would also be a useful back channel to his close friends Rumsfeld and [Vice-President Dick] Cheney when you are Prime Minister, or even before'.[8]

Keenan was impressed by Allen's email and United States government links. He proposed straightaway that they arrange a meeting between Brash and Allen in the near future. He checked Brash's schedule and within a few hours Hooton had phoned Allen on their behalf and reported back that he was keen to meet Brash, though 'also very keen that the meeting be utterly secret'. He warned that 'this guy is seen as a neo-con ultra even in the US (there are websites attacking him) and he wouldn't want any word to leak for Don's sake'.[9]

There were good reasons to keep contacts between Brash and Allen secret. Richard V. Allen represented the far right of United States politics. He had been a founding member of the Cold War Committee on the Present Danger, which strongly advocated American nuclear superiority and opposed all types of arms control in the 1970s and 1980s. He went from there to be the president's top security adviser in the midst of Reagan's nuclear build-up and his administration's support for repressive regimes in Central America. Other official roles followed, and also leading roles in Washington thinktanks including the Heritage Foundation (long-time critic of New Zealand's nuclear-free policy). More recently, Allen had been one of a who's who of the United States far right who were part of the Project for a New Century, which was credited with being the main American lobby behind the 2003 invasion of Iraq. Various New Century members, including Richard Armitage, Dick Cheney, Donald Rumsfeld, Robert Zoellick and Dick Allen, went on to implement their agenda as officials in the George W. Bush administration.

People who have met Allen describe him as charming and intelligent. But this man, with whom Brash and his staff were rushing to establish contact, was also a particularly hard-line American hawk. The *Washington Post* once interviewed his three daughters and asked them each to give one word describing what their father had instilled in them. One was reported to have said 'Win', the second 'Rule' and the third 'Conquer'.[10] Allen was the American who appeared with Kim Hill on her first television current affairs programme in March 2003 defending the American invasion of Iraq.[11] He told a New Zealand journalist at the time that 'The United States is not a bully, it is a liberator' – 'a benevolent nation eager to protect and help its friends'. He said the problem with France and Germany, which opposed the invasion, was that 'they are full of envy and fear'; the United Nations, for its part, faced 'the dustbin of history'.[12]

Early 2004 was not the best of times for National to be pursuing closer United States ties. A year after 'winning' the war in Iraq, the United States was bogged down in the war of resistance. There were dozens of attacks in Iraq each day, the American death toll was rising inexorably and the first stories of American and British torture and abuse of prisoners were appearing. Any plan to water down the nuclear-free policy for the sake of closer military relations with Washington would need to be pursued by stealth.

Hooton told Sinclair, 'I said you would call him, but that you would keep it to yourself.' He advised him to keep the meeting confidential: 'It's probably best for you just to set it up, and not let others in the office know'. He said that when he worked for Lockwood Smith 'we used to put "Catch up with Matthew Hooton" in the diary when arranging meetings like this'. Finally, he urged that they try to have the meeting at Allen's Queenstown house, 'to see how the "other half" live! It's a beautiful holiday home.'[13]

By chance, Brash had a trip scheduled just a few days later, 'taking his "one law for all" message to Queenstown and Invercargill'.[14] Brash's staff cancelled a planned walkabout in Queenstown and a visit to St Joseph's Catholic Primary School to make time for seeing Allen. The meeting occurred at about 10.30am on Monday 23 February 2004. Brash was in a confident mood, after hearing that morning that a *New Zealand Herald* poll had estimated National at 45.5 per cent, with Labour down at 37 per cent.

There is no record of the meeting, but Allen's earlier strategy email to Brash gives an idea of his thoughts. He said his credentials for offering advice were that he had 'participated in two long and arduous national campaigns in the United States in the past 35 years, both successful and both with candidates who had been written off as "finished" or "unelectable" by pundits, the chattering class, scribes and pointyheads'.

He pointed to similarities between Brash's campaign and what he helped achieve for Ronald Reagan in 1980. 'My interest is in grand strategy, foreign and domestic,' he wrote. 'Confidentially, I see there are plans for a series of powerful speeches in the weeks and months ahead, which I consider a great idea.... In 1980, as Reagan steadily mowed down the other candidates in a grueling series of primary elections, my domestic policy counterpart and I (we had been stablemates in the Nixon campaign of 1968 and in the Nixon White House) vowed to take charge of the policy agenda.' They formed a policy platform with 'the simple title "Family, Neighborhood, Work, Peace, Freedom".... Reagan liked it. We then made sure that every speech, every statement, every move was closely coordinated with these five themes.... This message led to his crushing defeat of [Democrat President Jimmy] Carter.'[15] This advice was where Keenan got the idea of presenting Brash to the public with blue backdrops showing the words 'Family, Security, Work, Community, Freedom'.[16]

Allen then proposed how Brash should deal with accusations that his policies were right-wing. The answer was to insist that he was 'mainstream'. 'Never mind if you are called "extremist" or anything else,' Allen said, 'that is so easily countered with the simple statement, "these views represent the mainstream of New Zealand values and thinking". Were we really "right wing" back in 1980, as the press charged?' he asked. 'You bet we were, but [we] responded only by the flat statement "Governor Reagan sits squarely in the mainstream of American politics", and we would not be knocked from that perch.... We never let them get away with that charge.' This idea of claiming to represent the 'mainstream' would be National's central idea for the 2005 election campaign.

Allen boasted, justifiably, about just how successful the neo-conservatives had been in dominating American politics. 'Forty years ago,' he wrote, 'as I was just beginning my professional association with the world of public affairs and academe, we could have held a national convention of mainstream American conservatives in a telephone booth. Now that movement, if we call it that, dominates politically, and it is to its agenda that the Left must respond. Never dreamed I'd see it this way.'

Allen had a small agenda of his own in offering the strategy advice to Brash. 'The only thing I would urge,' he said, referring to Brash's planned speeches, 'is the addition of a thoughtful speech on "restoring" New Zealand's place in the international community.' He explained that this was 'an oblique way of talking about trying to make things right with the United States', which for 20 years of American officials had meant changing the nuclear-free policy. He suggested using the threat of 'being left behind by the Aussie advantage in a [Free Trade Agreement] with the US' to argue for change.

Finally, he offered Brash 'a five CD set of Ronald Reagan's five-minute radio addresses recorded from 1975 through 1980. You should listen to these in drive time, and absorb the lessons,' he wrote. The email ended by wishing Brash good luck and predicting that Brash would 'be successful and Kiwis will be pleased'.[17]

Brash followed up their Queenstown meeting with a letter: 'Dear Dick, It was a great pleasure to meet you in Queenstown last Monday, and I appreciate your sparing the time'. He had not yet had a chance to listen to the Reagan CDs, 'mainly because I have not had any long car rides in the last week. But I will certainly keep them nearby, so that I can hear them when the opportunity arises.' Most importantly, he would like to try to take up Allen's 'kind offer to suggest people I should contact in Washington when I visit there, again probably in June'.[18]

Brash and Allen would meet again in Washington two months later and Allen would continue to offer strategy advice, which Brash and his staff took seriously. For instance, on arriving back from Washington Brash wrote to Sinclair: 'Bryan, as you know, we have been giving thought for quite some time about how to attract the votes of ex-pat Kiwis'. He said that 'Dick Allen suggested we should look at advertising on websites like Stuff, which lots of ex-pat Kiwis access regularly. Sounds like a good idea to me. Could you check out the cost of such ads please? Don.'[19] Yet National later prepared scripted denials for any questions on whether it had received campaign advice from the United States.[20]

The next sign of Brash's covert foreign policy discussions came a month later when the top United States military official in the Pacific region visited New Zealand. On Thursday, 11 March 2004 Prime Minister Helen Clark had a formal 45-minute meeting with Admiral Thomas Fargo, commander of the United States Pacific Command, at the Sheraton Hotel in Auckland. The official statement said Fargo had raised the Americans' wish to see an end to New Zealand's nuclear-free policy.[21]

In contrast to the prime minister's short but publicised meeting, Don Brash had had a secret meeting with Fargo the day before. Brash's private diary records that at 8.30pm on Wednesday 10 March, he arrived at the United States Ambassador's residence in Lower Hutt for a 'Private Dinner with US Ambassador Charles Swindells and Admiral Thomas Fargo'. Fargo's official programme mentioned visits to military bases and meetings with officials, but nothing about meeting the National leader. What they discussed is not known, but as with Clark's meeting, the nuclear-free policy would have been on the agenda.

It will never be known, either, where these secretive discussions would have led because some of Brash's manoeuvrings became public in early May 2004 and he never made it into government in 2005 to carry them out. The idea had been that the relationship-building could go on without public knowledge, but the secrecy was breached.

In early May National was preparing to release an internal party review of the nuclear-free policy – essentially, how to change the policy to allow closer military relations with the United States without antagonising the New Zealand public too greatly. Then, out of the blue, just before release of the review, the Labour-led government released details of a private meeting between Brash, Lockwood Smith and six United States Republican congressmen in January of that year. Asked a question by another Labour MP in Parliament on 4 May, Foreign Minister Phil Goff dropped the news that Brash had told the congressmen that 'if National became Government the nuclear ban would be gone by lunchtime'. Goff said, 'That statement was made by Dr Brash, who now claims he has made no decision on the issue.'[22]

To make matters much worse for National, this was by chance the exact day when the first shocking images appeared of abuse of Iraqi prisoners in the soon-to-be-notorious Abu Ghraib prison. The idea of watering down the nuclear-free policy to be closer to the Americans suddenly seemed less attractive than ever.[23]

The Labour ministers had clearly sat on the gone-by-lunchtime minutes for months, ready to use them when National released its nuclear policy review. Brash looked duplicitous and was attacked with accusations that he had a secret pro-nuclear agenda. He could not credibly deny the reported words and lamely responded that he could not recall saying them.

As Labour had intended, the revelations were damaging. This was the first time that Brash had been shown to be less honest and straightforward than his publicists presented him. He had been given the benefit of the doubt over the motives behind the Orewa speech, but this time the behaviour was plain to see. It affected the opinion polls and could later be seen as the start of a slide that continued over the next twelve months.

National knew there was no way they could win a public debate on changing the nuclear legislation. They had to say and do whatever was necessary to close down public debate as quickly as possible. On the day after the 'gone by lunchtime' revelation a thousands-strong hikoi was due at the Beehive, protesting at the government's foreshore and seabed policies. While attention was on the people gathered outside in Parliament grounds, National used this timing effectively to bury its long-awaited nuclear review. Richard Long sent out the instructions: 'Release time 4pm. No press conference.'[24] Brash welcomed the report 'as a useful contribution to the public debate', then immediately said there was no intention to change the nuclear-free policy, unless there was a public mandate to do so in the future.[25] A subsequent press release said, 'The National Party caucus has decided to leave unchanged the anti-nuclear legislation banning visits to New Zealand of nuclear armed and nuclear powered ships', only mentioning further down that they would consider a referendum if it was 'in New Zealand's national interest'.[26]

The main objective was to have the review forgotten as quickly as possible. Commentator Colin James, usually sympathetic to Brash, saw the decision as timid and cowardly and called it the 'pusillanimous nuclear retreat'.[27] Commentator Chris Trotter put it more humorously: 'To coin a phrase, the National Party's new-found attachment to US policy objectives was "gone by lunchtime" '.[28] Well, in public at least. While the National strategists did everything they could to close the issue down publicly, Brash's discussions with the United States government continued out of sight of the public.

The review was called the New Zealand National Party Taskforce on the Relationship Between New Zealand and the United States. New Zealand's nuclear-free policy consists of bans on visits by nuclear-armed and nuclear-powered ships. The review concluded that New Zealand could improve its relations with the United States by dropping the part of the legislation relating to nuclear-powered warships but then, to reduce public opposition, not actually having any visits from such vessels.

On 10 May Brash received a friendly but blunt private email from former New Zealand Deputy Secretary of Defence, Dick Gentles, who said the taskforce level of research was 'so shallow' that the members obviously did not understand the implications of their proposal. He was not convinced that the United States–New Zealand defence strains had 'had any real effect on New Zealand's security' and that the report's 'so-called Danish Solution has proven to be a thoroughly discredited approach' and 'had not worked in keeping Denmark nuclear free'. Gentles concluded: 'I think you would be wise to distance yourself from this idea while you still can'.[29]

Brash and Keenan had a private meeting planned for 4pm the following day, 11 May, with former Defence Secretary Denis McLean, one of the most outspoken opponents of the nuclear-free policy. They presumably urged McLean to co-operate in letting the subject go quiet. The meeting had been in the diary since before the 'gone by lunchtime' phrase had entered the national vocabulary.

From then on National did everything it could to bury the issue. The media staff were sensitive to anything, however obscure, that might raise the matter again and worked hard to ensure that the words 'nuclear' and 'Brash' were not seen together. When the National Party media staff heard that Wellington Labour MP Marian Hobbs had a fundraising evening screening 'Michael Moore's controversial anti-George Bush flick *Farenheit 9/11*', press officer Jason Ede wrote a concerned note to Don Brash, Murray McCully, Lockwood Smith and all the media staff saying, 'I have warned Lockwood and he agrees we should keep our heads down on it.' Ede drafted some platitudes in case the media approached Lockwood Smith – 'the Government needs to be very careful about protecting the New Zealand national interest on behalf of all New Zealanders' – which he 'figured' would provide 'the safest out as a last resort'.[30] Brash replied: 'I agree'.[31]

When the United States Secretary of State for Agriculture, Mike Johanns, was coming to New Zealand in 2005 and asked to meet the leader of the National Party, it was a meeting they would usually have welcomed. But Long intervened: 'Let's have Lockwood and David Carter do this. Better to keep Don as far away as possible from trade for nuke ship deal suggestions.'[32]

On other occasions there were urgent emails with titles like 'Nuke ships AGAIN!!' and 'Agreed lines on nuclear ships', warning National Party staff to be careful about media calls. The media staff advised Brash to keep away from any questions about National's nuclear policy. They even drafted 'lines' for why he was not speaking on the subject. 'Why isn't Don fronting?' they asked. 'We see no reason to distract Don from his busy timetable with this Labour Party nonsense,' the prepared answer said.[33]

Everyone else was reminded regularly to stick to the agreed no-plans-to-change line about the nuclear legislation. For instance on 3 August 2005 Ede sent an email to all National MPs and their secretaries, saying 'TV is doorstopping National MPs to talk about nukes.' 'If you're caught,' he advised, 'there's only one answer we can give... we have a very clear policy [of] no change without a referendum, and we have no plan for a referendum – Full Stop!'[34]

Their concern, as Richard Long put it, was that it would be 'a dream for Labour propagandists' to use the ' "Gone by Lunchtime" comment in election advertising in an attempt to discredit National as stooges of the US imperialists'.[35] But any moves to change the nuclear-free legislation relied on getting past the election without a public reaction derailing them.

After the May crisis Don Brash naively believed he had successfully disposed of the issue. In September 2004 he wrote to his colleagues about their goal of 'getting potentially contentious issues off the agenda well ahead of the election': 'Nuclear ship visits, I think that that has been dealt with'.[36] As we saw earlier, Keenan was not so confident. He warned Brash that one of the 'losing issues' they needed to 'inoculate' was nuclear ships, 'plus the possibility that we may ourselves get nuked a day or two out from the election by further releases of alleged comments made to US Senators'.[37] But Brash had underestimated how much the 'gone by lunchtime' would harm his public support during the election campaign.

The words had been recorded in a file note by a New Zealand foreign affairs officer sitting in on the meeting with the United States congressmen. That note gave a very clear picture of what Brash and his foreign affairs spokesperson told the Americans on Saturday 10 January 2004. Following introductory remarks, the note said: 'Dr Brash explained his political history and philosophy and introduced Dr Smith', who 'explained the current study being done by the National Party'. He said that 'If the study came to the same conclusion as it did in 1992' – which was that the nuclear propulsion ban should be dropped – 'then National would look at the nuclear legislation'. The official then wrote: 'It was here that Dr Brash made the throw-away comment "If the National Party was in government today, we would get rid of the nuclear propulsion section today – by lunchtime" '.

Lockwood Smith then asked 'if getting rid of the nuclear propulsion issue would guarantee an FTA [Free Trade Agreement] with the US' and 'whether it would be worthwhile for a US think tank to assist with the public campaign in New Zealand following the National Party study review'. The notes concluded: 'Dr Smith noted that he is regularly in the US and met with [James] Kelly, [Richard] Armitage and [Ralph] Ives to discuss these issues and he hoped that he is able to count on the Senators for further discussions in the future. [Senator Don] Nickles replied he was retiring but he was sure that his colleagues would be happy to meet him again in the future.'[38]

Foreign affairs officials do not write down verbatim reports of what a senior politician says unless they are sure. Brash was clearly signalling a willingness to change the nuclear policy and Smith was seeking collaboration from the Americans in successfully pushing through the policy changes. Their plan had obviously been to say as little as possible about their intentions until they were safely in government. That January meeting, and the sentiments behind the gone-by-lunchtime assurance, had led naturally to Brash's eagerness to meet Dick Allen and his extraordinary decision to allow him, an official from another country, to arrange most of his Washington trip, scheduled for early June.

When Brash and Keenan flew to Washington, the itinerary listed as the contact person not some National Party staff member, but Allen himself; and email communications show that most of the meetings were ones that Allen had organised.[39] During their three days in Washington, Brash and Keenan were introduced to several of Allen's neo-conservative colleagues, all of them opponents of New Zealand's nuclear-free policy. Meetings specifically arranged by Allen included the far right Heritage Foundation,[40] the American Enterprise Institute for Public Policy Research (which collaborates with the New Zealand Business Roundtable),[41] the Cato Institute[42] and the United States Institute of Peace. At the AEI they met Jeane J. Kirkpatrick who, as Reagan's ambassador to the United Nations from 1981 to 1985, had been an outspoken critic of New Zealand's nuclear policy. Besides being in the Reagan administration with Dick Allen, Kirkpatrick had also been prominent in the Committee on the Present Danger and the Project for a New American Century.

Allen also arranged a meeting with special assistant to the president, Michael Green, a lunch with former White House economic adviser Larry Lindsay and a 'dinner (informal) at Metropolitan Club with State, Defence [and] White House officials'.[43] Most of these meetings were not mentioned in the National Party press releases about the trip (a release on the day they left New Zealand announced disingenuously that Brash's 'detailed programme has yet to be finalised'). Brash and Keenan also met senior foreign policy hawks United States Deputy Secretary of State Richard Armitage, Assistant Secretary of State James Kelly and United States Trade Representative Robert Zoellick. All the people they chose to see were politically well to the right of the National Party. A few were the obvious State Department officials a foreign politician would meet, but mostly Brash and Keenan were actively choosing to forge links with the far right of American politics.

Afterwards, the National Party staff had second thoughts about mentioning the Armitage visit. Ede wrote: 'My advice is to keep quiet on the Armitage meeting and I have conveyed that to Peter [Keenan]. In his release Armitage mentions both Afghanistan and Iraq. All the media will do is make Don Brash feel uncomfortable about National's policy on Iraq. I do not think that is in our best interests at this stage.' He was also reluctant about having to release the photo of Brash and Armitage together, saying 'Note Armitage lack of neck'.[44] The only press release issued described Brash's meeting with Robert Zoellick and said 'the recently released National Party taskforce report on US/NZ relations was not discussed'.[45]

Discussions within New Zealand on the United States relationship were also conducted with care. During the three days in Washington, Brash had met the New Zealand ambassador to Washington, John Wood, a long-time bureaucratic opponent of the nuclear-free policy. Six weeks later, at 3.20pm on Monday 16 August 2004, John Wood met Brash again in his parliamentary office during a visit to Wellington. Lockwood Smith was also present for the meeting. A note in Brash's diary said 'No MFAT [Ministry of Foreign Affairs and Trade] Official will accompany Mr Wood'.[46]

The next time Brash met the United States ambassador, Charles Swindells, they did it well away from both Parliament and the embassy. Instead they had a private three-hour dinner at the Oriental Bay home of former National Party Defence Minister Max Bradford. Bradford had been using his contacts to help National with United States relations and to circulate copies of National's nuclear review, including arranging some meetings for Brash in Washington through New Zealand-born Bush administration official Peter Watson.[47] In an email to Bradford, Watson said he had 'spoken to Rich' (Richard Armitage) and 'a meeting date is being addressed'. Watson had earlier worked for Armitage as senior legal adviser at Armitage Associates. Watson also 'saw Jim Kelly at the Secretary's morning briefing... and he confirmed he is likewise making contact'. 'Issue fully engaged,' said Watson. Although National's nuclear taskforce report had been buried and dismissed by Brash within New Zealand, Bradford had used his channels to ensure the Americans saw it. Watson thanked Bradford for sending him a copy of the report and said, 'Will get a copy also to [James] Kelly.'[48] The possibility of amending the nuclear legislation was apparently still on the agenda for Brash's Washington meetings and presumably if National won the election these private negotiations would continue. The relationships Brash was building in Washington and whatever undertakings he had already privately given would have made this almost inevitable. Brash had left the door open for this on 23 June 2004: 'If we reach the judgement that it is in New Zealand's best interests to make a change [to the nuclear legislation], then clearly I would want to lead a constructive public debate on that issue leading up to a referendum'.[49] It all relied, of course, on winning the election.

When that did not happen, National MPs decided that the political cost of trying to change the nuclear policy had been too high. Some believed that even the suspicion of planning to change the policy had cost them crucial votes. Brash's secret policy plans appear to have reached the end of the road: in early 2006, foreign affairs spokesperson Murray McCully signalled that they were abandoning any plans for a policy change.[50]

The 'gone by lunchtime' revelation had been the public's first sign that Brash might not be the person they had thought. In politics the best guide to future behaviour is not what people say. It is who they have their private dinners with, whose advice they take most notice of and who they regard as their friends. It is the same with domestic policies. The best guide to the Brash team's political intentions was not their carefully planned 'messages', but the people and groups within New Zealand with whom they quietly built alliances as they prepared for the election. The same party that had so scathingly attacked Maori special privileges set about cultivating the support of many of the most powerful interests in New Zealand to help it into government.

CHAPTER 7

FOR THE MANY, NOT THE FEW
Special interests

By April or May 2004, when National's strong opinion polling seemed secure, Brash and his team began wooing all the special interests that might be willing to support them in the 2005 elections. Peter Keenan had urged this approach in December 2003, calling it a long-term 'constituency-building' strategy.[1] Little of this was visible to the public, but Don Brash's appointments diary revealed who was getting National's attention during 2004.

At the end of the 'gone by lunchtime' week, Friday 7 May 2004, Brash had a busy morning of meetings in Auckland. A parliamentary car collected him from home at 7am and took him to the first appointment at the Hyatt Regency Hotel, where he was delivering a breakfast address to the Property Council of New Zealand, the industry body for developers, construction companies and owners of commercial property.[2] His regular message about economic growth and removing obstacles for business would have fitted comfortably with the council's simple political stance of being 'committed to ensuring the continued growth of New Zealand's economy to help create a vibrant commercial property market'.[3] Property groups featured regularly on Brash's itineraries.

He left the breakfast meeting at 9am and went straight into a meeting in the Hyatt Regency's twelfth-floor boardroom with the Private Hospitals Association, which lobbies for government policies that help the growth of private health and private hospitals.[4] The meeting was organised by Diane Foreman, one of whose companies owns the Mercy Ascot private hospitals. The meeting followed another between Brash and the Private Hospitals Association a few weeks earlier where they had discussed 'growing the private sector to relieve the public sector'.[5] There were similar meetings in the following months. At the end of the private hospitals meeting, chief of staff Richard Long had arrived from Wellington to brief Brash on his next appointment, with the New Zealand head of the Fairfax newspaper company.[6]

Busy days like this continued, constantly and often exhaustingly, over the following months. During May 2004, between routine parliamentary and party business, Brash talked to a public relations agency political breakfast and the Real Estate Institute (12th), corporate advisers PriceWaterhouseCoopers (13th), a lunch at a Wellington infrastructure company (20th), the Auckland Chamber of Commerce (21th), a business breakfast at Ellerslie (28th) and more.

In each meeting or speech, the aim was to give reassurance that a National government would deliver the sort of policies that group wanted. The 21 May Chamber of Commerce speech, for example, was aimed at the Auckland roading lobby. Bryan Sinclair read over the draft speech for Brash the day before and sent him comments. 'Good speech Don, it "opens the door" and is an effective first step in the whole public/private funding debate as it relates to infrastructure. There is enough in it to keep the Auckland Roadhogs (main players!) happy.'[7] Brash replied by email a few minutes later: 'Thanks Bryan, I am hoping that Tony Garnier and his boss will be happy with it also. Fingers crossed!'[8] Garnier was organiser of the Auckland Business Forum pro-motorways lobby and his boss, Michael Barnett, was chief executive of the Auckland Chamber of Commerce.

The following year, 2005, National allowed Garnier to help write Brash's major 1 April roading speech. For instance, his was a key line that would be quoted in the *New Zealand Herald*: about the 'crying need' to complete Auckland's strategic roading network.[9] Garnier had questioned the need for a line in Brash's draft speech: 'I am not going to get into the business of promising particular roads because it is clearly undesirable for political pressures to become the main driver for the allocation of road investment funds'. he proposed that Brash should say: 'Clearly there is a crying need to complete Auckland's long-agreed strategic highway network as fast as possible'. Garnier's line was inserted straight after the one saying that Brash would not promise particular roads and that 'political pressures' were an undesirable basis for decisions. Garnier ended his email to National's transport spokesperson, Maurice Williamson, by saying: 'Yes, positive media support is being arranged.'[10]

A speech to the Property Institute likewise promised industry-friendly policies. The institute represents people involved in the property industry, including professional landlords. Brash told them he supported reviewing the tenancy laws, which were 'too heavily weighted towards tenants at the expense of landlords' and said National would renew its 1990s programme of selling off state houses 'to promote home ownership'. The speech finished with the question of capital gains tax. New Zealand is unusual in the developed world for not having a capital gains tax, which makes property ownership one of the most profitable (albeit unproductive) business areas. 'Do you support a capital gains tax on property?' the speech notes asked rhetorically. 'Rest assured,' he said, 'I do not support a capital gains tax.'[11]

There was a break in the business speeches while Brash made his Washington trip, then they started up again. On 30 June, for instance, Brash had a lunch meeting with the board of the Swiss-owned concrete company, Holcim New Zealand (formerly Milburn Cement), then went to an afternoon meeting, together with MP David Carter, with seven of the top managers of British American Tobacco (BAT).[12] In June 2004 the company was lobbying against increased tobacco taxes and working on plans to introduce new candy- and alcohol-flavoured cigarettes, a move criticised by the Public Health Association as trying to get children hooked on smoking.[13] The meeting was arranged by BAT's corporate affairs manager, Carrick Graham. Later that year he was invited to National's caucus party in his capacity as a BAT representative, and, as is seen in Chapter 14, he paid for two ten-person tables to National's main election-year Auckland fundraising dinner early the following year.

On 14 July Brash spoke to 200 people at the Wellington Chamber of Commerce,[14] then attended a Local Government Forum briefing arranged by Business Roundtable head Roger Kerr. The forum was established in 1994 to lobby for privatisation of local government activities. He went from the briefing straight to a meeting with Business New Zealand head Simon Carlaw and others to discuss changes to the Resource Management Act wanted by the business lobbies.

Over the following weeks Brash also had private meetings with the free trade lobby (Trade Liberalisation Network) and the head of a pharmaceutical company; private dinners with private health insurance CEOs, executives from New Zealand's largest beer company and timber industry heads; two other meetings with forestry companies, which were lobbying against climate change controls; and the annual dinner of a private schools group, which he hosted in the Parliament complex's Grand Hall.[15] And between the specific lobby groups was an endless series of general speeches to business and finance audiences.[16]

The private health insurers (the Health Funds Association) were lobbying for compulsory private health insurance for anyone earning over $38,000 a year, subsidised with public health funds through tax rebates

– a massive privatisation of health.[17] The Lion and DB meeting was organised by the Beer, Wine and Spirit Council, which was lobbying against controls on alcohol advertising.[18] On 4 August Brash had dinner with Rod Deane and Peter Shirtcliffe, two of the most influential of the National Party donors.[19] When National hosted its annual caucus party in August, the invitation list told the same story as the leader's itinerary. Excluding media and National and ACT people, the 140 or so attendees included over 40 representatives of industry lobby groups (eleven from the liquor industry alone), 35 public relations company consultants, over 20 public relations staff from large companies and a smattering of other industry associations and corporates.

In the middle of the year Brash had also his first contact with the wealthy Maxim Institute thinktank, a relationship that blossomed during 2005, and in August a series of meetings began between National and insurance companies.[20]

Brash's appointments diary from May to November that year gives a clear picture of the organisations and lobbies that National saw as its key constituencies: the finance industry, the roading lobby, forestry and fisheries companies, the private schools lobby, the private health lobby, law firms, property developers and owners, any business sector groups and, town by town, the local business clubs and associations.

There was also a smattering of Rotary clubs and such groups, but, unlike the election year, the emphasis throughout 2004 was on business groups. During this time Brash hardly spoke at all to people from public education or public health – and the few public schools he visited were decile 9 or 10 schools in affluent areas. Nor was he meeting the 90 to 95 per cent of New Zealanders who work for, bank with, buy or rent homes from and are otherwise affected by the business groups he was visiting. Brash said publicly that he was meeting and talking to thousands of people all around the country at this time, but he was talking to 'the few, not the many' – the same 5 to 10 per cent in each town and city who owned and managed the private businesses.

While 2004 was the year of business constituency building, the National Party strategists knew they also had to maintain momentum in the polls. They still needed the votes of 'the many'. They set about planning the next of a series of big populist speeches they hoped would repeat the Orewa poll surge. They knew that the speech could not be about increasing private health and education, or producing policies that would please property developers or tobacco companies. So they chose another well-worn populist issue that they hoped would fire up the emotions of the 'punters': law and order.

As he had with the Orewa race speech, Keenan wrote the speech specifically to achieve the desired political purposes. It is a textbook example of manipulative political communication: fear, anger, blame, retribution. When Keenan sent the draft to Brash he explained his thinking behind the 'approach and tone' of the speech. 'Most expectation is that this will be fairly hardline,' he said, 'so I have written it to emphasise the softer side first, and it gradually gets tougher as it goes, finishing on a bit of a rhetorical upswing.'

Keenan's plan was that they aim the speech at groups where, their polling told them, support for National was weak. 'I think we should be thinking of this as a key part of our pitch to the female and elderly constituencies. I removed some material related to speed cameras for that very reason.'[21] In its place were emotional buttons for the target groups. The speech began by giving statistics for murder of women and children and spoke of 'appalling family violence, resulting in death and disfigurement for women and children'. 'And what is our response?' the speech asked. 'Not much.... We have created a society where women and older New Zealanders are forced to significantly modify their behaviour because of the threat of violence. Our children are much less safe than they should be. All of us are at risk.'[22] The 'solution' was the usual prescription of tough welfare reform and more people in prison for longer.

Keenan was hoping not only for a repeat of the Orewa speech's large public reaction but also for its headline-grabbing controversy. 'With any luck all the liberal-pinky-lefty criminologists and psychologists and their flocks of friends in the chattering classes and the media will vigorously attack the speech,' he told Brash. 'That should whip the issue along for a while.' He advised his colleagues to be ready for the big public reaction. 'We will have paragraphs prepared for the front office to reply to all the mail that is likely to come in,' he said confidently. 'They are worried that we might do another Orewa to them.'[23]

Brash might have seen problems coming if he had thought about the comments he received on the draft of the law and order speech. A Palmerston North police officer and National Party member had sent Brash an email saying he was 'very pleased with the speech' and proposing ways to make it tougher.[24] But, as Brash wrote to Keenan, while he thought the speech was 'looking pretty good' his wife Je Lan had 'more fundamental worries I'm afraid'. She was 'surprisingly uneasy' about lowering the age of criminal responsibility to twelve, questioned why they were not look-ing at the influence of alcohol on young people and crime and 'worried about the realism of our "prison to work" recommendation'. He said she had pointed out that 'as a country, we haven't been terribly successful in getting people from welfare to work. What makes us think that we can do any better with prison to work?' Je Lan Brash was part of the female target demographic they were targeting and one of the only women shown the draft. But there was no sign that her concerns were taken seriously in the final speech. Certainly, her alcohol concerns would have been unpalatable to the liquor industry.

This time the speech was a flop. The front desk was not deluged with mail and the liberal-pinky-lefty criminologists had heard plenty of law and order grandstanding before. Brash found himself arguing over whether his figures were correct and the cost of doubling the prison population. Editorial reaction was largely sceptical, with such comments as 'why did National not do all these things when it was in power? The answer – promising is easy, delivering is another matter.'[25] The race speech at Orewa had got away with claiming to be a reluctant and principled act. But a second blatantly populist speech was seen for what it was. The issue died within days, reinforcing a decline in the National Party's polls that had begun within weeks of the Orewa peak. A couple of weeks later, in late July 2004, National slipped behind Labour again. The Orewa speech had shot them into the lead from February to July, but by then the race issue was swaying fewer and fewer people and a tough speech on law and order did not excite great passions.

What followed was a period of floundering and confusion until the party finally got a grip on its strategy not long before Christmas 2004, ten months before the election. Peter Keenan eventually realised that they would never be able to 'do another Orewa'. As he wrote to Sinclair, 'there is a bit too much of a feeling about the Party that Don can keep recreating an Orewa style momentum (sorry folks, it's back to normal hard-slog politics from here)'.[26]

Behind the scenes, Brash and his team were being run ragged by the constant schedule of speeches to the different business groups. The strain started to show in June. On the 15th Brash discovered that his programme included a non-essential event – a Plunket radiothon. 'Say guys, what the hell is going on?' he asked in an email to his appointments secretary and other staff. 'How do I get to be doing a Radiothon on Monday morning (what is a Radiothon???)... I thought I had requested that extra engagements be kept to a minimum.'[27]

As the polls slowly dropped, the theory within National's strategy team was that Brash needed 'more exposure'. On 17 August, he wrote to his colleagues: 'I am under some pressure from the Party to get more policy "out", with growing concern that we only have two policies – Treaty and law and order'. He asked that they be able to discuss strategy issues soon.[28]

The strategy committee discussed this problem the following week. Richard Long circulated by email their plan for 'a concerted effort to increase [Brash's] exposure'. This included 'local and regional human interest photo ops whenever possible' and Brash 'fronting major issues when feasible to gain TV and radio traction'. Long said this would, at times, 'mean that Gerry [Brownlee] and the spokespeople may need to relinquish good soundbite material to Don'. Murray McCully would explain this to the caucus. There would also be more regional tours, where 'women's groups and organisations will be a particular focus of attention'.[29]

One Sunday in the following month Brash and Sinclair discussed the problems across Auckland by email. Sinclair had kicked off the discussion by urging Brash to have a strategy discussion with the whole caucus. 'I can name half a dozen members of your Caucus who I understand have become quite unhappy with what they see as a "lack of strategy", and the quality of the advice you are receiving.' He named ten MPs and said, 'Ask them to bluntly say (a) what they understand our "strategy" to be; (b) whether they are confident we're on the right track.'[30]

For Sinclair the main obstacle to a caucus discussion was the National Party's arch political operator, Murray McCully, who, he believed, wanted to keep control of strategy to himself. 'Let me jump the gun and predict that Murray will counsel you firmly not to let strategy be the topic of a detailed discussion with the rest of your Caucus.... To be persuaded by Murray's advice here would, in my view, be a serious mistake.' He finished his email by saying, 'Sorry to piss you off first thing on a Sunday morning!'[31]

Brash replied: 'Bryan, sobering stuff. Now the question is, what to do about it?' He said he intended to take a more 'hands on' role in strategy from then on.[32] Sinclair responded that 'there is no easy answer of course. But I think you have hit the nail on the head right there – and that is the need for you to take a more hands-on role with strategy.' Sinclair urged that 'You should be seen as firmly in the driving seat' and, in particular, 'Caucus might feel a little more comfortable if they saw that you were on top of McCully'. He thought Brash 'should have a proper strategy session with your full Caucus – but not one that is facilitated (or dare I say impeded, controlled or directed) by your "strategists"'. He advised Brash to give himself time away from McCully's influence and talk to other MPs, listening 'extra closely to the views of the "new breed" – those MPs who are not the National Party of old. Each week you should pick three different MPs to talk to (that is only half an hour for each sitting day) and go to their office, pull up a chair and have an informal chat with the door shut. Work through all of them and visit their turf.'[33] Brash replied: 'I'll think about all those suggestions Bryan'. He was, however, not too convinced about the caucus strategy session. 'As you know,' he said, 'the place has a tendency to leak.'[34]

In that same week of early September Brash received another email from a supporter concerned that National was directionless and did not know what it stood for.[35] He forwarded it to the strategy team: 'Guys, the email below from [a supporter], just received, is exactly the message I am getting from an increasing number of our supporters. Where is National and where is Don Brash?' He voiced his own concern about the ongoing poor media coverage and expressed his unhappiness with party strategy: 'I think we need some action and I think we need it fast'. But, he ended rather ineffectually, 'Having said that, I am not myself sure what that required action is.'[36]

By early November, the polls looked worse, the same problems remained and Brash was still rushing constantly between engagements. It had been Keenan's intention that as the election approached they would 'move away from business audiences',[37] but he realised that wooing the business audiences had probably been helping to turn off two of their two key voter group targets, 'the elderly and women'. The problem, as he expressed it in a strategy paper, was 'the perception of National as a club for older white male business people'.[38] Murray McCully agreed with him: 'We do look like a bunch of conservative, honky males in suits'.[39]

Looking at Brash's daily appointments for that week, it was not hard to see why people might have that impression. On Wednesday, 3 November, Brash spoke at a business breakfast in Wellington arranged by Colin James's company, the Hugo Group, through which James provides political briefings to corporate and lobby group clients,[40] and had speech delivery training arranged by Keenan with coach Harry Mills. The next day he spoke to the Venture Capital Association's annual conference and then a VisionSchools (previously the Association of Bulk Funded Schools) seminar. The day after that, Friday 5 November, there was another early Hugo breakfast meeting in Auckland, followed by three morning meetings in a row with different private health companies and advocates. On the Friday afternoon, while Brash was at a lunch event, then opening a printing works, Peter Keenan and Bryan Sinclair discussed their growing concerns back and forth by email.

The discussion began when Keenan sent an email to Sinclair suggesting that, 'in light of concerns that Don is looking exhausted', they cancel an unimportant press release that day. 'By the way, how did the speeches go yesterday?'

'Badly,' Sinclair replied. 'He is exhausted, and it is showing – from Wednesday's snap debate [in Parliament], to his public addresses. From what I have observed, Don becomes extremely focussed on minor detail when he is under pressure. This is not where his headspace should be at the moment.' He said they needed to 'work on culling things from his diary, and give him time to manage Caucus, deal with the big picture... maintain waning funder support [and] focus on his presentation and delivery in the House and on the road'.

Sinclair said that Brash also had 'some very significant issues, that only he can address, with a growing bloc of Party funders and core supporters who have signalled very clearly in the past few weeks, in a number of forums, that, irrespective of their commitment to Don, they simply will not back the Party in its current guise. I know this better than most, because I have received the same ear bashing that he has been receiving... if the state of my ears in recent weeks are anything to go by, Don must have had his all but chewed off!!' He ended: 'we do need to collaborate on how best to support him before he really throws his toys'.[41]

'Thanks,' Keenan replied. 'Will keep this to myself, but I agree that we are at a crucial point.... It would be worthwhile you me and Don getting together for a session asap – you might want to suggest it to him.' He ended the email by asking Sinclair, 'What do the funders mean when they say they won't support the Party in its current guise?'[42]

Sinclair wrote back an hour later: 'They don't think Don is in the driving seat'. 'National's redeeming feature is its leader, and all his inherent potential lies in the perception of him as a "non-conventional politician".' But, he said, 'This year, I have seen him become (or at least gain the perception of becoming) a conventional National Party politician. To his detriment. Minus him, it is seen as largely the same house of cards as it was when Bill was running the show. We have to deal with this perception (of both funders and voters).... If we do not, Don might as well pack up now and move on.'[43]

The weekend interrupted their discussion but on the Monday Keenan sent a long reply, admitting many of his own worries about National's political prospects. He thanked Sinclair for his comments – 'all just between you and me' – and said 'there's quite a bit to discuss here'. First, he questioned whether the quality of the campaign team was really the problem. 'I think it could do the job for [Brash] if he does his part properly.' But he doubted Brash's part. 'You should get a copy of the Dominion Post article 6 November on what went wrong with Kerry,' he said. ' "The Senator was so obsessed with getting advice from a multitude of advisers that an aide confiscated his cellphone." In our case that would be Don's email. It was, apparently, a shambles internally, with Kerry not getting one simple channel of advice. And that is how I see Don operating. We have had our time wasted all year by assorted ideas from the thousands of wanna-be advisers out there who have Don's ear.... He will never have a clear head.'[44]

Keenan thought the party president Judy Kirk was 'not that important in the scheme of things' and the campaign manager Steven Joyce was 'doing a pretty good job... especially if he gets the Aussies on board'. National was in negotiation at that time to hire the Australian election strategists Crosby/Textor. As for the other National MPs, he had a very low opinion of them. 'The caucus!!' he exclaimed. 'The election will upgrade it – I hope.'

On the election campaign itself, he said, 'It will be a presidential style election, whether we like it or not – and we like it. TV interviews play to Don's strengths. Keeping on message will be the major problem.' On Brash's image, he argued, 'Clearly Don is pivotal to all this – without him National are stuffed. But I would not be so confident about his main strength being as a "non-conventional politician". It is only true to an extent. Equally you could argue that the more the electorate has got to know him the less they like what they see: somebody who cannot foot it in Parliament, who often seems to lack energy and charisma in interviews, who looks tired, and who often talks about things the voters actually don't like (like selling Kiwibank, TV2 etc).'

Keenan ended their discussion summing up where National stood less than a year out from the election. 'What I see is a lot of people running around like chooks with their heads off, Don letting far too many people get into his ear, some of whom are complete idiots... [and] not enough careful building on our strengths and eliminating our weaknesses.' He went on: 'Think of this from Labour's side. If I was in Labour's campaign team, I would keep encouraging the media to have National make some more big policy announcements, so that you would have maximum time to defuse them as issues. I would be confident that we had Brash's measure in Parliament (but know full well that most of the electorate don't really know this), but very nervous about his effectiveness on TV in a campaign. I would be confident that we had enough negatives on National to win, and hoping that Brash was foolish enough not to innoculate himself on them by going more centrist.... I would be nervous that National is holding back on policy, while remaining only 4–5% behind on average over the past 3–4 months. And you would be hoping the next Orewa speech is a flop.

'I think our task should be to keep Don positive, focused on fixing our weaknesses and always looking forward. For better or worse, he has his team, and the job is to make it as effective as possible. This works as a team game or it doesn't work at all.'[45]

Don Brash was of course also very aware that they had problems. At the end of that first week of November he received yet another exasperated email from a party official in one of the Wellington electorates. 'By now you will be aware that you have the night off on 18 November... the night that we were to have run the $500 per head fund-raiser at the Duxton Hotel, here in Wellington. We sent out some 230+ invitations to the so-called movers and shakers in this town... the net result was two positive responses.... Most disappointing, indeed!! Even the Wellington Mayor and one or two local body politicians declined.... I am VERY disappointed.

'Why, I ask myself are we not able to rouse these people to the cause?? Frankly Don, I think it is because the "strategists" in the Party are wrong, wrong, wrong.... We have dropped off the radar.... The momentum from Orewa has been lost, and, in my humble opinion... we have allowed small party people to make political capital from issues we should have made our own. We keep hearing, in this electorate about our standing as a "Gold" electorate... how winnable it is, how much a key electorate it is, how we just have to ask for help and it will be given. BS... it seems our MPs are more interested in action elsewhere... it is bad enough being reduced to mere fund-raisers, but to be apparently ignored has, I'm afraid, pricked my balloon!!'[46]

The email ended on a friendly note. 'I'm sorry Don that you have copped a wrathful email from me, but I'm sure that you will understand that we are both rather frustrated and disillusioned at the failure of 1) the fund-raiser dinner and 2) a fund-raiser cocktail party in the [local] branch area, both brought about by the lack of interest by our electorate members and others. We both want nothing more than for you to be the next Prime Minister leading a strong National Government.' They offered to talk these things over with Brash, offering him a 'healthy meal and, perhaps, a not so healthy drink or two' at their home.[47] But Brash was usually far too busy for dinners with people like these, who are the heart of any political party.

By now Brash had had enough. After months of vacillating he formally requested that each member of his strategy team, staff and MPs, write him a paper on what was needed – using the party officials' phrase – to put National back on the radar. He asked that all the strategy papers be sent to him on Monday 8 November 2004. This did not mark the beginning of Brash taking control of strategy – he never achieved that – but the papers, written ten months before the election, provided a rare insight into the thinking of the people who did. At the end of this November 2004 strategy review, most elements of National's election campaign were in place.

CHAPTER 8

EXCRUCIATING COMPROMISE
The election strategy takes shape

In an early episode of the American cartoon series *The Simpsons*, the local nuclear power plant owner, Montgomery Burns, decides to stand for election as state governor. He assembles 'the finest campaign team money can buy' to come up with a strategy. They advise him on how to 'neutralise' unhelpful issues (notably the three-eyed fish Bart Simpson caught in a contaminated stream flowing from the nuclear plant); how to identify popular messages that should be repeated over and over again to win the support of the average 'Johnny Lunchpail'; how to 'turn your average Joe Sixpack against [sitting governor] Mary Bailey'; and how to build his own image with staged photo opportunities and paid election advertising ('brought to you by the Friends of Montgomery Burns'). Soon Burns can be seen everywhere repeating his lines – promising lower taxes and attacking 'those bureaucrats down there in the state capital'.

The night before the election Burns arrives with a media entourage for a 'casual dinner' with the Simpson family, to show voters he is in touch with the 'common man'. In the kitchen, Marge Simpson tells her daughter, 'Lisa, you're learning many valuable lessons tonight, and one of them is to always give your mother the benefit of the doubt.' Marge takes a covered dish from the oven and presents it to Mr Burns: it is the three-eyed fish cooked on a platter. Burns tries to eat it, but gags and spits it out and his campaign is lost before the mouthful hits the floor.[1]

The strategy advice that arrived from each member of Don Brash's strategy team on 8 November 2004 was strikingly similar to that of their cartoon cousins. Their plan was to dispose of any actively unpopular issues, not mention most other issues and flog a small number of issues that, though unrelated to the party's core objectives, would work as easy vote winners.

The National leader's strategy advisers at that time were staff members Peter Keenan, Bryan Sinclair, Richard Long and Steven Joyce, and MPs Murray McCully, Gerry Brownlee and, briefly, Katherine Rich. As he did for all critical political decisions, Brash also sought advice from his friend Ruth Richardson, meeting her privately in Christchurch the day after the other advisers' papers arrived. McCully, who saw himself as the strategy mastermind, submitted two papers, one on strategy and one on 'campaign structure issues'.

Each strategy paper was addressed only to Brash, not the other strategy team members, so each person could raise concerns and express opinions frankly and confidentially. People in these positions usually choose to be face to face to discuss strategy, with no minutes taken, so this offers a rare opportunity to observe how they think. Each paper was written according to the adviser's personal view of politics. Richard Long focused on managing the news. Peter Keenan was concerned with big picture issues about how the National Party is perceived. And, in contrast to Keenan's frequent likening of politics to war, Murray McCully referred to politics repeatedly as a 'game'.

The advisers first needed to tackle how Don Brash was feeling – tired and barraged with criticism of his performance. In the presidential-style campaign they were planning, everything relied on the leader appearing confident and optimistic. Keenan accordingly began his contribution by urging Brash to 'stay positive'. 'Don't panic,' he urged. 'It is easy to concentrate too hard on what is not going so well. And you are in the position where all you hear are the complaints, grizzles and whining – people will tell you you should have done this, you should have done that. And I imagine that it gets to you eventually, so that you start to feel besieged.' His advice was: 'Tell some of these people to bugger off'.

He encouraged Brash, telling him that what he had achieved so far was 'really quite extraordinary'. Brash could take credit for 'the resuscitation of a dead Party to about the point we would have been hoping for at the end of 2003'. 'This electorate is incredibly volatile,' he said, 'and Labour have every reason to worry.' He reminded Brash that since taking over the leadership 'you have added 10% points to National'.[2]

Bryan Sinclair concentrated on securing funding and hiring campaign advisers. 'This has to be the most well-resourced campaign National has fought,' he wrote. 'You need to collect the booty now' and 'donors must also see something tangible for their money'. This was 'a mix of better calibre people (heavy artillery), evidence of campaign machinery, evidence of a communications strategy being delivered, and evidence that potential voters are seeing and hearing you and your message.... Most importantly, the donors want to fund Don Brash the Prime Minister.'[3]

Sinclair believed that the most urgent need was to buy in an 'A team' of professionals and specialists, 'each with different but complementary skill sets, and each with track records in their respective fields'. This team needed 'to be put in place now and each member has to be the best, not the second best'.[4] As pollsters – who would 'market research... on key issues and constituencies' – Sinclair proposed the controversial Australian Crosby/Textor company, whom he had taken Brash to meet in Canberra on 17 June that year. Sinclair's other key position was a 'policy wonk', someone who could 'distil complex policy into saleable chunks geared towards vote-winning'. Sinclair's suggestion for the role was Peter Keenan, who mostly was already doing it and had his functions in that area formalised in early 2005.[5] Around this time National also approached ACT Party organiser Brian Nicolle, who had been paid by National to assist its Tauranga electorate campaign in the 2002 election. The plans for him to do campaign organisation were dropped after Nicolle was caught out co-ordinating the covert smear campaign against Auckland mayoral candidate Dick Hubbard in September 2004.

Sinclair, who had little respect for what he saw as National Party hacks like McCully and Long, argued that if National would not choose the best staff itself, the A team should be arranged anyway using donors' money. McCully was obviously aware of criticism of the strategy team. His second paper, on 9 November, told Brash he must make a decision on whether he had the right team in place. If it was not, he should change them. And either way, he must 'then give the annointed team [his] confidence'. 'In Steven, Richard and Peter I believe you have a mix of skills you would not easily replace.'[6] As it turned out, the Joyce-McCully-Long-Keenan campaign team remained in place, but outside experts were brought in to help.

The National Party team's next priority was to neutralise issues that would lose them votes. McCully expressed this in his 8 November paper when he advised that they needed to 'fairly urgently make the decisions about those issues on which we intend to pick our fights and those we intend to inoculate'.[7] The National strategists use the words 'neutralise' and 'inoculate' to talk about taking vote-losing issues off the political agenda.

National MP Nick Smith had brought this subject to prominence in a report he wrote after observing the final days of the Australian election campaign. The report, on lessons National could learn from the 2004 Liberal Party's election victory, noted that 'the Liberals were most vulnerable over the Iraq war'. He said 'it could have evolved into the issue of the campaign and polls indicated the majority of people did not support Howard or the Liberal's decision to go to war with the US'.[8] Learning from the Australians, Smith concluded that 'we must identify our weak spots' and 'neutralise them early on'. He was 'concerned about potential for us to be targeted on 4-week holidays, asset sales and superannuation. I think we have already successfully neutralised the nuclear issue and tax cuts for the rich.'[9] National's strategy committee had taken his points up at its next meeting, noting there were 'several major vulnerabilities on our part which we need to address prior to Christmas'. Notes from the meeting said 'the most significant of these is a "back to the 1980s" image which had gained traction'. There were also 'a number of specific issues we need to inoculate before election year – superannuation entitlement, privatisation, four weeks holiday etc'.[10]

Richard Long's 8 November paper agreed with Nick Smith's idea about getting their inoculations out of the way quickly. 'We are constantly being seen to embrace Act, or employers, and being worker unfriendly (eg four weeks leave) which means we frighten off many of those blue collar male Labour voters that Don dragged across the divide on Orewa.' Before getting on with vote-winning policies, they needed to 'dispos[e] of [their] "inoculation" issues'. His list was the same as Smith's.[11] McCully's paper reinforced this, urging that before Christmas they 'target voters over 60, offering reassurance (inoculation) in relation to superannuation'.[12]

National had long known that 'taking away the extra week's annual leave that Labour had legislated for' would, in Keenan's words, be 'a clear losing issue for us with the voters we need to attract'.[13] A year earlier Matthew Hooton had advised Brash that sooner or later he 'was going to have to find an economically-acceptable way of backing off' on the issue but it had taken dropping polls to persuade the strategy team to act. (Hooton's deeply cynical proposal on how to do this is reproduced in the notes in full, as an example of the thinking behind deliberately ineffectual 'voluntary industry codes'.)[14]

They did their 'flip-flop' a month after the policy review, as one of a series of inoculations at that time. The only workable inoculation was backing down and accepting the Labour government's position. A National Party press release on 9 December 2004 announced that the party would now support 'a statutory minimum of four weeks annual leave'. They justified the policy change by saying that 'currently, employers and employees are negotiating contracts in good faith that will include four weeks leave as a minimum requirement. Forcing another round of change on business would be costly, and unfair to staff.'[15] They softened the back-down by saying they would offer employees the right to cash in the extra week of holiday. Being forced to back a Labour policy, against the wishes of their business allies, brought no joy to the National Party strategists. Peter Keenan described the move as being required to 'swallow a dead rat'.[16] But the main concern was that the issue would be gone for the start of election year, which it was.

The subject of privatisation was trickier to inoculate because, as Brash had written privately to his colleagues in September 2004, he did not want to suggest that they would 'never ever' sell a government-owned asset.[17] In a speech to the Screen Directors Guild in October 2004, he had tried to defuse speculation that National would privatise Television New Zealand by saying that the key issue was whether 'changing the ownership of TVNZ [would] make the New Zealand economic boat go faster', and that he believed selling might just cause disruption.[18] But his attempt to deal with the contentious issue went awry when he refused, in answer to a question, to rule out selling TV2 and noted that it was 'very commercial'.[19]

This led Long to say in his 8 November strategy paper that 'the leader and media team/strategy advisers need to work closely together on key messages and one-liners for sound-bites, especially before major TV appearances'. In some areas, notably on selling TV2, 'we have had an alarming tendency to go off message'.[20] But he made it plain that, at least in his mind, inoculating the privatisation issue was purely about public appearances and not about National's eventual plans. He expressed dismay at Brash 'musing aloud about selling TV2', not because National would not do it, but because 'we are trying to give the impression we will not push asset sales'.[21]

A few months later National Party finance spokesperson John Key took over the job of inoculating on privatisation. In a speech to the Ellerslie Rotary Club in March 2005, he said that 'the days of wholesale asset sales are gone' and, using Brash's line, that National was more interested in 'what will make the boat go faster'. This time the lines worked, gaining National the desired headlines: 'Nats rule out state asset sales'[22] and 'Nats do U-turn on selling Kiwibank'.[23]

Some commentators took this as Key having pushed Brash into a more moderate position on privatisation. But actually he was using the same lines as Brash to do the planned inoculation before the election campaign began. Richard Long sent Key a congratulatory email: 'Well done this morning. You were superb on Morning Report and the Dominion and NZ Herald pieces are excellent. It's gone across as a sensible, moderate approach and another sensible inoculation.'[24] Key had actually promised very little on the subject. He had not ruled out National government privatisations and even signalled that they would proceed with partial privatisations in various areas. He had simply said that they would not proceed with the main privatisation targets such as TV2, state energy companies and Kiwibank 'for at least our first term in office',[25] which was the compromise Peter Keenan had proposed to Brash ('Sort out privatisation in the second term!'). But they had gained the headlines they wanted, which was the whole point of the inoculation.

The other area for immediate inoculation was National's unpopular policy of raising the age at which people were eligible for superannuation. As Keenan had written, the policy was 'a huge political negative for us – we simply have to neutralise the political damage as best we can'. This was achieved in a speech by Brash to the North Shore Rotary Clubs three weeks after the policy review, entitled 'New Zealand Superannuation is secure'. Again the messages were driven entirely by expediency. The draft speech, as emailed back and forth between Peter Keenan and Don Brash, had the file name '<Superannuation Innoc speech>'.

With the inoculations dealt with, the strategists' next issue was choosing their key messages for the election campaign – in Murray McCully's words, 'those issues on which we intend to pick our fights'. Up until then there had been various possibilities for the main election issues, including law and order and education. But the National strategy team worked their way to the same conclusion as Montgomery Burns' strategists.

It was Bryan Sinclair who voiced the approach that won the day. In choosing the election policy, he argued in his 8 November strategy paper, 'You need to be sloppy, soft and wet – i.e. open up the cheque book, as excruciating as this will feel.' 'Soft centre voters are inherently self-interested, and will vote according to what they can get out of you. Election winning behaviour requires you to slosh those funds around and buy your way to the Treasury benches.' This sort of thinking ran utterly counter to their free market beliefs, but Sinclair noted that winning the election 'will mean some very hard ideological compromise at times'.[26]

Sir George Chapman, the former National Party president, wrote to Brash and Steven Joyce at this time recommending the same approach.

'The reality is,' he said, 'that most voters only take an interest in policies that directly affect their lives. [Prime Minister Keith] Holyoake's constant theme was "that every election is a pocket-book election", an approach that produced four election wins in a row. The thing affecting the lives of most voters, 'or at least their pocket-books', was the 'rates of personal taxation'.[27]

Richard Long, too, proposed the idea of tax cuts as National's main election policy. 'In my view our second big issue of the election campaign, after One Law for All, has to be tax cuts. I would vote for a bold statement promising big tax cuts, maybe even a flat tax, but without the detail.' The best approach for National, he believed, was to announce the general intention before Christmas but to delay providing any specifics until much closer to the election. 'We would have to find a formula of words saying this is our intention, our work over many months shows it is feasible, but that we will not produce details till we see the state of the books next year.... If we are looking for the topic for summer barbecue talk, this is it, more than welfare or education.'[28]

It was far from clear or unanimous that it was wise to focus the campaign on tax cuts. Long acknowledged in his paper that there were various counter-arguments. 'I know it is fraught with a thousand problems, and that Cullen will seek to discredit any promises, say it will be inflationary, will be funded at the cost of superannuation security, that it is tax cuts for our mates the rich etc.' The *New Zealand Herald* commented that Brash would like to campaign on issues like tax cuts, 'but it does not win votes'.[29]

But the tax cut view prevailed. Keenan wrote a speech for Brash promising tax cuts, called 'Getting Ahead With Lower Taxes', which he delivered to a National Party audience at Auckland's North Shore Stadium on 10 December 2004. This speech and the inoculations were the main moves made by National at the end of 2004 to set itself up for election year.

Why were tax cuts an 'excruciating... ideological compromise' for Brash and his colleagues? Surely they are standard new right policy? What this group had consistently pushed for, however, was tax cuts at the top end of the income scale – what their detractors called 'tax cuts for the rich'. The theory is that tax cuts for high income earners stimulate economic growth while tax cuts for low and middle income people do not, and may cause other economic problems. So when Brash was first elected as leader and talked in his first interviews about tax cuts, he was referring to high income earners and expressing a view he had long espoused. Since then, his staff had gone to great efforts to expunge the 'tax cuts for the rich' image before the election campaign. The December 2004 tax cut promise, in contrast, included low and middle income earners and was old-fashioned chequebook politics.

Partly because of chance and partly because of good planning, this tax cut promise would become the main election issue for many voters and played a large part in nearly winning the election for National. Tax cuts for low and middle income people were not why people like Brash, Sinclair and Keenan were in politics; they simply believed they were necessary to gain power, though they denied such motives. The media reported Brash as saying his 'tax cuts before Christmas' promise 'was not an election bribe to buy the votes of middle-class New Zealanders'.[30]

Although the tax cut decision was crucial, the strategy team knew that one or two policies were not enough on which to base the whole election campaign. They needed to be able to give a more general explanation of what the National Party stood for. McCully took up this subject in his 8 November paper and set down some of his views on the game of politics.

The big media coverage is always devoted to situations where there is a game on. Media invest most heavily in stories which will go somewhere, providing them with ongoing opportunity. The Orewa speech fell into that category. There was a game on with the commentators lining up to bag you, your opponents lining up to condemn you and the public lining up to support you. The polls then gave the media something they hadn't had for four years – a political contest, generating its own momentum. That situation was always going to be difficult to maintain....

In order to dominate the public stage from time to time we need to give the media a sense that there is a game on. That means ensuring that we roll a story out over several days or weeks. In a macro sense, the campaign build-up is such a game. The media will provide good coverage when they are convinced that there will be follow-through from us (and therefore good stories and interesting column fodder for them). This process is important because the subliminal message is that we are earning our success, not having it gifted to us.

It is in the nature of creating such a game that there must be debate and contest. In order to achieve the above, we need to be clear about the issues on which we wish to have those debates, and where we wish to avoid them. We then need to map out a range of initiatives which will give the issue life over a period of time (policy proposals etc). Then, it is our ability to manage our message which will be critical. So... I suggest that we need to be clear about our 'story' as a basis for determining our next steps.[31]

The strategy team had already accepted the need to sort out its 'story'. Steven Joyce had prepared a report on his and party president Judy Kirk's 'whistle stop trip' to Australia in early October 2004 to observe the Liberal Party's election campaigning. The report said they had met Mark Textor of Crosby/Textor and Liberal Party officials, who made three key points about what National should be doing at that stage of the campaign. These were to 'make sure the funding is right', to get the organisational 'mechanics' of the campaign set up well and to 'sort out a simple message for change, and do it prior to Christmas'. Joyce said he was advised that 'the message just has to answer the question, why will voters want to choose Don Brash over Helen Clark?' That was 'the context that the campaign will be fought on'. The story needed to be tested with focus groups and thereafter repeated 'relentlessly'.[32]

At the next Campaign Strategy Meeting, on 19 October, the agenda included this subject under the heading 'The National "Story"'.[33] The 'action points' from the meeting noted 'Murray [McCully] and Steven [Joyce] to arrange focus group work on the "National Story"', which would include 'the six points as discussed as well as one on tax relief'.[34] The draft six points were:

Why choose Don Brash over Helen Clark? Because Don Brash will...
1. Stop us going down the path to rampant political correctness.
2. Put an end to the treaty grievance industry.
3. Make our community safer by locking away violent criminals.
4. Ensure your hard-earned tax dollars are spent on Education and Health and not wasted on Labour's pet projects and bureaucracy.
5. Put in place economic policies that will lift all our incomes closer to those of Australians.
6. Tighten up welfare and ensure that everyone that can work does work.[35]

National's reasons for choosing these particular six points as its 'story' are discussed in Chapter 11.

Bryan Sinclair's 8 November strategy paper reinforced this approach, saying that Brash needed 'Five key policy planks (maximum)'. 'This is your product and you have to take it to the market (ie get it right into the homes and workplaces of voters) using a wide range of channels.'

This belief probably came directly from the Australian pollster/strategists Crosby/Textor, who also advised Australian and British parties to stick to an 'easily digestible' five priorities.[36] Mark Textor was hired soon after to investigate public reactions to the draft National story.

The other policy question facing the National strategists at that time was what subject to choose for Brash's next Orewa speech, scheduled for late January 2005. Peter Keenan, in his 8 November paper, told Brash 'I guarantee you a cracker of a speech'. But they could not agree on a subject. McCully was arguing for education, 'despite Peter [Keenan]'s reservations', with a welfare speech before Christmas.[37] Gerry Brownlee agreed it should be a welfare speech before Christmas,[38] but Katherine Rich thought it should be education. 'It can't be welfare this close to Christmas,' she said, 'because announcing any centre-right policy will only present you as being a Grinch.' She said the welfare speech, which Brash's staff had already begun working on, 'has to be post-Christmas'.[39] That view won the day and a welfare speech was agreed on for Orewa.

The next element of the strategy was attacking Labour. It is worth repeating Peter Keenan's explanation for this: 'Unless we create a public perception that this Government is not up to the job, <u>we will not win</u>'.[40] Their main target was of course Helen Clark. One of Keenan's strategy emails gives an insight into the thinking behind the attack strategies. He told the other strategy team members of an 'interesting comment I came across today' which 'fits with us attacking Clark on her integrity'. He explained the idea, which came from George W. Bush's strategist Karl Rove, as follows. 'Rove is an acknowledged master of negative politics, though it's important to understand what's worth going negative on and what's not. When the neophyte Bush ran against Ann Richards, the popular incumbent governor in Texas, she responded with the same cracks she'd made about Dubya's dad – pampered rich boy, born with a silver foot in his mouth, etc. Bad move: Rove believes there's no point attacking a candidate on his weak points; you attack him on his strong points. Do that right and there's nothing left.'[41] National would attack Helen Clark over her integrity on every possible occasion. The same applied for her image of strength. This led a second attack strategy, which was, as Nick Smith put it, that they 'must characterise Helen as arrogant'.[42]

The next element of the strategy, after attacks on Helen Clark, was building Don Brash's reputation. There were several parts of this. The first, as with the election policies, was dealing with the negatives. Keenan's ongoing worry was that Brash polled well with middle-aged men, especially those in suits, but not so well with women and young people. His 8 November paper advised that they needed to work on a softer, more caring image, working 'to set up perceptions of what is important to you'. The desired perception would come from 'visiting childcare centres, engaging with women's issues, visit[ing] Maori business groups and small towns with heavy welfare dependency problems'.[43]

A Campaign Strategy Meeting paper made the same point: National had to 'present a contemporary and modern face on the Party/Leader'. It said 'steps have already been taken to modify the Leader's programme to secure more coverage in softer, more human situations and expose him to audiences outside the business/Rotary sector. Broadening and deepening the Leader's image remains a priority.'[44]

The other negative was Brash's right-wing image. Again for Keenan the issue was managing impressions rather than changing their political goals. They needed 'to decide whether we are a centrist Party or not, because if we aren't we haven't got a chance'.[45] This repeated his urgings to Brash of a week earlier, when he had emphasised the need to 'deal with some negatives this year... repositioning as a clearly centrist party in late November'.[46] 'You have plenty of issues that you will be talking very straight on,' he said. 'But what you and I think we know about the economy and social policy is not where the electorate is, yet. You can only go as far as the electorate wants, and only change what they want gradually.'[47]

As usual, Sinclair's ideas about Brash's image were focused on marketing. 'Party Vote National', he wrote, essentially meant 'Vote for Don Brash'. 'You need a slick public relations outfit around you, stage managing your every move. Your movements and messages must revolve entirely around the key target constituencies identified – eg women, over 65s, soft centre swingers in both provincial and urban electorates.' He emphasised presidential-style campaigning. 'Your name and image needs to be everywhere across New Zealand. Not a single communication should go out between now and the election without you featuring somewhere in it/on it.'[48]

Brash took his point to heart. A couple of weeks later he wrote to campaign manager Steven Joyce: 'being a modest kind of guy, I hate to raise this issue, but feel I must! If Party Vote National is in fact synonymous with "Vote Don Brash rather than Helen Clark", shouldn't all of our campaign material, including brochures, business cards, etc, feature the handsome face of yours truly? The stuff I have seen so far does not do that, and it seems to me that that is a wasted opportunity.'[49]

Joyce replied tactfully that 'in general terms' he agreed with Brash's comments. 'However, the only stuff you have seen so far is the candidate's personal stationery – business card and calling card. On balance I think that is fair enough for it to be them' – that is, for candidates to have their own photographs on their business cards and stationery. 'The stationery is quite small,' he added. 'You will be pleased to see tomorrow that the over 60s brochure has your smiling face on it at least five times!!' [50]

Besides the main strategy areas, the strategy team had a few other pieces of advice in their 8 November dispatches. Keenan told Brash he needed to 'spend much more time on how you deliver your messages, and what they are. You should rehearse informally with the press team before significant TV interviews. You should always know what crisp message you want to get away.'

He also wanted Brash to be better at not answering questions. 'You should become more adept at not going with a line of questioning that doesn't suit your purposes. As you do that people will say, where is the genuine straight-talking Brash? That you are starting to sound more like a politician, that your handlers are getting to you, your strings are being pulled etc etc.' But, he said, 'Politicians sound like politicians because the ones that don't, don't survive'. For example, when media asked Brash about National's election strategy he should not try to answer but 'just fake extreme confidence'.

'You need to ensure you are not tired,' he continued. 'A good TV interview is worth hundreds of worthy speeches.... I think we should continue working with ['artful persuasion' speaking coach] Harry Mills (or somebody else if you don't feel he is right). We don't need to change much – just work on the delivery of written speeches (for the next Orewa and other set pieces) and on the times when you have to perform in Parliament (it is essential your Parliamentary performance improves).' He finished his paper by anticipating how Brash might be feeling in the face of all the frank advice. 'It seems to me that politics is the ultimate team game,' he commiserated, 'everybody, including the Leader at times, feels like just a pawn in the game.' [51]

MP Katherine Rich began her 8 November paper by saying, 'I have read Murray McCully's paper which was submitted to you and I endorse that as an excellent overview of what the strategy is'. She suggested Brash be 'more discerning' about what he gave his time to – 'You know my views on the weekly call to [Wellington lawyer–lobbyists] Chen and Palmer, lots of effort for little gain' – and noted that 'much of the Liberal's campaign was fought via targeted direct mail' advertising. She suggested that they 'survey each electorate as soon as possible so that information from those surveys can be collated and entered' into the party database.[52] Rich also noted that 'the team would be stronger if everyone was working. This is not the case. There are many coasters and the Chief Whip needs to get involved in encouraging certain colleagues to carry more of the load.' In conclusion she said, 'Finally, this may sound ironic given this comment comes by way of "advice", [but] you need to follow your gut feel more and listen to disparate views less.'[53]

A final strategy issue featured in one of Steven Joyce's internal election strategy papers: while National's primary goal was 'to be the party with the largest share of the vote', a 'subsidiary objective' was 'to see the Greens drop below the 5% threshold'.[54]

When all these strategies and plans were put together, and when agreements with the major donors had ensured the necessary funds, that November strategy review had laid the foundations for nearly everything that happened in the election year. Having swallowed the necessary rats to help reposition National as a 'centrist' party, the anything but centrist Brash could head off on a summer break that included joining a Business Roundtable retreat on Waiheke Island and hosting his old friend and free market mentor Milton Friedman when his cruise ship stopped in for a day in Auckland on 24 January.[55]

The overall strategy, as Keenan summarised it in his 8 November paper, was to 'get our inoculation done pre-xmas; keep focus on attacking the government; and keep hammering the same messages' – 'repeat repeat repeat'. If they did that, he said, they should 'prepare [them]selves for a huge 2005'.[56]

After the inoculations and tax speech, the next big event for the National team was Brash's 2005 speech to the Orewa Rotary Club, which Keenan predicted confidently 'gives you the perfect platform to launch the year and define the campaign'.[57] He was wrong. Just as Mr Burns's all-male strategy team had appealed to the 'common man' but forgotten about the views of women, National's usually all-male campaign team had never come to grips with the fact that many women did not like their more divisive and right-wing policies. And months later, in the midst of the election campaign, Brash's staff would be overheard by journalists referring to him behind his back by a special private name: Mr Burns.[58]

CHAPTER 9

TROUBLE WITH WOMEN
Orewa II and female votes

It was Richard Long who noticed that they might be heading for trouble with the Orewa II speech. In a section of his 8 November strategy paper called 'Damage Limitation', he warned: 'To my mind a "splits and divisions" story would be more damaging to National than the current party view that we are being inactive. We are very close to this on welfare. In my view the leader and spokeswoman [Katherine Rich] need to sit down together and compromise on the outstanding issues. I suspect the gaps are much wider than the leader may anticipate.'[1]

First, there were risks of alienating women voters. He argued that 'we may not be well served by having a welfare policy which is too hardline. For women, it may be better to have a policy which is compassionate overall, but which has a core of steel, pledging to remove the rorts.'

But the immediate problem concerned National's sole woman front-bench MP, Katherine Rich, and the potential for 'splits and divisions'. (National's other talented front-bench woman, Georgina Te Heuheu, had been dumped a year earlier when she disagreed with Brash's Orewa race speech.) 'We cannot afford to have Katherine, the young, liberal, articulate women's face of the party, walking away from the [welfare] portfolio,' he said. 'This will be hugely damaging in terms of media coverage and public perception.'[2] The National Party's first internal polling for the election year began on 25 January, just in time to record the reaction to Brash's 25 January 2005 Orewa speech. The impact of Orewa I had been immediate and hugely gratifying but this time the confidential polling brought them bad news. The 'rolling average' graph line had traced National gradually dropping in support all through 2004 until a low point at the start of December, when finally it had started to rise again for the two months up until Brash's hardline welfare speech. After this it dropped sharply to a new low.

While Helen Clark was judged to be doing an above average job by over 50 per cent of respondents, only 23 per cent felt that way about Brash and 38 per cent rated his performance as below average. It was a disappointing start to the year. But the most telling figures were, yet again, the gender breakdown of the results. Looking just at male voters, National was actually slightly in the lead. But for female voters National was hopelessly behind, more than 15 per cent below Labour.[3]

Peter Keenan had been watching the National Party internal polls month by month throughout the previous year and reminding the strategy team about what he called 'our women problems'. (When any journalists asked Richard Long about National's internal polling, which was being conducted weekly at that time, his prepared lines were that 'Unlike Labour we do very little polling. Too expensive. Labour is poll driven, we are principled.')[4] In 2005 Keenan continued telling Brash that 'if we want to close the gender gap, which is really what this election is going to be all about... then we had better focus on the issues that matter to females.... It is as simple as that.'[5]

Keenan does not, however, appear to have felt genuine sympathy for the opinions and concerns of women voters. He wanted their votes. 'Polling data is sketchy,' he said on one occasion, 'but the impression I get is that we do pretty well with middle-aged mothers (they get more conservative once they have some ankle-biters to deal with). The problem is younger liberal greeny ones and the elderly ones who, if they had the energy, would get their gear off for Winston.'[6]

Keenan felt he may have found a solution when he came across an article in the *New York Times* in September 2004. Called 'What Women Voters Want', it was written by Republican pollster Lance Tarrance and former Bush administration official Leslie Sanchez. Their answer for getting women voting for George W. Bush lay in what they called 'feminine appeal'. They said Bush could achieve this by 'building an emotional connection, humanising himself and portraying himself as the candidate who can keep America safe', which meant including special women-friendly messages in his speeches. 'In this presidential election,' they concluded, 'it is becoming more and more clear that the female voter is the true swing voter'[7] – which, to a pollster and political adviser, meant susceptible to last-minute manipulation by campaign tactics.

Keenan sent this 'very interesting article' to Murray McCully and the media staff, telling them to 'note especially' the comment about female voters being the 'true swing voters'. 'Worth our while to all try and work the right sort of language into speeches and press releases.'[8]

A week later Keenan sent Brash another American article, highlighting a paragraph that was 'interesting on how Bush pitches to the female vote'. The article, called 'Wooing mom', said Bush had 'toned down the cowboy rhetoric and begun presenting his daddy/hubby side to female audiences'. Bush, it reported, said the 'W' in his name 'stands for Women'.[9]

National decided to commission some focus group research on female voters. They hired the services of Auckland 'consumer insight special-ist' Sandy Burgham, who had begun market research for the party in the 1990s when Jenny Shipley was leader. She presented her results to Brash and the strategy team in the Leader's Lounge at Parliament on the evening of 5 October 2004.[10] Brash would later tell the strategy team that he 'thought the research was good, but we have made no decisions to act on it at all to my knowledge. But this is not from any reluctance on my part.'[11] The truth, however, was that Burgham had told them things they did not want to hear.

Keenan summarised her results for the strategy team. First, he wrote, 'the Sandy Burgham focus groups on women showed that Kiwi women value New Zealand independence (nuclear free, GE free, no Iraq war etc)' – all of which ran counter to National's preferred policies. Second, the research found that the women studied were 'worried about strong Asian immigration', which had more potential, though it clashed with National's immigration-for-economic-growth policies. Third, the women felt 'that Green credentials are increasingly at the heart of New Zealandness' and they 'like the idea of New Zealand taking a stand on environmental issues'. Keenan noted: 'National's Kyoto stance a problem here'.

The interviewed women believed 'that because New Zealand is doing OK they would not be worried about another term for Labour'. Their impressions of National were that it was 'old-fashioned', 'a boys club' and that 'the female MPs are invisible'. They thought that 'National doesn't have a big idea' and was 'too corporate oriented', and they worried that National 'might take away free childcare for under 6 group'. In fact, they thought 'National doesn't like free anything'.[12]

Burgham found the National strategists were polite and interested but not really connecting with what she was telling them. Keenan summed up her results to his colleagues with the understated comment that the women had a 'pretty flinty perception of National'.[13]

All of this was relevant to the vexed question of what subject to use for Brash's January 2005 speech at Orewa. In late October 2004 Brash told Keenan that he was 'not absolutely confident' that 'the big education speech scheduled for Orewa' was 'the right decision'. The other option, he said, was to 'save welfare for Orewa'.[14]

When Keenan responded a week later, he argued that 'a tough welfare speech would actually reinforce the... very significant negatives' National already presented to voters. Citing the Burgham research, he said that 'people almost always see [Brash] in suits and at business gatherings. No women, no children.... The message that gets through is what you see if you turn the sound off on the TV.' An Orewa welfare speech would reinforce the negatives 'especially [with] a speech in the form recently drafted', referring to a first draft Brash had written a few days before. 'I suspect that we might even achieve a 3/3 poll decline,' he said, referring to all three main media polls moving against National, 'instead of just 2/3'.[15]

Thinking of the women voters, Keenan said that a tough welfare speech would need to be timed nearer to the election and 'presented in a "tough-love" context, preferably linked to tax and benefit reform, and well-publicised job creation measures for the long-term unemployed'. These would be 'best linked to some "innovative" environmental schemes – saving wildlife via a huge expansion of funding for establishing pest free zones such as the Americans are doing at Cape Kidnappers, and has been done in Karori; Kyoto-alternative policies of substantial tree planting around the country using the 20,000 long term unemployed, as part of a beautify NZ programme – New Zealand makeover!!'[16] In his political mind, they could marry welfare reform with softer environmental issues to make it more palatable to women. He suggested they bring in environmentalist Guy Salmon (a National candidate in the 2002 election) to help on this and announce him as a list candidate in the election to boost their environmental credentials.[17]

Keenan carried these thoughts further a couple of weeks later in a paper about the strategy for the Orewa speech. He said it was essential that they counter the negative perceptions of National (corporate-oriented, old-fashioned boys' club etc.) and that their next opportunity to do this was at Orewa. 'That suggests that a tough Welfare speech is not the right topic for now. It is a better one for close to the election, once we have done some softening of the Brash/National image.'[18]

Instead, he toyed with the idea of choosing an Orewa topic that 'nobody is suggesting or expecting – an Environment speech'. Even better, they could 'make the environment a large part of a broader Vision speech', a 'very nationalistic speech'.

'The environment would add some punch to a Vision speech like this by putting a lot of emphasis on the environment.' They could announce some detailed environmental policy 'which would be a surprise move to most people'. This policy could include 'a five-year ban on growing GM Food (ie the Sustainability Council policy recommendation – Nick Smith not impressed with this idea), but strong support for the science and for medical applications; plans to deal with hazardous waste sites; [and] over time, replac[ing] all Government cars with petrol-electric hybrids'.[19]

But the strategy team did not agree. Brash had spent the year promising a different kind of policies to the business lobbies and there was no great enthusiasm for doing anything different.

Keenan suggested the vision speech idea in mid-December and the strategy team reached the Christmas break still without a decision. But Brash was being encouraged by other members of the strategy team to go with welfare. He sent Sinclair the latest draft of the welfare speech: 'I have drafted it on the assumption that I might use it at Orewa, but of course I may decide to use something on vision which Peter [Keenan] is drafting, and will have ready for me to read when I get back from Hawaii. If you get time, I'd be interested in your reaction.' He said, 'I don't yet have Katherine [Rich's] comments on the policy specifics.'[20]

Brash was heading off for an unpublicised ten-day holiday in Hawaii and other staff were scattering for a much-needed break. The last thing Brash did before leaving on holiday was to send a copy of his draft welfare speech to Michael Bassett. 'Michael, I attach a very preliminary draft of a speech which I MIGHT use at Orewa on 25 January. I may yet go with a different speech altogether, as I mentioned to you the other day.' He noted that 'some of the policy positions in it need a bit more thrashing out with my social welfare spokesperson, so I'd ask you not to share it with anybody else at all at this stage please. I may decide to make substantive changes.' But 'any comments you care to make would be much appreciated'.[21] As had happened with the Orewa speech on race, Bassett would have far more input into the text than any member of the National Party caucus except Brash and possibly McCully.

Bassett wrote back to Brash the next afternoon. 'Don, I'm working on your speech, but thought the enclosed that I did in August might be useful.'[22] This was a speech Bassett had given at an ACT Party welfare symposium on 14 August 2004, where Roger Douglas and Centre for Independent Studies head Peter Lindsay also spoke. Bassett had told the symposium that 'Bureaucrats, church groups, and private and publicly-funded social workers like welfare because farming beneficiaries gives purpose to their lives, and provides an income for many'. He said that 'the overwhelming number of beneficiaries have been lured into this life style by the ready availability of easy money'.

Brash replied from Hawaii: 'Michael, yes thanks – I had a copy of your August piece beside me as I wrote my draft! You will, I think, recognise the odd statistic!' He also thanked Bassett for information on 20th-century Maori leader Apirana Ngata's views on welfare, which he included in the speech delivered at Orewa.[23]

When the strategy team reassembled in January, the use of welfare for the Orewa speech won over Keenan's vision idea. The majority, and notably Murray McCully, wanted another contentious, headline-grabbing (and poll-raising) Orewa bombshell.

Looking through the succession of drafts of the speech, which stretch over a three-month period, the input of different people can be clearly seen. The final speech has an introduction written by Murray McCully, a closing paragraph and title written by Bassett and in between a patchwork written by Brash, Bassett, Keenan, McCully and others. As he often did, Brash also showed the speech to the Business Roundtable's Roger Kerr, who advised him, on political grounds, against using it.

Brash wrote the first draft on a Monday 25 October 2004, a few days after he first raised the idea of using welfare for the Orewa speech. 'I woke up this morning and decided to try my hand at a speech on social welfare reform,' he said in an email to twelve of his colleagues. 'I suspect the speech could gain us some media coverage, and might even gain us some political support.'[24]

This first draft was the one that Keenan had feared would merely increase National's 'negatives' with women. It included a 'life-time limit on eligibility for the DPB [domestic purposes benefit, actually single parent support] of six years' and no DPB for women under 18 years. 'Children born to young women of 17 and under should be made available for adoption or supported by the mother's family,' Brash had written.[25] Richard Long helped to have this section removed after pointing out in his 8 November strategy paper that 'suggesting in the welfare speech that we would rip babies off young mothers' breasts to place them for adoption... would be the only target for media uplift if it remains included'.[26]

Brash also wrote a long justification for why 'the economic reforms of the eighties and nineties' were in no way responsible for unemployment and beneficiary numbers today (this section is reproduced in the notes).[27] His advisers rewrote these paragraphs in various ways over the following weeks to try to strengthen them before finally deciding they were 'too defensive' and cutting them completely. It was a case of 'don't mention the war'. The last thing they wanted was something that reminded people of Brash's free market past in the context of poverty and social problems. In fact, the final speech made no mention at all of poverty or low wages or their social impact, instead insinuating that the welfare system itself was the primary source of the problems.

Michael Bassett sent Brash a rewritten version of the speech on New Year's Eve. 'Don, I'm sorry it has taken so long, but I re-typed that draft and made it a little more political.'[28] This was an understatement. Bassett had added inflammatory phrases about beneficiaries 'ripping off the system', using 'stand-over tactics' to get benefits and welfare policy being 'the most destructive aspect of the political correctness that Labour would engulf us in' – phrases that made their way into the final speech.

Some of Bassett's other 'more political' language did not make it to the final version. His accusing descriptions of a 'dependency army', 'bludging off the rest of us' with its DPB and beneficiary 'rip-offs' were later removed by the woman-voter-sensitive Keenan and the increasingly uncomfortable welfare spokesperson Katherine Rich. Bassett's vitriolic characterisation of 'politicians and others in the welfare industry whose careers depend on farming the problems of the disadvantaged' made it through many drafts before being dropped a week before the speech was delivered.[29]

Bassett's email to Brash said that he and his wife Judith thought 'this a good, even a powerful speech... [with] considerable bite'. He said, 'if it were mine, I'd make it a bit more political. Muldoon would have Labour writhing on the floor with less. The useless [Social Welfare Minister Steve] Maharey deserves to be punished!'

He also gave some political advice. National should find 'a few real people' to pop up supporting the speech 'when the critics pounce' ('the so-called "caring industry": the Waldegraves [social policy researcher Charles Waldegrave of the Family Centre Social Policy Research Unit and his wife Kasia] and [Auckland University lecturer] Susan St John, and others who make their money arguing for "more" '). He also proposed that National organise 'news stories about rip-offs that could be brought to life before the 25th' to 'give the speech even more topicality'. The National Party media staff later prepared five press releases of this sort for release under Katherine Rich's name in the month before the speech.[30]

Bassett said he would be 'grateful if you shifted the text across to a page of your own and "owned" it from this point on. I'd rather not be linked with any form of authorship'. He said he did not mind being quoted, 'not that it will help you with your audience'.[31] Brash thanked him warmly for his assistance.

When Brash arrived back from holiday in early January, he emailed Sinclair saying that he had had a 'very helpful series of suggestions from Michael Bassett'. But he also gave the first indication that Katherine Rich did not agree with parts of the speech. He had received 'an indication from Katherine that she is not at all happy with time limits' (referring to the 'life-time limit on eligibility' for DPB and other benefits). 'That will need to get sorted out!'[32] Two weeks later he told Sinclair he might need to change 'the tone' in a few places to 'meet concerns expressed by both Katherine Rich and Peter Keenan'.[33]

By mid-January, less than two weeks before delivery, the speech had been worked on by Keenan and other leader's office staff. Some of Bassett and Brash's more extreme sections had been removed and in places there were 'alternative wordings' as they tried to resolve differences between Brash and Katherine Rich over how hardline their welfare reforms should be. For instance, a DPB 'life-time limit' of six years had, as an alternative, a requirement for single parents to start part-time work when the youngest child went to school, with DPB support ending when that child reached the age of fourteen.[34] Subsequent drafts incorporated the less strict version.

But at the same time as they removed some of the more extreme language, they made sure to include the kind of political 'war of emotions' language that had marked Orewa I. Keenan's belief in 'manipulat[ing] the public's feelings' and 'mobilising passions of fear and resentment' was seen in these sorts of phrases: 'Why should Kiwi families battling to get ahead in life... have to support numerous people who are not making a similar effort?'; the system makes 'mugs of those who do the right thing and take responsibility for how they live their lives'; 'hard-working New Zealanders' have to support children with DPB payments because of the 'mistakes' of their parents. These 'real kiwi battlers' were, in a phrase contributed by MP Tony Ryall, 'the people Helen Clark has forgotten'.[35]

In these ways the speech was honed for political impact, with additions to the final drafts focusing on Maori beneficiaries and referring to 'the hard luck stories we see in the media about people who have no jobs, poor living conditions and many children'. McCully's introduction said that Labour's only response to welfare problems was to 'create more committees, institute reviews, develop plans, establish boards, expand regulation and maintain an expensive Beehive spin machine' whereas National had 'the determination to make the changes that are needed'.[36]

As the date of the Orewa speech approached, it appears that it was this 'tone' (anti-beneficiary stereotyping and simplistic anti-welfare attacks) as much as the detailed policies that finally caused a rift between welfare spokesperson Katherine Rich and Brash. She had done her share of taking a 'tough' stand on welfare issues in the past, but the Brash team, including informal members like Bassett, were finally too much for her.

It had not happened overnight. Four months earlier there were questions around the parliamentary press gallery about differences between Katherine Rich and Brash over welfare. Press secretary Jason Ede drafted lines on how National should respond to media enquiries. 'Splits and divisions on welfare?' his notes asked rhetorically. 'Absolutely not.' He said 'the National Caucus is signed up to the direction of welfare policy. Katherine Rich put together an excellent discussion document that will provide the basis for future policy'.[37]

Brash was leaving some of the negotiations with Katherine Rich to McCully. A week and a half before the speech, McCully reported to Brash that he had had 'a further discussion with Katherine who is very constructive and positive re welfare speech'.[38] Brash replied: 'That's great thanks Murray. I especially appreciate your liaising with Katherine – having her broadly supportive of the speech is obviously pretty important.'[39]

Less than a week before Orewa, Brash wrote to several advisers and Rich with a near final draft of the speech. 'This draft is a composite of my previous one and Peter [Keenan's],' he began. 'It also incorporates Murray's suggested introduction.' He felt they were 'getting close to a final version. I have further time to work on this tomorrow, but from that point on my time is getting very limited with other commitments.'

This email reveals an ad hoc and last-minute approach to making policy. First, Brash said he did not agree with three suggestions from Keenan for toning down the more hardline proposals. The new draft did not 'pick up the three points which Peter made to me in his note of yesterday afternoon about deleting reference to adoption (I see no reason to do that, since it is only mentioned as one option), about deleting reference to vaccination (we have a footnote making it clear that people can object to that if they wish), and about suggesting that having kids outside marriage isn't such a bad idea after all'.[40]

Then he proffered a new idea of his own. 'I have added a possibly outrageous suggestion that we provide free contraception to women between the ages of 16 and 30 on a doctor's prescription, on the grounds that it might appeal to women, and could well be "self-funding" in terms of a reduction of DPB disbursements. Is this a totally stupid idea? Might it attract all the media headlines?' The strategy team overruled the idea and it did not appear in the final version.

Again Brash relied on McCully to check that Rich was happy with the speech. 'I don't know whether Katherine is able to access her Parliamentary email from Melbourne. Could you check that she is able to gain access to this text please Murray?' [41]

The National staff assiduously 'conditioned' the media in the days before the speech, trying to build up expectations – but not too high expectations – of another powerful speech that would 'seize the political agenda' in the election year. There were headlines the week before such as 'Nats set to fight on welfare' and 'Orewa is Brash's bash' about the 'much-anticipated' speech. [42]

National made preparations to create the impression of a strong public reaction. Key points from the speech were to be emailed to 'all party activists' straight after it was delivered and the whole speech to be sent to all 'party office holders, electorate offices and other individuals/businesses that have expressed an interest in getting information from us'. Campaign manager Steven Joyce was co-ordinating 'people throughout the country writing letters and ringing talkback'. 'Ideally we will have a lot of people willing to put their names to letters and just a few people writing them,' one of Brash's staff told him. [43]

Ordinary members of the public would probably not realise that political parties plan and orchestrate apparent signs of public support for their own actions, but National (and undoubtedly other parties) have organised groups to write letters to the editor, phone talkback radio and appear as crowds and audiences.

National hired an autocue machine to help improve Brash's public speaking and Sinclair gave him last minute encouragement on his delivery. He offered 'two little wee reminders for tonight's speech delivery, if you don't mind me saying'. He advised Brash to speak slowly and deliberately and to increase his 'overall volume by 10-20%' – 'it creates the atmosphere of a powerful man making a powerful speech.... That is all you need to do, and you will be absolutely great, I know it.' [44]

The initial publicity was all they had hoped for, with headlines such as 'Orewa II: a sequel that delivers' and 'War on welfare – no more free lunches'. [45] Jason Ede sent an email to all National Party staff talking about 'their dream run with Welfare coverage', but warning that everyone should be careful about 'attempts now to find differences in National ranks over details'.[46] Then everything went downhill.

First, it had turned out that one of the speech's most dramatic statistics on Maori benefit numbers had been incorrect – a figure popped for extra effect into the 'close-to-final' 19 January draft. The *New Zealand Herald* commented that 'this rubberiness over the use of statistics does nothing for the National leader's image.... Couple that with the pumped-up numbers Brash used at last year's Orewa speech to underpin his attack on Maori privilege and the impression is one of policy being made on the hoof, with numbers picked out of the air for their shock value, rather than a sophisticated attempt to delve behind the figures and grapple with the reasons behind some disturbing trends.'[47]

Then the long-predicted, 'splits and divisions' problem came to a head when journalists found the differences over policy they had suspected. Four days after the speech the *Dominion Post* reported 'Rich cagey on Orewa II support'. Three days later Brash precipitously called a lunchtime press conference at which, according to Richard Long's lines, he was 'fine tuning' the National Party caucus line-up. Brash sacked Rich from the welfare portfolio and removed her from the party's front bench for refusing to publicly endorse everything in the speech. He gave the job to an MP called Judith Collins, whose views on welfare would have fitted comfortably into the ACT Party.

The 2 February 2005 headlines told the story: 'Brash's sacking of "star" riles MPs', 'My compassionate conservatism didn't fit', 'No women left on National front line' and 'Rich's replacement a welfare hardliner'.[48] The result was an abrupt dip in the polls. Katherine Rich revealed publicly that she had 'found herself out of step with Dr Brash's thinking on welfare some months ago and asked to be relieved of the portfolio'. She did not agree with 'DPB bashing' or a 'punitive approach to welfare'.[49]

In the view of the *Dominion Post*, 'Ms Rich's dumping is the worst possible start to National's election-year campaign and has overshadowed any gains Dr Brash received from Orewa'. There had been 'rumblings for months about the influence of his advisers, in particular party strategist Murray McCully'.[50] Brash and McCully apparently just did not understand. They felt that Katherine Rich had been consulted and had won concessions, then still gone against them. They did not seem to grasp that the tone of the speech – caricaturing and blaming people receiving benefits – mattered at least as much as the specific policy proposals.

There were large and long-term differences within the National Party on these issues. Back when he was still Reserve Bank governor, Don Brash made a speech suggesting time limits on all state benefits for the able-bodied, or even scrapping benefits altogether.[51] In 2002 John Key had said that people on the DPB had been, 'for want of a better term, breeding for a business'.[52] Katherine Rich, by contrast, had said in 2002 that 'most of the people I meet on the DPB are pretty motivated people who have the same dreams and aspirations as the rest of us. Beneficiary bashing is a most unsatisfactory practice. It doesn't really take you anywhere.'[53] Another competent woman National MP, Lynda Scott, who stayed at Rich's side through the day after her sacking, had already announced her retirement from Parliament because she was unhappy with the direction of the Brash-led National Party. The origins of National's 'women problems' were obvious to anyone with eyes to see.

On the Friday before Brash sacked Rich, he received a relatively rare communication from National MP Bill English, the person he had deposed as leader fifteen months earlier. English sent his email at 10.30 in the evening, at the conclusion of a two-day caucus meeting of all National MPs planning for the year ahead. Events during the gathering had convinced him to put his concerns to Brash.

The email began by discussing two presentations that MP Judith Collins had made to the caucus, one on health policy and one on family. 'I thought the health presentation at caucus was awful,' he wrote, 'and I am told Judith's family presentation was worse. I am not one the caucus complains to, except for today, so it must have been pretty bad.'

'There are a few lessons here,' he said. Brash's strategy team had been 'pushing Judith [Collins] as a star' but she was a second year MP 'pushed beyond her capacity' into a hard portfolio and 'with an unfortunately high estimation of her own competence'. Collins, 'with apparent backing from the top', had 'spent too much time cultivating the media herself and believing the resulting publicity. She will find it hard to recover her credibility in caucus where she has been a tough critic of her colleagues behind the scenes and they know it.'

'The star strategy is crap,' English said, 'and the Leader's office ought to drop it. Katherine's difficulties are a product of the same process. She has two young children and a tough job and she has been oversold instead of supported. Now you are getting the backlash.'

He said that the caucus meeting's defence presentation was also awful: 'no policy in one of the most contentious issues in the National Party in the last 5 years'. He believed MP John Carter had been promoted 'beyond his capacity' into the defence portfolio when Brash had fired MP Simon Power. The 'saving grace' was that Power was 'a good enough whip to start filling the large gaps left by the deputy and the last whip'.

English painted a picture of a party with a lack of talent and where skills of the more competent were being mismanaged or wasted. 'I hope by now you can see the tragedy of losing Roger [Sowry] [who had also announced his retirement from politics] and Linda [Scott].' 'They were trashed by people who are now showing they cannot fill the gap. Their resignations were both avoidable, and I hope Katherine does not head in the same direction.'

He came to his point. 'Unfortunately the middle of the road caucus people are coming to the conclusion their fate is largely in the hands of McCully, who is happy to burn off anybody who gets in the way, Long who just pushes stars and Brownlee who looks after his own interest not theirs. You cannot afford to be seen to allow these guys to burn off the talent we have and reward self promoters who turn out to be incompetent.'

English also argued that 'the bad presentations in the last few days were also the result of a lack of decent process around policy. Your office should have known Judith and John were off track. No one from the management spoke a word to me as a presenter in the run up to this caucus – that is very unusual. Writing policy is hard for anyone but particularly inexperienced MPs. They need direction and support to do it and they don't get any.'

He said, 'McCully appears to have persuaded you it doesn't matter. He's wrong and Judith's and Katherine's problems this week show what happens when policy is not under control.' Brash needed to 'slow down some decisions and force the strategy team to talk to people' or else he would 'end up hitting a credibility wall in the campaign and become government with an odd shaped cabinet which doesn't know what it's doing. Competence matters more than spin in government.'

He finished the email with a warning. 'You need to know now that the experienced people you have will NOT work in a government run by McCully. I and others will not tolerate him exercising the same influence he does now.' He signed off, saying, 'Hope this helps, Bill'.[54]

Brash replied the next day in a jaunty and strangely disconnected way. 'Bill, thanks for these comments. Yes, there were one or two presentations over the last couple of days which were not up to scratch – and your own was masterly by comparison with all of them. Happy to give you a few additional portfolios!' He was 'happy to discuss some of the issues you raise at some stage this coming week, though I won't do this by email'.[55]

It is not clear that the discussion took place. Over that weekend Brash was apparently persuaded by McCully to take the tough stand against Rich over the welfare speech. Furthermore, Brash showed no sign of having heard what Bill English was trying to tell him. Instead he continued to allow McCully more and more influence, and he never worked out how to solve National's problems with women. There seems to have been at least some connection between the two.[56]

Months later Keenan was still trying to persuade Brash that he needed to take account of women voters. In May 2005, for instance, he again tried to tell Brash 'that we have to be very careful about the way we use some of the harder-edged issues'. He said that 'while they may energise the base and swing some male Labour voters across to us, we face a much more serious problem. And that problem is our massive negative with women – and we don't have a show unless we change that negative.'

It was the same problem with the same causes. Keenan said 'women rate National poorly on being "focused on their issues", on Health, and (this the same also for men) as hugely negative on "helping families". Women also have more negative views of National on "keeping promises" and "doing what's right". These are all issues that are rated as amongst the most important. The biggest divergence of view is on Fixing the Treaty – where we lead with men by about 7%, and trail with women by about 17% – a massive 24% gap, the biggest of the lot.'[57] But Keenan was wasting his breath. Brash and McCully believed the best strategy was to fight the election on race and tax cuts.

McCully's dominance over Brash was already visible in early 2004, when Brash began deferring to him on many issues. By the time of the first Orewa speech, Brash's staff began going to McCully for sign-off on public statements before they could be released. As time passed, his influence spread to more and more areas of the party's business.

One continually unhappy with McCully's influence was Bryan Sinclair. He tried to warn Brash about McCully assuming more and more authority. 'Remember he is an operator,' he wrote to Brash in an email. 'His role has expanded from assisting you with House strategy to advising on who should attend your mid-Winter Caucus parties, what your receptionist should look like, and now the shape and style of National's election campaign. I recall wise advice last year – along the lines that he is great for parliamentary stuff, great for digging dirt, for keep[ing] a finger on the political pulse, but don't let him near your communications and don't, whatever you do, let him determine National's campaign strategy or influence the appointment of your key people in the lead up to an election.'[58]

McCully's influence seems to have come from offering support to a succession of inexperienced or unconfident National MPs who had arrived in politics without the skills to operate successfully. He presented himself as the one who knew how to play the game, used his media influence to build the profile of his annointed stars and gradually assumed authority for all manner of party business and decisions.

McCully had entered Parliament in 1987 as a National Party supporter of Roger Douglas's free market policies. His arrival in politics epitomised a movement of professional public relations people into New Zealand politics at that time. A Young Nationals chair and the National Party's communications director in the 1970s, he had worked as a public relations consultant in the 1980s. His PR firm, Allan Fenwick McCully, included Rob Fenwick (later of National's Blue Greens) and Michelle Boag as its Wellington manager. Boag went on to be National Party president, McCully ally and PR woman to merchant bankers Fay Richwhite in the 1990s.[59]

When National became government in 1990, McCully was soon being described as the Minister of Politics, devoting most of his time to spin and information control. He instituted a system where all information requests to government were channelled via him so that he could delay or otherwise thwart them as required to make life easier for the government. He also assumed responsibility for media spin doctoring for the government. To this day, when you see a news report quoting an unnamed 'National Party insider' or 'National Party strategist', it is quite likely to be McCully. These roles were later formalised into his becoming chair of both the government's communications strategy committee and the party's executive campaign group, which managed day-to-day election strategy.[60] In Brash he had found another leader ready to rely on his advice.

By election year Brash was deferring to McCully on most important matters that arose and by the last fraught couple of weeks of the campaign McCully was escorting him continuously. When Brash was finalising his election-year conference speech in June 2005, he explained that he had set aside nearly all of his own speech draft in deference to a draft written by McCully. 'Guys, attached is the latest draft of my main speech for the conference. It is essentially the one which Murray drafted, with a couple of paras added from my draft of last Sunday. I liked some features of my own draft a lot, but they didn't fit well into Murray's draft, which I also thought was very good, so I have stuck fairly closely to his draft.' He asked for comments on the minor changes he had made, saying he would 'particularly appreciate' them from Murray.[61]

The same thing happened with Brash's election campaign launch speech, where again McCully took over the writing. (He had displaced Keenan for these major speeches.) 'Murray, I have made virtually no changes to the text you sent me,' Brash wrote, 'though have added a couple of paras near the very end.'[62]

At the same time, however, McCully was also one of the party's liabilities. It was he more than anyone whose attitudes and advice were alienating women from the party. An example of this was his fixation with attacking the presence of women in the Labour-led government. When he attacked Labour, it was as often about the gender of its leader as its policies, with bitter and sarcastic ridicule of the 'Sisterhood'. This grated even within the National caucus.

In late 2004, for instance, Brash received an email from National MP Phil Heatley, who had seen McCully's latest weekly newsletter, with its usual use of the word 'Sisterhood' instead of 'government'.

> I have been thinking about this for some time Don, so I finally raise it this time. I don't know what the readership is of [McCully's] regular update, but I have to tell you my wife Jenny is 33, a lovely woman and intelligent. To women like her this is lame stuff. The 'sisterhood' idea is a great joke the first time, maybe even the second, a bit blokey but forgiveable. But if women are receiving this all the time it is not going to help our female vote. Clearly National does not like women in leadership, we believe in the glass ceiling, we feel threatened. This sisterhood message is sexist and Neanderthal so National is sexist and Neanderthal.

Heatley said, 'I would raise it with Murray directly but he just would not see it.' He hoped Brash would do something about this 'when thinking about projecting our image to women voters'.[63] Brash wrote back five minutes later: 'Phil, many thanks for pointing this out. Perhaps surprisingly, I didn't think of the point myself – and should have done.' Brash was not anti-women, merely oblivious to the viewpoint of anyone different from himself. He promised to 'find a way of raising the matter at some stage' with McCully.[64] Heatley replied: 'thanks Don, it's been bugging me for some months believe it or not'.[65] It is not known if Brash acted on the letter.

Machiavellian though some may have considered him, McCully was just an amateur compared with the Australian campaign strategists who had recently begun working for National. They would take National's bid for the Beehive to a whole new level of manipulation.

CHAPTER 10

THE MANIPULATORS
Leveraging doubt and fear

During the 2005 British election campaign there was controversy about the Australian campaign strategists hired by the Conservative Party to direct their campaign. The Australians – Lynton Crosby and Mark Textor – were accused of advising Conservative leader Michael Howard to use such issues as immigration, asylum seekers, gypsies, law and order and abortion to exploit fear and prejudice to win voters.

The *Economist* described this phenomenon. 'Over the past few weeks a new expression has entered the Westminster lexicon: dog-whistle politics. It means putting out a message that, like a high-pitched dog-whistle, is only fully audible to those at whom it is directly aimed. The intention is to make potential supporters sit up and take notice while avoiding offending those to whom the message will not appeal.... It seems likely that Lynton Crosby, the Tories' Australian campaign director, is responsible for importing dog-whistle politics to Britain.'

The magazine said that 'when not shamelessly pandering to prejudice, the Tory campaign has been a series of hit-and-run ambushes on the government's record.... For a couple of days, immigration dominates the headlines, then hospital waiting lists, then abortion, then tax, followed by gypsies and tax again.' It explained how these tactics work.

> Nothing that Mr Howard... said could fairly be described as racist.... Yet it is also true that racists, bigots and the millions of people who are neither of those things but whose fears are fanned daily by a mendacious press will have pricked up their ears and listened to a message aimed squarely at them. And just in case there was any question about who and what the Tories were appealing to, Mr Howard issued his statement on gypsies astride a platform emblazoned with the party's rather creepy campaign slogan: 'Are you thinking what we're thinking?' Thinking, but not quite saying, in other words.[1]

Shortly after this article was published in early 2005, news appeared in Australia that Crosby/Textor's next stop, after the British election, was helping the National Party in New Zealand. National's campaign manager Steven Joyce was asked about the rumour but assured the reporter that, although they were getting 'some assistance' from strategists associated with Australia's John Howard, there were 'no plans' to bring Lynton Crosby to New Zealand.[2]

In July 2005, Don Brash was asked in a *New Zealand Herald* interview, 'Is Lynton Crosby's firm advising National?' Brash was reported to have turned to Richard Long and asked, 'What's our answer to that one?' Even if Brash had momentarily forgotten the name of their strategists, Long was well aware of them. But Brash turned back to the journalists and replied, 'I know Lynton Crosby has not been working for us at all. I've never spoken to or met Lynton Crosby. To the best of my knowledge he is not involved.... I don't know about his firm. That's something you'd have to check out with Steven Joyce on.'[3] Contrary to what he said, Brash had first met and been briefed by Lynton Crosby in Canberra a year before this interview, and would have been fully aware that Mark Textor and some of their staff were playing a major part in National's election campaign. After reading Brash's answers in the *Herald* interview, I sent the paper's journalists a copy of National Party December 2004 board minutes that referred to work being done by the 'Crosby/Textor Group'.[4] This made it impossible completely to deny that the company was involved in the campaign. So the next time the question of Crosby/Textor involvement was raised by journalists, the National staff slightly changed their tune.

Richard Long emailed Brash, and others, to warn him that 'Steven [Joyce] has just had an "aggressive" interview... about our use of Crosby Textor'. Long explained that Joyce said the company had done 'some polling' for National but that they did not formulate policy. 'Steven was asked if you [Brash] had met Crosby,' Long said. 'Steven said he didn't recall and they would need to ask you.' Long advised Brash: 'You'd better say, if caught, that you had met him in passing a few times when he was over here polling'. However, if he was not 'caught', Long advised that Brash try to avoid answering questions. 'It would be better to answer anything we have to through a spokesman.'[5]

Joyce wrote back to Long, saying that 'the questions around Don were how aware would he be [about] our involvement with Mark Textor (not Crosby this time). Had he met him?' Joyce said he had replied that Brash 'may have' met him as 'Textor is another of our suppliers'. Joyce explained to Long that he had fudged on the question of Brash's knowledge because he did not know what Brash had already said publicly. 'I said that you would have to ask Don,' he said, 'not remembering what Don had said previously.'

Joyce gave advice on how much Brash should be willing to say. He told Long he was 'quite comfortable with Don remembering he had met [Textor] a few times' and Brash saying he was aware Textor did 'a bit of polling work for us'. But he said that when the reporter rang back asking about Crosby/Textor doing work beyond polling, he 'got a bit short with her at that point and said that [he] felt the conversation was going around in circles and it was time to wrap it up'.[6] Then, confirming that they all knew exactly what was going on, Long sent an email to Brash: 'The inquiry was about Textor, not Crosby this time'.[7]

National had two reasons for wanting to play down or to avoid mentioning the involvement of the Crosby/Textor company in their campaign. The first and obvious reason was the strategists' controversial reputation. But, equally important, Crosby/Textor was doing much more in the campaign than 'just a bit of polling'. The company's slogan is 'Research, Strategies, Results': research and strategy advice are two halves of the same role.

The company's founders and partners, Lynton Crosby and Mark Textor, got to know each other when Crosby was the Australian Liberal Party's federal campaign director and Textor its pollster. They worked together on successful Liberal campaigns in 1996, 1998, 2001 and 2004. Their company, formed in 2003, has an office in Melbourne headed by Textor, one in Sydney headed by Crosby, a research office north of Melbourne in Echuca and a Canberra office located a stone's throw from the Australian Parliament House. The company's chair is Robert Champion de Crespigny, previously owner of a mining company and currently a director of the same Centre for Independent Studies that is the meeting point for the radical right in New Zealand.[8]

The Crosby/Textor website states that the company offers 'high-level strategic advice, based on opinion research, to clients who need to run campaigns targeted at various stakeholders such as customers, voters or politicians'.[9] Their work has been summed up as 'a clever synthesis of polling and pitching the message to suit the polling';[10] and identifying and focusing resources on the 'most persuadable "swing" targets'.[11] But there is more to it than that.

National formally approached Crosby/Textor to help with its election campaign in October 2004. Lynton Crosby had recently relocated to London for seven months to head the Conservative Party campaign so Mark Textor took on the National Party contract. Chapter 3 discussed the proliferation of expedient political advisers who often shift back and forth between political jobs and corporate public relations, using the same skills and contacts for both. Textor is an outstanding example of the type.

He describes himself as 'Australia's most successful pollster and campaign strategist'.[12] He built his reputation working for the United States public relations and 'strategic research' company Wirthlin Group, whose founder, Richard Wirthlin, was a pollster and campaign adviser to Republican president Ronald Reagan. Wirthlin, for which Textor served as Australasian managing director, specialises in the same research-based strategy advice to political and corporate clients now used by Crosby/Textor.

Wirthlin has a long record of working for tobacco company Philip Morris and Mark Textor was a consultant for them in Australia. There is a glimpse of Textor's work for Philip Morris in some of the internal tobacco company documents that the United States courts ordered to be released to the public following American anti-tobacco lawsuits in the 1990s. For instance, Textor conducted market research for Philip Morris and presented the results at its 1998 Corporate Affairs Conference at the Hyatt Regency Sanctuary Cove Hotel in Queensland.[13] The Crosby/Textor website also lists British American Tobacco as one of Textor's clients.

When Textor moved into politics, there were allegations in the Northern Territory and Canberra about his arranging push polling, in which a supposedly independent telephone poll interviewer asks questions containing damaging allegations about an opposition politician to turn voters off that candidate. Following a 1995 Canberra by-election there was court action against Textor and others for alleged push polling to discredit the Labour party candidate Sue Robinson. Australia's Radio National obtained a tape of the polling questions used against Robinson. They included the following: 'Would you be more or less likely to vote for Sue Robinson and the Labor Party if you knew she has publicly stated that she supports the right to abortion up to the ninth month of pregnancy?' She had never said that. Textor subsequently made a written apology to Robinson and, together with the then director of the Liberal Party, paid her $80,000 in an out-of-court settlement.[14] She lost the election.

A British newspaper profile of Textor described him as a 'far more controversial figure' than his partner Crosby. It called him an 'unashamed promoter of wedge politics... credited with putting anti-Aboriginal sentiment into the mainstream of Northern Territory politics at a time when the former One Nation leader Pauline Hanson was still running a chip shop in southern Queensland'. In the 2001 elections, 'it was Textor's polling advice that crystallised Howard's decision to run a xenophobic scare campaign based on fear of immigrants and terrorism'.[15]

As Australian journalist David Marr explained to Anthony Hubbard of the *Sunday Star-Times* in August 2005, Textor comes from Northern Australia where 'race is not a fringe issue but a fundamental issue'. In a state where half the people are black, 'every aspect of the politics of the Northern Territory is permeated by race. That's the dark expertise of [Crosby/Textor].'[16] Campaign manager Steven Joyce contracted Textor to work for National in late 2004.

Don Brash first met Mark Textor and Lynton Crosby on 17 June 2004 during a short trip to Australia. Brash visited them at their Canberra office at Engineering House, 11 National Circuit for a two-hour early evening meeting. Textor had written in advance to suggest that their discussion points, 'after a get to know you chat', should be:

1. 'Mega' social and political trends over the last 5–10 years in Australia, New Zealand and in the rest of the world
2. Comparative approaches to political strategy around the world (with our current clients in UK, USA, NZ and here)
3. What's working / what's not around the world (what's 'best practice' in advertising and communications) – lessons from our campaigns
4. Various approaches to polling
5. Recent New Zealand Qualitative (focus group) polling and comparisons to Australia
6. New Zealand next steps – 'locking in' your lead.[17]

When Steven Joyce visited Australia to observe the Liberal Party election campaign in October that year he was briefed by Mark Textor on the campaign strategy. Joyce said in his report on the trip that Textor was 'keen to help [National] on a commercial basis'.[18] Textor and other Liberal advisers had advised Joyce to secure the campaign funding and sort out a 'simple message for change' and test it with focus groups. Soon after Textor was advising National on these things.

Textor did not move to New Zealand as Crosby had to Britain. But for the ten months, between late November 2004 and the election in September 2005, Textor and his staff made about fifteen visits to New

Zealand, as well as consulting by telephone and sending written reports. About half these trips were Crosby/Textor research staff visiting New Zealand to conduct focus groups and the other half were Textor visiting the National Party in his capacity as consultant on campaign strategy.

Most of Textor's advice was given orally so there is no record of it. However National Party insiders say that early on he persuaded the National campaign strategy team that 'securing the campaign funding' meant raising enough money not just for one election campaign, but for two. His argument was that after a close election, in which the New Zealand First Party, Maori Party and Green Party might be part of a coalition, there was a good chance the government would collapse after a short time. Textor's argument was that National would then be the only party with millions of dollars ready to fight a new campaign and therefore would be well set up to win.

Textor recommended to National that his company immediately do some 'benchmark' research into New Zealand public beliefs, against which all the subsequent research could be compared as the campaign progressed. One of his staff, Mark Domitrak, visited New Zealand and oversaw two focus groups in Auckland on 30 November 2004 and two in Hamilton on 1 December 2004. On 10 December, National received its first report from Crosby/Textor, based on the findings of this research.

The report, called a 'Strategic Memorandum', provides the first ever inside view into the techniques that have become standard practice in a series of Australian, British, American and New Zealand elections. You might imagine that focus groups are designed to find out what groups of people think and want. Sandy Burgham's focus groups on women were like that, and might therefore assist policy formulation or the language used in campaign speeches, but the Crosby/Textor groups had a completely different purpose and revealed a deeper level of political manipulation.

Each Crosby/Textor research report makes this difference clear at the start: 'it should be kept in mind', says the first page, that this qualitative research is designed to 'uncover ideas and persuasive creative leads.... It is not designed to quantitatively define the marketplace.'[19] The intention is to 'uncover' perceptions and feelings of which the people concerned may not be consciously aware – or even just potential perceptions and feelings – and find ways to use these 'persuasive creative leads' to influence target groups of voters.

These techniques were more obvious in subsequent reports, but even this initial benchmark report identified some of these 'leads'. It stated that 'voters in Auckland and Hamilton believe that, overall, things in

New Zealand are heading in the "right direction" '. They were concerned that National would be 'too harsh' on social services, with 'less money for health and education', and that Brash was a bit 'arrogant', might not 'think things through' and that he was a 'rich man leading a rich man's party'. Interestingly, they found that 'voters believe that tax cuts "miss the point" as they will only be a temporary solution'. Textor and Domitrak then reported on ideas that the focus group people had not raised but about which, 'once prompted', they had potentially been concerned. For instance, they were happy about the state of the economy but 'once prompted' were uncertain about whether Labour had a plan to keep the economy growing: 'no forward plan for the economy is a concern for voters, once prompted'. 'Herein... lies an opportunity to use the economy to demonstrate, in a practical way, what a lack of incentive in New Zealand means.' Crosby/Textor took this 'prompted' concern and used it to justify National's existing tax and welfare policies in the following proposed words: 'In New Zealand, if we continue not to encourage people to work (through the welfare system) and if we don't start rewarding people who work hard and earn some extra money (through the taxation system) our economy will stagnate and this means we will slip behind the rest of the world'.

In this way they strategise the possibility of moving voters from, for instance, thinking that tax cuts 'miss the point' to the 'prompted perception' that tax cuts are necessary in response to uncertainty about the growth of the economy. The Crosby/Textor word for this is leveraging. The report summarises this and other findings: 'a significant opportunity exists to leverage the (prompted) perception that New Zealand has lost its initiative and that under the Labour Government there is no incentive for New Zealanders to better themselves, be it through the welfare system, the taxation system or the education system'.[20] Such perceptions may have little to do with how people feel and the leveraging messages may not even be true, but they may still provide 'strategic opportunities'.

These words about getting the right incentives in tax, welfare and education policy were seen in numerous National Party messages during the election year, starting with the Orewa welfare speech. The campaign recommendations in the report included 'consistent message and core values need to be repeated at every opportunity'. A second persuasive opportunity Crosby/Textor identified was to build the perception that such government initiatives as the civil union legislation, which obviously did not affect most people, were evidence that Labour was 'distracted' from more important issues.

As was predictable from strategists involved in the Australian and British elections, Crosby/Textor also pointed to immigration and security as useful issues for National. The increase of migrants in Auckland was 'perceived' to have put significant pressures on the infrastructure of the city, 'evidenced through increased class sizes, lack of hospital beds and traffic congestion'. They found that the voters were 'concerned that the current intake policy lets "just anyone" come in without regard for the skills and education they can bring. As a result Auckland voters believe that they are "paying" for these migrants as they go "straight to the welfare queues".'[21] Crosby/Textor recommended that National use the same policy as the Conservatives did in Britain: to say they would allow immigration only by 'skilled migrants'.

Keenan picked up the immigration suggestion and wrote to his colleagues a few days after the Crosby/Textor report arrived. The 'Textor focus group work shows that Immigration is a major hot-button issue – as Winston Peters knows all too well'. He continued: 'We need to toughen up our line on that. If we don't, we could find NZ First grabbing 5% of our support in the last month of the campaign. We are well placed to grab back NZ First's elderly constituency; but we also need to do enough to not leave ourselves too exposed on immigration.' He suggested that they 'could work a tougher line on immigration' into a future speech.[22]

Don Brash made just such a speech, timed six weeks before the election, that used the negative feelings that Textor had 'uncovered' on immigration in his focus groups. 'There is resentment,' Brash said, 'that too many immigrants, and especially those who arrive as refugees, go straight onto a benefit, and live for years at the expense of the hard-working New Zealand taxpayer.' Taking up the Textor suggestion, Brash announced that the 'first' plank of its immigration policy was that 'National will focus priority on skilled migrants'.[23]

Brash declared: 'Nor, frankly, do we want immigrants who come with no intention of becoming New Zealanders or adopting New Zealand values. We do not want those who insist on their right to spit in the street; or demand the right to practise female circumcision; or believe that New Zealand would be a better place if gays and adulterers were stoned.'[24]

New Zealand Herald writer Claire Harvey described the speech as 'classic dogwhistling'. 'Notice,' she wrote, 'he doesn't actually say that these habits are Asian, African and Islamic – although that is what we hear at a subtler level.' As she noted, 'anyone who had visited Southeast Asian countries... has seen plenty of people spitting in public. But then so has anyone who's ever watched a game of rugby in New Zealand.'[25] Her article, titled 'If you listen carefully you'll hear the real message', said, 'Let's have a look at the verbs. Who ever "insisted" on their right to spit in the street? Who is "demanding" the right to practise female circumcision? And shouldn't proud New Zealanders be allowed to believe whatever they like?'[26] Brash was playing the politics that Crosby/Textor have become famous for, presenting himself as reasonable and mainstream – the speech was called 'A balanced middle way' – while appealing to stereotypes and prejudice. When Textor highlighted concerns about immigration policies that let 'just anyone' into New Zealand, he was signalling the 'opportunity' of appealing to racist feelings.

The other thing worth noticing about the benchmark Crosby/Textor report, and all later ones, is what kind of person they were targeting. The research methodology specified that the people 'stratified and recruited' for the focus groups were all 'politically non-affiliated voters'. This means they were not interested in talking to the majority of people who were pretty clear about which way they would vote. They were interested particularly in the undecided, uninformed and indifferent voters, the ones they called 'soft' voters. Significantly, they were not interested in studying the opinions or feelings of people on superannuation or state benefits. Although they wanted a representative mix of 'blue and white collar households' and men and women, the directions specifically 'excluded people who derive the majority of their income from Government sources, eg Unemployment benefits, disability or... pensions'.[27]

In countries with first-past-the-post voting systems like the United States, Britain and Australia, this highly strategic campaigning involves focusing a large part of the campaign effort on relatively few soft voters in key marginal electorates. In New Zealand, with proportional representation, the targets must be broader. But the principle is the same. When National spoke of 'hard-working New Zealanders', the 'special privileges' going to Maori and the welfare free-loaders taking money that belonged to struggling taxpayers, these messages were aimed specifically at a relatively small percentage of the voting age population who were judged to be susceptible to this emotionally loaded rhetoric. Much of National's election campaigning was interested only in that area of greatest potential gain, the soft voters.

Textor made his first trip to New Zealand for five days in December 2004, a week before Christmas. This was the first meeting where the big strategic campaign issues were discussed. At this meeting Steven Joyce and Textor discussed a list of 'key messages' National should use to attract soft voters away from other parties.[28] These would become the foundations of National's election campaigning.

Work had begun on the key messages after Joyce first met Textor in Australia in early October. Joyce came home with advice that National urgently needed to agree on its simple 'story'. A first draft of six key messages was worked out at a campaign strategy meeting in mid-October 2004 and it was these ideas that were tried out on the focus groups at the end of November. A revised set of key messages was then written based on the Crosby/Textor report and it was these that Joyce and Textor discussed on 20 December in Wellington.

A lot of the words in this message plan (reprinted in full in the notes) come straight from the first Crosby/Textor report. It repeated the leveraging opportunities:

* While the economy is going well currently, it has nothing to do with the Labour Government. They have been lucky.
* Labour has been distracted by its social reform agenda, and is doing nothing to ensure a strong economy going forward.
* We have lost the New Zealand Values of Initiative and Rewards for working hard and 'Getting Ahead'.
* There is no incentive for individuals to better themselves, be it through the tax system, the education system or the welfare system; and
* If we don't put in place plans for a stronger economy now, we will suffer badly in the next economic downturn.[29]

Textor returned for more meetings with National on 23–24 February 2005. These included 'Peter Keenan and Textor meeting with Leader [Don Brash] on styles of lines to use and language re framing/positioning'.[30] This is another important part of the Crosby/Textor technique. Textor explained that by 'framing' he meant 'setting a notion not about the issues people think about but giving them a WAY to think about the issues in question, that is giving them a model or a structure or equation'.[31]

According to Textor, framing was becoming critical in campaigns for several reasons. First and obviously, by framing the debate, the party could 'ensure that [its] issues... naturally come to the fore and are automatically considered'. An example of framing for National was putting all discussion of welfare and tax cuts into the frame of 'incentives' and more generally defining the 2005 election as being about tax cuts. Second, he said, in a 'scrappy' election campaign framing gave 'indifferent voters a guide or a roadmap on how to think about issues and think about them on your terms'. For instance, since Ruth Richardson's reign as finance minister in the early 1990s, tax cuts had been associated in the public mind with cuts to social services. Framing tax cuts in terms of 'incentives' for 'getting ahead' could take people's minds off social service cuts and replace these associations with a way of thinking about tax that was advantageous to National.

Third, framing could 'take the form of an "opening statement" or big claim'; and making a 'radical' claim would allow National to 'refocus the campaign back to your issues'. 'Big' or 'radical' claims were ideas like privileged Maori, criminals getting an easy ride from the legal system and 'hard-working' people being held back by welfare bludgers. Textor explained that a lot of the impact of such claims comes from being attacked for making them. 'Hopefully your distractors will turbo-charge by drawing attention to the issues that you have raised, forgetting that they are in effect drawing attention to your issues and your areas of strength.'[32]

There was a second 'wave' of focus groups in early April 2005, which formed the basis for the second major Crosby/Textor report. All the techniques discussed so far were much more blatantly evident in this 'Qualitative Track Wave II' report, given to Brash on 8 May 2005. It focused intensely on the search for 'persuasive creative leads' to win over soft voters.

Like the December 2004 benchmark report, the report began by assessing how the target voters were currently feeling. There was 'an overall belief that things in New Zealand are "generally" heading in the right direction, due predominantly to perceptions about the "strength of the economy" '. It said that 'an emerging trend in this wave of research is the sense that New Zealand is heading in the right direction because of a perception that more money is being spent on "social" issues, such as health and education'. And, where there were issues of concern, the voters were 'not holding Helen Clark or her Ministers accountable for the perceived problems they believe exist, nor do they necessarily believe that the Government is responsible'.[33]

Textor and Domitrak then moved on to 'strategic opportunities'. Some 'emerging trends were identified in this wave of qualitative research which, if leveraged effectively, can provide the National Party with real opportunities in the lead up to the next general election.' There was a strategic opportunity in 'an underlying sense that things in New Zealand "COULD" be heading in the wrong direction due in part to mounting financial pressures on families and a concern that "PERHAPS" not enough attention is being paid to "hard working" New Zealanders'. They said that 'these sentiments are reinforced by an underlying perception that those in the "middle" who "work hard" are being overlooked, at best, and, at worst, their concerns are being ignored'.

A look at the confidential focus group 'moderators guide' – the list of questions to be asked in the focus groups – shows how 'underlying' sentiments like these are found. For instance, after open-ended questions about the Labour Party and its leader Helen Clark, the moderator asked, 'What could the [Labour Party] be doing better at the moment – that is in what ways do you think the New Zealand Labour Party is performing poorly at the moment, even if it is begrudging blame or discredit?' The questions then moved on to Clark: 'regardless of your overall view of Helen Clark, what would you acknowledge are her weaknesses at the moment, even if they are slight or begrudging weaknesses?'[34] The idea, of course, was that even slight and 'begrudging' feelings, that only came to mind 'once probed', could potentially be sown and cultivated more widely.

It was the same with questions about Labour's Working for Families social support package. The moderator asked, regardless of their overall view of the policy, 'what is not so good about this package – that is in what ways is it not beneficial to you personally?' This was followed by: 'What does it say to you about Helen Clark and the Labour Party?'[35] And so on.

The findings gave Textor and Domitrak what they had been looking for. They found that the people saw Helen Clark as 'articulate', 'aware of what is happening', 'a thinker', 'experienced' and 'strong'. 'However,' they wrote, 'an emerging trend was identified that "PERHAPS" Helen Clark was too busy with "other people" to worry about "working families".' This included trying to cater to beneficiaries and 'focussing too much on minority issues'. Once again they emphasised that in order for these 'hesitations or concerns' to be effective, 'the National Party must leverage them'.

Back in the 'strategic opportunities' section of the report, the findings from this questioning were put to work. 'One of the new learnings from this wave of qualitative research is an emerging perception that Helen Clark is too busy with "minorities" and "other people" to worry about the concerns and the pressures on "working families".' But they did not pretend these were strong feelings. 'It must be stressed that this sentiment is embryonic and must be consistently demonstrated and leveraged if it is to be effective.' In fact, what they were talking about was potential more than actual feeling: 'These perceptions will not exist and mature on their own'.[36]

Textor and Domitrak put it to National that the way to build these perceptions was 'to continually demonstrate, in ways that are practical and have meaning to ordinary families, how Helen Clark and the Labour Party are focused on the "noisy" minorities at the expense of hard working New Zealanders and what the consequences of this are on those in the middle (in terms of higher taxes and no real incentives)'. This advice would subsequently be seen in numerous speeches, public statements and campaign messages during the election campaign.

The report concluded that 'If the National Party is to be successful in leveraging such sentiments, and building on these embryonic perceptions, part of this process will involve linking Helen Clark and the Labour Party to concerns that people have with important issues'. They recommended that the best issues for leveraging these feelings were, first, immigration, followed by the treaty and then health, education, taxation and defence. 'At present,' they wrote, 'this sentiment does not exist', which was why the National Party must encourage the community to hold Helen Clark or her ministers accountable for the 'perceived problems the [public] believe exist'.[37]

The Crosby/Textor technique was to take these non-existent sentiments and use them as the basis for campaign messages that, once repeated often enough, could arouse those sentiments in the target soft voters. So in National's 'First ten things we will do' election brochure, Brash said, 'National is very focused on tackling the issues of mainstream New Zealanders that have been ignored and neglected by Labour for so long'. Likewise the brochure emphasised that National would provide the 'right incentives' for people to stay in New Zealand, work hard and get ahead.[38] These two ideas – the mainstream ignored and getting incentives right – had come, respectively, directly from the second and first Textor reports.

Ideas like Helen Clark being 'too busy' or 'distracted' for ordinary people were 'framing' the discussion – setting the agenda and giving the indifferent voters a structure in which to evaluate the election contenders. National could then 'bridge' from those manufactured ideas back to its core issues by claiming that Labour was not tackling issues like tax cuts that mattered to mainstream voters because it was too busy with minorities. After a while it all starts to sound like truth and a reality check is needed to appreciate what is really going on.

The defining character of these techniques is that they attempt to get voters to act in ways that might not be in accord with their interests or even beliefs. The aim is not good policy, or leadership that unifies a country; the objective is manipulating enough voters, at the right time, so that their clients can achieve power.

These techniques show little respect for the citizens concerned. The research sets out to unearth 'prompted perceptions', 'embryonic perceptions' and even just 'hesitations' that can be turned into ways to influence them. The aim is not to understand what these people might believe in and hope for. It is purely and openly about manipulation.

In keeping with this approach, the report also reminded National to bring commercial interests into the election campaigning by encouraging business lobbies to make public statements that reinforced the campaign messages. For instance, the campaign recommendation section of the report said they should 'encourage third parties (business groups) to publicly state their concerns for jobs and investment in New Zealand if the taxation issues are not addressed'.[39]

And so it went on. After that there were focus group sessions each month up until July 2005, then two sets of focus groups in August and in September as the election approached. All the focus groups were held in the North Island, mostly in Auckland and Wellington but also in New Plymouth and Hamilton. During the last two weeks of campaigning Textor was in Wellington twice, being briefed in detail by staff on the progress and problems of the campaign and giving last-minute advice about staying on message and deflecting crises as the election day approached.

After the second Crosby/Textor research report, the strategy for the election messages was mostly set. Textor then shifted his emphasis to imposing 'message discipline', ensuring that the agreed messages were heard clearly and repeatedly by the target voters, with as little distraction as possible. Keenan reminded Brash of Textor's directions about how to achieve this. 'If you recall the session with Textor,' he wrote, 'he suggested you should have an A6 card in your pocket at all times (as did Howard) with your core message printed on it – and that you have it memorised.' The idea was 'to use it as a reminder to "keep repeating it endlessly"'.[40] Crosby and Textor had given the same advice to Australian Liberal leader John Howard, and, presumably, to Michael Howard in Britain. After a while the endless repetition of simple, emotionally loaded slogans by a politician can have a faintly sinister, brain-washing quality, but it drills some simple ideas into the heads of soft voters. And, at least to an extent, it seems to work.

Peter Keenan followed Textor's suggestion and prepared two A6-sized cards for Brash. The 'short version is designed for the max 11 second TV "grab"', the long version 'for about a 20 second statement in an interview situation (TV or radio)'. The objective 'is to have a crisp line that people will start to recognise – repetition is good!' 'I think Textor's point is to help make these statements as crisp as possible. You should rehearse the key message points so that you can deliver them assertively, and with punch (on stage with some assertive hand movement).'[41]

Another aspect of message discipline pushed by Textor was the concept of 'bridging' – using any issue that arises, all media questions and every other opportunity to bring the subject back to the key messages on the A6 card. Peter Keenan reported that he and Brash 'had a terrific session with Textor' on the subject of bridging during Textor's February 2005 visit. [42]

When new issues arose, the National Party strategy team would seek Textor's advice on the best messages to maintain message discipline and 'bridge back' to the agreed lines. One such occasion was in June 2005 when the government announced that New Zealand's Kyoto climate change commitments were going to be much more costly than previously estimated. Steven Joyce wrote to Long, Keenan and McCully saying he had just been speaking with 'Tex' in order 'to tidy up vote message'.

Joyce 'told him of the Kyoto scandal (Kyoto-gate anyone?) and his view was that it is an unbelievably good story for us'. Textor thought it would be easy to bridge from that to various of their key election messages. Joyce said Textor 'encouraged us to be all over it as it had all the ingredients of what we have been saying about Labour'. By then, three months before the election, the key messages were that Labour were 'profligate wasters of taxpayers money, wrapped up in trendy issues that cost the money of mainstream kiwis'. Joyce passed on some 'suggested wording' from Textor for how to handle the issue.

They 'framed' and 'bridged back' the Kyoto issue as follows. First, it was 'typical of Labour – they like the nice trendy issue but they don't look properly at the serious numbers beneath the surface that affect mainstream New Zealanders who end up paying the bill'. Next, it was 'Labour and Cullen... overspending and wasting money so you can't have a tax cut' – 'an insult to the hardworking middle New Zealanders who pay the taxes in the first place'.[43]

In other words, the Kyoto issue was being framed as just another of Labour's trendy 'distractions' off the important issue of tax cuts. Talking about efforts to deal with climate change in this way is, at the very least, distasteful, but according to this strategy anything and everything is an opportunity to repeat the key messages. Economy going well? Tax cuts to share benefits with hardworking New Zealanders. Economy going badly?

Tax cuts to give right incentives for economic growth. People struggling on low wages? Tax cuts to put extra dollars in their pockets. Climate change? This is how Joyce and Textor related the Kyoto news to tax cuts:

Q. Your tax cuts now don't look affordable Dr Brash?

A. If anything they are more important. In the last few weeks Labour has been revealed as scandalous wasters of taxpayers money. We will eliminate their waste and mismanagement in short order; and provide tax relief to mainstream New Zealanders. This government has OD'd on a wall of money, they are spending and making commitments like drunken sailors without seeking any accountability, and they show complete disregard for the people that work hard to pay them that money. That must stop.[44]

The Crosby/Textor-style campaign tactics may be manipulative but, as John Howard's four wins in Australia demonstrate, they can work, by producing a short-term reaction from the so-called soft voters that can swing elections. So, does this mean that we must accept this type of political manipulation as an inevitable part of politics? The answer is no. The first response should be publicity and criticism. If enough people recognise and understand the tactics, naming them for what they are, they can be counter-productive and backfire. No one likes being obviously manipulated. Second, people within parties can insist on higher standards and take a longer term view. As former National leader Jim Bolger said in 1990 about using racism to win votes, 'Playing the race card may help us win – then come Monday how do we run the country?'[45]

But most importantly, a party like National can become government without deception and manipulation: it can sort out its philosophical foundations and present a set of policies that both the politicians and the public can believe in. Changing the policies makes it possible to change the tactics.

The question no one seems to ask is 'why?': why is a major political party basing its 'story' and election campaign on rather empty and incoherent policies like 'stopping' political correctness and 'putting an end' to Maori special privileges? Is that really what they believe is important? And why, apart from election bribes and policies wanted by commercial special interests, is there so little serious policy addressing the big problems of our times? Next we look at the philosophical hole in which the party has found itself and some of the reasons why it got there.

CHAPTER 11

THE HOLLOW MEN
Emptiness at the core

Political correctness used to be a self-mocking phrase on the left of politics. It referred to an excessively strict or self-righteous attention to a political principle, and use of language such as 'personhole' instead of 'manhole', and to a holier-than-thou attitude towards anyone who was not as strict. But the right-wing usage of 'politically correct' is quite different. It starts with mocking silly liberal stands – or misrepresents things so they look silly – then slides into a general attack on liberal beliefs and values.

The term is used to mock measures to promote equality for women and gay people, human rights legislation, environmentalism and efforts to reduce racial prejudice and poverty. In 1997 former Labour politician John Terris dismissed the welfare state as politically correct, characterising it as a 'whole army of thought police – conciliators, commissioners and other highly paid public servants – administering laws designed to make people feel good'.[1] In a National Party publication in June 2005, even measures to control climate change were described as 'another of [Helen Clark's] PC crusades'.[2]

A populist radio journalist inveighed in the *Sunday News* against the 'PC police', describing an occasion when someone had questioned his parking in a disabled carpark, even though he had checked that no 'cripples' were needing it at the time.[3] The power of the political correctness term is that it bundles together all kinds of unrelated things – the seemingly ridiculous, the prejudiced and general attacks on policies with which they do not agree – with each seeming to gain legitimacy from the label.

It is dog-whistle politics again. To one audience the messages purport to be a common-sense dismissal of silly excesses; to others they are an invitation to sneer at feminism, to feel comfortable talking about 'cripples', 'faggots' and 'coconuts' and to put the boot into Maori. As Australian academic Damien Cahill wrote about his country, the power of the anti- PC idea 'lies not in its reflection of reality but its ability to mobilise real fears, anxieties, resentments and insecurities'.[4]

Significantly, the anti-PC campaigning reached its greatest intensity under the Brash-led National Party. A search of the Newztext database shows a steady increase in the use of the term from the early-mid 1990s, but the high point is the 2003–05 period, especially the 2005 election year.[5]

Dozens of National Party public statements talked of 'rooting out political correctness', stopping 'politically correct pandering to violent criminals', 'cringing politically correct Treaty nonsense' and much more. Most National MPs joined in the chorus – even those who should have been aware that much of the so-called political correctness was normal policy for maintaining a fair and tolerant society.

Political correctness, according to the National Party publications, was 'rife', 'stifling', 'rampant' and 'engulfing'. Those responsible were the 'thought police'. Then there were the 'special interests' that got priority over 'mainstream' people, the 'chattering classes' with their trendy issues and the different types of 'grievance' industries. The first clue to the origin of the anti-PC campaign was that exactly the same exaggerated and emotive language was being used by right parties overseas. For instance, the British Conservative leader Michael Howard said in March 2005 that their education system had been 'engulfed in a tide of political correctness'. He was going to 'strike out political correctness, which was running rife'.[6] In a law and order speech he attacked a 'stifling culture of political correctness and red tape' in the criminal justice system. Like the law-abiding majority, he had had enough of political correctness.[7] Keenan had kept in touch with the Howard adviser responsible for the law and order speech, whom he and Brash had breakfasted with in June 2004. 'We all have mutual interests, and so have swapped the odd draft speech.'[8] The anti-PC campaign did not arise in New Zealand. It was adopted completely from overseas political parties.

These ideas, as used by the National Party, were formulated by those United States neo-conservatives who, Dick Allen said, could have met in a telephone booth 40 years ago and now dominate American politics. Right-wing thinktanks in the States started talking about political correctness and the rest during the 1980s Reagan era and it spread from there. The package was picked up by like-minded people to become the 'Aboriginal industry' in Australia, the 'Treaty industry' in New Zealand and so on. The political objective was to delegitimise left-wing social justice ideas and reverse the polarity of blue-collar politics from left to right.[9]

There are many books and articles discussing the rise of political correctness and related ideas in United States politics. John Wilson's *The Myth of Political Correctness* noted that in 1985 there were no recorded uses of the term on the NEXIS database. There were 15 in 1990, 1570 the following year and 6985 in 1994.[10] Left-wing politicians, human rights advocates, unions and environmental groups were portrayed as powerful and selfish zealots, outside and hostile to the 'mainstream', who used the PC causes to gain access to public money and influence. In a clever reversal of the truth, the critics of political correctness were painted as embattled and intimidated.

In the early 1990s the American right was adjusting to the fall of the Berlin Wall, which had taken with it their Cold War anti-communist framework. Led by thinktanks such as the Heritage Foundation, the Republicans shifted their strategy away from attacking socialism to attacking the 1970s and 1980s liberal movements – feminism, civil rights and so on. Combating political correctness became the banner of convenience under which the neo-conservatives could cut welfare programmes, reduce environmental protections and attack civil liberties. Australian writer Mark Davis, who saw the same PC campaign in that country, summed it up. 'What better way to stifle real dissent than an all-purpose pejorative such as "political correctness", which amounts to little more than a blanket way of discrediting anything that looks like a progressive idea, without having to resort to argument?'[11]

A few weeks after Brash became party leader his staff began work on upping the anti-PC campaign. Head of research Phil de Joux wrote to Richard Long advising that 'The team have compiled a list of PC Government Actions for the year.... I have saved it on the J drive, under J:\Research\Govt PC Actions.doc'.[12] Long sent the list to the rest of the office, asking 'staffers recalling awful PCnesses by Helengrad's team [to] please refer them to Phil for adding to this list'. 'We need a trail of social engineering/PCness examples.'[13]

And what were the awful PCnesses they had found? The meagre eighteen items on the list included legislation banning smoking in bars, the Employment Relations Law Reform Bill that allowed complaints on pay equity and protections for contract staff, a proposal to allow public access across private property to significant waterways and a proposal for a telephone hotline where gay people could report discrimination.[14] If political correctness was rampant and rife it would have been a better list than this. Some may disagree with these policies, but that would be a political difference, not evidence of political correctness engulfing New

Zealand. There are of course occasional instances of political silliness that can legitimately be criticised, but they generally deserve a groan, not the concerted attention of a major political party. Political correctness neither describes a major problem nor suggests any solutions. It is a purely political tactic, imported into New Zealand as a ready-made formula whose proponents can then find 'evidence' to justify.[15]

The most comical case of National seeking out 'evidence' to fuel their anti-PC campaign was in December 2004, when MP John Key's secretary sent a breathless email to all the National Party staff looking for information about a stunning new example of PC madness. 'Does anyone know what programme interviewed a guy who had made a Maori porn movie and received a $100,000 Government grant to do it?' she asked. She checked that no other MPs had got onto the case before them: 'Is anyone's MP already looking into this?'[16]

The story turned out to be true. A man had indeed been interviewed a few days earlier on television about government funding of his porn movie, which had the appalling title 'Anal Mana'. It was exactly what Long had been encouraging them to find – combining a careless attitude to spending taxpayers' money with allowing Maori to do things that Pakeha would never get away with. The only problem was that the interview had been part of the comedy programme *Eating Media Lunch*, which was lampooning the anti-PC campaign. *Listener* television reviewer Diana Wichtel declared the programme Best Hoax for 2004 and noted that 'Incredibly, some people actually believed that an indigenous good time called *Anal Mana* would be coming to an adult section near you. Time for another of those shows where they test the IQ of the nation. Quick.'[17]

Why did the National Party make political correctness and the special interest grievance industries a centrepiece of its political platform? When Brash became leader and announced new portfolio allocations for his caucus, he stated their mission as turning back the tide of political correctness.[18] Two years later, as he refocused the party after its election defeat, he created a new portfolio called Spokesman for Political Correctness Eradication. What was going on?

The answer to this becomes clearer if some of National's other prominent policies are examined more closely: reducing the bureaucratic red tape for businesses, stopping the Resource Management Act (RMA) from blocking economic development, and strengthening defence. Each had been the subject of numerous speeches, parliamentary debates and press releases.[19] First, red tape and costs for business. According to National, businesses were being 'stifled by red tape and over-regulation' and the country needed 'a bureaucratic bonfire to do away with the excessive red tape that is crippling businesses and cutting profits'.[20] John Key said the government was 'drowning business in red tape'.[21] Comments like this were repeated hundreds and hundreds of times.

But it was not true. Five years into the term of the Labour-led government, the World Bank conducted a worldwide survey of business-friendly government policies. Of the 145 countries studied in the 'Doing Business in 2005' report, New Zealand came top, ahead of all the others. Judged on regulations and policies that encourage or discourage investment, productivity and growth, New Zealand was the most encouraging country for business in the world.[22] The right-wing Heritage Foundation's annual *Index of Economic Freedom* likewise had New Zealand ranked fifth in the world in 2005, ahead of the United States and Australia.[23] An Otago University survey of small businesses completed in 2004 likewise found that 'perceptions of the time spent on compliance issues are often exaggerated'.[24] Yet National had said the regulations and policies were stifling and crippling and drowning businesses.

Key grudgingly acknowledged the World Bank survey, saying it 'reflected past policies'.[25] This was partly true but only underlined the fact that in the balance between social and economic regulations ('red tape') and business freedom, the past policies from the 1980s and 1990s placed New Zealand far across on the side of business. And a few days later Key was back to exactly the same lines: New Zealand businesses were 'living with the red tape nightmare every day' and it was 'strangling our small and medium enterprises'.[26]

It was the same with the RMA which, according to Brash, was slowing down and blocking projects affecting 'traffic congestion, power prices, housing costs, key sporting events, jobs and exports'.[27] According to National, the RMA was 'quite simply madness – a riot of political correctness rampaging through our statute books'[28] which 'has created a whole industry of consultation, and of special interest lobbying'.[29] National MPs regularly attacked the RMA madness 'which is crippling so many of our communities throughout the country with unwarranted costs'.[30]

But again the evidence did not fit the National Party story. After years of this criticism, the Ministry for the Environment began collecting statistics about the impact of the RMA. It found that out of a total of 54,658 resource consents in 2003–04, only 404 were not approved (less than 1 per cent). Furthermore, 95.2 per cent of the applications were not 'notified', which means there was no public consultation, special interest or otherwise. For this non-notified group, the average cost of applications was about $500. For the minority of larger applications that had public consultation, the cost was on average a few thousand dollars.[31] Yet anyone hearing the stream of anti-RMA statements in the news from National could believe it was a large and important issue.

And international comparisons do not support the National claims about the RMA obstructing roading projects. Another Ministry for the Environment study found that, on average, major roading projects in the United States took twelve to fifteen years for planning and approval, Britain and Sweden ten years and France and New Zealand eight years. Obviously it takes time to go through the processes before pushing motorways through residential suburbs or countryside, but New Zealand was not slower than the others.[32]

Finally defence. 'The National Party says New Zealand's defence force has been badly run down by the Government,' the defence spokesperson said during the 2005 election campaign.[33] New Zealand was 'bludging on defence', the prime minister and defence minister were 'peaceniks' and they had achieved 'mainly inactivity' during five years in government.[34] 'We dishonour the memory of the Anzacs if we allow our defence forces to atrophy in what is clearly an unstable international environment.'[35]

There are military issues over which a right party might have disagreed with the Labour government, but definitely not defence spending. Labour had ordered several new navy ships, was replacing or upgrading all the air force planes (except strike aircraft, which in the previous 30 years had never been used in combat), had bought many new vehicles and weapons for the army and was even funding a long-planned new defence headquarters building. Billions of dollars were being spent on the military after nine years of National government neglect – in many cases replacing equipment last funded by the 1984–90 Labour government, which had been similarly generous to the military. An Institute of Strategic Studies report concluded in 2005 that 'after substantial reductions in expenditure (in real terms) by previous administrations, plans and political commitment are now in place to rebuild the New Zealand Defence Force'.[36]

There are policies voters agree with and those they disagree with. But these National policies were something different altogether. Each was in fact more like a non-policy. They did not relate to serious needs or problems and, leaving aside the symbolic value of reversing another party's policies, they offered no clear benefits for the country. Of course politicians do sometimes grandstand on relatively meaningless populist causes like 'fighting crime', but there was more going on here.

There was, and still is, a curious policy vacuum in the National Party. All the determination and political efforts to become government were not matched by a clear philosophy or plan explaining why National wanted to be in government. There were, of course, various policies adopted to please specific special interests, such as the private health and education lobbies, and there were ad hoc policies such as abolishing Maori seats in Parliament adopted tactically to back up the attack on Maori privilege and other parts of the anti-PC campaign. But there was no coherent philosophy to take to the nation, nothing to address many important issues affecting New Zealand – for instance the uncontrolled house price inflation that is making it impossible for many younger urban people to own a home, and the damage done to society as the gap grows between rich and poor in New Zealand. There were three reasons for this – one concerning the public, the second concerning National's political allies and the third, and most important, concerning the party itself.

First, political correctness, Maori separatism and stifling red tape provide easy political fodder when politicians do not want to talk about their real agendas. This is the other side of the tactics of inoculating, de-emphasising and hiding their unpopular political intentions. While Don Brash and his staff were avoiding talking about privatisation and tax cuts for the rich, the anti-PC, Treaty industry and red tape themes could harmlessly pad out speeches and press statements, filling the political airtime. Meanwhile, attacking 'left' policies as being PC, overregulating and tax-grabbing, avoided the need to present viable policies for dealing with social instability, inequality, injustice and crime.

Second, rhetoric about political correctness, Maori privilege and special interests was a highly effective way of shifting attention away from the real privilege and special interests in our society, which mostly meant the organisations and individuals with whom National was politically aligned. This is the tactic of accusing your opponent of what you prefer to hide about yourself. The powerful interests in New Zealand are not teachers, unions and iwi organisations; and the claim that Labour pampered them more than other sectors, such as business, is not supported by evidence. The powerful elites are large corporations, finance companies, PR and law firms, property developers and so on, who wield an influence far out of proportion to the numbers of voters they represent. These are the people to whom Brash and other senior National Party people gave most attention in 2004–05.

Third, and most importantly, emphasising these sorts of issues helps National to avoid confronting a deep and fundamental rift within its own ranks. For most of its history, the party was a combination of conservative and interest group politics (in the same way that the Labour Party has combined progressive and interest group politics). Since the 1980s National has had two very different and incompatible philosophies at work: conservative and radical free market right. There were vigorous fights within the 1990s National government between the two camps, represented by Ruth Richardson on one side and ministers such as Philip Burdon and Winston Peters on the other, with leader Jim Bolger in the middle. The Burdon/Peters group was concerned about social stability and protection of community and family life; Richardson's group believed that its purist market policies would be best for the country in the long run. This fundamental conflict has never been resolved.

This is where the anti-PC package of ideas has its main function. In the United States, Britain, Australia and New Zealand, the attacks on political correctness and so-called special interests have provided rhetorical weapons, a shared enemy and at least the appearance of a common policy framework upon which both the conservatives and radical right factions could work together.[37] Thus very different National Party politicians such as Don Brash, John Key, Bill English and Katherine Rich could be united in attacking Labour's supposed political correctness, possibly unaware that the main function of this campaign was to prevent them from having to confront their differences.

In the period after 2003 this politicking on relatively unimportant issues served as a protective cover to help the free market radicals secure dominance in the National Party, and to prepare to continue their unfinished business whenever they gained power, without having to show their hands. For the whole party – radicals, conservatives and don't knows – it was easier to go along with a philosophical fog, flimsy policies and unresolved hidden agendas than to try to face up to clarifying what the party really believed in.

The problem is that the two factions are truly incompatible. There is almost no discussion of this difference in New Zealand, but in other countries there is vigorous debate. In Australia, for instance, former Prime Minister Malcolm Fraser, who in his day was a reactionary, anti-union Liberal Party leader, later became one of his country's strongest opponents of free market or 'neo-liberal' economics. He also criticised the New Zealand reforms: 'The worship of market power has not led to a strong and prosperous country.... The economic rationalists... would prefer to sacrifice the country than their theories.'[38] He wrote in 2002 that 'our generation is without a political philosophy relevant to our time and circumstances. We have a theory of globalisation but, baldly stated, it is cold and technical.... We need an idea of how our society will develop and how, in a more global society, people will relate to each other. We need a philosophical framework.'[39]

In Britain, Professor John Gray of the London School of Economics was once close to Margaret Thatcher and a favourite of the New Right. He wrote books on John Stuart Mill and the theoretical father of the New Right, Friedrich Hayek (in whose honour Brash gave the speech mentioned in Chapter 4). He now believes that these ideas, variously referred to as New Right, neo-liberal, neo-conservative and free market, are a threat to the traditional conservative values of social cohesion, order and stability.

Neo-liberalism is the process whereby power, resources and responsibility for the provision of services are transferred from the public to the private sector; from the state to markets.[40] Free market believers argue that markets are 'natural' and should ideally not be obstructed. 'The truth is that free markets are creatures of state power,' Gray wrote in 1998, 'and persist only so long as the state is able to prevent human needs for security and the control of economic risk from finding political expression.' He wrote of the collapse of social cohesion in a purely market-driven society. 'The free market is most recklessly short termist in its demolition of the virtues it once relied upon. These virtues – saving, civic pride, respectability, "family values" – are now profitless museum pieces.'[41]

Gray now argues that neo-liberal policies such as outsourcing have contributed to the disappearance of entire occupations and career structures. Job insecurity, the growth of casual, part-time and contract work and the end of loyalty to a single employer erode a settled life: 'How can families meet for meals when both parents work on shifts? What becomes of families when the job market pulls parents apart?' He believes that 'only a framework of global regulation – of currencies, capital movements, trade and environmental conservation – can enable the creativity of the world economy to be harnessed in the service of human needs'.[42] Deregulated trade and foreign ownership of a nation's productive enterprises make it more likely that their operations will fit the interests of transnational corporations and be less subject to national democratic institutions and democratic decisions about what is best for society.[43]

This of course sounds very similar to 'left' criticisms of free market policies. This is because the conservative emphasis on social cohesion and stability has more in common with the left's emphasis on social justice than with the free market destructiveness to all these values. The right/left labels confuse rather than assist understanding of this new political landscape, which helps to explain why many in a party like National do not know what to make of their feelings of discomfort about the free market programme.

In New Zealand businesspeople express concern about head offices and decision-making shifting overseas and ordinary people talk about the social effects of the 1980s and 1990s reforms. But there is almost no critical discussion of these issues from people on the right of politics. There needs to be. Currently it is 'not done' for either the free market right or the conservatives of the National Party to talk openly about their beliefs. The result is a kind of philosophical paralysis, waiting for new leaders with the intellectual wherewithal to articulate a new direction for the party. Overseas conservatives like Malcolm Fraser and John Gray have been working on such ideas. But as long as the National Party is led by the free market right – and a more or less severe version of their philosophy is the only serious contender to underpin a future National government – a combination of philosophical ambiguity and phony policies serve a useful purpose.

The difference between conservative and free market policies is seen clearly in attitudes to social problems. One of the striking differences between conservative and neo-liberal philosophies is how they view people who are less wealthy and privileged. In traditional conservatism, people can acknowledge their own privilege and feel it carries with it a responsibility to the rest of society. The free market view tends to blame those who have failed to be successful and refuses to acknowledge that social inequality, including people's feelings about having less wealth and opportunity than others, batters their self-esteem from a young age and can be the origin of personal and social problems. This is why the free market philosophy has no real answers to crime, poverty, failures in education and other social problems.

Tax cuts also highlight the difference. There is nothing about traditional conservatism that is inherently anti-regulation and anti-tax. Years of campaigning by the radical right – in New Zealand more than most countries – have attempted to demonise tax, portraying it as government grabbing ordinary people's money for its own wasteful purposes. But this characterisation is dishonest and misleading. The opposite view was summed up by Oliver Wendell Holmes, former justice of the United States Supreme Court, when he said that 'Taxes are what we pay for a civilized society'.

Tax and regulations are essentially democratic tools, providing the means and resources with which citizens can shape the future. They are the tools with which governments can control socially harmful activities and provide the parks, clean beaches, libraries, roads, schools, policing, healthcare and all the rest of the social infrastructure that gives us our quality of life. Together these justify the proportion of the national income that goes to providing them. The lack of voices in the National Party defending tax-funded social services shows that the conservatives are confused and disorganised. But, as this chapter argues, they are also distracted.

Damien Cahill wrote that 'the general unpopularity of neo-liberal policies in practice has meant that governments the world over have often bolstered their economic regimes with a conservative social agenda'.[44] Rather than advertise their free market plans, they appeal to voters with a platform of Christian right-style moral conservatism, xenophobia, law and order and 'family', while at the same time attacking ideals of equality and social justice as Political Correctness and the clamouring of special interests.'

He said the Australian Liberal party's 'experience of the 1993 campaign, in which the [Liberal–National] coalition lost the "unlosable election", demonstrated that an electoral strategy based primarily on a radical neo-liberal agenda was unlikely to win broad appeal. Strategically, the coalition needed something more to knit together a stable electoral majority. The "something more" was the construction of a series of "others" – "special interests", "politically correct elites", [refugee] "queue-jumpers", the "guilt industry", "terrorists" – who threaten the mainstream.'[45]

It was not surprising that National, which employed the Liberal Party's election strategists (Crosby/Textor) would use the same strategy. Don Brash gave an election year speech on 17 April 2005 – by which time Mark Textor's influence over campaign strategy was well established – which leaves no doubt that they were following the same road. He told National Party delegates in Auckland that the Labour government was a 'seething mass of minority agendas' and that 'New Zealand is not being governed by mainstream New Zealanders, or in the interests of mainstream New Zealanders'.[46]

This is a government which panders to fringe groups and special interests. Which is great if you happen to be a trade union activist. Or part of the

Maori caucus. Or a member of the Rainbow caucus. Or the inhabitant of a university common room. But if you happen to be Mr and Mrs Average New Zealander, earning an average wage, struggling to educate your kids, pay the mortgage, and save a little to improve your lot and that of your family, this... is not your sort of government....

The hard-working, over-taxed, over-regulated people of this region know... this Clark Government is not made up of people like them. They know that middle class welfare and stultifying political correctness are not the path forward for this country.[47]

It might just as well have been John Howard or George Bush reading the speech. It would not have mattered what the Labour Party had been doing in government. The words would have been exactly the same.

CHAPTER 12

IWI/KIWI
Award-winning propaganda

In March 2005 Murray McCully described to Brash the challenge National faced to be able to win the election. 'Our own polling, with the new Textor questions, tells us that: the favourable economic conditions provide a very fortunate backdrop for the government [and] their tight management and vigorous damage control is working for them. We have not broken their hold. Our credibility as an alternative government had taken a hammering.' The 'task ahead is formidable but by no means impossible.... We need to invest heavily in a bounce back prior to the budget. If we do not... the Government's momentum [will be] potentially unstoppable.'

The first sign of this investment was the dozens of large billboards that began appearing around the country in late April 2005. After twelve months of floundering, this campaign helped at last to lift National's poll ratings. With two words – 'Iwi/Kiwi' – they achieved what Brash had done with his 4973-word Orewa race speech the year before. National again looked capable of winning the 2005 election.

The billboards were designed by an advertising writer who had worked for the Labour government in the 1980s and 1990s, moved to the ACT Party for three elections and then decided to help Don Brash and the National Party in the 2005 election. John Ansell made his initial approach to Don Brash via a mutual friend. He wrote her an excited email on 29 October 2003, the day after Brash was elected as National Party leader. Brash looked 'honest' and 'untainted', 'the anti-politician' who was 'not being afraid to talk straight to the public'. He predicted Brash would become prime minister in 2005. 'He'll preach the same sermon as Roger Douglas, but without getting people's backs up.' She forwarded his email to Brash, explaining that Ansell was the person she had told him about who was interested in 'promoting a campaign' for National.[1]

A few weeks later Ansell wrote directly to Brash to introduce himself. He explained that he had worked for Labour in the 1987, 1990 and 1993 elections. 'The first was for Labour in 1987 when I was at Colenso. I did the radio ads – a series of spoofs of the TV show "Soap".' One of these, 'delivered by a deeply ironic American voice', attacked National leader Jim Bolger, Ruth Richardson and the former leader Rob Muldoon.

> Why are Jim, Ruth and Rob so concerned? Rob says they're concerned about people – that they care and Labour doesn't care, even though Labour brought in Family Care, which Ruth doesn't care for. Will Ruth really have young girls' babies put in someone else's care, and will old people be left to care for themselves? Could it be all the Nats care about is getting elected? Who knows? Who cares?[2]

He told Brash that these radio ads won the Mobil Radio Award for campaign of the year. He also described a local government election campaign he ran for his then wife in 1994, in which she got the highest per capita vote. 'It's an awful thing for a politician to admit, but the advertising was everything.' Ansell stayed with Labour until 1993, but then 'couldn't in all conscience carry on doing ads for Labour since they seemed determined to return to their roots'.

He explained the political beliefs that he would be bringing with him if National hired him for its 2005 campaign. 'I should put my cards on the table about ACT. I really click with most of their policies and have supported them since turning down Labour in 1996.' However, like many ACT supporters at that time, he was willing to move because of Brash. 'While it's fair to say I'm a fan of ACT policies, I'd be more than happy if National won the election as long as they implemented those policies. I prefer the [Roger] Douglas approach of doing what's right for the country, and trusting the public to come round. This, I'm picking, is the way you operate.

'Don, if I could design a role for myself it would be to prepare advertising messages. I truly believe you can win in 2005, but only if you package your policies in ways that shock the soft centre voters into reassessing their prejudices. It's got to be quite a powerful approach – not leaders walking down beaches and talking to phoney election meetings.'

Ansell said he was already known to Richard Long 'who seems quite keen on my letter writing on behalf of the Taiwanese'. Ansell was a regular writer of letters to the editor which, besides supporting Taiwan, where his wife is from, had called New Zealand a member of the 'Coalition of the Weaklings' and France 'the nation that caved in to Hitler' for not supporting the 2003 Iraq War.[3]

He ended his email to Brash by proposing that 'What the media are fond of labelling "right wing" is nothing more than what good parents or good Christians would do'. He bemoaned the fact that 'neither National nor ACT is saying this. The hypocrisy of Labour's so-called "caring" policies needs to be exposed, and I believe I can do that as well as anyone. I've had success with humorous messages in the past, but would recommend that National start to adopt a tone of moral outrage.'[4]

Brash wrote back, saying he was 'not sure if we could afford you' but that he would be 'keen to talk to you at some stage, sooner rather than later'.[5] Nothing happened quickly. Ansell sent Brash a bundle of his ideas and wrote a second email a couple of months later, at the end of February 2004, saying that ACT wanted to use him for its campaign but that 'I'd rather work for National now'. He explained what he could offer to a National victory. 'To fully support your policies, swinging voters will need to understand them clearly. Yet these people are allergic to long, complicated explanations, no matter how sensible. The media are unlikely to help simplify them for you. The key, I would suggest, is pictures. As any accelerated learning guru will tell you, the brain remembers in pictures. Yet politicians nearly always use words. I think a combination of simple words and strong graphics is the best way to create a lasting impression of a new idea.'[6] This, in a nutshell, would be Ansell's approach for National's election year advertising.

Brash apologised that he had been 'struggling' with email since his Orewa speech and said he would like to have a meeting with Ansell and his key advisers.[7] Brash asked his secretary to arrange for McCully, Brownlee, Long, Keenan and Sinclair to be present. The meeting went ahead at 9am on Wednesday 31 March 2004, with Ansell showing his ideas in a powerpoint presentation.

Within weeks, Richard Long had allocated money from the parliamentary office budget for a $5000 a month payment to Ansell to work part time for National from home.[8] But this was 2004, the year when National gave its attention to the business lobbies more than the public. Ansell worked quietly on election ideas and by the start of 2005 had the first big plans ready.

Ansell, incensed at criticism of Brash following the Orewa welfare speech and Katherine Rich's demotion, sent the National leader an email headed 'Bold as Brash' to encourage him about how they could change

National's fortunes. A stream of ideas and advice poured from the email.

'Don, I can't believe what I'm reading. I hope you make it clear to these dissenters that the public see National as a one-man band. That man is entitled to choose his instruments, and play them as he sees fit.' He went on: 'Winning elections is easy. All you have to do is say the right thing, in the right way, at the right time.' That right thing 'needs to be highly original, properly crystallised, and endlessly repeated.... I'm also hoping my first slogan, "The guts to do what's right", will be, if not chosen, then at least true!' Passionate in his support, Ansell continued: 'This country has one last chance to avoid being entombed in socialist permafrost. You're it, Don. For all our sakes, keep fighting.' He assured Brash he could help. 'From one "one-man band" to another, I'd love to show you some ideas for how you might crystallise that message.'[9] This was 21 February 2005, when Ansell had just completed the mock-ups for the billboard campaign.

Ansell had spent most of his working life in advertising, rising to running his own ad production studio in central Wellington during the 1990s. When the studio got into difficulties, he shut up shop, moved home and mostly devoted himself to a new life of writing humorous poetry, public speaking and other personal projects. It was the force of his ACT Party-style political beliefs that brought him back to advertising for National. He later said, 'I thought I'd retired from advertising, but when I saw Don Brash on the horizon, I just had to put my hand up.'[10] It was the combination of the advertising industry's 'sell fridges to Eskimos' expediency and Ansell's personal hardline politics that would produce an especially potent style of election advertising for National.

Based on his belief on 'simple words and strong graphics', Ansell came up with the idea of billboards in two halves, red on one side for Labour and blue on the other for National. The Labour side, with a confused-looking photo of Helen Clark in one corner, would portray Labour as focused on minorities, wasting taxpayers' money and generally lacking competence. The National side, with a confident-looking photo of Brash, would portray National as solid and possessing strong policies on Maori privilege and tax cuts – the two key election policies – plus a set of secondary policies including education and crime.

Ansell worked on the ideas; Phil O'Reilly of Auckland's 20/20 Design Group made the ideas into the billboards. Brash selected the photograph of himself for the billboards but his attentive assistant Sinclair made sure the photo was retouched to convert some slightly ruffled hair into the proper conservative image: 'Phil [O'Reilly] should be able to photoshop his "scary hair"'.[11]

The first billboard to go up concerned roading policy, promising that National would spend all money from road taxes on roading. There is a revealing story behind it. When the billboards started going up, press officer Jason Ede circulated the lines providing the prepared words that National spokespeople could say about them. The billboards were 'part of a pre-election campaign designed to point out the many clear differences between National and Labour' and 'to emphasise National's focus on the issues that matter for mainstream New Zealanders'.

The roading billboard arose from a debate in the campaign strategy committee, not about how National was different from Labour but simply about what policies they could use to win election support. Allocating all road taxes to roading was not party policy at that time but an email to Brash from a supporter helped prompt a rethink. 'As a long time supporter of ACT and now National,' the correspondent wrote, 'I think a National Party policy to dedicate all revenue from taxes at the petrol pump to roading would be a great platform for getting the support of the country. ...I actually think the surpluses should be returned to those who pay them, but the policy outlined above will get the support of the masses and that is the first priority.'[12]

Bryan Sinclair, who handled Brash's parliamentary emails, forwarded the letter to Brash and others saying, 'I hate to revisit this issue, and I know the fiscal and political issues surrounding this sort of commitment, but I really do agree with the substance... in terms of vote-winning.' He proposed they have a policy saying 'National will, within 5 years of becoming Government, apply all petrol tax revenue raised *solely* to roading and transport infrastructure across New Zealand'. 'I think we would make a killing, particularly in the metropolitan centres.'[13]

Maurice Williamson wrote to Brash, agreeing with Sinclair's proposal. 'I think it's a real winner. It's been John Key that doesn't agree and we have had several meetings and caucus presentations to get us very close to this point – but we're not quite there yet.'[14] Sinclair wrote back to Williamson, reiterating his November 2004 argument about the need to 'slosh those funds around' and the support of 'inherently self-interested... soft centre voters'.[15] He wrote, 'The fact is we have to spend to win votes, and this is a credible area in which to open the cheque book.' He knew Key was 'not comfortable' but he would 'continue to lobby Don'.[16] Williamson replied with a one word email: 'Cool'.[17]

A few weeks later the chequebook view prevailed and Brash announced the new policy at an Automobile Association conference in Napier on 1 April 2005. It was referred immediately to John Ansell and the campaign team. The petrol tax billboard was designed and produced rapidly in mid-April and erected on Friday, 22 April 2005, next to Karangahape Road in Auckland. Don Brash was there 'putting the last staples' in the huge 12- by 4.8-metre billboard for the media.

The heading on the billboard read 'What's your petrol tax for?' On the red Labour Party side was the answer 'Hip-hop tours, welfare bribes, prisoner compo, twilight golf, sing-along courses, taniwha, more bureaucrats, NCEA inquiries, Treaty lawyers...'. On the blue National Party side, it said 'Roads'. Anyone could see this was highly effective advertising. But it was not really about differences between National and Labour. Three months later Brash admitted to his colleagues that he was speaking to the Contractors Federation that afternoon 'and at the moment [Labour minister Pete] Hodgson is winning the "who will spend most on roads" battle'.[18]

The second billboard had a similar theme and style. 'Education priorities' read the headline across the top. On the Labour side there were four four-letter acronyms: 'NZQA, PPTA, NCEA, NZEI' – the New Zealand Qualifications Authority, the Post Primary Teachers Association, the National Certificate of Educational Achievement and the New Zealand Educational Institute. On the National side it said 'Kids'. As the next chapter shows, it would have been more accurate to write Business Roundtable, private schools lobby and Maxim Institute on the National side. But, again, the billboard seemed decisive and convincing.

After that the new billboard slogans came quickly. Steven Joyce wrote to Brash on 25 May 2005 showing him copies of 'the final eight billboards the team had settled on for June'. He said that in total, including the roading and education designs, they were using 90 billboard sites around the country.[19] For election winning, they certainly looked like the 'right thing' Ansell had promised Brash. 'Dial 111 for....Cabs [Labour] / Cops [National]'; 'Violent criminals... Out in no time [Labour] / Do the whole time [National]'; 'What's best for your kids? Excuses [Labour] / Exams [National]'; 'Health spending... Pen-pushers [Labour] / Patients [National]'; and so on.

The billboard that produced the strongest public reaction, both positive and negative, and which will be remembered the longest, was simply headed 'Beaches'. On the Labour side it said 'Iwi'; on National's 'Kiwi'. This billboard was probably John Ansell's greatest achievement of the campaign. Some of the billboards had a shred of truth, some very little, but this one, besides saying almost nothing genuine about Labour and National's policy difference over beaches, was a pure example of calculated emotional manipulation.

The billboard was so dishonest that even Brash-leaning commentator Colin James was concerned about it. His first reaction had mainly been to applaud the political impact of the billboards. Shortly after the Iwi/Kiwi one appeared, he wrote: 'Watching Brash, the man of principle, do populism is spellbinding (and disjunctive).... [National] has backed this with brilliant billboards grossly, but slyly, overstating Labour-National contrasts. That initiative suggests its election advertising will be the strongest since 1975.'[20] A month later, however, he wondered whether 'National and Labour are undermining themselves by playing dirty and reminding voters how rotten politics can be'.

> Don Brash feigns anger (or maybe is actually angry) at being misrepresented when his Iraq and nuclear policy words are quoted out of context. With hand on Presbyterian heart, he declares his billboards just point up differences with Labour. Well, test him on his 'pen-pushers' versus 'patients' billboard. The 'difference' stated there is that Labour ministers care only for bureaucrats while Nightingale National cares deeply for patients. Misrepresentative? Yes. So are the rest. The 'Iwi/Kiwi' one is divisive to boot.[21]

Mostly, though, the media commentary was not interested in the accuracy or integrity. 'National's hit billboards' were 'striking', 'iconic', 'clever' and 'short, punchy and easily recognisable, if somewhat misleading in their simplicity'.[22] The *New Zealand Herald* described the billboards as 'elegantly simple and humorous and perfectly designed to catch the attention of the drive-by voter'. The 'Succinct messages... cleverly presented the essence of a problem and its solution'.[23]

Did they really? Labour's political problems over the foreshore and seabed were not that it was giving the beaches away to iwi, but because it was seen by Maori to be taking them away. And as for 'Dial 111 for... Cabs/Cops', here are four out of dozens of news articles on the 111 emergency call service when National had been last in government: 'Right street, wrong city for 111 police call-out', '111 computer breaks down again', 'Failure of 111 angers victims of Loburn fire' and '[Police Minister Clem] Simich refuses inquiry into troubled 111 call system'. These stories started not long after Telecom was privatised and all governments since have faced the same problems. It was not about a 'clear difference' between National and Labour at all.

Striking, clever and perhaps iconic the billboards were, but primarily they were misleading and manipulative. This is what we expect, and take for granted, in commercial advertising. It is illuminating to look at some of the theory of propaganda, since it explains why National's billboards felt so clever and compelling.

The first point is no surprise. Repetition works, and endlessly repeating simple slogans works precisely because they do not strongly engage our brains, meaning that we do not apply our experience and intellect to consider whether they are true. It works this way, according to an American textbook on propaganda, because 'we see and hear many, many persuasive messages each day, and we see and hear them over and over again. It is difficult to think deeply about each and every one of these communications' and 'repetition is thus left to create its own truths'.[24] Complex messages and reasoned two-sided debate have a completely different effect on our brains. They stimulate thought and help us to reach our own judgement. That is the basis of genuinely democratic politics but it is not the aim of propaganda.

Some commentaries on National's billboards noted that, despite their dubious truthfulness, they 'do have a small saving grace: they have a tinge of wit'.[25] Advertising and propaganda must find methods to get around our natural scepticism about sales talk and our tendency to think of counter-arguments when someone is trying to persuade us. The simplest solution found for this is mild distraction. Research has found that when simple, repeated messages are accompanied by 'distractions' such as music, humour, striking images or fast-moving film, it blocks or reduces our natural tendency to construct counter-arguments and so makes the message more persuasive.[26] Big distractions do not work, because they get in the way of our even noticing the message; and even mild distractions do not work with complex messages. The ideal messages to bypass our intellects and get inside our heads are the simple repetitive ones where our attention is caught (distracted) by the music, moving pictures, surprising images – or clever humour.

A well-designed billboard, like a short television ad, is therefore made for propaganda. A *Dominion Post* feature described how National campaign manager Steven Joyce 'struggled to hide his delight' with the billboards. 'Generally, politics can be too complicated for people,' he said.

'Some people perhaps don't read the paper every day and don't consume everything.'[27] The billboards particularly had these people in mind.

The special power of Iwi/Kiwi – which made it the most influential of the billboards – came from the use of an extreme claim (that somehow public access to beaches was at risk) combined with the simple elegance of the words iwi and Kiwi being so alike. It also relied on another well-documented phenomenon: most people's innate wish to be part of a group and their easily aroused feelings against people who are not in the group.[28] This is apparently the case even when the 'group' does not exist in any practical way and is created only by political rhetoric such as 'hardworking' New Zealanders. The Iwi/Kiwi billboards encouraged 'non-Maori' to feel separate and threatened by Maori who wanted to take away their beaches, even though there was never a real risk of this.

Negative stereotyping often employs anecdotes as 'proof' to build or reinforce prejudices. This is why National's selection of outrageous Labour government spending – 'Hip-hop tours, welfare bribes, prisoner compo, twilight golf, sing-along courses, taniwha....' – tended, coming after years of similar publicity, to bring to mind a Maori or Polynesian face. After a while, a regularly maintained negative stereotype can become an enduring myth, as repetition creates its own truth.

John Ansell worked from home or, when in town, in a spare office shared with surplus office equipment at the back of the National Party's four-teenth-floor headquarters. He worked rapidly, trying out new ideas in succession. He was proud of the billboards, which had been released in stages through June and July to maintain public interest, but he was working on very different ideas for the election campaign itself. With the tried and true techniques of advertising and propaganda in mind, it is not difficult to see what was going on when the election campaign advertisements began to be broadcast in August 2005.

National's most effective advertisements during the election campaign proper were the 'Taxathon' leaflets and 30-second television advertisements. On 16 August 2005, when political television advertising could legally begin, Richard Long invited all National leader's office staff to the caucus room to view 'a clever little election advert which will go to air on TV1 tomorrow night'.[29] He also wrote to McCully and Brownlee to let them know the parliamentary journalists were 'being invited up for a drink and screening at 4.30pm and communications staff are invited to join in and chat to them'.[30]

The *New Zealand Herald* reported 'Clever election tricks that fit the bill' while the *Dominion Post*, in a more critical news story headed 'Nats' new TV ad "all good fun" ', quoted Steven Joyce making comments similar to those he had made about the billboards. 'When you've got an audience who is not necessarily deeply involved in politics, you've got to get them interested in an entertainment style they are used to.'[31] The *National Business Review* described the ads as 'aimed at an emotional rather than the intellectual response'.[32]

The 30-second Taxathon television advertisements had all the text-book characteristics of effective propaganda: fast-moving images, catchy music and humour to distract from questioning the messages. There was a cartoon stage, in Labour Party red, decorated like the set of the Telethon charity fundraising events of an earlier era. 'It's the Clark-Cullen Taxa-thon, with your hosts the Prime Moneywaster and Wastemaster General,' the announcer declared, as puppets of Helen Clark and Michael Cullen danced onto the stage, throwing handfuls of money into the air as they sang 'Thank you very much for your high taxation, thank you very much, thank you very, very, very much'.

National's target voters appeared one by one for a line of the song. An angry 'Kiwi battler' Auckland man shook his fist from a motorway on-ramp as he sang 'Thank you very much for your petrol levies'. A young woman in a car had to hand across an armful of money to a police officer as Labour's police minister sang 'Me and my revenue gathering team!' A blue-collar man in his 60s in a pub pushed a small mountain of dollar notes across the bar as he sang 'Thank you very much for your tax on bevies'. Helen Clark quickly hid a glass of wine behind her back as she sang the chorus. Then a middle-aged woman was seen terrified in bed at night as a man in a black mask appeared in her room and robbed her. She tried to dial for help as a voice in the background sang 'Dial 111 and Screeeeeeam!'

The advertisement ended with Clark and Cullen pushing a wheelbar-row of money across the stage followed by a conga line of Labour MPs who had got in trouble in the previous years, two of them portrayed as drunks. Near the end of the advertisement the scene switched abruptly to a blue (for National) set, where a friendly Don Brash puppet was standing quietly, without all the distracting movement and sound. 'Time we had a new government,' the announcer said. Brash replied 'Thank you very much' and gave a broad wink to the viewers.

The advertisement was effective, award-winningly effective, but dishon-est. It felt true and evoked feelings of resentment, fear and anger as the images rushed across the screen. But it had almost nothing to do with real differences between the two parties. National and Labour's past records and policies on petrol and alcohol taxes and the 111 system were almost identical. Misdemeanours and drinking in one party were no better or worse than in the other. The National strategists had realised that 'proposals for tax cuts need to be combined with effective attack on wasteful public spending, otherwise the electorate will equate tax cuts with cuts to public services'.[33]

The Taxathon advertisements were paid for from public money, part of an allocation to all parties for their broadcast advertising. The National Party had written a submission to the Electoral Commission early in the election year arguing to retain or increase its share of the public money and eventually received $900,000 (up from $615,000 for the 2002 election) and eighteen minutes of free television time. What was its justification for getting this public money? To allow 'a balanced and fair presentation of [its] alternative policy platform to the voting public'.[34]

American film director Charles Guggenheim once wrote: 'Ask any seasoned media advertiser and he will tell you what he can do best in thirty seconds. Create doubt. Build fear. Exploit anxiety. Hit and run. The thirty and sixty second commercials are ready made for innuendo and half truth. Because of their brevity, the audience forgives their failure to quantify, to explain, to defend.'[35]

The worrying thing about the Taxathon advertisements is that they were treated as acceptable. Thirty years earlier, National's 'dancing Cossack' advertisements had been controversial and widely discussed. The 1993 anti-MMP advertisements – with their black and white images of babies left crying and a strait-jacketed, faceless politician – also caused disquiet and debate. But in 2005 the advertisements were just clever, part of the 'successful' campaigning. A party could become government not because of its policies or candidates, but purely because it had the cleverest advertising people and the biggest budget.

A month before Ansell decided to return to advertising to help Brash, he published a book of poetry including a long fourteen-verse poem called 'Political careering'. Four verses can serve as a tribute to Brash's years as National Party leader. It is fitting that Ansell, who nearly got him into power, provides a well-crafted epitaph.

Wanna be a politician,
Follow me I'm on a mission,
Gotta get a strong position
On the party list.

Leader of the Opposition,
Keeper of a strong tradition
To articulate a vision
People can't resist.

One embattled politician,
I'm a picture of contrition,
Honestly to God I'm wishin'
I did not exist.

Soon-to-be ex-politician,
Step aside on one condition
'Leavin' of my own volition' –
Think you get the gist.[36]

CHAPTER 13

GO THE BLUE TEAM!
Lobbyists join the campaign

Early in election year a highly complimentary biography of Don Brash appeared, published by the reputable Penguin Books. As the *Sunday Star-Times* summarised it, the book found that Brash possessed 'gravitas... commanding self-assurance... a concern for all humanity, regardless of race, gender or class'; that he was 'unflappable under pressure', 'a perfectionist' with a 'first-class temperament'; that he was remarkable for his 'honesty, integrity, tenacity and sheer nerve'; and that he had a fetching sense of humour.[1]

Shortly before the book's release, the author Paul Goldsmith was selected as a National Party election candidate, raising questions about the independence of the biography. But Goldsmith assured the New Zealand Press Association that the book 'was not commissioned by the National Party' and would 'stand on its own merits'.[2] Goldsmith presented the biography as being his own initiative, though 'written with Don Brash's cooperation'. In the introduction Goldsmith thanked Brash for 'his trust in letting me see his papers and for his interviews'.[3]

This explanation was misleading. He had been offered the job of writing it by the National Party staff and they provided him with a prepared collection of papers for the purpose. They later checked and approved each page of the text he wrote, selected the photos and even signed off the things that would normally be the publisher's prerogative, such as the front cover and the back-cover blurb. It was, in other words, part of the party's election-year marketing activities. They just thought it would work better if this fact was not admitted to the public.

Goldsmith was not, however, strictly telling an untruth when he said the book was not commissioned by the National Party. The money to pay Goldsmith, though a contribution to the party, appears never to have gone through the party's accounts. Goldsmith was paid for this election project by some of National's wealthiest donors, in addition to their other contributions. It appears they cooperated in the fiction that this was an independent biography by paying the tens of thousands of dollars for writing the book directly to Goldsmith.

Goldsmith and the biography were an example of National's biggest advantage in the election campaign, which was that it had access to very large sums of money from business interests and extremely wealthy individual donors. Much of the rest of the book is about how they used unprecedentedly large sums of money and gained other types of assistance from the special interests that wanted a National government. The first big budget item in the election year was the biography.

The use of a biography to promote a politician was not a new idea. Journalist Vernon Wright published one about David Lange before the 1984 election. Eight months before the 2002 election, the Labour Party leader's media adviser Brian Edwards brought out a similarly uncritical biography of Helen Clark.[4] However, unlike Edwards, who was open about being a Clark supporter, Goldsmith did not declare that he was doing it for money and the National Party tried to hide its involvement.

The first sign of the biography is an email from Brash to Richard Long in May 2004. 'The book proposal from Willson Scott LOOKS quite good,' he wrote, referring to a Christchurch publisher. 'But you obviously know more about the quality of their work, and about what other options might be better.'[5]

Long had already moved on. 'Re the book,' he replied, 'I've subsequently talked to Paul Goldsmith, who is a known quantity, and who is putting something on paper for us. Shall we hold fire till then.' Goldsmith had earlier been press secretary for John Banks when he was a National Cabinet minister and later an Auckland PR consultant and supporter of the National Party. Long said that they should be careful not to let the project take up too much of Brash's time, pointing out that 'a huge amount of material has been documented already'.[6] Brash answered: 'I lean in the direction of using Goldsmith, though don't know really how he compares with the Christchurch option, or with somebody like a Michael Bassett'.[7]

They decided to give the job to Paul Goldsmith, with the payment organised from the National Party donors. Later that year, when National was considering a joint launch for the biography and fundraising event, Brash wrote to his colleagues that they might 'need to donate a couple of tickets to those who have funded the writing of the biography itself.... I'm not sure... that we should expect somebody who has contributed heavily to the writing of the book, and whom we expect to contribute substantially to campaign funds, to also pay $600 for a ticket to the launch.'[8] (Later they split the fundraiser from the book launch because they were having trouble selling tickets to the former and also, as Brash wrote, having 'the book launch become something we do with the rich and famous... is arguably exactly NOT the image we are trying to cultivate'.)[9]

Goldsmith was supplied with the already prepared materials and in July he began a series of interviews with Brash at his home in Auckland.[10] The idea was to produce the book for early the following year, so only a few weeks later Brash and the National Party staff began receiving draft chapters from Goldsmith for their 'perusal'. This went beyond checking accuracy – Goldsmith was, in effect, working for the National Party. But he had been well chosen. His drafts were so complimentary that Brash found little to change. 'Paul, I think all your changes are improvements,' he wrote about the final chapter, 'The Unfinished Story', which talked of Brash's 'honesty and credibility' and ended saying that 'most would acknowledge Don Brash is a true patriot'. 'I like the way the chapter now looks,' Brash said. 'Indeed, I do not have a single word I would change, though I would delete or add the odd comma!'[11]

By November 2004 Goldsmith was feeling sufficiently collaborative to offer Brash help with writing the Orewa welfare speech. Brash accepted his offer and sent him the draft. Goldsmith replied on 10 November 2004 with the draft 'Marked up [with] some ideas you might find useful'. He thought 'some of the policy is very exciting' and 'in my humble opinion, the welfare policy is the key to the election'.[12] He added some lines that made it through to the final version.[13]

During November Brash's staff spent a large amount of time gathering photographs and, with Brash, made the decisions about which ones would be included in the book. Brash wanted more pictures than Penguin was prepared to fund, so he personally paid for extra photographs to be published. Goldsmith wrote the back-cover blurb and checked it with Brash, then Brash and his staff were given the choice of which photograph to use for the front cover. When Penguin finished the layout of the front and back covers, they sent them by email to both Goldsmith and Brash's assistant Bryan Sinclair, saying, 'Could I have your sign-off today please?'[14] The publisher appears to have been increasingly aware that National was a partner in the project, but that was never declared in the book.

Once the book production was under way, the National Party team looked at how, in Brash's words, to use the biography 'as a significant marketing tool'.[15] Sinclair was concerned that if they did not get organised they would 'miss opportunities to effectively market "Brand Brash" via the book launch and subsequent sales campaign'. He spoke about this to Brash, who agreed to him 'picking up the reins' for promoting the book.[16] From then on Sinclair took over most organising for the book launch. He reported later that 'the budget side looks to be under control and it will all be catered, music, lighting etc.'[17]

Meanwhile, Goldsmith had written to Brash, concerned about how they handle the subject of whether National was really behind the book. 'I think we should think very carefully about how you want to handle the publicity around the book.' He liked the idea of a big launch in February or March 2005, but he was worried about how it would look if Brash did book signings. 'If you go around the country doing signing, then you're effectively saying it's "your" book – it is an authorised, or even "commissioned" biography.'[18] That is, of course, what it was. But they decided to avoid book signings and maintain the desired impression.

Goldsmith had a reason to be feeling sheepish about possible inferences that it was a commissioned book. On the same day as that email to Brash, Goldsmith informed Penguin that he had just been accepted as a National Party candidate for the elections. Sinclair wrote to Long, Keenan and press officer Jason Ede: 'I have been told by Penguin that a couple of editors have gone cold on the book since the Goldsmith candidacy was announced. This makes our jobs with this a bit harder.'[19] Long replied that he had 'warned the party and Goldsmith months ago that his candidacy would undermine the authority of the book and I urged him to hold off till next time'.[20]

When the time came to arrange publicity, Ede wrote: 'I don't think it would be too smart for the leader to be sending out releases about the book from this office (might be better coming from Penguin) since we are going to be marketing the book separately from the National Party'.[21] Richard Long responded, telling Sinclair that 'It would be good for the advisory and press release from the book launch to come from the publisher (even if written by you) so that it is clear that it doesn't come out of this office'. Long said that 'Don needs to be squeaky clean in this area' and, blithely ignoring the fact that he had helped arrange for the book to be commissioned in the first place, noted 'it's best that we are not seen to be promoting a commercial venture'.[22] Frantic work then began on promoting the venture.

Campaign manager Steven Joyce approached PR woman Jenny Raynish, a friend of the National Party. Raynish agreed to donate her company's time to prepare an email to go out from National to its supporters promoting the book. Joyce explained that they wanted the email to have a link through to the National Party website where people could both order the book and offer support to National. He sent her the Textor-inspired National Story so she could incorporate the agreed language into the mailout.[23] Her staff prepared the email, which was sent to about 31,000 email addresses on the day of the book launch, resulting in a large spike in visits to the National website over the following five days.[24]

The launch was arranged for early evening on 28 February 2005 at Unity Books in Auckland. Although it was nominally a Penguin book project, Sinclair made all the arrangements. The guest list of 60 fell into distinct groups. Brash had argued that, since the aim was marketing, the 'highest priority names' were the 'media and glitterati'.[25] There was a small number of each. PR man Greg Shand was present, invited because he had 'read [the] draft carefully'. Then there was a handful of friends and family of the writer and Brash, and a small number of National Party people. Brash's staff had been keen to have Katherine Rich present, but she declined firmly.[26] Finally, invitations had been sent to about a dozen of National's main donors, the unseen force within the party. Of this group, Alan Gibbs, Craig Heatley and Michael Horton turned up.

In a sense it was the donors' biography. It is not certain who paid Goldsmith to write it, but it is possible it was the National Party donors Doug Myers, Alan Gibbs, Craig Heatley and David Richwhite. When Goldsmith sent National a list of those he would like to be invited to the book launch, these four names came straight after his wife and parents and before his friends. He was 'not sure if the above 4 will be able to come, but need courtesy to invite'.[27] National's big donors even paid for the book launch. Goldsmith mentioned in his email that 'Rod Deane said he would contribute to the cost of the launch'.[28] Others did too.

The National Party records show that Sinclair got Brash's electorate secretary Anna Tripp to ask the catering company to send their invoice not to Penguin, nor the National Party, but to a company called Silverbeat.[29] Silverbeat was Bryan Sinclair's personal company, which he used for his marketing work before starting work for Brash. Sinclair had reported three weeks earlier that the budget side of the launch was under control, including catering. Insiders confirm that Sinclair arranged for the money from the National Party donors to be paid into his company accounts and that he then paid the book launch costs.[30]

After all that, the biography was only a partial success for the election-year marketing. It gained Brash a sympathetic article in *Women's Day* magazine and an interview on TVNZ's *Good Morning* programme, which the producer had promised Brash would be 'very very light and personal and will not mention much political stuff'.[31]

But other publicity was not so good. Steve Braunias, in the *Sunday Star-Times*, pointed out that Goldsmith, when asked about his National Party candidacy, had said that people know the difference between a good book and a bad book. 'Yes,' Braunias agreed. 'His book is so bad – so unquestioning, so puppy-eyed, so on side with its subject – that it hardly matters that Goldsmith has nailed his political colours to the mast.'[32] The *Dominion Post* ran excerpts from the book for three weeks, headed 'Days of our (leader's) lives', which highlighted odd personal insights about Brash from the book, such as his obsessive cleanliness and a period he spent living off meals of defrosted corned beef and Kentucky Fried Chicken.[33] John Campbell irritated the National media staff by instituting nightly readings of similar passages from the book on TV3's *Campbell Live*.

On 7 March, however, Don Brash received a phone call from columnist Colin James, who said he had just finished reading the book and thought it was 'very good'. Brash reported to Richard Long and Bryan Sinclair that James 'totally disagreed' with the journalists who had criticised the book as 'sycophantic' and 'said that to him it correctly described the Don Brash he had known for years'. He told Brash he had referred to the book in his column for the *New Zealand Herald* the next day. Brash forwarded his email, with James's comments, to Goldsmith, saying, 'Take a bow Paul!'[34]

In an interview with his local Remuera newspaper, in an article headed 'Speech inspires Brash book', Goldsmith explained what had led him to write the biography. 'With the dramatic success of National at the start of last year,' he said, referring to the Orewa race speech, 'I thought there was something unusual going on. I wanted to get to the bottom of what was driving Don Brash.' He approached him 'and he was comfortable with me doing it. We worked up a pretty good relationship.'[35]

The biography is just one example of the ways National worked to arrange third-party publicity leading up to the election. 'Third party' is the term used by the public relations profession for getting seemingly independent individuals or organisations to say and do things that support their clients. The target of the next third-party campaign was 'punters' – in this case literally the punters who follow horse racing plus others involved in the racing industry.

National collaborated with racing industry lobbyists to arrange extensive pro-National publicity aimed at the punters in the weeks before the election. Much of it should have been declared to the Electoral Commission but was not. The publicity was not anonymous but otherwise it had many features in common with the Exclusive Brethren advertising campaign.

National Party racing spokesperson, MP Lindsay Tisch, had been liaising with the racing industry over a long period and had written a policy for the party that was identical to what the racing industry lobby wanted. For years there had been an anomaly that allowed casinos to pay only a small fraction of the tax paid by other forms of gambling. National's new policy, rather than raising the casino taxes to match the rest, was to give the racing industry the same extremely low tax rate – meaning tens of millions of dollars less tax to pay on gambling income each year. Racing industry interests were willing to spend a lot of money and organise publicity nationwide to support their campaign for lower taxes. National was keen to be the beneficiary of this effort.

Since the beginning of election year a racing lobby group called Fairtax had been lobbying the political parties and preparing its election campaign. Already, they had gained national exposure with signs saying 'Fairtax' stencilled on the rumps of racing horses. The group was chaired by a well-known race horse owner and bloodstock agent, Rob McAnulty, and was made up of racing industry people. Their political leverage came from the claim that they could swing large numbers of ordinary punters behind a party that promised the lower tax rate. 'If you get the punters on side,' spokesperson Mary McCarty said publicly, 'we're talking 100,000 plus votes.' [36]

National and other parties announced their policies at a 16 June 2005 meeting at Te Rapa racecourse in Hamilton arranged by the New Zealand Thoroughbred Association. To National's horror, McAnulty told the meeting that 'the racing industry should block vote for New Zealand First'.[37] (New Zealand First had long had a pro-racing industry policy.) Brash was furious. He shot off an email to Lindsay Tisch.

'Lindsay, what the hell does this idiot mean "use your party vote for NZ First"? Does the numb-skull not understand how MMP works?' He said: 'Do you need to talk to him, or should I??'[38] It is not clear which of them spoke to McAnulty, or what was said, but a few days later Richard Long wrote to Bryan Sinclair asking him to 'please talk to Lindsay about a Racing Industry offer to help us win the election!'[39] This was the beginning of intense contact between National and the racing lobby representatives.

Once again, Brash used Sinclair to handle sensitive private negotiations on his behalf.

Something had changed almost overnight in McAnulty's attitude to National. The day after Long's email, Sinclair contacted Brash's appointment secretary. 'Anne, please make a tentative note to have Don in Christchurch on Friday August 12th (to present the Mercedes Benz Horse of the Year award). This is the major event on the thoroughbred calendar. Details to be confirmed following my meeting with them.' He also asked her 'to have Don in Hastings on Saturday 28 August to present the winners prize for the "Fair Tax Stakes" (formerly the Mudgway Stakes). This is arguably the biggest event on the racing calendar, and is being renamed this year to help our cause. Details on this also to follow my meeting.' He explained that 'both these form part of our racing industry schmooze. They don't want the PM this year, they want Don.'[40] He then wrote to Tisch and Long to let them know he was 'meeting with Rob McAnulty at his home in Auckland tomorrow [about] their strategy. Will update you as things progress.'[41]

Meanwhile, campaign manager Steven Joyce was also having meetings with the Fairtax lobby. According to insiders, Joyce offered to help Fairtax prepare an extensive direct mail campaign to different racing networks. Apparently Fairtax had accepted an offer from Joyce that he would write their letters for them, targeting race horse breeders, owners and racing club members – in addition to messages sent to Fairtax's own members. Fairtax would have its name on all these communications and National would not have to pay anything. The racing lobby representatives said privately that they had up to $100,000 to pay for the election activities. A lot of these plans were finalised at a private meeting between Joyce and the Fairtax group on or about 1 July 2005.[42]

Altogether the potential racing lobby contribution to the National election campaign was very substantial. It combined direct mail to thousands of people working within the racing industry with publicity at race courses aimed at hundreds of thousands of punters – most of them exactly the low- to middle-income conservative Labour and New Zealand First party-type voters that National wanted to reach.

And National made a very specific suggestion to Fairtax about its messaging. The proposal put privately to the racing industry lobbyists in a series of meetings was that the crucial words they should use were 'Change the Government'. The National Party staff explained that if Fairtax said 'Change the Government', then National could complement this in its own publicity by saying 'and the only way to change the government is to vote National'.[43] This was the same slogan that the Exclusive Brethren, in their advertising to win party votes for National, chose for their brochures. In the end the racing lobby preferred to keep its Fairtax message but they arranged a formula of words that just as effectively linked the Fairtax messages to voting National.

Brash was also having private meetings with the racing industry representatives about how they could help the National campaign. One such meeting was at the Te Pania Hotel in Napier, where Brash met John McGifford and Jeff Drinkwater of the Hawke's Bay Racing Club and race sponsor Wayne Mudgway on the evening of 13 July 2005. Mudgway was sponsor of the $200,000 prize money Mudgway Partsworld Stakes, which he had allowed to be renamed as the Fair Tax Stakes for election year. The purpose of the meeting was 'to run through plan for [the] Fair Tax Stakes race on Saturday 27 August'.[44] Drinkwater wrote the following day to say 'the guarantee of tax parity given by Don is tremendous.... Please be assured, we will be spreading the positive message given by National.'[45]

Sinclair contacted the National Party head office staff on behalf of Brash to explain what input was expected from them in support of the racing lobby activities at the 27 August race meeting. 'Don, after his own meeting with Hawke's Bay Racing Club officials last month, is very keen to ensure that the opportunities that flow from this race meeting are maximised.' Although Steven Joyce 'no doubt has it in hand', for 'ease of reference, here is a summary of what we are supposedly supplying them. My understanding is that this was all agreed by Lindsay and Steven at the Ellerslie meeting they had with the FairTax guys recently.'[46]

The racing lobby's plan was to use 27 August as the occasion for every possible bit of promotion of the National Party. Sinclair's list gives an exact record of the level of collaboration to achieve this goal. This was a deliberate effort to gain votes for National, and it appears to breach electoral laws, as will be seen in Chapter 15.

First, it was agreed the National Party staff would design a full-page ad to be placed in the race book for the day and supply it to the Fairtax group. Sinclair said, 'note, ad placement is being paid for by Fairtax'. Second, National would produce and print thousands of copies of a pro-National postcard containing both Fairtax and National Party messages. Fairtax would pay to have these handed out to everyone attending the races. Third, National would supply an electronic slide saying 'Vote National For Fair Tax', which Fairtax would arrange to be shown on 'the on-course big screen'. Fourth, 'Party vote logos/correct colours [would be] supplied by National to Fairtax for winning post signage and miscellaneous signage' around the race grounds. Fifth, National would provide '"Message from Don Brash" copy for [racing newspaper] Friday Flash front page'. Finally, there was the 'Direct mail item, supplied by National to Fairtax for mail-out to their database (Steven [Joyce] was negotiating arrangements for this).'[47]

National Party operations manager Jo de Joux replied that she had 'now had a chance to talk to Steven' about these arrangements. She confirmed that all of them were what Joyce had arranged, except that the party had 'no budget' for the postcard. It was too close to its maximum election spending level. So instead the postcard was designed by the graphic designer in Brash's parliamentary office,[48] and printing was paid for by the taxpayer from Brash's parliamentary office budget.[49] There are rules about not being allowed to use parliamentary money for publications 'with the purpose of supporting the election of any person'.[50] Given the context, this was obviously the purpose of the postcards (like all the other materials being arranged). The race ground had various 'Vote Fairtax' banners and other publicity materials; the Parliamentary Services-funded postcard said 'National stands for Fair Tax' on one side and, on the other side, a list of pro-racing industry policies that 'the next National Government' would implement. It ended with the words 'Make it happen'. The message was clear.

Only the month before, Brash had criticised the Labour government's use of public money to promote itself. 'In recent years, all political parties have pushed the boundaries on the use of taxpayer-funded advertising,' he said. 'The time has come for someone to take the lead in pushing the boundaries back. My personal view is that, if political parties want to tell the public to vote for them, they should be using their own money to do it.'[51] When the National leader's office designer saw a copy of a Fairtax cartoon showing a horse race between Brash and Helen Clark – Brash riding a horse with 'Fair Tax' written on its rear as he crossed the finishing line first – he said ironically, 'I guess the National "brand" is being pushed to its limit anyway so why not push it over the limit to meet its doom?'[52]

The combined effect of all the publicity materials on 27 August was a huge party vote National promotion. All the Fairtax messages on banners, signs and the horses themselves – plus the race name itself – linked with the postcards and banners saying 'National Stands for Fair Tax'. The combination of large banners saying 'Vote for Fair Tax' and others saying 'National stands for Fair Tax' and 'Vote National For Fair Tax' were saying 'Vote National' loud and clear. On top of this there were overtly pro-National billboards and the race book advertisement; and in addition to the Fair Tax Stakes, the final race of the day, at 2.44pm, had been renamed the Party Vote National Stakes.

Although the banners and other materials saying 'Vote for Fair Tax' did not mention National, there was no doubt that this third-party advertising was encouraging votes for the National Party. The organisers also arranged for National to bring a large contingent of MPs and the party president to be visible with Brash during the day as special guests of the race organisers.

Sinclair had written to all National MPs saying 'the Leader encourages you to rework your travel plans and attend this event if at all possible.... A very big effort has been made by the Fairtax group to secure prime exposure for the National Party... [It] promises to be a big campaign event for the National Party.'[53] Besides the thousands of people at the racecourse, the races (with banners placed strategically in the background) were broadcast on television and into all TABs around the country.

The value of the advertising to National's election campaign was enormous. But this is what the electoral laws are for: to stop vested interests helping a particular political party by supplying undeclared election advertising on its behalf. But as with the Exclusive Brethren, everything was arranged privately so National could retain the appearance of distance from what was going on.

The racing lobby invited Brash and his colleagues to other race meetings as well and the Fairtax publicity campaign continued strongly. The direct mail advertising also went ahead, as did full-page advertising in racing industry publications. For instance, the *Harness Racing Weekly* and the bi-monthly *Pacing and Trotting Guide* ($1250 per ad) carried advertisements headed 'Christian Cullen Supports Proactive Racing Policy'. Christian Cullen's owner, Ian Dobson, was quoted in the advertisement saying that since the famous race horse was not old enough to vote for himself, he would have to vote on his behalf. Written in bold across the bottom of the advertisement were the words 'I'm backing a winner, by Voting for National'.[54] Although this was clearly political advertising, there was no name or address to show who had authorised it.

Rob McAnulty emailed Sinclair nine days before the election, describing their plans for the last weekend. 'We will have the Fairtax message out big and bold this weekend,' he said. 'Trots at Auckland on Friday night, gallops at Ellerslie on Saturday, when the favourite for New Zealand's longest race the Great Northern Steeplechase will carry the Fairtax colors, watch the TV1 & TV3 news that night. Also signage at those two meetings stating Vote for Fairtax. The trots or Harness meeting at Methven will also have Fairtax colors and signage for their Sunday meeting.... Good luck next week, we are in there beavering away.'[55] Fairtax secretary Jo Davis wrote to National MP Lindsay Tisch 'and team', predicting they would all be celebrating on 17 September. 'Go the Blue Team!'[56]

The racing lobby, like all such groups, insisted publicly that it was non-partisan. So did the right-wing thinktank, the Maxim Institute. From the outside, its election year activities appeared independent and relatively neutral, despite the organisation's obvious conservative politics. It is only when the hidden collaboration with National is examined that this looks like yet another effort aimed at changing the government.

Maxim had been established in 2001, based on the model of right-wing United States thinktanks. It had Auckland and Christchurch offices, a large staff and very large privately funded budget. Since forming, Maxim had energetically opposed the Labour-led government over a series of issues, such as the Civil Union Bill, and upped its effort still further for election year. It is unlikely that its conservative backers would be willing to spend large sums of money on politically neutral election year activities. There were two parts to Maxim's plans: release of a series of reports on education, strongly attacking Labour's policies; and an extensive campaign encouraging people to vote and educating them about their voting decision.

It was clear from the start that the education project was intended to influence the election. Sinclair reported on the project to Steven Joyce, Peter Keenan and Richard Long at the end of March 2005: 'I have been meeting over recent months with Maxim in Auckland, at Don's request'. He explained that the education project was 'designed to grab headlines and make education a big election year priority'. A Maxim press release on the project said 'Political parties that ignore what parents want' – meaning parties that ignored what Maxim said parents want – 'will face the music on Election Day'.[57]

Sinclair reported that Maxim would be 'releasing four research reports to the media, boiled down into saleable chunks, starting at the end of April, as scene setting material for the election. I recently gave Peter [Keenan] a summary of their education policy points and they are almost entirely consistent with our own,' he said.[58] 'Needless to say it would be very advantageous for us to work in harmony with their initiatives in this area in order to see biggest (and most sustained) bang for our buck in the education area.' He emphasised that the project would work best if it looked independent from National. 'This does not, of course, mean that we do things hand in hand with Maxim. They are well aware of our need to maintain distance.'

Brash had recently met with Maxim's director Bruce Logan and been briefed on the plans – referring to a meeting in Christchurch on the morning of Friday, 4 March 2005.[59] Shortly before Logan had showed his support for Brash in a *New Zealand Herald* article defending the Orewa welfare speech,[60] and during this meeting he offered 'to put together a meeting of up to 1000 "flammable" parents on the North Shore of Auckland', so Brash could present National's education policies to a large and sympathetic audience.[61]

Two months later, in May 2005, Maxim prepared to release the first of four education reports. Policy manager Nicki Taylor offered an advance copy to National and proposed that they meet to discuss their planned communications strategy. She and managing director Greg Fleming would be more than happy to brief the National team and 'talk about how we can best support you in terms of giving you profile, talk about media angles, etc'.[62]

Maxim even delayed the release of their report after hearing the National staff would be busy on the budget so 'we can have the briefing for you guys a bit later when you are not dog tired after the budget brouhaha. It really doesn't make a lot of difference to us when we release the first report,' Taylor wrote.[63] 'I hope the budget goes well for you guys,' she signed off a subsequent email.[64]

Maxim arranged a separate briefing for National's education spokesperson, Bill English, so that they could 'confirm exact details of [National] press releases, questions in the house, tabling of reports and which stories he can use at which time'.[65] None of this collaboration between a lobby group and political party is exceptional, but it shows that Maxim's protestations about being non-partisan were not sincere – and sets the scene for the institute's supposedly neutral education campaign in election year.

This project took up a large part of Maxim's $1,000,000-plus budget in staff time, polling, consultants and production. Whose political agenda was at work? The answer comes from a mention in the education reports that Maxim had begun the research in 'late 2003'. By chance, the leaked National Party papers used for this book included a November 2003 email from Richard Poole, of the Business Roundtable-backed October 2000 'brain drain' campaign, who was working for the Maxim Institute on the early stages of fundraising and strategy for a major education project. He said the people behind the project were 'Peter Shirtcliffe, John Graham, Michael Friedlander and Michael Whittaker'.[66]

John Graham was an obvious person to be involved. He had spent his career in education, most notably as head of Auckland Grammar, had helped to found Maxim and was chair of its board of advisers. He was also a political supporter of Don Brash and had sent him a congratulatory message when he became National leader, offering 'any support' he could give, 'in educational planning or otherwise'.[67]

Peter Shirtcliffe and Michael Friedlander were something quite different. Friends of Brash, radical right activists and two of the main funders of the National Party, they came from very different political backgrounds to Maxim's managing director, evangelical Christian Greg Fleming. Their presence suggests an alliance of the conservative Christians who started Maxim and the not noticeably Christian free market right of the 1980s and 1990s reforms. These people were not organising and funding a major research project out of academic interest. Shirtcliffe had fought and funded the anti-MMP campaigns and similar very focused political efforts. Friedlander had been a major ACT Party backer. Just like the racing lobby, they were keen to get a National government elected so it would implement the policies, including education, that they wanted.

The Maxim education reports were released in the last four months before the election, on 29 May, 28 June and 4 September 2005 and, as predicted, each dovetailed neatly with the education policies upon which National was campaigning. This appears to have been their purpose. Brash referred to the reports, without saying they were from Maxim, in his main televised election broadcast. 'Helen Clark has suggested this election will be about trust,' he said. 'Well, New Zealanders trusted Helen Clark to fix the education system and we've had two reports on that system in the last month or two which really indicate that the Labour Government has totally failed in that area.'[68]

During election year National was talking about being the party of 'mainstream New Zealanders' and its education policies being for the children, 'not the interest groups'.[69] So it is interesting to see where the Maxim/National type of education policies were most strongly supported. When Brash gave his long-planned address on education policy, 'Excellence in Education', on 13 April 2005, the speech had been sent in advance to a select group of organisations and individuals who had been asked to chime in with supportive public comments. On the list were the Business Roundtable and its Education Forum, Independent Schools (the private school association), the VisionSchools group (previously known as the Association of Bulk Funded Schools), Business New Zealand and the Maxim Institute.[70] In other words, mostly the private education lobby. The only non-partisan group was the School Trustees Association. Don Brash had sent an email to the National Party press staff suggesting one more name for the list – Peter Shirtcliffe: 'I have sent him a copy myself and got back a very positive response already'.[71]

Indeed, the Business Roundtable's Education Forum policy adviser, Norman LaRocque, had helped to write the speech. Brash mentioned in an email earlier that year that 'it was decided some time ago that Peter [Keenan] would work on an education speech, in conjunction with Norman LaRocque' and others. After the speech had been delivered, Sinclair contacted LaRocque on Brash's behalf to say 'he was very hopeful that you personally would approve of it, and NZBR too.... Many thanks from Don for your own contribution to this – your thinking has had a very direct effect.'[72] (The interesting correspondence between LaRoque and Sinclair is included in the notes.[73]) Sinclair wrote to Brash: 'Norman likes it. That is good.' Brash replied: 'Yeah, very pleasing indeed'.[74] Both National and Maxim's education policies were being pushed by the same grouping of lobbyists.

Maxim's main election year collaboration with National was its NZVotes voter education campaign. This was centred on the nzvotes.co.nz website – a 'one stop shop for voters offering objective information and not pushing any political agenda'[75] – with a large advertising budget to attract voters to the site. Maxim received an award for its election year projects (education and NZVotes) from the United States Atlas Economic Research Foundation, the thinktank upon which Maxim models itself (Maxim staff regularly attend Atlas conferences, including one where Greg Fleming spoke on 'Successful Think Tank Efforts to Communicate the Message of Liberty to Sceptical Audiences').[76] The Atlas Foundation promotes free market policies and devotes itself to encouraging the establishment of similar thinktanks around the world.[77] Maxim won its Templeton Freedom Prize for Initiative in Public Relations for the 'innovative advocacy campaign, New Zealand Votes',[78] but the question is, what was the advocacy campaign advocating?

In November 2004 the Maxim employee in charge of the election project, Scott McMurray, who had worked in the National Party research unit for five years in the 1990s, contacted Brash's office to suggest a meeting to discuss the plans for their 'major election project'. After Christmas delays, Sinclair replied for Brash, saying that he would be 'very keen to meet to discuss the nzvotes stuff as soon as possible'. Sinclair said, 'I have some thoughts on this, and it is certainly timely.'[79] McMurray replied that there would be 'fresh coffee and donuts' for Sinclair's visit to the Maxim headquarters on 14 March 2005.[80] Between the invitation and the meeting, Brash received an email from his friend, and former ACT Party candidate, Michael Coote, who regularly sent him advice. This letter, which Brash referred to Sinclair, seems to have cemented Sinclair's thoughts.

Coote's email drew Brash's attention to the large numbers of expatriate New Zealanders entitled to vote in the election, many of whom he suspected would lean towards National, and questioned what the party was doing to appeal to them. 'I wonder if National has developed any election strategy to alert at least the most significant concentrations of these people... to their voting rights and the correct procedures they need to follow to get their votes collected and counted as valid?' He pointed out that 'there seem to be a few hundred thousand votes going with ex-pat kiwis, which could mean a lot of extra party votes for National'. He recommended 'an advertising campaign in those cities around the world (probably primarily in the UK and Australia) to have ex-pats register to vote and send them their instructions on how to do so'.[81] This was the idea Sinclair took to Maxim.

There is no record of the coffee and donuts meeting, but a few days later Sinclair followed it up with a letter to McMurray. 'Further to our discussions, attached is a summary of a more weighty document on the ex-pat community' which highlighted what 'we' would need to do to target this group.[82] His paper, called 'Expatriate Add On', said that 'anecdotal evidence suggests that expatriate New Zealanders have a strong interest in the values and messages espoused by centre right political parties'. By far the biggest numbers were in Australia and Britain – amounting to over eight electorates worth of votes. He suggested adding extra pages onto the Maxim NZVotes website with information for expats and then advertise in key publications in these countries to generate traffic to the website.[83] Sinclair was proposing that Maxim take on the job of encouraging the votes of these supposedly centre right-leaning expatriates.

McMurray replied to him a couple of hours later. 'I am now building into our budgets some decent exposure in Australia and the UK.' He signed off his email saying, 'Back to putting the frighteners up the [Labour] government on hate speech.'[84] Shortly after receiving this, Sinclair wrote back to Michael Coote. 'Michael, Don has asked me to reply to you on this expat stuff. There are a couple of initiatives occurring outside of the Party to generate interest from the expat community, including encouraging them to enrol and to subsequently vote. We will be discreetly supporting these initiatives.' It was 'more efficient' to have these done externally than to 'initiate them from scratch from within'. He assured Coote that 'the suggestions you make are very consistent with where I understand these external initiatives will lead, including the advertising side of things'.[85] Coote replied that he thought expats would be 'more attuned to what National is trying to do than sympathetic to the socialist ostriches and their various lobby group leeches.... Cheers and death to socialism!'

Having got this in motion, Sinclair reported on the NZVotes initiative to the National campaign strategy team. The aim of the website, which would be 'extensively marketed', was 'to encourage voter turnout and to ensure more "informed" voting'. 'I have reviewed most aspects of the site, and I have offered a number of suggestions to them.' He explained his suggestion of 'an Expatriate New Zealander add-on' to 'target the message to expat Kiwis... the site will now be marketed in targeted publications in Sydney, Brisbane, Melbourne and London also'. Maxim later said, in response to a query, that it 'did not specifically target expatriates with any direct advertising',[86] so if this advertising went ahead, it may have been funded separately by some of National's big donors. Sinclair said that Maxim had also given National 'a head start on other parties in collating information to supply to nzvotes.org.nz'.[87]

This correspondence leaves no doubt about the Maxim–National collaboration, but it is still not clear what had moved Maxim to spend very large sums of money on general voter education within New Zealand. Many months later, when Maxim was approaching candidates from other parties, telling them that the NZVotes project was 'non-partisan and aims to present information in an objective and impartial manner', they said they wanted to 'reduce the staggering figures which have found that nearly half of voters did not know they had two votes on election day'.[88] The website, which contained lists of candidates and policies supplied by each party, did appear neutral, but this comment about people not understanding MMP voting hints at the underlying thinking.

The website and associated advertising were not the only parts of the NZVotes campaign. Maxim had paid the charismatic Christian Family Television Network to produce 500 three-minute DVDs that were sent free of charge to selected churches and 'community groups' to play to their congregations and members. According to Maxim, these DVDs explained MMP and 'encourage[d] people to make sure their vote is not discarded'.[89] This may be the concern that prompted Maxim to organise the NZVotes campaign.

Following the 2002 election, conservative Christian groups had been very aware that many of their supporters had voted for parties, such as Christian Heritage, with 27,492 votes, that did not make it above the 5 per cent threshold and so gained no seats in Parliament. These were the 'discarded' votes. Then there were other conservative Christian votes that went to United Future, only to have that party go into relatively ineffectual coalition with Labour. Certainly the Maxim NZVotes' 'key message' was 'know what you are voting for and make your vote count'. As Fleming said, they 'did not want a repeat of last election, where over 99,000 votes were discarded'.[90]

Maxim disseminated this message through conservative Christian media, such as Vision Network and Radio Rhema, and offered editorials to other publications saying, 'A vote for a third party is a wasted vote. It is not only a wasted vote, it is actually a vote for a party you may not like on the basis that any party that doesn't make the 5% threshold (or win a seat) has its vote redistributed among the parties that do cross the threshold.'[91] Not voting for the third parties implied voting for National. Brash's appointment diary shows him appearing weekly on Radio Rhema and doing the rounds of other conservative Christian media.

Maxim also organised 29 Political Forums around the country, which about 6200 people attended to hear the local candidates speak and have a briefing from the Maxim staff on effective voting.[92] The *New Zealand Herald* described how meetings began with the national anthem and reported that United Future and National got the biggest cheers and Labour, the Greens and Progressive Party the biggest boos. It sounded very much as if the meetings were drawing out the conservative Christian audiences at whom the vote wasting message was aimed. The *Nelson Mail* reported that candidates got only two minutes to speak and Maxim specified these speeches should be on 'compulsory education, tax and welfare spending'. Then the Maxim representative gave a long presentation on voting before 45 minutes were allowed for questions to the candidates.[93]

The largest of the meetings, with 800 people present, was held in Epsom at the Greenlane Christian Centre, one of the most politically active evangelical churches in New Zealand, which Maxim managing director Greg Fleming attends. The candidates spoke in front of a backdrop of New Zealand flags. Ensuring this congregation voted correctly was consistent with the strategy of concentrating the conservative Christian vote on National.

The NZVotes campaign is reminiscent of an earlier campaign called VOTE (Voters Organisation for Tactical Education). The VOTE campaign, a response to 'widespread misunderstanding about MMP', had the goal of informing voters that they had two votes and would throw one of them away if they did not vote tactically. They used large newspaper advertisements to spread this message, insisting that these were 'educational, not political'. VOTE spokesperson Alex Swney was adamant the campaign was 'politically neutral' and that they had 'no political affiliations'. Specifically, he denied suggestions from journalists of a link to ACT, which had long been pushing the same message.[94] Whether or not he was then involved in ACT, a couple of years later Swney was being referred to openly in the *New Zealand Herald* as an 'ACT party activist' and at the following election he was the ACT Party's candidate in the Tamaki electorate.

As it turned out, the United Future vote collapsed and, as Maxim said in a press release after the election, the number of wasted votes to small third parties had dropped from 4.9 per cent in the 2002 election to 1.3 per cent in 2005. Fleming said that this had been 'one of Maxim's objectives in participating in the build-up to the 2005 election'.[95] It is impossible to say how much effect the Maxim campaign would have had on this.

None of this, of course, is as dramatic as the Exclusive Brethren advertising campaign or as blatant as the racing lobby campaign. But the involvement with Maxim was still a major election activity. Sinclair told the National campaign strategy team how much money Maxim was spending on its election year activities. 'As an indication (and this is entirely confidential), they presently have a $800,000 confirmed budget for advertising alone, to market nzvotes.org.nz in New Zealand. Further advertising budget for the overseas ads is being confirmed.'[96] Sinclair also reported that Maxim had 'recently upped staffing numbers and have nearly all of their 22 strong team (15 Auckland based) working almost solely on these two projects [the education campaign and nzvotes.org] at the moment'.[97] Approached during the research for this book, Maxim said that its NZVotes project had cost $135,000,[98] to which must be added a share of the other staff's salaries and expenses. It seems, therefore, that Sinclair overestimated the amount but, together with the education reports, it still adds up to a large sum.

Richard Poole later told Sinclair he was working with Maxim to approach some 'good old donors' to fund the overseas advertising – one of whom may have been Diane Foreman, whom Poole met about the project on 15 April 2005.[99] The presence of Shirtcliffe, Friedlander, Poole and possibly Foreman around the major Maxim election year projects suggests that the thinktank was in part being used as a new front for this familiar grouping of right-wing activists.

The NZ Votes project was co-ordinated by a former National Party staff member who liaised with the current National Party staff throughout. Overall it seems that, like the Exclusive Brethren and racing lobby, the aim was to change the government – a government that Maxim had been vigorously fighting over a series of issues ever since it formed four years earlier. In closely fought elections, moving even 2 or 3 per cent of the vote could be crucial to determining the government. Moving a small percentage of the vote in National's favour would probably have been seen as good value for money by the donors who financed Maxim's election activities.

Maxim publicises some of its donors, but those who matter most are not usually acknowledged. The unnamed donors are described vaguely as 'a clutch of retired and semi-retired businessmen',[100] which certainly includes Peter Shirtcliffe and Michael Friedlander and probably other influential and anonymous National Party donors.

As usual, National's links to the Maxim projects were kept secret and the Maxim staff stuck firmly to the line that they were being non-partisan. National was also careful to avoid being associated publicly with the thinktank. When *Sunday Star-Times* reporter Ruth Laugesen contacted National about an election feature on moral issues, Richard Long sent a note around Brash's staff saying, 'we wouldn't want to over egg the links to Maxim'.[101]

Anonymous political donors, with hidden motives, do not fit comfortably in a democratic society. The next chapter reveals, for the first time, many of the anonymous donors behind the National Party. These invisible political players tried to guarantee a National victory by providing it with the biggest election budget ever seen in a New Zealand election.

CHAPTER 14

THE INVISIBLE HANDS
Money in politics

A short article in Wellington's main newspaper in early 2006, headed 'Big money backed up National's campaign', reported that the party 'poured more than $2.1 million into its election campaign, more than twice its 2002 budget and the clearest sign big-money backers have flocked back to the party under leader Don Brash.'[1] But it could only be a 'sign' as no details were available. The article was relegated to page five. A subsequent news story reported that National received twice the declarable donations in the election year as Labour – $1.88 million to $930,000 – but again there was no detail.[2] If journalists ask political parties for information about who is providing the large sums to fund their campaigns, and the nature of the relationships with those donors, they are politely told it is none of their business.

Politicians and party officials have come up with an outstandingly absurd excuse to explain why there is no need for public declaration of such donors' names. Such people do not give their money in order to gain influence, they insist, but merely as a contribution to 'democracy'. The parties stick firmly to this lame explanation because to admit otherwise would sound bad and they want the money the donors are offering. And they need everyone else to go along with the fiction. Otherwise the current system of faceless donors funding democratic elections is indefensible.

Back in 1852, when New Zealand first started to hold elections, the richer citizens really did decide the government. The privilege of voting was only for wealthier men owning or renting sufficient property, and some particularly wealthy men had more than one vote. But the early settlers and gold miners objected to importing British-style politics based on wealth and class. In 1879 all men got the vote and in 1893 all women, establishing the principle of one person, one vote.

Straight away the authorities recognised that, to protect the integrity of the electoral system, they needed to ensure that the candidates with the most money could not spend their way to power. In 1895 the Corrupt Practices Prevention Amendment Act imposed limits on the amount a candidate could spend and required a post-election declaration listing the candidate's election expenditure and the sources of their funding – with no anonymous donations allowed.[3]

This principle was confirmed by the Royal Commission on the Electoral System in 1986, which said that 'if elections are to be fair and our democracy is to prosper, it is important that the effects of [economic] inequality are minimised'.[4] The commission recommended that there should be full disclosure of all major donors to political parties, which would 'give valuable information to voters about the character of the parties' and 'provide healthy confirmation that political parties and candidates are not dominated by big business'. The commissioners stated: 'we believe that these considerations over-ride any right large donors may claim to privacy' and proposed that any donations received anonymously or through 'front' organisations (such as private trusts) should have to be returned to the donor or, if that was not possible, passed to the Electoral Commission.[5]

Unfortunately, the subsequent electoral donation law was written by the same politicians who wanted the money that big business could provide. They ignored the recommendations and produced the present mess of anonymous and third-party election funding.

The power of the big donors is evident from the National Party's election budgets. The party spent $1.9 million in 1996, $1.6 million in 1999, $1.1 million in 2002 and over $2.1 million in 2005. The huge dip in 2002 was the result of a financial boycott of the party by the big donors, who were unimpressed with the centrist policies of then leader Bill English. As we have seen, Don Brash won the party leadership the following year in part because he said the donors were backing him. It is worth repeating what he told his colleagues, in the privacy of the 28 October 2003 caucus meeting, about what he would 'bring to the table as leader'.

'The business community can't give us enough votes to win, but [they] can provide us with money. As you and I both know, the Party is currently very short of money, with no obvious willingness on the part of those who could do so to write out big cheques. We need money badly. Indeed, without a substantial injection of funds in the near future, we are in big trouble. I believe that attracting that money would be substantially easier with me as leader.'[6] Minutes later he was voted leader. A couple of news articles quoted English supporters complaining about the influence of big donors in his election, but no one had any way of knowing who those donors were and therefore whether it was desirable that those people had so much influence over the selection of a possible prime minister. National's 2005 election campaign manager, Steven Joyce, began working full time for the party as general manager in April 2003. One of his first jobs was to review the party finances and figure out how to lift their donations from the 2002 low point. He presented his conclusions to the National Party board in August 2003.[7]

In a section called 'Funding Imperatives', Joyce noted the falling funds for the 1996, 1999 and 2002 elections and said that 'given the relative successes of the three campaigns, a budget of $2 million at least seems an appropriate target for 2005'. But that was just for the campaign period. He said, 'it has become apparent that under MMP the lead-up for the campaign is just as important as the campaign itself.... It is imperative that National maintain a high level of activity and build its polling share during the next two years *prior to* the commencement of the campaign proper.' He estimated this would require a further $400,000 of campaigning money each year.

Joyce concluded that, before the election, 'we need to look at raising about $2.8 million dollars from fundraising activities, over and above electorate levies and the President's appeal'.[8] This would be achieved by targeting different types of supporters in different ways. Most important were about a dozen very wealthy 'high value' donors. Then there were a set of 'medium value' donors (businesses and wealthy individuals) and last what he called the 'low value donors'.

A clear hierarchy was apparent, in which donor levels and their influence were linked. In terms of money given and how seriously they were taken by the National Party leadership, the three groups were like first class, business class and economy on an aircraft. The wealthy donors did not need to be members of the party but would have a high level of influence.[9] Low level donors mostly referred to the party membership and electorate organisations, who contributed by paying their subscriptions, arranging electorate fundraising events and being targeted once each year by the President's Appeal fundraising letter, but in practice they had minimal influence. This is not the basis for a democratic organisation.

When Brash was elected as leader later that year, the first priority was wooing the higher value donors. This began three weeks after the coup with a special dinner party on Monday, 17 November 2003 at the home of Jenny Gibbs in Auckland's Paratai Drive. When Peter Keenan began work for Brash soon after he advised Brash that it was 'critically' important that he 'find the time to make a funding pitch to wealthy supporters'. This, he argued, was 'a hundred times more important than us inching our poll ratings up 1–3% at the moment'.[10]

Brash and Keenan made this a priority when they travelled overseas a few months later, in June 2004. During three days in London, they met two potential high value donors and other medium value donors. First they were hosted at a French restaurant in Chelsea by former New Zealand beer baron Doug Myers, who used the occasion to introduce them to some of his free market political associates. On the evening of 8 June 2004 they met another super-wealthy expatriate, Alan Gibbs, at a dinner organised by PR consultant David Broome.[11] At a third meal they met with an old workmate of Keenan's from CS First Boston, Russia-based New Zealander Stephen Jennings, who donated $20,000 to the party.[12] *New Zealand Herald* journalist Fran O'Sullivan subsequently wrote that the trip was 'said to have levered open a few more significant wallets', including money to fund the election billboard campaign.[13]

As the National Party donors are documented in the coming pages, the important question to ask is whether this feels like a one-person, one-vote system (nowadays two votes each under MMP). These few hundred people – and in particular the dozen or so high value donors – had a far greater influence on the result of the 2005 election than did their individual votes, which together amounted to only about a fiftieth of one percent (0.02 per cent) of the 2,286,190 eligible votes cast.

The first level of medium donors were those invited to attend a series of special corporate fundraising dinners held in the main centres. These were aimed at businesspeople willing to pay $500 for a seat and major companies willing to buy a table (seating about ten people) for $5000. For this they would have a meal and hear the party leader speak, but the main purpose was giving the donation. These sums are all below the radar for election declarations and so the identity of these few hundred donors would remain private.

The first dinner was held in Christchurch on 25 November 2004, at the Fendalton home of McDonalds fast food franchise owner, Bruce Davis. The evening event brought together about 40 wealthy Christchurch businesspeople and National Party supporters, raising about $20,000 for the night.[14]

But at that point National was in the political doldrums. There were to have been dinners in Auckland and Wellington earlier that month but both were postponed for lack of interest.[15] The dinners were rescheduled for February 2005 but again had to be postponed. Steven Joyce told the 17 February 2005 National Party board meeting that 'there had been a drop off in interest following the Katherine Rich issue' so 'a decision had been made to postpone the Leader's Dinners given the timing of the adverse publicity right on the peak selling period'.[16] The dinners were finally held in June 2005 after the nationwide billboard campaign had lifted the polls and supporters' spirits.

The Wellington corporate fundraising event, renamed the Leader's Dinner, was held at the Academy of Fine Arts on the Wellington wharves on Thursday, 16 June 2005. Guests arrived at 6pm, when they were greeted by party president Judy Kirk, Don Brash and a band, the Hep Cats, maintaining an upbeat mood. Brash spoke after the entrée and before the main course. The band then played on until 11pm.

A list of most of the 70 attendees was sent to Brash in advance so he would know who was there supporting the National Party. The Wellington event was more a party fundraiser than corporate fundraiser: most seats were filled by former politicians, party faithful and staff. The list includes a whole table sponsored by lawyer and former party president Geoff Thompson, another by lawyer and election candidate Christopher Finlayson and a third by campaign manager Steven Joyce's company, Joyce Investments Ltd, with the seats given to party staff. Apart from them, the main group consisted of property developers and investors and a few other businesspeople. The full list was:

Table 1 Sponsored by Geoff Thompson (Kiely Thompson Caisley)
Table 2 Judy Kirk, Don and Je Lan Brash, Terry and Sue Wood, Bill and Joan Young, Shane Ardern, John and Helen Hayes
Table 3 Sponsored by Christopher Finlayson
Table 4 Sponsored by Joyce Investments Ltd: Steven and Suzanne Joyce, Greg and Nickie Sheehan, Phil and Jo de Joux, Sean Sheldrake and Victoria Heine, Briony Ellis and Roger Wood
Table 5 Roger Bridge, Doug and Jane Kidd, Richard Worth, Deborah James, Bill and Katrina Shanks, Rosemary Bradford
Table 6 Mark and Corinne Blumsky, Richard Francis, Joshua Harris and Kate Angus, David Bradford, Mr and Mrs Ian Cassells, Chris Parkin and Partner

Table 7   Denis and Verna Adam, Ralph Stewart, Stuart and Jennifer
            Young, David Farrar, Herbert Van Veen, Richard Montgomery.[17]

The Auckland fundraising dinner, held on Saturday evening, 11 June 2005
in the Sky City Casino complex, was twice the size of the Wellington dinner and much more of a corporate event. There was a line-up of current
and retired CEOs and company directors, plus free seats given to some
of the high value donors. Again they were greeted at the entrance by the
party president and leader and could dance to the band Super Highway
until midnight.

The guest list sent to Brash is not as complete as the Wellington one, but
gives an idea of who was booked to support the National campaign:

Table 1   Sponsored by Diane Foreman
Table 2   Roger and Judy Kirk, Burton and Jenny Shipley, Don and Je
            Lan Brash, Craig and Katherine Heatley, Scott Simpson, Alan
            Towers
Table 3   Sponsored by Carrick Graham
Table 4   Sponsored by Carrick Graham
Table 5   Evan Davies and Heather Shotter, Lockwood Smith and Alex-
            andra Lang, Michael and Rosie Horton, Murray and Lynda
            Crisford, Mark and Cecilia Fitzgerald
Table 6   John and Margaret Tapper, Thomas Song, Samford Maier,
            Richard Rowley, Lindsay Fergusson, Steven Wong, Peter and
            Lyn Menzies, Mike and Beverley Cotton
Table 7   Sponsored by Pfizer NZ Ltd
Table 8   Sponsored by Joyce Investments Ltd
Table 9   Hosted by Richard Worth
Table 10   Hosted by Richard Worth
Table 11   Hosted by Richard Worth
Table 12   Hosted by Pansy Wong
Table 13   Hosted by John Key
Table 14   Hosted by Peter Kiely
Table 15   Hosted by Peter Goodfellow
Table 16   Hosted by Moira Irving.[18]

The very high value donor Craig Heatley was seated with the party presi-
dent, the leader, former leader Jenny Shipley and senior board members.
Another high donor, Michael Horton, shared a table with Sky City CEO
Evan Davies and Citigroup head Mark Fitzgerald. Table 6 likewise had a

range of past and present high executives. But it is the sponsored tables that are most interesting.

Table 7 was sponsored by the pharmaceutical company Pfizer, which stood to gain from a review of the state pharmaceutical purchasing organisation if National were elected.[19] Tables 3 and 4 – costing $10,000 – were sponsored by Carrick Graham, son of former National Party Cabinet minister, Sir Doug Graham. This may have reflected Graham's personal generosity, but another explanation could be that the event organisers decided for reasons of good taste not to write down the name of the company – British American Tobacco – for which Graham worked as corporate affairs director. He had arranged Brash's visit to the BAT head office in Auckland a year earlier, when Brash and MP David Carter met all the top executives.[20]

If this is correct, National had invited BAT to be part of the fundraiser and accepted tobacco industry money for the campaign. It would have meant that when the senior National Party people looked out across their special fundraising event they could see the head of the largest casino company and the tobacco and pharmaceutical industries, there helping to fund their election bid. It is an almost universal rule that people who give donations to political parties want those at the highest levels to know to whom they are indebted. (To Sky City's credit, it made its main donation to National openly: unlike most other donors, it appeared on the 2005 official declaration form.) Recall the 1986 Royal Commission's view that the public should know all major donors to political parties so it is informed about 'the character of the parties' and has 'healthy confirmation' that they are not dominated by big business. The reason for this is obvious. When National MPs oppose measures to control smoking or gambling, or to allow greater subsidies for or advertising of pharmaceuticals, the public has every right to know whether those interests have been giving the party money.

The other sponsored table had been paid for by Diane Foreman. She was also given the honour of proposing the vote of thanks at the end of Brash's speech. Foreman had been lobbying National on behalf of the Private Hospitals Association, whose goal was to 'grow the private [health] sector to relieve the public sector'.[21] Again, with the party leadership well aware that she was prominently involved in funding the party, obvious questions arise about the effect this might have had on National's pro-private health policies.

Brash's prepared speech for the Auckland and Wellington dinners began by thanking everyone for being there and for their generous support.

'Without you, we would not be where we are now – running neck and neck with Labour in the polls, with an increasingly widespread view among the public that National can and will win the election.' He continued: 'We haven't got all the resources we could usefully use, hence this fund-raising dinner tonight, but we are already better resourced than for many elections past. And you can see the result in, for example, our current billboard campaign.... That campaign has been made possible by the support of people like you.'

Interestingly, this speech was quite different from what the rest of the country was hearing. There was no mention of political correctness or the 'welfare industry'. Brash was not sticking to the glib Crosby/Textor lines. Instead he was telling his people the parts of National's policies that were being de-emphasised for the rest of the country. A National government would 'use the private sector to provide solutions to problems in the health sector, and let private hospitals compete with state-run hospitals'; it would 'reduce the size of government'; and it would 'not be ashamed to support business'.[22]

The 70 Wellington and 160 Auckland guests at the corporate fundraising dinners provided about another $100,000 towards the election – but still only a tiny fraction of what would be spent. The larger sums had to come from elsewhere.

The next level of donors could be expected to give in the thousands. Steven Joyce and his staff established six regional Party Vote Fundraising Teams, in Auckland, Hamilton, Hawke's Bay, Wellington, Christchurch and Dunedin, which had the job of locating local big donors. Since this initiative was organised locally, most of their names do not appear in the leaked National Party papers, but it is evident from the documents that as senior MPs travelled the country in the election year they gave priority to spending time with these donors. For instance, on a trip five weeks before the election in August 2005, John Key was scheduled to be 'Meeting with loads of big donors in Northland with John Carter (full day and night)'.[23]

When a campaigning trip by Brash to Queenstown was being arranged for 22 July 2005, National's Otago candidate Jacqui Dean suggested that he could have a meal with 'the big donors that gave to the fundraising lady [Deborah James] who was in Queenstown earlier this year'.[24] Her campaign manager Paul Anderson replied that 'the "big donors" include Barry Thomas and David Broomfield who are lunching with Don et al on Friday'.[25] That Friday Brash shared a meal with them and the local mayor at Queenstown's Tatler's Restaurant.[26]

Thomas and Broomfield are probably typical examples of National Party donors around the country. Thomas, a Rich List multi-millionaire, was chair of Queenstown's Skyline Enterprises Ltd and Christchurch Casinos Ltd, director of two other casinos and involved in a range of other business ventures. He was an active member of the Business Round-table. Broomfield was a Queenstown property developer and outspoken critic of efforts by other locals to control overdevelopment of the area. A 2002 *Southland Times* editorial described Broomfield's views on council planning as 'extreme' and called for balance between development and 'preservation of the resort's picturesque landscape'.[27] There is little doubt about what types of policies such men would want from a National government.

Other medium value donors included South Islanders Tim Wallis, from the deer hunting and aviation industries, Fred Willett, steamed pudding manufacturer, and Peter Talley from the fishing industry – all described as 'strong backers of the Party'[28] – and Raumati Beach physiotherapist Robin McKenzie, author of the bestseller *Treat Your Own Back*. McKenzie wrote to Brash in May 2005 pledging $10,000: 'I voted ACT at the last two elections but returned to National after the Orewa speech. I made in the past substantial donations to ACT.'[29]

The following month Business Roundtable chair Rob McLeod approached Brash and Key to help arrange a donation to National from heirs to the Spencer Family fortunes. 'Berridge and Mertsi Spencer have been talking with me about the possibility of increasing their financial contribution to your election campaign,' he wrote. 'They are also very keen to meet John [Key] after hearing about him from you. I was therefore wondering whether it might be possible for the three of us (Berridge, Mertsi and I) to have dinner with the two of you at some stage in the near future at their residence at Clifton Rd in Takapuna? ... you guys are doing great – keep it up.'[30]

Even though the election campaigning was under way, Key replied: 'Sure, love to do that. I will speak to Don and see if we can get a date that suits all of us.'[31] Brash agreed and the three of them – Brash, Key and McLeod – had breakfast with the Spencers at their home on Saturday, 9 July 2005. Politicians regularly claim that they do not get involved in fundraising, so as to avoid possible compromise, but with National at least this is not true. Until the diary got too full in the last weeks of the campaign, collecting the money was always a priority. The night before this breakfast, Brash had been at a Taiwanese businesspeople's fundraising event at Si Chuan Restaurant in Remuera, where he gave a ten-minute speech translated by MP Patsy Wong.[32]

For a lot of this fundraising Key and Brash worked as a team. On 9 August 2005, John Key's birthday, the pair attended another fundraising dinner, this one co-ordinated by party fundraiser Deborah James. It was hosted by Bill Birnie at his plush offices on level 18 of IAG House at 151 Queen Street, Auckland. This is a memorable location, as it was previously the offices of merchant bankers Fay Richwhite, whose remaining New Zealand business interests were overseen by Birnie.[33] He had worked in Fay Richwhite's Wellington office in the company's 1980s heyday and by 2005 was chair and managing partner of FR Holdings Ltd ('FR' standing for Fay Richwhite) and a director of Fay Richwhite Holdings.[34] Rod Deane hosted a similar lunchtime corporate fundraiser in Wellington on 8 December 2004. It was obviously an event for soliciting funds because party president Judy Kirk came to Wellington to accompany Brash to the event.[35]

There were many other fundraising events. Eventually the MPs were told by Steven Joyce not to agree to any fundraising dinners after the first week of August as they were getting in the way of the election campaigning. At a meeting just before Christmas in December 2004, the National Party board had discussed 'the extent of the Leader's involvement in fundraising activities'. The minutes record 'it was generally felt that a certain degree of cautiousness should be exercised in the Leader's direct participation, as any direct fundraising activities could be misinterpreted'.[36]

These were sensible feelings but, as the above examples have shown, they were largely ignored. Brash, Key and the other main MPs were all involved in numerous meetings, lunches and dinners with potential donors for the simple reason that their presence helped in raising the money. They may not have literally collected the cheques, but they were personally involved in appeals for money, they knew exactly who the donors were and – very important for getting the money – the donors knew that the politicians, who might soon be running the government, knew who was helping to get them into power.

The other major National Party scheme for securing medium value donors was an initiative called the President's Council. Party president Judy Kirk's October 2004 invitation letter told prospective donors that 'with input from the Leader of the National Party Don Brash and other National politicians I have developed a list of people we would like to see become foundation members'. These people would 'be encouraged to use their membership as a vehicle to express their views and make political comment on New Zealand's future. Our aim is to acknowledge support-ers of the National Party by giving them personal access to the President to voice any political issue.... You will also have the opportunity to meet the Leader of the National Party and other National Caucus members as my guest.'[37]

The plan, explained by Deborah James, was to 'sell' at least 100 mem-berships at $10,000 per annum. Ten thousand dollars is a special sum: it is the largest donation that can be made without having to be declared by the party. Donations of $10,001 or more must appear on the yearly declarations, even if just as anonymous donations, whereas a $10,000 donation disappears quietly into the party accounts. 'Our target market is aimed at the medium level donor,' James wrote, 'more specifically the business/corporate sector and individuals identified as strong financial supporters of the National Party.'[38] Each regional Party Vote Fundrais-ing Team was set the task of trying to locate ten to 20 of these $10,000 per annum donors.

The glossy President's Council brochure said that 'Elections are not just won on Election Day – they are won in the months leading up to it through preparation and hard work. The President's Council will play a large role in providing the resources necessary for a successful Party Vote campaign.' Members, by giving their money, would be 'making a critical contribution to the future of our party and our country'. The council's 'simple self-assigned mission' was 'to ensure that the New Zealand National Party is financially competitive in every general election'.[39] Page after page, the brochure is about the role of money in elections and a reminder that having most money helps a party to win.

Together all these donors must exert a strong but invisible influence over National Party policy. When senior MPs are considering a policy, these are the faces likely to come to mind – not ordinary people with ordinary concerns and priorities. The influence of these donors is also greater than that of all the party members combined. The funding imperatives cre-ate a hierarchy that determines who gets visited by the leader and senior politicians, who is invited to the lunches and generally – in the words of the President's Council brochure – who gets 'an opportunity to have a say and to be heard'.[40] The more money that is given, the truer this is.

The council memberships and most other medium value donations are not over the $10,000 limit and so do not need to be declared. This has three consequences. First, of course, it means that all the donors' identi-ties are kept from the public (for example, British American Tobacco's

20 sponsored seats at the Leader's Dinner conveniently came to exactly $10,000). Second, it means that most of the medium value donations are in addition to National's declared election year donations of $1.88 million, bulging the purse to an extent that will never be made public. Finally, it means that much of the $1.88 million came from people who donated more than $10,000 – some of them much more than $10,000 – and it is this small group that deserves the most scrutiny.

The dozen or so high value donors are a little understood force in New Zealand politics. As previous chapters have shown, hired strategists, pollsters and advertising whizzes – plus lots of money for billboards and other advertising – can be enough to swing an election. These high value donors are the people who can provide the money. With money comes influence, as when some big donors used their financial muscle to help clinch the National Party leader's job for Don Brash.

Each donation from one of these 'super-rich' individuals was usually worth more than the entire takings of a large fundraising event. The attention they received from the National Party leaders and the influence they wielded was, as a result, equal to dozens of ordinary donors and thousands of ordinary party members. There is only ever a small number of these very wealthy donors. At the February 2005 National Party board meeting, seven months before the election, Joyce distributed a confidential report on fundraising and Kirk who, as president was dealing only with the main high value donors 'reported on her conversations with approximately ten committed pledgers'.[41] News stories about the big National Party donors usually refer to them with such phrases as 'wealthy business interests'. But this misses the point. What is significant about National's main donors is not so much their wealth (and they are very wealthy) but their political beliefs. These are not well-heeled businesspeople who happen to lean a bit to the right. This small and distinct group comes mostly from the radical right of New Zealand politics and business.

The identities of the major donors is a closely guarded secret, and it was difficult to confirm how much the donations were for or even whether they were definitely sent.[42] Based on several sources, however, there appear in 2005 to have been the following eight high value donors and four other probable high value donors:

Alan Gibbs
Craig Heatley

David Richwhite
Diane Foreman
Doug Myers
Michael Friedlander
Peter Shirtcliffe
Rod Deane

and probables:

Barry Colman
Colin Giltrap
Michael Horton
Trevor Farmer.

The first and most obvious thing about them is that they are some of New Zealand's richest people. Doug Myers was for many years listed as New Zealand's richest individual. David Richwhite comes close behind, followed by Alan Gibbs. Colman, Heatley, Foreman, Horton and Friedlander are all well above the $100 million mark in the *NBR* Rich List. Deane is a more ordinary millionaire, but still very wealthy. It was their money that helped National to outspend all its rivals outside the three-month election campaign period and in non-advertising expenses. Apart from former *New Zealand Herald* owner Michael Horton and car sales magnate Colin Giltrap, all these people are prominent radical right proponents. Their lifestyles and homes have been extensively profiled, but their political influence is not well understood. Together they represent much of the pro-free market reform lobby of the 1980s and 1990s period, as it tried to renew its crusade in the new century.

In the 1980s and 1990s Doug Myers was as much politician as corporate executive. He was a founding member of the New Zealand Business Roundtable in 1983 and chaired the lobby group from 1990 to 1997. In 1986 he chaired a major Roundtable sub-committee that drafted a 75-page submission on industrial relations, which contained the seeds of the National Government's 1991 Employment Contracts Act.[43] Described as 'the embodiment of New Right ideology', he was a fervent advocate of continued privatisation and the removal of all social or environmental barriers to business activity.[44]

In 1992 Myers told an Australian audience that the availability of the unemployment benefit in New Zealand 'reduces the pressure on wages to adjust to competitive pressures' (meaning, of course, the downward pressure). Later he criticised church leaders who had suggested that free market reforms increase social inequality: 'The poor on average have not got poorer and the rich have barely got richer'.[45] In 2000, still New Zealand's richest man, he opened the ACT Party's annual conference, attacking the Labour government's policies, including raising the minimum wage, and reportedly saying that 'Individual freedom was being curtailed in the absurd pursuit of reducing inequality'.[46]

Merchant banker David Richwhite was a vice-chair of the Business Roundtable and another spokesperson for the free market reforms. As public resistance to the reforms grew in the late 1980s, he called New Zealand 'a nation of knockers' with a 'lack of willingness to face up to change as a good thing'.[47] Together with Gibbs, Myers and Deane, he was a funder and trustee for a New Zealand branch of the radical right pro-free market Centre for Independent Studies, established in 1986. The early research subjects of the CIS included removing the minimum wage and privatising state houses.[48] Its first Auckland seminar, in June 1986, was on takeovers – specifically, opposition to government controls on the activities of the corporate raiders who were making huge profits but causing massive damage to many New Zealand-owned companies at that time.[49]

Alan Gibbs has been described as 'perhaps the most radical voice in the Business Roundtable'.[50] A long-time member of and donor to Britain's free market thinktank the Institute of Economic Affairs, he initiated and funded its New Zealand equivalent, the CIS, and in the early 1990s set up the World Service New Zealand radio station, run by libertarian Lindsay Perigo, as a vehicle for his free market beliefs. Gibbs was assisted at the station by an economist he employed during the 1990s named Rodney Hide, who went on to be leader of ACT, allegedly after Gibbs and Myers, as major donors, put pressure on the party hierarchy to promote him.[51]

Gibbs gained notoriety in the 1980s when he presided over the Hospitals Task Force that looked at the steps needed to move towards privatisation of health services in New Zealand. The 1987 Gibbs Report proposed that the crucial first step was separating funding from provision of healthcare and then placing public and private 'providers' on an equal footing to compete. These recommendations were the basis for the shambles created by the National government health reforms of the 1990s. Gibbs went further at a 1988 conference organised by the CIS, suggesting that a social welfare system based on general taxation was immoral.[52] He was appointed to chair the establishment board of the state-owned Forestry Corporation from 1987 to 1990 as it was prepared for privatisation.

Gibbs's long-term business partner, Trevor Farmer, was also a likely National major donor.

While the business activists mainly lobbied from the outside, Rod Deane was a leader of the reforms within the public service. In 1979 he returned to New Zealand from a job at the International Monetary Fund to become chief economist, then deputy governor of the Reserve Bank. He co-authored a 1980 report called 'The stabilisation role of fiscal policy', which argued for the introduction of free market 'monetarist' policies, a view that would underpin Roger Douglas's post-1984 monetarist reforms. After he was appointed State Services Commissioner in 1986, he instituted equally radical state sector reforms, particularly the process of public service corporatisation, during which large numbers of people lost their jobs, which earned him the nickname 'Dr Death'. He said in 1994 that 'Although one does these things because, in a sense, they have to be done for organisations to continue to progress... it doesn't give one any pleasure to be involved in having to reduce staff numbers.'[53] Deane then became chief executive of the corporatised Electricorp, laying off thousands of staff as he prepared it for privatisation. In 1992 he became chief executive of the newly privatised Telecom, with Peter Shirtcliffe as chair of the board. He was also a vice-chair of the Business Roundtable.

Lawyer and property investor Michael Friedlander was another Business Roundtable member and long-time supporter of the local Centre for Independent Studies. Together with Myers, Richwhite, Gibbs and Deane, he was one of the participants at the November 1989 Christchurch meeting of the free market Mont Pelerin Society.[54] The society, whose early members included Friedrich Hayek and Milton Friedman, is linked to the United States Heritage Foundation and British Institute of Economic Affairs thinktanks.

Friedlander was also one of the anonymous funders of the ACT Party leading up to the 1996 election. A small group of very wealthy donors provided $2.8 million for the recently established party – more than any other party received – and demonstrated that, with enough money, they could effectively buy their way into Parliament. In 2001 the *Sunday Star-Times* was leaked details of an elaborate 'money maze', designed as a legal mechanism to avoid Electoral Commission declarations, through which eight main ACT donors siphoned their money to the party.[55] Besides Friedlander, the 'money maze' donors were Myers, Richwhite, Michael Fay, Gibbs, Farmer and – the next member of the anonymous 2005 National donors – Craig Heatley.

Heatley was a more recent arrival to the free market cause. He became involved in politics when the ACT Party was being established by Roger Douglas and Brian Nicolle in 1994. Heatley was a founding member, joined the party's board, became the main fundraiser and travelled the country with Douglas and Derek Quigley promoting the party's message. He said later that he had been attracted to the ACT Party by Douglas's book *Unfinished Business*: it 'just sort of turned on a light for me'.[56] In this book Douglas spelt out his plans such as 100 per cent privatisation of all public schools and hospitals.[57]

Diane Foreman, although a relatively recent arrival, was vice-chair of the Business Roundtable and firmly part of the small CIS political circle. Her combined roles of donor, private health lobbyist and personal friend of Brash were demonstrated when, in a single email to Sinclair, she discussed her private hospital, mentioned having given Brash a personal tour and sought ideas on how to make her next donation to National: 'I understand that you are visiting my hospital tomorrow, it will be very slow as most doctors away for holidays and we try to send everyone home for the weekends. Don has seen the whole place previously as I gave him a personal tour before it opened. Hope you enjoy the visit. I have still to make my final donation and not keen to just put it into Stephen's pot so any ideas you know where to find me.'[58]

Barry Colman was owner of the *National Business Review*, part of his investment Liberty Group. He used the *NBR* as a campaigning tool on free market issues and to attack those with different views or support those with whom he agreed. He was the social liberal in this high donor grouping and had a role as a director of Amnesty International's Freedom Foundation.

As we have seen, Peter Shirtcliffe was a personal friend of Brash and had been a determined radical right campaigner since the early 1990s.

These, then, were the main individuals who worked together to help fund the Brash-led National Party into government. Like Peter Keenan, Sinclair and other players, they were not automatically National Party supporters. They were motivated by the idea that a Brash-led National Government would provide the right leadership to get on with the unfinished business.

Throughout the period covered by this book, there was constant interaction between Brash and these key donors. This meant private dinners with Deane and Shirtcliffe,[59] a stream of helpful emails from Myers, Heatley arranging a top American campaign expert to visit and help National,[60] Foreman acting as friend and political confidante, Colman sending early notice of *NBR* polls and funding Brash's media training,[61]

Deane and Shirtcliffe sponsoring Brash to become a member of the Wellington Club,[62] Brash taking an evening off from election campaigning to attend Friedlander's birthday at the Northern Club[63] and so on. Probably few of them belonged to the National Party, but because they were writing the cheques they had a major role in the business of the party.

Their relationship with National is illustrated by a letter Deane sent to John Key in March 2005, copied to Brash, expressing 'increasing' concern about some recent policy positions National had taken. As documented in the next chapter, Deane had been in discussions with the party president a few months earlier about making a substantial donation, and now he was writing directly to the finance spokesperson and leader to express concern that the economic policies of the possible next National government might not be the ones he had been led to believe it would pursue.

'From private conversations with Don and yourself, I had been greatly encouraged that the National Government might in fact pursue not only sound macroeconomic policies on the monetary and fiscal fronts, but also undertake a set of microeconomic policies which would assure us of a sustainable growth path for the future.' (Such microeconomic policies would include privatisation and deregulation.) 'However,' he said, 'I have followed with interest and increasing consternation the range of policy pronouncements with respect to economic policy issues which seem to part company with the principles I have always associated with the National Party and potentially with a National Government.'[64]

Deane had apparently mistaken the pre-election year expedient of 'swallowing rats', as the National strategy team called it, for a fundamental change of direction. The policies about which Deane was 'gravely disconcerted' were the 'inoculations' on four weeks' annual leave, 'no nuclear ship visits' and superannuation that had been made at the end of 2004, plus the language both Brash and Key had been using to try to avoid National's plans for privatisation becoming an issue during election year.

For Deane, the 'most important source' of economic growth was 'halting and reversing... the pervasive regulation.... I hope you will thus understand how disconcerting it is to read that a National Government, which many had hoped would stand for lower compliance costs and greater flexibility for the private sector... is in fact backing off these types of policies in a range of areas. In this context,' he said, 'I use a broad-based definition of regulation to effectively encompass government ownership of commercial assets.'

Having reminded them of the importance of privatisation, he stressed how harmful these inoculation statements were. 'It is becoming increasingly difficult for those of us in the business community to understand how a National Government would actually differ from the existing Labour Government and how National would undertake policy changes which might actually contribute to a faster and more assured rate of economic growth.' These policies would 'only lead to disillusionment amongst your business colleagues'.

He ended by saying, 'I do hope you will accept this letter in the terms in which it is offered. You have many well wishers in the private sector and it is important in the interests of democracy and economic growth that New Zealand has a strong Opposition and a really credible alternative to any existing government. I am left rather mystified as to just where you stand in this respect now.'[65]

This fascinating letter shows Deane making his displeasure known when public statements from the politicians were not consistent with what he had been told privately about their economic plans. Note that he was calling them to account for relatively small deviations from the free market line, such as accepting that New Zealanders should have four weeks of holidays each year, and saying that certain contentious privatisation targets would not be sold 'for at least our first term in office'.[66]

This letter could be read as showing that National under Brash was centrist, but that would be to mistake election expediency for beliefs and intentions. The policies Deane was objecting to were exactly the four inoculations that Brash reluctantly agreed to in the late 2004 strategy discussions. That Deane, one of the main architects of the 1980s and 1990s reforms, had been 'greatly encouraged' by his private discussions with Brash and Key seems a more telling indication of their private beliefs on economic policy, and their intentions if they became government.

Deane's concerns in early 2005 were very much the same as Brash's frustrations in November 2004, when he was telling Keenan he had not come into politics just to be 'Helen Lite'. Keenan had patiently assured Brash that the inoculations were politically necessary and would not prevent them getting on with the policies they both believed in once they were safely in government – 'Sort out privatisation in the second term!'[67] It can be assumed that much the same explanation and reassurance was given to Deane after his letter; that this was still the party he believed it to be when he wrote his cheques. Indeed such a discussion likely occurred on the very day Deane sent the letter, 14 March 2005, when he and Brash had a long-scheduled dinner together at the Roxburgh Bistro in Wellington.[68]

It should be clear by now that these were not ordinary National Party supporters. What set them apart was not their wealth but their politics: they were not funding National to achieve particular policies to benefit their businesses. Their agenda was much bigger: they were seeking a return to radical right government in New Zealand.

In contrast, some other major donors such Horton and Giltrap were examples of traditional National Party supporters. Both of them apparently made substantial donations to the 2005 campaign,[69] but there is no sign that they were linked to the free market lobby.

Other typical National Party donors were the property developers like David Broomfield, who wanted the RMA changed to avoid neighbours objecting to their projects, or the company owners who were not keen on unions and wanted more business-friendly employment laws. But they were not driven by a fervent belief in slashing the size of government or privatising hospitals. As discussed in Chapter 11, political language in New Zealand is not very helpful for recognising the difference between conservatives, commercial vested interests and the radical right, each of which has separate political goals and motivations.

The wealthy radical right donors were very much a group. As we saw, they had numerous links through their membership of right-wing think-tanks, joint funding of the ACT Party and other concerted political activities. They were also linked through their businesses and personal friendships. When Richwhite and Fay left New Zealand in 1998, for instance, Doug Myers threw the farewell party for them and other members of this group, including Alan Gibbs who flew in to be there.[70]

They were also, in different ways, beneficiaries of the deregulated and privatised economy they championed. This is not saying they championed the policies for personal gain, but merely that they grew rich (or richer) in the environment they helped to create. Richwhite earned large consultant's fees and commissions from arranging the privatisation of various state assets and also helped to form consortia to buy some of the state assets. The consortium that purchased Telecom New Zealand in 1990 included interests associated with Richwhite, Michael Fay and Alan Gibbs. According to sharemarket analyst Brian Gaynor, between them these three had earned $600 million on top of their initial investment by 1997.[71]

For the purchase of New Zealand Rail, Fay Richwhite again put together a consortium with foreign companies with a 28 per cent share for themselves. The railway system was cut back and run down as the consortium extracted maximum value before selling the company again. Gaynor estimates that by 1997 Fay and Richwhite interests had made a profit in excess of $800 million from Telecom and Tranzrail and Gibbs' interests had made more than $300 million – sums that account for most of their estimated personal wealth.

As chief executive of the privatised Telecom, Deane received a record-breaking salary package that had risen to $1.8 million per year by 1999.[72] Peter Shirtcliffe, who as chair of the board decided Deane's pay, was also paid hundreds of thousands of dollars a year. Later Deane retired as CEO and took over as chair of the Telecom board, receiving an annual director's fee of $400,000 (by 2005) for the part-time job. When he stood down from the position in 2006 he received a golden handshake of over $600,000.[73] Thus the 1980s and 1990s reforms indirectly provided this group with the spare finances that would allow it to bankroll the 2005 National campaign.

Members of the National Party donors group also benefited greatly from the deregulated business environment following the 1980s reforms, notably the lack of sharemarket rules that allowed powerful investors to benefit at the expense of smaller shareholders. A particularly controversial case occurred in 1998 when Doug Myers and his fellow Lion Nathan directors sold most of their stake in the beer company virtually in seconds, before other shareholders could realise what was happening. As a result they 'pocketed most of the takeover premium' while retail investors, according to the *Australian Financial Review*, 'were left battered and bruised in the dirt'.[74] Myers's assets, according to the *NBR* Rich List's estimate, increased in value by 50 per cent to $500 million as a result of that transaction.[75] The following year Myers announced he was leaving New Zealand.

Strangely, after having helped to create one of the most unregulated economies in the world, many of this donor group did not continue to live in New Zealand. When Brash was soliciting the financial support of Myers and Gibbs, he visited them in London. Fay and Richwhite likewise sold their Auckland homes (Richwhite's setting a record home sale price) and their $100 million Queen Street building and moved to Geneva in 1998. Heatley, as Brash put it in September 2004, 'spends a large amount of time out of the country!', and Deane, at the time of writing, was considering moving to Australia.

In 1999 Deane gave a speech in which he claimed that New Zealand had 'persecuted' and 'driven away' people like Fay and Richwhite.[76] Shortly before leaving New Zealand, Myers complained that not only was the reform process incomplete but 'middle New Zealand that still... mourns the demise of the egalitarian society' was anti-business. 'Who's the most hated group in New Zealand?' he asked, and then provided his own answer: 'the Business Roundtable'.[77] As the National-led government headed for defeat in the 1999 election, people like Myers and Deane were bitter and disillusioned with the public for not appreciating their achievements or wanting to carry on with the crusade.

But as their 2005 election donations to National showed, that was not the end of their political efforts. Like Ruth Richardson, Peter Keenan and Brash himself, their support for the Brash-led National Party represented another attempt to regain some control of the political agenda in New Zealand. Even from their homes on the other side of the world, their money was able to have a huge influence on the outcome of a New Zealand election.

CHAPTER 15

THANK YOU VERY MUCH FOR YOUR KIND DONATION
Election finances

When questions arose in the midst of the election campaign about foreign donors to the National Party, Don Brash gave the simple and firm assurance that he did not have 'the faintest idea' where the party's money came from. Fundraising was handled by the campaign manager and party president and 'it is not for me to ask who is contributing to the National Party.... This is something handled by the Party, not by the politicians.'[1] He repeated the 'haven't the faintest idea' phrase twice in the interview, emphasising the point and deviating slightly from Richard Long's suggested answer: 'I simply don't know'[2]. Later, in October 2006, the party president Judy Kirk told Nick Venter of the *Dominion Post*: 'Our MPs have no idea where the money comes from. We keep that absolutely secret, absolutely confidential. It's better for the MPs not to know. Then they can't be accused of tying policy together with a donation.'[3] As this chapter will show, this was all far from the truth.

One of the surprises of the National Party papers was discovering the extent to which the senior party people, including MPs, were aware of the identities of the big donors and talked openly about donor negotiations. Later, when the party's declaration of election year donations was provided to the Electoral Commission, none of these names were listed. The party was not only secretive and deceptive about its election finances; some of its activities appear to have breached both the electoral laws and the parliamentary spending rules, and it seems to have been a party to others' breaches of the election legislation.

In the public's mind, an anonymous donation would be something like a bank cheque that arrived in the mail without any indication of who had sent it. It is common, however, for parties (not just National) to invent ways by which they can solicit and receive donations from known people without ever having to disclose the donors' identities. Brash and his staff had regular contact with the main donors and discussed their donations. Many of the highest donors were personal friends of the leader. And, of course, the donors themselves had no intention of being anonymous since they wanted the party hierarchy to know exactly to whom they were indebted.

Despite this, the National Party official disclosure of donations showed only 7 per cent of the declared donations in 2005 coming from known donors ($140,000 out of $1,881,793) – accounting for only four medium level donors. A report from the party's December 2004 board meeting shows up the absurdity of this declaration. The minutes record that Judy Kirk 'briefed the Board members on the HQ's streamlined procedures of maintaining relationships with donors, including sending flowers, letters of appreciation and Christmas cards'.[4] The party staff dispatching the flowers, letters and cards knew perfectly well where they were sending them.

To convert known donations into anonymous donations National used private trusts – in particular the Waitemata Trust. This trust received money from National supporters during 2005 and then sent a cheque for $1,254,845 to the National Party, meaning that only this 'Waitemata Trust' donation was shown on the party's official donation declaration, not the people who actually gave the money. Some other donors got their lawyers to send the cheques from their law firm trust funds. All this is legal, but the reason for passing the money through these trusts is apparently to keep the donors' identities secret from the public.

Kirk told the *New Zealand Herald* in May 2006 that 'she knew little' about the Waitemata Trust. 'It was set up to support centre-right campaigns and we apply to them and ask them for funding. I don't know how it is done, I don't know who they are. They've been doing it for years.'[5] (In an article some months later, she gave a slightly different story when she 'refused to disclose' the names of the Waitemata Trust trustees.)[6] Steven Joyce said he had 'no knowledge' of who donated to the trusts. 'They don't tell me who gives the money so I don't know.'[7]

But common sense tells us that the Waitemata Trust, like the Free Enterprise Trust before it, was created to assist the National Party and was under the control of National Party faithful. The president and the campaign manager were making formal approaches to potential donors, securing their support and reporting back to the board on their progress in securing much-needed election funds. It defies belief that some of these donors would then, of their own volition, decide not to give their promised donations to National after all and instead give them to an independent trust run by people whom Kirk claimed not even to know. Why would National want its precious donations sent elsewhere, beyond its direct control, unless it knew perfectly well that they would all be reliably passed on to the party?

The history of National's use of anonymising trusts can be seen from its election returns. The first National Party-linked trust, called the New Zealand Free Enterprise Trust, appeared in 1999. It provided $570,000 for that year's election, making it the main donor to National's election campaign. It was also the main donor in 2000 and 2001, but it disappeared in the 2002 election year when it was replaced by the Waitemata Trust. The disappearance of one and appearance of the next can hardly be a coincidence.

The Free Enterprise Trust was chaired by the 1970s National Party president Sir George Chapman and, despite calling itself an 'independent thinktank',[8] appears to have been fully under the control of National. Throughout that time Chapman was thoroughly a National Party man. Even in the period covered by this book, the elderly Chapman regularly provided organisational and political advice to the party leader and officials.[9] In one email to Brash eight months before the 2005 election Chapman mentions that he 'met with Judy and Steven last 10 days ago'.[10] Kirk and Joyce may have been seeking political advice, but it seems quite possible that Chapman had moved straight from involvement with the first trust to the second. If Chapman were not involved, the trust would presumably have been in a similarly safe pair of party hands.

The only public face of the Waitemata Trust was its accountant, Robert (Bob) Browne, of the Auckland accountancy firm Mabee Halstead & Kiddle. He told the *Sunday Star-Times* that the trust was 'a professional client for us'.[11] This was undoubtedly true, but Browne had had links to the National Party for decades. In fact, he was electorate chair in East Coast Bays in 1980 where Don Brash first stood for Parliament.[12]

None of the top donors – Alan Gibbs, Barry Colman, Craig Heatley, David Richwhite, Diane Foreman, Doug Myers, Michael Friedlander, Peter Shirtcliffe, Rod Deane, Colin Giltrap and Michael Horton – were declared as being donors. But passing the money through a party-linked trust fund does not stop a donation from Craig Heatley to the National Party being a donation from Craig Heatley to the National Party. The legal loophole that allows this anonymising defeats the purpose of donation declarations.

There is ample evidence of the National Party staff and politicians discussing donors whose gifts were subsequently directed through anonymising trusts. As described in the last chapter, in February 2005 Judy Kirk knew by name and reported to the rest of the party board on ten major donors.[13]

In September 2004, during secret negotiations with Peter Talley and lawyer Nick Davidson over a million-dollar plan to assist National's election campaign (discussed below), Bryan Sinclair wrote to Brash: 'It would be helpful for you to perhaps facilitate the introduction of Craig H, Diane F and Roderick D to Peter T and Nick D (or at least give them Nick D's phone number and suggest they call him to discuss a "very draft concept" he is confidentially working on.... They are all likeminded on this stuff from what I can see).'[14] Brash agreed to ring them and noted 'all the people you mention have already contributed pretty generously, or (as in the case of Roderick D) are in conversation with Judy about doing so'.[15] In other words, Brash knew Craig Heatley and Diane Foreman had made big donations and even knew the stage of negotiation between the party president and Rod Deane.

Similarly, in December 2004 Brash asked, concerning a fundraising dinner, 'should we be confining our invitations to the 'second rank' of Auckland supporters (in terms of money) [and] specifically NOT invite the Colin Giltraps, the Craig Heatleys, etc?'[16] In the same email Brash, who had no hesitation about micro-managing donor relations, said that National 'may want to donate a couple of complimentary tickets [to the corporate fundraising dinners] to those, like Craig Heatley, who have already contributed substantial funds'.[17]

Then there was Diane Foreman, who talked openly about her donations with Bryan Sinclair in July 2005. Sinclair had approached Foreman about her funding some election advertising 'focused on the hip urban city magazine reader type'. This would not officially be part of the National Party campaign, but instead – as Sinclair described it to Foreman – 'some "change the government" stuff that could run alongside National's marketing'. Foreman replied that she did not want her 'final donation' to go to National campaign manager Steven Joyce and the official party accounts so she was receptive to his suggestions.[18] She was casually discussing how to support the National Party financially without going through the party accounts and donation declaration regime. It appears her donations were no secret in the inner circles.

Brash and his staff were also involved when Berridge and Mertsi Spencer wanted to 'increase their financial contribution to [National's] election campaign'. As we have seen, both Brash and finance spokesperson

John Key took time off election campaigning to breakfast with them and secure the donation. It is very unlikely they made the special visit to one of New Zealand's richest families for a donation of $10,000 or less. If any bigger donation went ahead after their meeting, it was presumably via an anonymising trust. Similarly, Brash wrote to Sinclair and Joyce: 'I think Fletcher Building may have already contributed, but in case not I'm copying Steven into this correspondence'.[19] Again, it is abundantly obvious that Brash and his staff took an active role in fundraising and the public claims about not having 'the faintest idea' about donors were not true.

A February 2005 email exchange between Brash and Joyce about the high donors illustrates well how casual the division was between party and the leader on fundraising. Brash initially wrote to Joyce, Kirk, MPs Gerry Brownlee and Tony Ryall, and to staffers Keenan and Long. 'I think we should be giving a very high priority to fund-raising at this point. Key potential contributors are accessible now, and are understood to be in a reasonably receptive frame of mind. That may not be true for long.'[20] Joyce replied just to Brash that the staff and MPs 'can't be directly involved in that – but we are moving on it'. The operative word was 'directly'. He then added as an aside: 'Incidentally, I have a call in to Craig Heatley'.[21] This conversation shows that the party and politicians did maintain some formal lines between the party and politicians over fundraising – there had been a board discussion about exercising 'a certain degree of cautiousness... in the Leader's direct participation',[22] – but they did not stick to this decision.

There are good reasons for the conventions within political parties about keeping politicians away from fundraising. It means that they cannot be influenced by who is giving money and there cannot be accusations that donations influenced their subsequent actions. If they have not the faintest idea, there cannot be influence. But in reality National, Labour and probably other parties use politicians to solicit funds for the simple reason that the donors want to meet the people they are supporting. When this is combined with donation laws that make it easy, in fact routine, not to declare the identities of most donors, the basic purpose of the laws is thoroughly undermined. At the time of writing the whole structure of party funding has built-in incentives for party officials and politicians to be secretive and deceptive about the sources of their money. It is legal to avoid declaring donors and secrecy helps political fundraising. This is obviously an unhealthy situation: the only solution is to put an end to both anonymous donations and anonymising trusts.

There are also cases where the National Party breached the laws and parliamentary rules covering election finances. In 1995 there were three important changes to New Zealand's election campaign finance rules: an overall cap was placed on each political party's election spending; each party was required to make a public return setting out its expenditure for each election; each party was also required to make a declaration of donations and donors (although only covering donations above $10,000 and allowing donors to be listed as 'anonymous').[23] This system has two main purposes: to attempt to provide a 'level playing field' for election contenders so that some parties do not have much greater resources than others; and to try to stop political donations being used for influence buying or corruption. The cap on election spending also includes some spending by 'third parties', so that parties cannot outspend their rivals with the help of 'independent' political allies. The most controversial example of third-party advertising was, of course, the Exclusive Brethren campaign. The relevant part of the Electoral Act is section 221, which says that 'no person shall publish or cause or permit to be published in any newspaper, periodical, poster, or handbill... any advertisement which... encourages or persuades or appears to encourage or persuade voters to vote for a party'.

The only exception is that 'A person may publish or cause or permit to be published an advertisement of the kind described... if: the publication of that advertisement is authorised in writing by the Secretary of the party or his or her delegate; and the advertisement contains a statement setting out the true name of the person for whom or at whose direction it is published and the address of his or her place of residence or business'. As the act says, 'Every person is guilty of an illegal practice who wilfully contravenes any provision' of the above sections.

The primary offence would relate to the Exclusive Brethren men who arranged and paid for the pamphlets and advertisements. If the publications appeared to be encouraging votes for National – and in October 2005 Chief Electoral Officer David Henry concluded that one of them was[24] – then clearly the Brethren were committing an offence. If so, and if the National Party knew this and supported or encouraged them, it was very likely a party to that offence.

There is no doubt that National knew about the advertisements, that some of its MPs had seen them in advance and that Joyce had had discussions with the Brethren about them. A group of MPs were, for some reason, 'very nervous' after being shown the advertisements on 23 June 2005. On 4 May 2006 Gerry Brownlee made the vague statement to TVNZ that 'The Brethren had at various times attempted to show Dr Brash bits and pieces but there was no formal connection between us': those 'bits and pieces' sounded suspiciously like copies of Brethren pamphlets.[25] It was not credible for National to argue that they were unaware and uninvolved.

The police investigated after a formal complaint from the Chief Electoral Officer but decided not to prosecute. But these were the investigations where the police decided not to prosecute any party for anything: they did not even prosecute the Brethren for producing publications with false addresses. The second potential area of illegality was National exceeding its allowable election spending. If the advertising 'appeared to encourage' votes for National, then in practice it was adding an extra million dollars of advertising to National's campaign. But the law is complicated and on this point it is not clear that they technically committed an offence.

For the Exclusive Brethren themselves, there is a third offence of failing to identify who was publishing some of their brochures. The use of false addresses showed a deliberate effort to hide their involvement in the campaign and a flouting of the law. On this point, the church should have been convicted.[26]

The horse racing lobby's third-party advertising for National seems clearly unlawful. For example, National's authorisation should have appeared on the pro-National advertisements in the racing magazines. The same goes for the thousands of 'National stands for Fair Tax' postcards that were handed out. The banners and signs seem suspiciously like posters, which also have to carry party authorisation. National may well have committed an offence by 'permitting' these unlawful advertisements. At the very least it seems to have been a party to the racing lobby's breach.

Of course, if the advertisements had been formally authorised by National, then the party would have had to declare them as part of its advertising expenses. Its own spending on designing and printing the postcards, in particular, should have been declared. There is no sign that it was. It would not take much of this sort of undeclared election advertising spending to put National over its legal spending cap – another electoral offence. What's more, if any person or organisation in the racing lobby gave National more than $10,000 in money or goods, that, too, should have been declared as a donation.

In addition to the electoral law issues, there are also parliamentary spending rules. The National leader's office budget and staff were used to design pro-National advertisements and signs for the 27 August 2005 Hawke's Bay Racing Club meeting and to pay for the thousands of National Party postcards – bearing the parliamentary crest to show it was paid for from parliamentary funds – that Fairtax people handed out that day.[27] This appears to break the parliamentary rules and was exactly the issue on which National politicians were attacking Labour in Parliament in August–September 2006 – the issue they said showed 'a degree of corruption and dishonesty never before seen in New Zealand politics'.[28]

Brash's office staff and resources were also used for election activities at other times. In May 2005, for instance, National Party board member Alan Towers contacted party president Judy Kirk with a plan to target New Zealand voters in other countries. Tower said a personal friend, the managing director of a recruitment company, had been contracted by the Department of Labour to prepare a database of 7000 expatriate New Zealanders who could be surveyed on what government incentives would tempt them back to New Zealand. The friend had offered to use this database to send out National Party election advertising.[29] Kirk forwarded his offer to Brash, asking, 'Are you happy for this to happen?'[30] Brash replied: 'Absolutely happy to proceed'.[31]

He asked his office to prepare a suitable publication to be emailed to the database. Bryan Sinclair wrote the 'Postcard from Home' and office designer Andrew Slade did the design work. Sinclair sent it to Towers's friend with a note saying, 'Thank you very much for the opportunity to get this out to your database. Don very much appreciates your offer.' He copied the email to Kirk and Towers so they knew the project was successful.[32] Brash, Kirk, Towers and Sinclair all knew that there are strict rules prohibiting leader's office staff working on election materials – essentially, parliamentary publications cannot refer to voting for the party – but that is what they had done. The publication was presented as being from the National Party and said 'when you come to mark your ballot paper, remember that only a party vote for National can change the government'.[33]

Why was this not picked up by Auditor-General Kevin Brady, in his October 2006 report on parliamentary spending?[34] Brady certainly did look into the spending by the leaders' offices, which he said was of 'most concern'. He ruled that spending public money on 'party-generated advertising' (such as Labour's pledge card) breached the parliamentary spending rules, because it was plainly intended to win votes. But the scope of his inquiry was very limited. He was looking only at spending on advertising. He noted that 'some support staff may have spent time designing and arranging advertising for MPs and parliamentary parties' and that such taxpayer-funded activities might well fall foul of the rules – but nobody recorded it, so it was too hard to track.[35]

Both the 'Postcard from Home' and the designing of the Fairtax post-cards provide a window on exactly the sort of electioneering spending emanating from National's leader's office that fell off Brady's radar. But this also raises a serious question. The printing of the Fairtax postcard looks to be exactly the same sort of expense as Labour's pledge card. It was paid for out of National's leader's fund. Was the auditor-general told about it? Another possible breach of the election laws concerned the Brash biography which, as Brash said, was intended 'as a significant marketing tool' for him and the party.[36] He and his staff knew who had funded the book. They arranged it. Brash even thought that, as a courtesy, the party should donate 'a couple of tickets [to a National Party dinner] to those who have funded the writing of the biography', some of them 'likely to be major contributors' to National's election campaign.[37] If any person donated over $10,000 in a year, as seems possible for a twelve-month writing contract, this may be another case of failing to declare donations (which legally include both money and goods and services). The same applies to the free use of a helicopter that Peter Talley gave National in 2004 and 2005. If the various trips added up to more than $10,000 in value in a year, as seems likely, they should have been declared.

In a strangely casual attitude to party business, Bryan Sinclair per-sonally took donations from the National Party big donors for the cost of the biography launch while paying the bills in the name of his private company, Silverbeat. And Sinclair quietly arranged for Barry Colman to pay for Brash's speech and media training in December 2003, sought a private donor to pay for Brash's new clothes after he became leader and, generally – as he emphasised with the inverted commas in an email to National MP Sandra Goudie – worked to 'find some "assistance" some-where' to meet various 'Don-specific' expenses. Sinclair was asking for Goudie's help in contacting rich donors, arguing that 'Don is already contributing about $250K himself in lost salary for the cause [by which he meant the 'cost' of becoming an MP] so any offers from any quarters gratefully accepted... as I may have mentioned, Peter Keenan also has a source of assistance for other stuff we have in motion at the moment'.[38] This blasé attitude to inviting private donors' money into parliamentary business seems unhealthy, to say the least.

Politicians and their staff should make a virtue of being utterly strict about not accepting money or favours. Instead National was surprisingly loose about accepting all sorts of little favours, from gratis use of corporate jets and helicopters to free tickets to concerts and sporting matches.[39] Sinclair epitomised the attitude when he sent a boasting email to one of his workmates about gifts from Dean Schmidt of Telecom's government relations division. 'Dean is a good guy. He gives rugby tickets away to nice people.'[40] The workmate replied: 'If you got Lions vs All Black tickets I'm going to be very grumpy'.[41]

When donors are giving money in the form of goods, or in a series of smaller sums, it is hard to tell whether they have provided over $10,000 of donations in a year. Another difficult area to enforce is the law on election spending. How would the Electoral Commission ever know that National's spending declaration included all the costs of producing the election advertisements? For instance, the party's main advertising consultant John Ansell is recorded in the official return as costing only $1271 for his work on producing television campaign materials. Ansell spent many days filming Brash at his home and around the country to collect footage for advertisements. He then contributed to the design of the advertisements. Unless he donated his time, this does not sound like only $1271 of work at television charge-out rates.

The cost of election consultants, focus groups and polling do not have to be counted as election activity and included within the spending limits. In an era when such people and activities are often more important to 'encouraging or persuading voters to vote for the party' than the things like 'notices, posters and handbills' that do have to be declared, there is no good reason for this.[42] Even under the current law, however, election consultant costs do have to be declared when they are directly part of the development and conduct of a party's advertising campaign.[43]

As National's consultant campaign strategist, Mark Textor's advice was sought on all aspects of the campaign, including checking that the party's election advertising was consistent with the messages they had decided on. This was done during Textor's visits to New Zealand and by telephone. Obviously, the advertising-related component of his advice is easy to hide and impossible for the Electoral Commission to identify if a party does not co-operate. But one case with Textor was unambiguous. As the campaign launch approached in August 2005 the National Party staff contacted Textor specifically to seek his advice on the television campaign opening they had filmed of Brash reading a script prepared by John Ansell in his home. According to insiders, the broadcast was sent to Textor in Australia and he provided comments. The cost of this advice should have been declared, but was not. This appears to be another breach of the electoral laws.

Two other million-dollar-plus stories from National's 2005 campaign will probably remain mysteries but are worth mentioning as examples of what could happen to bring millions of extra dollars behind the National election campaign. Both stories date from late 2004, when the need to raise enough money for the election began to preoccupy the National Party inner circle. Sinclair told Peter Keenan that he and Brash had been receiving an 'ear bashing' from several 'traditional Party donors' – 'all super wealthy and probably not all that hard to figure out who' – who were 'absolutely unconvinced' when 'recently approached for further funding'.[44] The first story concerns one of those super-wealthy donors.

In an email to Brash in early September 2004 Sinclair had referred to Steven Joyce's recent decision to reduce his fundraising targets in view of the poor response.[45] Brash had replied: 'I plan to take a more hands-on role in terms of strategy, and I need your help brother!'[46] Then, only a couple of weeks later, Brash told Sinclair that, at the next day's National Party board meeting, he planned 'to tell Steven [Joyce] that I want him to work out how best to spend $4 million between now and the election, making some assumptions about when the election will be, and recognising that there are legal limits as to how much we can spend in the last few months'.[47] There was a problem with his campaign team being nervous about money but they needed 'to spend NOW if we are to avoid a self-fulfilling downward spiral – the sort of point that was made to us last Thursday at Talleys. You'll see me get a bit stroppy very shortly.'[48]

The sudden turnaround from fundraising worries and lowered targets to talking about spending $4 million – probably the highest amount ever spent in a New Zealand election campaign – followed a private meeting attended by Don Brash and Bryan Sinclair in Motueka at 3pm on 16 September 2004 – that is, 'last Thursday at Talleys'.

Talley's Fisheries head Peter Talley is a powerful man. For decades he has used his economic power to wield a large influence in the Nelson region and he wanted to have similar influence over national politics. In May 2004 Talley had been guest speaker at National's Canterbury–Westland regional conference, telling delegates what they needed to do to win the next election. He advised them to 'maximise their use' of Don Brash's image and exploit 'one-off publicity rich issues' such as immigration.[49]

Brash and Sinclair then visited Peter and his brother Michael Talley in July, when the Talleys were giving Brash free use of their helicopter and pilot for a three-day visit to Golden Bay and the West Coast.[50] Before he flew off, they took Brash to their company headquarters to give him their views on National Party strategy.

The 16 September 2004 meeting – again with Peter and Michael Talley, Motueka lawyer Nick Davidson, Brash and Sinclair present – got down to business on how Brash could win the election. Brash was told that National should start spending money to boost its election chances and the Talley brothers had a plan to help this happen. Davidson, formerly a partner in a Wellington law firm (and not the Christchurch QC of that name), had prepared a paper for the meeting with the title 'Bold and Simple Strategy'. It urged Brash to find better advisers than his current team and focus on 'a few key, sexy, issues' such as abolishing the MMP electoral system and the Maori seats.[51] If Brash was prepared to follow their advice, the Talleys were offering to provide money – lots of it – to see National elected.

It was five days after that meeting when Brash requested the $4 million election plan. Then, a day after that, Davidson flew to Wellington 'on Peter Talley's instruction' to put a specific proposal.[52] As Brash recorded in an email, Davidson brought an offer from Peter and Michael Talley that they were willing to provide $1 million to help get National elected – or, as he put it, 'they are saying that they can find a million dollars to encourage us to do certain things', such as hiring campaign consultants.[53] Sinclair confirmed this in a reply email: 'yes, they say they can source the million they have spoken of all by themselves'.[54] A million dollars is a huge donation in New Zealand politics – enough potentially to determine the outcome of a closely fought election.

The Talley–Davidson plan was based on the view that Brash's campaign advisers did 'not have what it takes' and proposed that they pay to bring in the best campaign consultants, such as market researchers, that money could buy.[55] Sinclair, acting in his capacity as Brash's right-hand man, gave Davidson the go-ahead to prepare a detailed proposal.[56] Brash and Sinclair discussed the proposal on 29 September, including the risk of 'possible adverse reaction' if the collaboration became public 'further down the track'. But Brash was comfortable enough with exploring the plan that he agreed to phone three of National's main existing donors to suggest they talk to Davidson and give their ideas on the best way to shape the plan.[57]

On 2 November 2004 Davidson sent an email to Sinclair containing the written proposal Davidson had prepared for Peter Talley. He told Sinclair he 'look[ed] forward to discussing the proposal with you and Diane [Foreman] tomorrow night'.[58] Brash had phoned Foreman to ask her to offer ideas for the Talley–Davidson plan.

The written proposal is, in its own way, as extraordinary as the letter setting out the Exclusive Brethren's $1 million plans. The proposal document, drafted by Davidson, was headed 'The repackaging of Don Brash'. It began: 'This is the outline of the mechanics for implementing the concept which we have put to Don Brash and Bryan Sinclair'.

The plan involved forming a company or trust, provisionally named 'VCo', 'the directors/shareholders or trustees of which would not be the source of finance'. 'That way,' Davidson explained, 'anonymity can be preserved for those who wish it.' The trust or company would then 'hire the people who would form the small, key, advisory team. Where necessary, they would be paid their normal professional fee for the work. We need the best people and should not expect to gain their services for nothing.'

The paid consultants 'would devise policy and strategy for DB and report directly to him. The style would be that of a presidential campaign... given the quality of caucus as a whole, no other approach is tenable'. The 'funding would go directly into Vco', which would hire the campaign consultants in its own name. 'Expenditure of those funds would be controlled in house, not by National.' By directing the campaign spending through the privately controlled VCo, they 'would avoid any declarations of political party funding'.[59]

The aim was to add another million dollars of grunt to the National Party campaign, which, because it would be spent on strategy advisers and other non-advertising expenses, would not have to be declared so could be an addition to National's $2.24 million legal spending cap. However, it is hard to see how they could do this legally if the plan was to 'avoid any declarations of political party funding'.

Like the Exclusive Brethren advertising campaign, the plan was based on the assumption that everything would be done secretly and no one would ever find out. Even so, it was bound to meet internal resistance once other senior National Party people became aware of it. As Davidson noted, 'what is needed is a mechanism which is totally under the control of the backers (working with Don Brash and Bryan Sinclair) and which can be halted and, if necessary, abandoned if it does not work. It would operate totally independently of the present caucus strategy team.'

The proposal considered that there 'may be one or two people from within the caucus group which has been advising on strategy who have the capacity and the desire to grasp what we are proposing. If so, perhaps they should be given a liaison role. However, the appalling failure to capitalise on the Orewa speech would tend to indicate otherwise. Hence my firm view that the new "Kitchen Cabinet" of advisers should bypass the present group. It is essential that interference from anyone in caucus who may suffer from a bruised ego as a result of this proposal is firmly dealt with "from above".' [60]

The plan was based on the view that the main obstacle to a Brash victory was the quality of his campaign advisers. The Talleys were willing to find $1 million to solve the problem. But the intention to sideline the existing campaign strategists was too audacious (or arrogant and unrealistic) and it seems likely that this derailed the plan.

There is no documentation concerning what happened next. After this proposal arrived in Don Brash's office, no other communications about the plan appear to have been put in writing. Whatever happened after that was discussed across restaurant tables and in private meetings. It seems likely that the Talleys wanted more control over campaign decisions than the National Party inner circle was willing to give away – even for $1 million. Or the proposal may have been reworked into a less ambitious and more realistic form.

We do know, however, that Sinclair promoted the plan enthusiastically and Brash, at least initially, knowingly went along with it – approvingly stating in writing his understanding about the $1 million offer. If the initiative did go ahead in some form, it was deliberately intended that the public would have no way of knowing, since the private trust and back-room assistance being proposed would be very hard to detect. Documents show that Peter Talley and Davidson continued to have close and friendly contact with the Brash team, including free on-call use of a Talley heli-copter for Brash throughout the election campaign: Davidson was listed in Brash's daily diaries as contact person for the travel arrangements.

The other possible million-dollar donation story is also unconfirmed. During the research for this book, a senior National Party figure provided details of various National Party funders and stated that the largest single election donation, believed to be well over $1 million, had come from the Insurance Council and was given to National because the party was known to be intending, if elected, to privatise the Accident Compensation Commission (ACC). [61] It is a believable story – the insurance companies specialising in accident insurance had billions of dollars to gain from privatisation – but that does not mean it is true. Like the Talley plan, the story will probably remain a mystery.

There was, though, a series of meetings between National and insurance companies over many months between August 2004 and July 2005, where privatisation of ACC and the details of how it would be achieved were on the agenda. (The background and details of these meetings are given in the notes.) [62]

When National released its ACC policy on 25 August 2005, 'offer[ing] Kiwis choice of insurer by allowing competition' (which meant privatisation), Insurance Council CEO Chris Ryan sent a private memo to insurance company heads announcing the news. He said the details 'were very positive for the industry'. 'The details of [National's] policy have been deliberately kept out of the announcement after consultation with the Insurance Council.'[63]

When this memo was leaked shortly before the election, National and the Insurance Council appear to have worked out their media responses together. Richard Long wrote to his colleagues warning about the memo and saying it would be 'used to further the conspiracy between National and big business' and 'Chris advises that we should refer queries to him'. He drafted lines for the National MPs: 'to questions about what is meant by deliberately withholding details, we should refer the question to the Insurance Council as it is their statement, not ours'. Mostly, however, he advised that they should just say, 'I have no idea what [Chris Ryan] is talking about.'[64]

Controlling secret election donations is probably the main area of potential corrupt political behaviour in New Zealand politics. The present laws, designed by self-interested politicians, have created a regime that, at its worst, is legalised corruption.

The 1986 Royal Commission on the Electoral System explained succinctly that the main aim of donation disclosure is 'to limit the potential for corruption by interests with access to substantial funds'. They quoted the United States Supreme Court Justice Louis Brandeis: 'Publicity is justly commended as a remedy for social and industrial diseases. Sunlight is said to be the best of disinfectants; electric light the most efficient policeman.'[65] To stop a handful of wealthy people from repeating in future elections what they did in 2005, New Zealand must urgently improve its electoral system.

The first step is to ban anonymous donations and the use of anonymising trusts. It is absurd to have legislation that acknowledges the importance of disclosure but includes loopholes that make it possible and lawful to name not a single donor. Parliamentary inquiries into each recent general election have repeatedly reached the same conclusion, that the donation declaration laws do not 'meet the purposes for which a public disclosure regime was established' and said there should be 'a fundamental review of electoral legislation'.[66] The time has come.

Deliberate withholding of information or deception over the identity of a donor should be a criminal offence. As the royal commission originally recommended, any genuinely anonymous donations received by a party should have to be handed over to the Electoral Commission. The reason for this strictness is simple: otherwise parties can deliberately encourage and facilitate anonymised donations to suit their own and their donors' wish to avoid publicity.[67]

The second change is to require all donations, except perhaps very small ones, to be declared. An appropriate level would be all donations above $25 or $50. This may sound unnecessarily low, but one of ACT's 1996 donors demonstrated why this is necessary. Alan Gibbs's business partner Trevor Farmer wanted to donate over $100,000 to ACT. His lawyers, Buddle Findlay, arranged twelve separate donations, all slightly under $10,000, which were contributed in the name of Farmer, several members of his family and four Buddle Findlay partners.[68] None had to be listed on the party's donation declaration. To avoid such tricks the minimum value for declaring donations must be very small. This and a ban on anonymous donations would bring New Zealand more into line with laws in similar countries.

The third change needed is for declarations of all election year dona-tions to be publicised *before* election day. Currently, the public cannot see the parties' donation declarations until months after one election but still nearly three years before the next. Under this system there is very little chance that information about, or lack of disclosure of, the donors will have any meaningful influence on voters' judgement of the parties. A change to the legislation could require all election year donations to be received by, say, a month before election day, with the details to be made public a week or two later.

A fourth important change would be to permit political donations only from New Zealand citizens and permanent residents. This rule has important symbolic value for reasserting the democratic basis of elections. Only these people are permitted to vote. People who are not permitted to be part of the election should not, instead, be permitted to influence it with money.

These changes to donation laws, although necessary, will not solve all the problems. The United States has strict donation declaration laws but the elections are still awash with big corporate money and become a battle between election budgets. To ensure democratic elections, different types of controls are also needed.

At present, donations, and the donors' expectations, remain secret but occasional cases have become public. In 1993, for example, Helen Clark, then Labour health spokesperson, released leaked correspondence between the Beer, Wine and Spirits Council and the National Party in which the council expressed dismay that the party seemed to be backing down on a key part of the deal that had opened the way for industry assistance with National's 'election efforts'. The council later noted that a proposal for a new Substance Abuse Council 'directly contradicted' past agreements and was 'a fundamental point of principle on which the BWSC cannot possibly be expected to compromise'.[69] National quietly 'reviewed', then dropped its policy of creating a Substance Abuse Council. In the 2002 election the Macraes Mining company offered election donations to Jim Anderton's Progressive Coalition and the Green Party at a time when the company was trying to reduce opposition to its goldmining operations: Progressive accepted and the Greens declined.[70] But the most serious example by far is the one outlined in this book: a group of wealthy radical-right businesspeople using their economic power to change the direction of the National Party and then, very nearly, the country.

New policies are needed. One option is to extend the three-month election campaign period to include the full year before an election. But this would not be enough on its own. A good option would be to place limits on how much any individual can donate to a party in a year. The maximum figure could, for instance, be set at the level a person on an average income could reasonably afford, which would mean only about $500 in 2006 values, with severe penalties for someone channelling their money via others.

At the same time the definition of 'election activity' needs to be extended to include crucial election-winning components such as campaign strategists and advisers, voter database systems, focus group research and polling and any other activities that have as their primary purpose gaining electoral support for the party or reducing electoral support for other parties. This is necessary to avoid parties outspending opponents in non-declarable areas.

It should also be made impossible for a wealthy group like the Exclusive Brethren to spend huge sums promoting their preferred party. The law needs to be tightened and breaches treated as serious crimes. At the moment, the police seem more likely to use a search warrant on a common burglar than on someone trying to steal an election. Police should be able to take action immediately and there should be greater penalties, powers to access bank accounts and party records and an extension of the time for laying charges well beyond the present six months.[71]

The final area where reform is needed is public funding of election activities. Currently, most of the costs of elections and election campaigning are already funded by the state. For months, as politicians travel around the country making election speeches and kissing babies, their airfares and accommodation are paid by the state, as are the salaries and expenses of all the minders, plus everyone's phones and other costs – not to mention the politicians' salaries and entertainment allowances. For instance, Richard Long, Bryan Sinclair and the other National Party staff were being paid by the public, through Parliamentary Services, as they worked from morning until midnight on the National Party election campaign.

While the politicians are on the campaign trail, back at the parliamentary and electorate offices most other business has given way to election work. Executive assistants help to prepare direct mail mailing lists, office stationery, printers and postal budgets are used to send out bulk mailings of information about the achievements of politicians and parties and so on. In other words, many millions of dollars are used, not on parliamentary business, but on the efforts of the politicians and parties to secure votes in the coming election. On top of all this, the party leaders' offices have a large budget to publicise their party policies and activities, which, though it should not, obviously merges into election publicity as well as the election approaches. Finally, there is $3.2 million of public money shared between all parties competing in the election to pay for the time and production of their election broadcast advertising. All the parties, whether they profess to be for or against state election funding, already accept all this money.

In reality, the controversy and potential problems that surround election donations and spending are mostly about a relatively small part of the cost of electioneering: the last few million dollars, across all parties, that has to be raised from private donors. It is worth putting this sum in perspective. Organising the information campaigns, voter registrations, electoral rolls, polling booths and everything else that goes into holding an election costs the public in the tens of millions. The existing public funding of election activities described above costs many millions more. Next to all this, complete state funding of elections would be a relatively small extra cost.

The argument in favour of more state funding is simple. If state funding went together with strict limits on donation sizes and election spending, it could reduce greatly the influence of the big individual donors, the tobacco industry, the liquor industry, unions, business associations, churches and any other lobbies on the elections. A second argument for state funding is that big donors kill political parties as mass-member organisations. As we have seen, money from big donors, together with paid election consultants, means election campaigns can be run by a small political clique around the leader of the party. This leaves little need for, and therefore little commitment to, party organisations or members.

The main argument against state funding is that it produces much the same effect on the party organisation as big donors. It increases the power of the party élite, who can run the election campaign with the help of their paid strategists and other consultants. At the same time, parties can become lazy and cease to bother much with members and internal processes. There is also a general dislike of the idea of giving public money to political parties. National was playing to these feelings when it boasted that its billboard campaign had been paid for by 'supporters of the National Party' while the spending on Labour's election pledge cards had been funded from the public coffers. This contrast does not sound quite so good when it is understood that the contrast is between publicly funded publicity and publicity paid for by special interest groups such as far right multi-millionaires.

In combining both public and private funding of elections, New Zealand appears to have chosen a sensible balance. Actually the opposite is true. There is abuse of the public funding (such as Labour's pledge card), elections are compromised by big private donors and both the public and private funding undermines the internal democracy of the political parties. A better way needs to be found to fund elections.

First, despite the problems with state funding, it makes no sense to allow a small group of donors to have a disproportionate influence over elections merely for the sake of saving a few million dollars of public money every three years. After all, the government that is elected will have control of tens of billions of dollars of public money.

As Otago University senior law lecturer Andrew Geddis has pointed out, state funding of elections has usually been introduced, as it was in Canada, in the wake of funding scandals. 'The public was prepared to wear [increased state funding] because they thought, "We don't really like giving money to political parties. But we'd rather they got it this way than doing the kind of dodgy things they were doing otherwise." '[72] New Zealand should not wait for more scandals before making the change.

Moreover, it is appalling to have a system that leads to senior politicians and party officials regularly misleading or deceiving the public about monetary matters. This institutional lack of integrity feeds into the rest of the political system. The best answer is probably to devise a way to make state funding work, while improving democracy inside political parties. This could mean, perhaps, modest state funding combined with relatively low spending caps (including for third parties), where any extra funds parties want have to be raised in small sums from large numbers of party members and beyond.

If there is an increase in state funding of election activities, it must be accompanied by strict limits on the size of donations and third-party activities to ensure that it is impossible for big donors or a group like the Exclusive Brethren ever again to affect an election as they did in 2005. If they want to participate, they can vote and make a small donation like anyone else. Under the laws at the time of writing, parties can receive million-dollar donations and raise as much money as they like as long as they do not spend more than the permitted amount on advertising within the last three months before an election.

Putting to one side the natural reaction of not wanting to give public money to political parties, the choices are stark. National Party members must ask themselves whether they want wealthy special interest groups to continue exerting so much influence over their party. If the answer is no, then they need to find new ways to fund their election campaigns. The public must ask themselves whether they want such influence over the outcome of elections. If the answer is no, then there need to be *fundamental*, not kneejerk and ad hoc, changes to the funding of elections in New Zealand and how donations and election spending are controlled.

CHAPTER 16

AS GOOD AS WON
Behind the scenes in the election campaign

National's election campaign slogan, 'Tackling the issues of mainstream New Zealand', was launched at its election-year conference at the end of June 2005.[1] Deputy leader Gerry Brownlee used the word 'mainstream' fifteen times in his conference speech and Brash repeated it more times in his keynote address. 'There is a concern,' he said, 'that the Labour Government has been pandering to minority issues for too long.'[2]

In the weeks that followed, as National suggested publicly that Maori and gay people were not mainstream, the party was vigorously pursuing the votes of a different minority: fundamentalist Christians. The decidedly irreligious senior National politicians and staff, some of whose cynical views are reproduced in the notes,[3] took care to ensure that their links to these churches remained below the radar, aware that if this alliance became publicly visible it could lose them votes elsewhere.

National MP Richard Worth raised the idea of collaborating with evangelical Christians in February 2004. 'Don, I've spoken to you about Terry Calkin in the past. He is the pastor of the Greenlane Christian Centre which is faintly evangelical with a Sunday congregation of 2,000. It was he who made the offer to Bill [English] which was never taken up to shift what he calls the "blue collar" vote to National. He is overtly National... [and] is very keen to meet you to talk about specific strategies which he can use through his church to advance our cause.' Worth ended the letter saying: 'P.S. He thinks it is unhelpful for you to say that you are not a Christian, if of course you ever said that'.[4]

The Elim Greenlane Christian Centre was one of the most outspokenly political churches in New Zealand: for example, it took a leading role in opposing the 2004 Civil Union Bill. It was also the church of Maxim Institute managing director Greg Fleming. National's Mount Albert candidate, Ravi Musuku, himself a Baptist pastor, had recommended the Greenlane Christian Centre to Steven Joyce as 'politically very active [with] regular political meetings'.[5]

There was some contact between National and Calkin at that stage, then detailed collaborations began as the election got closer. National staff met with Calkin about late June 2005 to discuss how he could help the election of a National government.[6] This was the same as other behind-the-scenes meetings occurring during that time, such as with the Exclusive Brethren and the racing lobby. It was agreed that Brash would give a speech to the Greenlane Christian Centre congregation at 7.45am on Saturday, 11 July 2005, without journalists present. His 'Morality speech' said there was a 'growing backlash' against the Labour-led government's policies and, particularly, that 'parents are crying out for schools that teach the values of their community'.[7]

He told the congregation that National would introduce policies that would help the Elim Christian College (a special Christian secondary school run by the church) and the Elim Ministry Training College and English Academy. This assistance would include increasing public funding for private schools and training establishments and shifting back to bulk funding of schools, which would also increase Elim's public funding. He was quite specific that the election of a National government would result in well over a hundred thousand dollars a year extra funding for the church.[8] He showed he was in tune with their concerns by saying National opposed the proposed 'hate' and anti-smacking legislation.[9]

Brash also made time for appearances on Shine Television and evangelical radio stations, as well as a regular weekly interview on Radio Rhema, the radio network inspired by American evangelist Pat Robertson, who was credited with turning the United States Christian Coalition into a conservative political force.[10] Victoria University Professor of Religious Studies Paul Morris commented the day after the election that, by appealing to a Christian moral conservative vote, National had succeeded in winning the votes of previous supporters of the Christian Heritage, Destiny and United Future parties. Christian moral conservatives, like the Exclusive Brethren, had been drawn to secular National because the party had championed their moral agenda and also had a realistic chance at becoming government. 'If Brash was openly Christian,' Morris said, 'it would be electorally disastrous.' Instead 'he's made the right noises, the right codewords, and the Christian leaders around the country feel he is addressing their issues'.[11]

Brash made a second appearance at a Greenlane Christian Centre-linked event later in the campaign, this time an evangelical youth leadership conference called Getsmart with the slogan 'You can influence this nation, you can influence your world'.[12] Bryan Sinclair, who co-ordinated the visit, said there 'should be about 1500 there, average age 18 years'.... Warm reception guaranteed. Tony and Sandra [presumably Tony Ryall and Sandra Goudie] did this today at the Wellington sessions and got standing ovations.'[13]

The day after their visit Sinclair wrote to the organiser, Caleb Standen, to thank him for 'accommodating Don's impromptu visit at such short notice'. Brash had 'appreciated the opportunity to speak to such a fantastic and sparkly bunch, and he very much enjoyed meeting you... and your team. Your organisation's aims... are aims consistent with Don's own, and with the values of the National Party.'[14] The main reason for Sinclair's email, however, was that he and Brash were nervous that a photo showing the National leader joining in the meeting might find its way into the mainstream news media.

'I only have one minor concern,' Sinclair went on, 'and that is the digital photo taken of Don during the prayer which immediately followed the national anthem.' He headed into a convoluted and not entirely frank explanation about why the photo should not be published. 'Don, as you might be aware, was bought up in a Presbyterian family. Since becoming the leader of the National Party, he has found some mainstream media organisations to be quite deliberately unhelpful regarding his religious upbringing, and I see some potential for this photograph of Don to be used out of context and in a way that attempts to deliberately embarrass both Don (in the lead up to an Election), and your own organisation. Publication of that image on a website or in printed material would inevitably lead to mainstream media, and our political opponents, picking it up, taking it completely out of context (as they have done on previous occasions) and using it in a twisted fashion to try and embarrass and discredit both the Getsmart team, and Don personally. I hope you don't mind me raising this red flag, and I would appreciate it if you could use your discretion on this matter.'[15]

The reason for Sinclair's concern was that when the meeting prepared to pray, the leader had asked everyone to raise both their arms in the air and Brash had been photographed in this not very mainstream pose. Standen reported back later that night that he had dealt with the problem immediately. 'We are embarrassed that this happened and have spoken to our team member who took the photographs. The photographer has given me her word that she has not distributed the two photographs that she took (actually digital images) to anyone and has not downloaded them to her computer and I watched her permanently delete the images from her camera this evening.' He asked Sinclair to 'please accept our apologies for this incident and let us know if you would like us to take any further action'.[16] Sinclair forwarded the news to Brash with a one-word comment: 'Hallelujah'.[17] Brash replied: 'Many thanks Bryan. You're a champ.'[18]

The National politicians adopted the same approach to all subjects they thought would be unhelpful for their campaign. For instance, whenever Labour raised National's policy on sending troops to the Iraq War, a genuine area of policy difference between the two parties, Brash simply evaded the questions. Asked by Radio New Zealand for his party's policy on sending troops, he replied: 'The key issue for the moment is Labour's incredible waste of taxpayers' money on the education sector.'

> Reporter: Sorry Dr Brash, Iraq's not about wasting money, it's a policy position. I mean...
>
> Don Brash: No it's not, but Helen Clark's raising it is a diversionary tactic. The difference between National and Labour in foreign policy is negligible.
>
> Reporter: The situation in Iraq is set to go on for some years - yes or no, would a National government send troops to Iraq?
>
> Don Brash: That's entirely hypothetical. The issue at the moment is Labour Party waste.[19]

This refusal to depart from the party lines and engage in debate – and National and other parties were guilty of this – contributed to the phoney, unreal feeling that the 2005 election campaigning had for the public. Here is Brash again with TV3's Duncan Garner a week later:

> Reporter: Would you have sent troops to Iraq?
>
> Don Brash: I say this is a diversionary tactic by Helen Clark. It's not relevant.
>
> Reporter: But would you have sent troops to Iraq, Dr Brash?

Don Brash: The issue right now today is about Labour's wasting hundreds of millions of dollars of taxpayers' money....

Reporter: My question was, would you have sent troops to Iraq if you were the prime minister?

Don Brash: And I'm telling you that the real issue of the day is not that issue of the past that's essentially gone [interrupted]

Reporter: It is the question I'm asking you today, though.

Don Brash: And I'm saying to you that the key issue today is the fact government is wasting hundreds of millions of dollars of taxpayers' money. That's the issue the media should be focused on....

Reporter: What about answering my question? As prime minister would you have sent troops to Iraq given some of the flyers that are out today by the Labour Party?

Don Brash: Look, the Labour Party is desperately harking back to issues which are no longer relevant at all.

Reporter: So are you saying you are not prepared to answer that question about whether you would have sent troops to Iraq or not?

Don Brash: That's not the issue today. The issue [interrupted]

Reporter: But it is the issue because I'm asking you it.

Don Brash: Well. I'm sorry. I want to focus on the issue which is important right now to taxpayers and that's waste of government spending to a huge degree.[20]

Labour continued needling National about foreign policy. A few days later Cabinet Minister Trevor Mallard claimed, without any apparent evidence, that the 'lead bag man' raising money for the National Party was an American and that Americans had been helping to write the party's policies. It seems unlikely any Americans had been doing this. Richard Long drafted the responses, vehemently denying the accusation about party policy.

In an email to his media staff, he said their reply to Mallard should be: 'This is another panicked and desperate attack by Labour to get the debate off issues that affect mainstream New Zealand. It is absolute rubbish to suggest that policy is written in America. It is homegrown. It is designed by National party politicians.' [21] When he came to the funding question, the prepared lines were suddenly more slippery: 'Any fundraising by Americans, and any Americans at head office? I simply have no idea. I remain at arm's length from fund raising, as do all our politicians. That is for a very good reason. That is handled by the party president and general manager.'

Long was particularly sensitive about the issue of Americans at the party head office. (National had at least two Republican campaign consultants from the US working out of its head office but their presence was kept secret until after the election.) [22] 'There will be multiple questions on the following. Do you have Americans working at party HQ? Do you have American advisors? How much backing does National get from the US? Do you have Americans fund raising for you?' He proposed the following line for the politicians if required: 'There are bound to be Americans who feel strongly about National's policies and who donate to the party. I simply don't know. In the same way, there may be some misguided Americans who donate to Labour. I don't know that either.' [23] In fact, National had been receiving advice from United States Republicans (some details are in the notes), [24] but these answers managed to deflect media questioning.

Long and his colleagues co-ordinated their denials with Julian Robertson, the American billionaire about whom Mallard had been hinting. Long emailed Steven Joyce, Brash and McCully with instructions. He said that Robertson's assistant Diana McCarthy had 'called from the USA and said Julian had been getting quite a few calls but wanted to keep a low profile unless Don thought he needed to say something'. McCarthy 'will talk to Steven Joyce' and, also, 'Steven, can you please call Julian?'

It is not known whether Robertson made a donation to National (which he is entitled to do) but there is evidence that he actively tried to help the party. When Brash and Peter Keenan went to the United States in June 2004, they saw Robertson during a one-day visit to New York. As Brash described it, 'When Peter Keenan and I were in the US last month, we met about 15 people over a lunch hosted by Julian Robertson in New York. Among those present were two guys who have been actively involved in various Republican campaigns and who have expressed a strong interest in helping with our campaign in New Zealand after the elections in the US are over.... From the fact that Julian Robertson has recommended them highly they are probably pretty good.'[25] When National decided against hiring the two consultants, Sinclair wrote to Brash: 'You will know best in dealing with Julian Robertson here but might be a good idea to drop a note and thank him for the intro... lest he think we didn't want the advice/help and quite possibly the funds for this!'[26]

Long continued his media advice, noting that 'there were some suggestions internally of using Gerry [Brownlee] as a battering ram against Mallard'. 'We have explained that we want to look superior at this stage and not play that game while things are running in our favour. [Foreign affairs spokesman] Lockwood [Smith] has also agreed to keep a low profile and not engage.'

Finally, Long explained that he had received the cooperation of a journalist in avoiding unwanted attention about the issue. 'Paul Holmes wanted to get Julian on,' he informed his colleagues, 'but I said we would prefer to downplay that side of it and upplay our statement of today about concentrating on the issues and policy rollout. Paul accepted that.'[27]

Besides all the effort to avoid saying things, the campaign strategy team tried to keep tight control over what the politicians could say. Anyone in New Zealand between June and September 2005 was guaranteed to hear the same sets of words repeated over and over in election publications, speeches and interviews. This is what the campaign strategists call 'message discipline'.

In April 2005 Steven Joyce summarised National's election campaign strategy for Brash and the key party spokespeople. The strategy consisted of 'key attack themes', 'reinforced by strong advertising' to build the 'image' of the Labour government's 'squandering and mis-managing'. The campaign strategy committee gave Bill English the job of co-ordinating the 'concerted "team" attack on Labour'. First on the list of attack lines were 'race-based discrimination' and social welfare, finishing with '111 calls' and the government squandering the public's tax money.[28]

Joyce followed this up a month later with an email on 'message discipline'. As part of 'a plan to create greater message discipline', he discussed 'setting up a text [message] group to inform candidates/MPs when a reporter is on the rounds, and providing the key messages to them'. He said 'we need hits on the economy and education, and we need to be planning for Don to re-visit the Treaty aggressively soon (as discussed with Murray)'.[29] Long instituted a daily meeting of National's communications staff at 9am so he could 'pass on the decisions/strategy each day so... we are all singing from the same songbook'.[30]

The 'message discipline' was soon obvious. Every opportunity was used to repeat the approved words. When a TV3 poll appeared two weeks later, showing the gap between National and Labour closing from 11 to 4 per cent in one month, Long wrote lines for Brash: 'The electorate was turning to National's policies to benefit middle, mainstream New Zealanders'.[31] For a Fairfax poll, Long drafted similar lines: 'National is producing policies for middle, mainstream New Zealand, including tax relief, and this is leaving a clear choice for New Zealand. Only National can change Labour's policies of over-taxing and wasteful spending.'[32]

When a *Sunday Star-Times* poll showed National equal to Labour, Jason Ede wrote 'Don's line's for poll' saying, 'I am certainly not pausing to take any pleasure from the current polling. However, these results do confirm that the public understands lower taxes and stronger incentives are the keys to a better performing economy.'[33] The following month Ede prepared for some upcoming polls by preparing two sets of lines – one for if the polls went up and one for if they went down – with Brash saying the same thing whichever way they went:

Q: National increases lead on Labour?

A: I am not pausing to take any pleasure from the current polling.

* Helen Clark is desperately trying to avoid talking about the issues that really matter to the majority of us – things like tax, a growing bureaucracy and the wastage of taxpayer money....

Q: National loses ground to Labour?

A: We expect the polls to bounce around between now and the election.

* Repeat bullet points above

In early August 2005 Joyce updated the message discipline with a new list of 'key vote messages' called 'What this election is ALL about' (reproduced in the notes),[34] with all the familiar Textor/National lines about giving 'ordinary New Zealanders the right incentives to work hard and to get ahead', about 'cutting personal taxes for mainstream New Zealanders' and about stopping Labour's waste of 'your hard-earned tax dollars'. The election was also 'about Kiwi, not just iwi', about the 'mainstream New Zealanders that have been ignored and neglected for too long'.

Long sent Joyce's list wider: 'FYI all, this is our approved core message for the election, which should form the basis of what our troops say'.[35] The publications had exactly the same messages. The personally addressed letters signed by Brash to every voter in the week before the election asked 'which party will provide the right incentives for people?' and replied 'If you want a focus on hard-working New Zealand values, lower taxes and less waste, then my simple message is – give your party vote to National.'[36] And so on.

Carefully controlled and scripted as it was, most of the detail of the campaign is not worth recording. It consisted of a series of essentially boring photo opportunities for the leader and candidates, the clever advertisements and insubstantial public statements repeating the agreed lines. A giant asteroid could have hit the earth and National would have responded that it showed that hardworking New Zealanders needed tax cuts to help them get ahead and that there was now no excuse for Labour's shameful squandering of taxpayers' money. The most interesting election events were those happening behind the scenes or when things went wrong.

Because the public receives so much of its election information via the news media, it is no surprise that political parties put enormous effort into trying to manage the news to their advantage. This management occurs at three levels: the daily 'lines' and message discipline, maintaining relationships with individual journalists and – a level at which there are only hints – maintaining relationships with the executives of the private media companies.

Political party attempts to influence journalists is a complex subject.[37] The National Party papers show various mainstream journalists and a good number of talkback radio hosts whom the leader's staff regarded as actively sympathetic to National. And other journalists, of course, are privately sympathetic to other parties. Problems arise, however, when party–journalist relationships lead the journalists to act unprofessionally, when political operators use aggression to pressure media organisations and when party media tactics get in the way of normal democratic election debate.

Journalists covering an election campaign are faced with an unhelpful wall of media minders, message discipline and prepared lines. As they try to do their job, and somehow get behind the spin before deadlines, they are up against a bevy of party strategists and media officers working full time to control the news. This has an obvious effect on the quality of news reaching the public. Since the journalists still have to produce stories every day or week, the news is inclined to revolve around the formulaic stories that are easy to get, such as the ups and downs of opinion polls and preferred leader 'stakes'.

Fortunately there is also good political journalism. But overall there is a trend in New Zealand, and many other countries, for election news to focus on each new poll, like the latest sports results, accompanied by spurious and often self-serving theories from commentators to explain the latest movement on the league board. In 2005, while Richard Long scripted the official responses (voters are responding to Labour's overtaxing and wasteful spending etc.), Murray McCully exploited journalists' shortage of real information by offering off-the-record insider briefings and interpretations of events that he hoped would find their way into the news stories.

The style of political journalism is an important issue as increasing political resources go into controlling news and there are fewer news media resources available to cut through the spin. Such a situation plays into the hands of the Crosby/Textor political manipulators. Their aim is not to create interested, intelligent and engaged citizens, because that is not in their clients' short-term interests. Their job is easier if the public is 'sick' of politics, 'bored' by the election and not thinking hard about the issues – and not challenged by a strong, independent media. Vote winning can then be the science of winning people over via vague feelings of self-interest, indignation, fear or jealousy.

An example of journalistic conflict of interest was the help given to National by radio and television personality Paul Holmes. One of New Zealand's best known media people, Holmes hosted the most listened to morning radio news programme in Auckland. In this role he regularly interviewed many politicians, including Don Brash, and his listeners had a right to expect a reasonable level of independence in the news reporting and interviews. As we have seen, back in July Holmes had already acceded to National's request that Julian Robertson not appear on his programme. In the crucial final week of the election campaign, he agreed to help Brash prepare for some important media appearances.

On the Wednesday before election day, Brash was scheduled to have a 45-minute interview with Larry Williams on Sky television in the morning, then a more challenging 30-minute interview with Kim Hill on TV1 at 9.30pm. A special 'Media/Debate Training' session was arranged for the day before, Tuesday 13 September 2005, at the Sky City Hotel in Auckland. Richard Long set up for the session in hotel suite 439, which had been booked under the name of a junior press officer. The item in Brash's diary was discreet, recording only that the training was with 'Paul H'. The room was set up with a private film crew and two lecterns, one for Brash and one for the practice interviewer. Holmes arrived in time to begin the two-hour training session at 3pm.

Other media people have trained politicians, most notably Brian Edwards, who was Helen Clark's media trainer for years. The essential difference was that Edwards did not hide his role, so the public could judge his media appearances in the knowledge that he regularly assisted Clark and was clearly sympathetic to her politics. Holmes was guilty of conflict of interest over the election-week media training because it was being kept secret from his listeners and viewers.

Long and his media staff, all of whom received good salaries paid by Parliamentary Services from public money, saw it as part of their jobs to assist journalists they thought would write sympathetic stories and obstruct those they felt might be critical. For a requested interview that might result in bad news coverage for National, the leader and other MPs were unlikely to be available and prepared lines would be supplied by Long or a press officer. Wherever possible, they avoided comment on difficult issues, saying between themselves that they did not want to give them 'oxygen'. Certain journalists were treated with suspicion whenever they requested an interview and some staff regarded whole news organisations as the enemy.

Long had been angry at Fairfax, owners of the *Sunday Star-Times*, *Dominion Post* and *Press*, ever since the *Sunday Star-Times* had likened Brash to Australia's One Nation leader Pauline Hanson after his 2004 Orewa race speech. Brash had worked to improve relations at a meeting with Fairfax corporate affairs manager Bruce Wolpe during a visit to Sydney in August 2004. But early in the election year, when Wolpe contacted National about a New Zealand Labour government tax proposal, Long's reaction showed his continuing strong antagonism towards Fairfax.

'My initial reaction to this is Fuck Fairfax,' he wrote to Sinclair. 'You should get back to Wolpe and tell him Fairfax should address their blatant bias in the Sunday Star Times and the Dominion Post (which has yet to run the child care policy in any detail) before we take any interest in their plight. Their company is doing more than any other (apart perhaps from State Radio) to keep Labour in power. I'm an APN [APN News and Media, publisher of the *New Zealand Herald*] man myself. May Tony O'Reilly rule.'[38]

This conversation was a continuation of ongoing disputes between Long and Sinclair. The latter replied tartly: 'Glad it's only an initial reaction, Richard, because were this your ultimate view then I would respond that such an arrogant and emotive stance is unlikely to improve the situation you describe, and would do nothing at all to assist the ongoing management of media relationships between the National Party and a significant player in the NZ newspaper market'. He continued: 'And yes, the matters you raise have been drawn to the attention of Fairfax, and higher up the food chain than Bruce Wolpe I might add'. They agreed on one thing, however: 'of course, in saying all of that,' Sinclair concluded, 'I agree with you on Tony O'Reilly'.[39]

Long's fondness for the *New Zealand Herald* was matched by his and Murray McCully's hostility towards Television New Zealand (TVNZ). They made no effort to hide this hostility. When TVNZ's *Agenda* current affairs programme requested an interview with John Key in May 2004, for instance, Long replied at 10pm, checking if the interview would be an ambush. That email had been sent for only seven minutes when Long sent another to 'Dickie', *Agenda* producer Richard Harman. 'I thought I was being reasonably direct, but in case you mistook the delicate phrasing of my message, see the message below from the dark prince'.[40] He had forwarded an email from McCully that said, 'Long, you omitted to mention that we regard them as a bunch of lying, cheating, duplicitous bastards.'[41] Harman replied, formally, that he had 'no idea what Mr McCully's comment refers to – I hope it is meant as a joke – but if it is not then I take exception to it'.[42]

Six months before the election Long and McCully were furious over TV1's news coverage of National's 'youth justice' policy, which proposed lowering the age of criminal responsibility to twelve years. Long complained that news reader 'Judy Bailey looked and sounded as if she had been personally offended by the policy', said he intended to 'take it up with someone' and sought McCully's help.[43]

Again the divisions in the campaign strategy team were clear. When he saw this correspondence, Sinclair wrote to Brash warning that involving McCully in the party's relationship with TVNZ was not going to help them in an election year. 'TVNZ loathe him and in my view this can only further deteriorate the coverage.' Referring to McCully, he said 'the man minding your media relationships cannot be the man who is charged with ripping that same organisation apart in the event of you becoming the government'. Long was 'perceived by these news organisations to be too close to Murray McCully (rightly or wrongly). Fairfax's worldview, you will recall, is much the same.'[44]

The internal conflicts between the National Leader's office staff had been brewing since soon after Brash became leader. The main tension was between Long and McCully on one side and Sinclair on the other. McCully and Sinclair were the two main political advisers on whom Brash relied, with Keenan sitting off to one side, and each was jealous of the other's influence and contemptuous of their ideas. While McCully and Long tended to squeeze Sinclair out of campaign strategy committee decisions, Sinclair accompanied Brash much of the time and appeared to be the person he trusted most.

The strains within the campaign team came to a head as the pressures of the election campaign grew. On 10 August 2005, Sinclair wrote: 'if we're not careful, before too long the shambles will appear obvious to the outside world [and] we'll look like complete incompetents'.[45] Shortly after, one of the leader's staff wrote this exasperated note to colleagues: 'Murray and Steven [have turned] into obsessive, over-reactive, knee-jerking prats in the last couple of days, and they won't let it rest. Fed by Richard at his worst, it's become overbearing and bully-ridden and if they could, they would probably hang every pratfall this week from feminism to Connell on "advance" [sending staff ahead of Brash to check arrangements].'[46]

The simmering hostility between Long and Sinclair spilled over at the same time. On 23 August, during an electioneering visit by Brash to some South Auckland businesses, an argument over who was responsible for a particular piece of work apparently became abusive, with a furious, yelling Long shoving Sinclair backwards.

On 22 August 2005 the party released its 'long-awaited' tax package – the centrepiece of its election-year policies. Crosby/Textor had been telling National it must show the public what it was offering them, 'meeting the positive expectations the paid advertising has built'.[47] Timed for the afternoon before the first major TVNZ leaders' debate, the tax policy was launched at the Sky City casino complex in Auckland. The *Dominion Post* reported that 'Dr Brash and Mr Key were in far from celebratory mood yesterday. Their grim faces said it all: National has a lot riding on its tax cuts reaching out to middle New Zealand in the same way that Dr Brash's Orewa speech did 18 months ago.'[48]

The tax policy had not been worked out for months; nor referred for approval to the party caucus or policy committee. Internal papers show that the campaign team, in the midst of the election campaigning, were still working out the details during the week before the announcement. What Peter Keenan described as a 'horror week or two... leading to a slip in the polls' led to a last-minute increase in the tax cuts even though it meant pushing 'an already heavily massaged fiscal impulse back up to the limits of credibility'.[49] The image projected publicly was of solidity and sound fiscal management, but behind the scenes the main calculations were about how to win votes (details are in the notes).[50] As Long instructed Brash: 'DON'T talk about this being done to influence the polls'.[51]

National's lines for the media were that the tax 'relief' – not 'cuts', a word that goes together with social service 'cuts' – was designed to give the right 'incentives' to hardworking New Zealanders. But what National was really thinking about was incentives to vote. And it worked. All over the country, people who had not been inspired or engaged by more important issues in the election campaign were quietly visiting National's Tax Calculator website, www.taxcuts.co.nz, to see what a tax cut might give them.

It was after the launch of the tax cut package, 26 days before election day, that the National team started to believe they could win. The Taxathon television advertisements were 'possibly the most talked-about political television commercials since the Nats' Dancing Cossacks 30 years before'.[52] The big 'Party Vote National' Hawke's Bay horse race was coming up the following weekend and two days after that the long-planned speech 'for Don to re-visit the Treaty aggressively',[53] designed to harvest the Orewa vote tree one more time. All the pieces were falling into place. Dick Allen wrote from the United States wishing Brash and his team the 'Best of Good Fortune' and the Exclusive Brethren leaders sent their 'urgent and unceasing prayers... for you in this critical election campaign'. (Sinclair answered the Brethren by saying that Brash 'very much appreciated your kind wishes'.)[54]

Moreover, the repackaging of Brash was complete. Launching the election campaign on 21 August, he had declared, 'I promise you a government of mainstream New Zealanders, for mainstream New Zealanders.'[55] Less than two years after becoming leader, his media-projected image included barely a hint of his far-right political beliefs. He had declared in a recent speech that 'a culture of evasion, deceit and half truth pervades the Clark-led government of this country', and presented himself as a straight-talking man who means what he says and says what he means.[56] And, mostly, the media believed him. The *New Zealand Herald* promoted the Honest Don image in an article titled 'Remarkable rise of Don Brash'. It spoke of 'classic Don Brash: unplugged, devoid of guile, with a hint of blunder lurking behind a political fragility and, often as not, startlingly frank. It is both his virtue and his Achilles heel.' The article concluded: 'No amount of planning by the experts will prepare Brash for the intensity of the election campaign.... He will be yelled at, challenged and provoked. A man who does not relish confrontation in the way his tough opponents do, it would test the temperament of any person. But as Brash has demonstrated, he is not just any person.'[57]

As events would reveal, Brash's Achilles heel was not his frankness, but the discrepancy between this sales talk and the reality. Despite the best efforts of politicians and their staff to plan and contrive events to suit their purposes, there are fortunately always unexpected events to disturb the script. The 2005 election campaign had begun with one of these: tax cuts expected in the June 2005 budget did not happen and earned Labour ridicule, which lifted National into the lead. The campaign ended with two other unexpected events that may have narrowly prevented a National election victory: leaked National Party papers about Brash's far-right politics and the revelations of National's secret collaboration with the Exclusive Brethren.

If there had been just one unexpected event, Brash would probably have shrugged it off, considering the momentum he had achieved by those final weeks of the campaign. But the leaks raised doubts about the guileless 'non-politician' image and warned the public of possible hidden agendas. The Brethren link, coming straight after, became a huge controversy as the public discovered that National had collaborated with an extremely non-mainstream church and saw Brash refusing to tell the truth. Perhaps equally important, both cases provided something real in a campaign of artifice and manipulation. It was a bit of democracy in spite of the election campaign and may well have cost National the election.

The leaked Brash papers were a result of the work on this book. A year of research had revealed some deep divisions within National. There were two main complaints: that Don Brash's rise to the National leadership had been, in effect, a takeover by the radical right of New Zealand politics, and that certain big donors of the same political persuasion were having too much influence over the party. The insiders provided documents, including those that make up part of Chapter 2, which supported their view.

It seemed irresponsible simply to save all the information for the book. The basic condition for a democratic election is that people know what they are voting for and here was some revealing information which suggested that the classic Don Brash image was, at least in part, false advertising. I offered a parcel of my research to the *Sunday Star-Times* and the story appeared on Sunday, 28 August 2005, under the headline 'How ACT helped Brash take over'. It described the role of people such as Brian Nicolle in the leadership challenge and Diane Foreman's proposal that her Business Roundtable colleagues lobby the National caucus with the line 'No Brash, no money'.[58] The story was picked up by other media and stayed in the news over the following week.

Brash had been tipped off about the story at least ten days before it was published and pulled strings to try to have it stopped. On the weekend of 20–21 August 2005, he nervously awaited the Sunday newspaper, unaware that publication had been delayed for a week at the last minute. When it finally arrived on 28 August, it was not the big front-page story he had feared.

Richard Long sent reaction lines to Brash on the Sunday morning. 'We need to be relaxed, shrugging off another dirty trick and saying let's get back to tax. The SST story of moment is the tax poll on page one. That is the news. National could win and bring us lower taxes. The piece inside is conspiracy theory stuff, somewhat damaging, but it goes nowhere. Most people won't read it. The idea today should be to get people back to tax.' He urged Brash to stick to Mark Textor's A6 'key messages'. 'Use the key, key point for TV [i.e. tax] and the series of key points for radio. (You still have that sheet?)'[59] Then he scripted some lines, demonstrating again the banal but effective arts of media management. When asked about his links to ACT and the Business Roundtable, Brash was to reply:

A. [This is] just another dirty tricks campaign – we have come to expect these, but we want to keep the debate on the issues that affect mainstream New Zealanders, such as fair tax and one standard of citizenship.

Q: But surely this is serious?

A: Not as serious as our tax message. When you can tell 85 per cent of New Zealanders that they will be on the lowest tax rate, that's a serious message and I can understand political opponents trying to divert attention from this.

I am here today to illustrate how easy it is to work the tax calculator which demonstrates... National's plan to reward hard work and initiative.... All Kiwis should plug into this to see how much better off they are under National. [60]

Long wrote to all the other National MPs as well: 'Good morning, Please avoid expressing concerns/outrage over the SST right wing conspiracy article. We want to keep attention on tax. This is just another attempted diversion etc.... Please note the lines below which Don will be using: National gets opinion from all across the political spectrum. The caucus decides the policy.'[61]

The *Sunday Star-Times* story had included an email in which Business Roundtable head Roger Kerr suggested a line, quoting Governor William Hobson, for Brash's 2004 Orewa race speech: *'He iwi tahi tatou.* We are one people.' Brash was scheduled to reuse the line the day after the *Sunday Star-Times* story came out, in his 'aggressive' revisiting of race issues. Keenan sent Brash a revised copy of the speech on the Sunday night saying he had 'deleted the quote from Governor Roger Kerr Hobson' as 'we don't want to revisit that tomorrow'.[62]

National hired a private investigator, Russell Joseph, to try to discover the source of the leaks. But his inquiries were inconclusive. By the end of that week, when no follow-up stories appeared in the *Sunday Star-Times*, Brash and his colleagues relaxed and were again quietly confident the election was won.

That was Sunday, 4 September 2005, with thirteen days to go until the election – back where this book began. During that weekend the pamphlets headed 'Beware!' and attacking the Green Party started arriving in letterboxes around the country. The radio news reported that 'National denies involvement in anti-Greens leaflet' and no one realised what an explosive issue it would become. The next day, Greens co-leader Rod Donald approached Don Brash as they both campaigned in Rotorua, asking him about the pamphlets. Brash replied that National had had nothing to do with them. The first brochures were attacks on the Greens and Labour and then, in the frantic last days before the election, they became more and more obviously pro-National. The electoral authorities were powerless to stop them.

You have read the rest. The scripting of lines by Long and his staff went into overdrive: this was another distraction from the issues of mainstream New Zealanders and so on. But this time it would not work. Coming on top of the leaks about Brash's undeclared right-wing supporters, the journalists were not prepared to accept his earnest denials at face value. He and his colleagues spent the week trying, with only partial success, to lie their way out of a political disaster. In the end Brash would only apologise for some 'confusion': 'Some people clearly think I misled the public deliberately, but I did not'.[63] No one ever really understands what makes polls move up and down and all the factors that affect an election result, but there is little doubt that the moment, a week before voting day, when Brash was revealed as slippery and untruthful over his Exclusive Brethren links was the moment National lost the election.

The Exclusive Brethren's million-dollar campaign could have remained anonymous, as had been intended. Their collaboration with National could also have remained hidden, at least until the election was safely over. The events that exposed the Brethren and guaranteed them a place in New Zealand's political history were genuinely unexpected. And yet these were exactly the issues on which Brash and National deserved to stumble. Since becoming an MP, Brash had built his political success on hidden political relationships and a political expediency that had somehow been disguised as 'startlingly frank' and 'devoid of guile'. It was fitting that some of his secrets and hidden alliances should trip him up just days from the finishing line.

But that weekend, one week before the election, the National team did not know they were losing. Their private polling showed the party ahead of Labour throughout the last ten days. Over that last weekend three polls were published: a TV1 News poll had National 2 per cent ahead, TV3 News had Labour 4 per cent ahead and Fairfax had National 7 per cent ahead. The *Sunday Star-Times* headline said 'National survives Brethren fiasco'.[64] National tried to change the subject on the Monday by promising a 5 cent reduction in petrol taxes within a fortnight of taking office, responding to public feelings about recent rises in petrol prices.[65]

On the Wednesday, with only three days to go, the last Fairfax poll had National 6 per cent in front of Labour. The *Dominion Post* said 'Don Brash is poised to become prime minister'.[66] Brash stuck strictly to his lines: 'Today, I say to New Zealanders: If you want to return to hard working New Zealand values, lower taxes, less waste then my message is simple. Give your party vote to National on Saturday, and my team and I will get on with the job.'[67]

On the Thursday morning a 'message from the leader' was sent to all National MPs and their staff. 'It is very important that MPs and staff show a level of humility and take nothing for granted,' it said. 'Please avoid making any comments that would contradict this view.'[68] It meant, of course, humility in victory.

For Don Brash, his staff and close supporters, it had been a two-year election campaign. From the moment Brash took over as leader, everything had been focused on getting into government. On election night they very nearly made it, but not quite. It was so close that Brash remained at home through the evening awaiting a clear outcome. At 10.30pm he and his advisers held a telephone conference in which they decided they were unwilling to concede defeat until the special votes had been counted. Brash was driven to National's election-night party to announce this decision to the cheering supporters. He also used his speech to have the final word on the long-running conflict between his advisers. When he reached the point of saying his thank yous, he only mentioned one of his staff, giving special thanks to Bryan Sinclair.

National might just as well have won. The difference between completely winning and completely losing was so little it could have been the other way. No real moral can be taken from the result – or maybe just a small one, which is that political manipulation and the biggest money do not always win.

EPILOGUE

Brash was in shock, various key staff were planning how to get away from each other as quickly as possible and some big donors were furious that all the efforts to secure a Brash-led National government had failed.

Close Brash supporters like Ruth Richardson knew how much had been lost. When the special votes were announced two weeks after the election and the Labour victory was confirmed, she asked, 'Is this the wisdom of the crowds at work?'[1] She was on her way to Georgia, as a consultant on economic reform, but she would see Brash at an Auckland Centre for Independent Studies gathering in the near future. 'Hope he stays on course,' she told Bryan Sinclair.[2]

The day after the election Brash had said, 'Political parties in New Zealand and indeed elsewhere don't normally continue with leaders who lose elections and I understand and respect that.'[3] But his leadership was safe at least for a while. There were 23 new National MPs and, as one MP told the *Sunday Star-Times*, 'Those who play games with Don Brash and chip away at him, at a time when he has brought so many new MPs into caucus, will find it doesn't look very good on their CVs further down the track.'[4] The same article, however, quoted one-term MP John Key poorly hiding his leadership ambitions: 'I have no intention of challenging Don,' he said, 'but you can't ever rule those things out.' There might be 'other circumstances' that caused his intentions to change, though they were 'not on the radar'.[5]

Richard Long stage managed the first National caucus meeting three days after the election. 'TV cameras will be lurking before tomorrow's caucus, looking for easy prey and loose quotes. This is the procedure agreed with Gerry and Simon [Power].... Don and Gerry will walk down the corridor together, from Don's room, to enter the caucus, to standing applause, at 10am. The cameras will follow them in to pan around the room to show the greatly expanded caucus.' He warned that 'difficult questions will include':

Q: Is Don Brash's leadership leadership safe? Do you think he should resign?

A: We are all here because of Don Brash (variations: National has doubled its vote. We have won 11 new electorates. We have 24 new MPs. National is back in a big way and we have sensible policies).[6]

At that first caucus meeting, or one soon after, John Key made a speech strongly criticising National's decision to work with the Exclusive Brethren in the election campaign. Those who knew that Key himself had been one of the people in contact with the Brethren commented wryly that he was doing a bit of personal 'inoculation' to avoid sharing criticism for the trouble that had resulted.

A month after the election, in mid-October 2005, the campaign team began to scatter. Bryan Sinclair, Richard Long and Steven Joyce all left their jobs within weeks of each other. Sinclair moved back to Australia, Long disappeared on an extended holiday and Joyce had a break, then did some part-time work in Brash's office before taking a job running a travel publication company.[7] John Ansell's work for National had finished with the election, but he resumed working for the party the following year when some big donors came forward to pay for him again. The only strategy person who remained was Peter Keenan.

Three months after leaving the National leader's office, Long approached Don Brash's arch rival, Winston Peters, offering to work for him instead. PR man Richard Griffin attended meetings with Long in February 2006 to argue why he was perfect for the job, but Peters, by then Foreign Minister for the Labour-led government, declined the offer. Matthew Hooton also quietly shifted camps, privately offering his strategy and speech-writing assistance to John Key. The loyal Sinclair returned to New Zealand to assist Brash when he needed help in September 2006.

Murray McCully had begun work on Brash to persuade him that the best course was to wait for a time that suited him, name John Key as his preferred successor and then bow out of the National Party leadership in a dignified manner. But all that would change over the Christmas break. Brash took his family to the South Island for a holiday, including a stay in Greymouth with ACT Party leader Rodney Hide.[8] The most important part of the trip, however, was Brash's unpublicised stay in Central Otago, with his long-time political friend and supporter Ruth Richardson.

He visited her at her holiday home at Eely Point, on the outskirts of Wanaka, a regular meeting place for New Zealand's small far right. Richardson argued forcefully to Brash that the best hope for achieving their shared goal of renewed economic reforms was still a National government with him as leader. They went off alone to a small island in Lake Wanaka for a long and private talk and Brash returned with his mind made up. He would stay leader and in 2008, or hopefully sooner, he would be Prime Minister.[9] There he would be in a powerful position to make the kind of big changes for which Richardson and his other old friends had encouraged him to enter politics in the first place. Richardson called the new plan their Ruby Island Pact, after the small island where they had gone to talk.

Brash headed back to the North Island fully committed to the new plan, but other friends, including Diane Foreman, were not so certain Brash had made the right decision. Having made up his mind, however, Brash was set on staying leader. He told journalists that the close election result and the 'Christmas break' had hardened his resolve to stay on. After 'overwhelming' positive feedback from the party, his colleagues and the public, he was determined to lead National into the next election.[10] Reinforcing this, a meeting of newly elected National MPs early in the new year, organised by Tim Groser and Chris Finlayson to discuss the leadership issue, agreed that Brash should be allowed to lead the party into the 2008 election.

The 2008 election campaign effectively began at that time. National held a three-day caucus meeting at Wairakei Resort in Taupo in early February to talk about campaign plans. These included further inoculation of issues they believed had cost them votes, including formally dropping the policy of a possible referendum on the nuclear-free policy and a proposal from deputy leader Gerry Brownlee for softening the party's Treaty of Waitangi policy. They also discussed Keenan's idea from a year earlier of softening the party image with new environmental policies and, as Keenan had proposed earlier, invited the help of Guy Salmon drafting these new green policies. But by far the most important decision, which would define New Zealand politics for the rest of that year and beyond, was to focus their energies on attacking the Labour Party's strongest asset in the 2005 election campaign, its leader Helen Clark.

The following month John Ansell presented plans to the National Party board for a new billboard campaign attacking the Labour-led government.[11] Ansell and other National campaign staff had recently received the *National Business Review* Advertising Campaign of the Year award for the 2005 election advertisements, accepting the award on board a yacht belonging to National donor Barry Colman. The board approved Ansell's 2006 plan and the same small set of Business Roundtable donors were approached to fund Ansell's salary and the nationwide billboards, which went up in May. Soon Ansell's hand could be seen in both party advertising and speech writing for Brash, including the principle versus corruption speech quoted at the beginning of this book.[12]

The first newspaper advertisement of the new campaign appeared in August 2006. Half the advertisement was a large photograph of Don Brash with just a single word: 'Guts'. The text beneath the photo described Brash as a man who refused to compromise his principles. 'The National Party is very proud to have a man like Don Brash as its leader. Time and again, Don has proved he's got the guts to do what's right for our country.' The advertisement had obviously been designed by Ansell, using the 'guts to do what's right' slogan we saw him proposing to Brash in early 2005. 'We stand with Don in choosing the more difficult path to power – the path of principle.'[13]

Brash and his colleagues began aggressive attacks on Labour and Helen Clark over their use of public money for the party's election pledge card. This was the attack that contrasted National's 'path of principle and per-suasion' with Labour's 'path of bribery and corruption'. For the first time since becoming leader, Brash was credited with performing strongly in Parliament.

Day after day there were orchestrated personal attacks on Labour politi-cians, driven in part by the hope of forcing an early election. The Labour government was described as being guilty of corruption and bribery, breaking the law and even, by Matthew Hooton, of being 'quasi-fascist'.[14] These sorts of tactics were developed by the United States conservative movement in the 1990s: 'a process characterised by the relentless trawling of politicians' private lives until "evidence" of moral turpitude, criminal wrongdoing or both is uncovered'.[15] The idea is to have an apparently unco-ordinated succession of accusations, personal attacks and news media revelations popping up one after another which are actually a deliberate campaign to undermine a political opponent. Commentator Chris Trotter interpreted the attacks as follows: 'The only way the far right can win is by default, by making people hate Labour so much that they cease caring what National's neo-liberal policies will do to them'.[16]

Brash also reused the populist politician's old favourite, the anti-immigrant speech. In a repeat of his pre-election 'tougher line' immigration speech, he said that immigrants who did not share New Zealand's core values were not welcome in the country. He questioned the idea of diversity, saying it 'is a bit like red wine. A certain amount is good for one's health; too much quickly alters your personality and can be thoroughly bad.'[17] Like the earlier speech, he did not need to be explicit about which immigrants he believed did not share core values: the dog whistle would be heard and understood by its target audience.

The Exclusive Brethren were still there too, looking down most days from the parliamentary gallery on the MPs below and, as the news media revealed, fuelling the personal attack politics by paying private investigators to collect dirt on Labour politicians. They showed signs of intending to repeat their election year election activities in 2008 as well.[18]

As Brash returned from Wanaka in January 2006 full of a new determination to become prime minister, John Key returned from a four-week family holiday in Europe and began sounding out caucus support for a leadership challenge. Some of his colleagues were unimpressed by his pushiness, describing him among themselves as being 'greedy for power'. The challenge attempt fell apart just before the February Wairakei caucus meeting, when an unnamed senior National MP (Gerry Brownlee, according to insiders) told journalists about Key's lobbying. The party's Auckland division had already privately expressed its support for Key when the unnamed MP told the *New Zealand Herald* that 'the caucus was "very, very angry" the leadership question was dogging the party again and believed Mr Key and other Auckland supporters were fuelling the stories'. It was 'being made clear to Mr Key that the caucus would not tolerate a "campaign of destabilisation", said the senior MP'.[19]

Colleagues who had been lobbied by Key and McCully about the leadership watched as they strongly denied the suggestions. 'I have very publicly on dozens of occasions outlined my unconditional support for [Brash],' Key told the press. 'I don't think I've ever made a public or a private comment that would indicate anything other than my support of him.'[20] McCully said there was not the 'slightest interest' in a change in the leadership.[21]

The publicity and resulting denial of Key's leadership ambitions happened just as an issue of *North and South* magazine appeared in the shops with a cover story promoting Key as National Party leader. The magazine cover had the modest headline 'National Velvet, The coming of John

Key' and the story began: 'You'd be scouring through New Zealand's political history to find an individual with the full leadership package: intellect, charm, compassion, vision, international experience and a successful private sector track record. But there's a rising star in National's ranks. Virginia Larson finds out why everyone's talking about National's John Key.'[22] As Key kept his head down in the following weeks, his face stared out from the magazine posters in shop windows as a reminder of the stalled leadership attempt.

But from then on whenever Brash stumbled or was criticised Key's name was likely to be raised in the media. Just as with Brash three years earlier, the media coverage was oddly uncritical, mostly describing the new 'star' in the words of his promoters. He was the 'state house kid turned millionaire merchant banker' (it could not say 'working-class kid' because he grew up in a middle-class family) who, presumably because he had once made lots of money, was automatically assumed to be politically competent.

According to Colin James, who had earlier talked up Brash's virtues, Key had 'a beguiling mixture of charm, affability, approachability, intelligence, determination and, deep behind the mirror glass, a glint or two of cold steel'.[23] ACT's Richard Prebble said Key was the 'the candidate from central casting – he never forgets his lines'.[24] It was at least not surprising that Prebble would promote Key, since he was the natural New Right successor to Brash. Key, it should be recalled, had a 'private conversation' that left Rod Deane 'greatly encouraged' that a National government would pursue policies, including further privatisation and deregulation, he believed were desirable.[25]

In the middle of 2006, Key and his backers began lobbying again for support within caucus. In September 2006, Richard Long turned against Brash publicly, writing in a newspaper column that 'Honest Don is beginning to look more like Mr Magoo'. John Key, on the other hand, 'is the leadership candidate straight from central casting and the anointed one.... He's the state-house-to-international-moneyman success story, media-savvy, fluent with business and the economy.' And, of course, as Long had once insisted in his lines about Brash, he said Key was a centrist. He repeated the myth that Key – who was part of implementing expedient inoculations decided by the campaign strategy team – 'played a big role in tempering Dr Brash's more hard-line economic stance before the last election'.[26]

As with Brash in 2003, the evidence was there for anyone looking beyond the media packaging. At the National Party's annual conference in late July 2006, Key spelt out his economic beliefs. 'If we simply muddle along as we have been, we will find we have slipped into a trough..... We will find ourselves in the position where many European countries are now, where excessive levels of tax, public spending, red tape, and overly-protective labour laws have sucked the life out of their economies.'[27] As Chris Trotter noted, 'this is pure Business Roundtable-speak.... In this regard, at least, Key is Don Brash's natural successor and the right wing of the National Party's insurance policy.'[28]

In other words, National looked set to continue along the same tracks, whether or not Brash was leader. It would continue with the same strategies, the same political alliances and the same hidden agendas. There might be a different frontperson, but many of the same people would be in the background. The near-success of the 2005 election and strong poll results during the 2006 principle versus corruption attack campaign had seemed like proof that nothing needed to change.

In a *Press* interview in July 2006 Brash explained what he believed was right and wrong in politics.

> Reporter: Much was made of your honesty and integrity when you became leader. Do you think it remains as strong in the public's eyes now as it did then?
>
> Don Brash: Yes, many commentators have accused me of not being a 'natural politician'. If what it takes to be a natural politician is to evade the question, give misleading answers and act deceitfully, then count me out.... I'm simply not prepared to sacrifice honesty in favour of a few votes.
>
> Reporter: How do you react when your performances in Parliament are interpreted as being uncertain compared to those of Prime Minister Helen Clark?
>
> Don Brash: I laugh. Helen Clark is a career politician; I, on the other hand, come from a background working in commerce. I'm not going to change and become deceitful and evasive because that's what too many politicians do. I think the public deserve better than that.[29]

Brash, like most politicians, knew the difference between right and wrong, and he knew what the public deserved: politicians with integrity; politicians who are not evasive, misleading and deceitful; politicians who will not sacrifice honesty in favour of a few votes. But National had not lived up to these standards during the period documented in this book: 2003 to 2006. Instead it had offered endlessly repeated lines rather than answering the question, election-winning policies and real policies for later, emotional button pushing and lever pulling, carefully scripted evasions and deceptions when confronted with things it would rather keep secret, slogans about representing the mainstream and shunning special interests while doing the reverse, cynical internal strategy discussions and aggressive attacks on the government over funding issues without owning up to its own dodgy election secrets.

In September 2006 the three politicians most likely to lead National into the 2008 election were again asked by journalists if they had told the truth about their links to the Exclusive Brethren. Commenting on Labour's statement that he had lied about his involvement with the church, Brash declared, 'That's absolute crap, that's a lie told by Helen Clark.'[30] When journalists suggested to deputy leader Gerry Brownlee that his party had colluded with the Exclusive Brethren, he replied, 'That is wrong and it is most offensive.' The Brethren 'exercised the democratic right they have under the current law, but they have not done that in collusion with us or with any particular sanction from us'.[31] John Key also repeated his public statement that the Brethren had not told him about their plans. He told the *Sunday Star-Times* he was unaware of any offer from the Brethren and, if they had offered, 'I would have rejected it. I wouldn't want to be beholden to any particular group anyway, and it's just not the way I operate. I run my own ship.'[32]

All politicians face the same dilemma and choice. They know that telling the truth, admitting mistakes, giving straight answers and facing up to tricky issues can make their lives more difficult. They know that openness is good for democracy but they also know that keeping things secret, or telling only the comfortable part of the truth, can save them a lot of trouble. Expediency is simply easier, which is why it is common.

It is also catching. When politicians evade questions, slide around the truth and play the sorts of games seen in this book – and are seen to succeed politically – others are encouraged to do the same. If journalists, commentators and the public stop being offended by such behaviour and come to see it as normal, there is even less reason for politicians to bother about being principled.

The most damaging consequence of this attitude is that ordinary people are put off politics. They may not know exactly what is going on, but they can tell they are being short-changed and that their concerns do not count. Good people are not drawn to become MPs or even to be members of political parties that are dominated by a small leadership clique. This is called cynicism but is really disillusionment. People lose hope about politics, which is a rational response to feeling excluded and manipulated.

But the response should not be to give up and leave the ground to the expedient. It can be different. The politicians who are respected and even loved by the public are not just successful in the sense of winning votes and holding power, like rodeo riders who can stay on the bucking steer longer than others. Such politicians have a longer-term view and a vision to offer the public; they demonstrate that they are living by their principles and have the skills to lead rather than manipulate.

For the National Party, the underlying problem has been the lack of a clear vision and philosophy to offer the public. Without these, the party is disorganised and ineffectual, and susceptible to being taken over by cliques and outside interests. Until new leaders find a genuinely conservative vision of their own, and, crucially, election funding from somewhere other than the same few radical-right millionaires and big businesspeople, the party will keep sliding back into the same two ruts in the road – a more or less extreme free market agenda that must be pursued by stealth and deception.

The party has some good role models of principled politicians. It was National who gave New Zealand its freedom of information law, the historic Treaty of Waitangi settlements of the 1990s, protection for many of the rainforests of South Westland in the 1980s and even the Resource Management Act. It has also provided a home for plenty of unscrupulous politicians. But the National Party, in the period covered by this book, was exceptionally unprincipled in the context both of New Zealand politics and its own history.

But it does not have to be that way. An exposé like this helps to explain why people feel disillusioned about politics and what it would take for that to change. The characters in this story largely got away with their actions not because the public approved of them, but because the public did not know. Once such behaviour is exposed, other, principled people have an opportunity to set a fresh example and to insist on change. That is why insiders were willing to blow the whistle and expose the inner workings of their own party. They did so out of a deep wish for the politics of this country to be different.

Major Party – Three poll rolling average
----- Labour   —— National

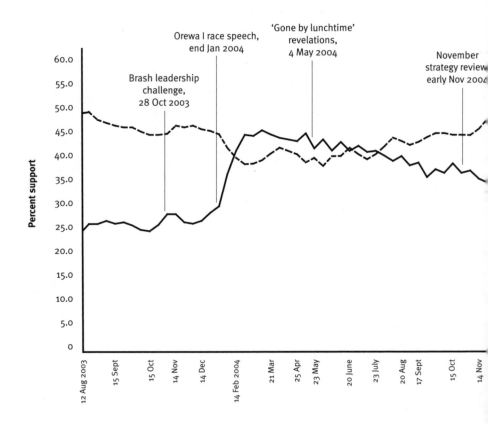

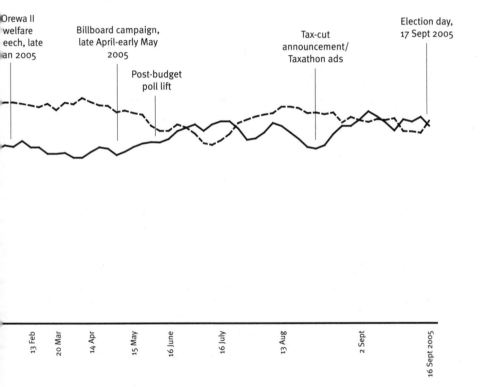

Orewa II
welfare
eech, late
an 2005

Billboard campaign,
late April-early May
2005

Post-budget
poll lift

Tax-cut
announcement/
Taxathon ads

Election day,
17 Sept 2005

13 Feb 20 Mar 14 Apr 15 May 16 June 16 July 13 Aug 2 Sept 16 Sept 2005

ENDNOTES

CHAPTER 1

1   Don Brash, Address to Christchurch Central Zonta Club, 7 August 2006.
2   'Clark stole election, says Brash', *New Zealand Herald*, 24 August 2006.
3   Don Brash, *Don Brash Writes* newsletter, No. 88, 25 August 2006.
4   Chapter 13 mentions these and other examples.
5   See Appendix.
6   Ibid.
7   This figure is found in reference 22.
8   Richard Long, email to Don Brash, Gerry Brownlee, Murray McCully, Simon Power and Tony Ryall, 5 April 2005.
9   Richard Long, email to Don Brash, 7 April 2005.
10 Thanks to Peter Wills for advice on the Exclusive Brethren.
11 'Veiled sect hails Bush, Martinez', Lucy Morgan, *St Petersburg Times*, 18 January 2005.
12 '"Inflammatory" flyer raises ire', Lisa Jorgensen and Rosalind Duane, *North Shore News*, British Columbia, 18 April 2005.
13 In late 2006 Exclusive Brethren election campaigns were discovered in Sweden and again in Australia.
14 See Appendix.
15 Bryan Sinclair, email to Don Brash, 9 December 2004.
16 The Brethren sponsors were Philip Win, Steve Wallace, Julian Anderson, Richard Judd, Geoff Smith, Eddie Stanners, Andrew Simmons, Doug Watt, Tim Lough and Andy Smith. The company was Aspect Interiors, jointly owned by Andrew and Neville Simmons.
17 Anne Small, email to Don Brash, 8 February 2005.
18 Richard Long, email to Don Brash, 24 February 2005.
19 National Party candidate profile for Fepulea'i Ulua'ipou-O-Malo Aiono, www.national.org.nz, 2005.
20 Emails between Fepulea'i Ulua'ipou-O-Malo Aiono and Bryan Sinclair, 21 April 2005.
21 'Brethren cost Nats win: Rich', Ruth Laugesen, *Sunday Star-Times*, 24 September 2006; Simon Power, quoted on *TV3 News*, 7 September 2005.
22 Ron Hickmott, letter to Don Brash and John Key, 24 May 2005.
23 Ibid.
24 'Unlocking John Key', TVNZ *Sunday*, reporter Garth Bray, broadcast 15 May 2005.
25 Don Brash, email to Bryan Sinclair, 24 May 2005.
26 Ron Hickmott, email to David Henry, 8 June 2005.

27 Ibid.
28 David Henry, email to Robert Peden and Irene Walker, 8 June 2005.
29 Simon Lusk, email to Bryan Sinclair, 8 June 2005.
30 On 19 June 2005, 'Poll favours ship visits', the *Herald on Sunday* reported that 'Most New Zealanders support allowing American warships back into our harbours now they no longer carry nuclear weapons, a privately-commissioned poll shows.' The poll was released by ACT Party MP Ken Shirley, who said it had been commissioned by a group of concerned New Zealanders. He said the concerned New Zealanders 'had offered the poll results to National, which was not interested, so they had instead given them to ACT.' In an email to Don Brash, Steven Joyce, Anita Ferguson and Gerry Brownlee the same day, Richard Long noted that the poll had been commissioned by the Exclusive Brethren, 'not the group of leading concerned NZ citizens that Ken Shirley suggested', and instructed media staff to keep Don Brash away from the story. He said that 'while Digipoll did the field work, they did not do the methodology... and some of it looked a bit like push polling to our people' and the full poll contained 'dodgy stuff... about people viewing China as a security threat etc'.
31 Simon Lusk, email to Bryan Sinclair, 9 June 2005.
32 Simon Lusk, email to Bryan Sinclair, 24 June 2005.
33 Others said, 'Use your party vote to put someone else in charge', 'Change the government with your party vote' and 'It's time to change the government'.
34 See Appendix.
35 See Appendix.
36 The first full-page advertisement dated 9 December 2004 looks and sounds like an Exclusive Brethren publication. The layout is basic and the language includes old-fashioned phrases such as 'union of a man and a woman', 'the sanctity of marriage' as a 'providential bond' and appeals to MPs to act in recognition of the 'Supremacy of God'. Five months later the layout of the 'Wake-up call' advertisements is still pretty basic and, again, the language does not sound like the work of slick political people. The anti-Labour message is almost lost in hundreds of words of unfocused pro-American text. These advertisements are reminiscent of the unsophisticated Canadian and United States Exclusive Brethren advertising. In the midst of the design of the election publications (13 June 2005), Don Brash received a lobbying letter from the same Ron Hickmott who authored the 24 May letter setting out the Brethren's million-dollar election plans. He asked the National Party to vote for a pro-nuclear ACT Party bill and an anti-single-sex marriage United Future Party bill 'so as to give God a basis to continue the increasing support the Party has enjoyed in recent weeks.... We would respectfully urge that the Supremacy of God is recognised in this matter.' Again, this is far from advertisements about All Black matches and Caribbean cruises. Then, shortly after the New Zealand election, the Exclusive Brethren resumed their lobbying activities. The next publication, signed by four of the leading Brethren behind the election advertising, was back to the pre-election style. The leaflet, called 'An urgent appeal to all MPs', returns to a moralistic tone of demanding attention: 'You must seriously consider your position on the "Marriage (Gender Clarification) Amendment Bill".' It also returns to the old-fashioned language: 'Your vote today will publicly signal your valuation of the institution of marriage'. This was being sent to MPs who would be more likely to take notice of something about flying to Aussie to watch the All Blacks.
37 Private communications from a confidential source.
38 In South Australia, researchers Peter and Bronte Trainor managed after the election to trace some Adelaide advertisements back to Exclusive Brethren members. One was a

full-page advertisement in the *Adelaide Advertiser* on the day before the election with the theme 'We are Happy John'. The advertisement was authorised by B. Hornsey, SAET School with the address 137 Davis Road. The SAET (South Australian Education Trust) school had actually been deregistered some time before and replaced by the Melrose Park School, run by the Brethren community, at 137 Dawes Road. Two other half-page advertisements were placed in the *Mount Barker Courier* in the issue before the election. They were anti-Green – 'Why The Grass Won't Be Greener On The Other Side – Keep Australia in Safe Hands'– and authorised by an A.K. Grace from a suburban address that turned out to be a rented domestic property, not far from Melrose Park School. Grace later confirmed that advertisements in both papers had indeed been placed by the same group of people associated with Adelaide's Brethren community. The Trainors found eight other advertisements headed 'John Howard provides strong leadership for Australia. Keep Australia in safe hands', which they say were almost identical to official Liberal Party election material. They were placed by a Mr D. Burgess from an address which they subsequently discovered was one of the campuses of the Exclusive Brethren Glenvale School in Melbourne. Personal communication, March 2006. There were probably many other advertisements in other states.

39 Stephen Win, Favona Road, Mangere, Auckland.

40 M. Powell, 30 Stephen Lynsar Place, Mount Roskill, Auckland.

41 'Anderton ad complaint', Vernon Small, *Dominion Post*, 30 September 2005. The name on the advertisement, which accused Anderton of championing big business, was M. Currie at 52 Somerset Crescent, Christchurch.

42 This company was incorporated as Business Information Limited on 9 May 2005, the day the 'Wake-up call' advertisements began. The name was changed to Strategic Information Services Limited on 6 September 2005 as the first election pamphlets were distributed. The three directors and shareholders of the company were, in 2006, Gregory Charles Mason, a wealthy Auckland businessman who has been described in the news media as head of the New Zealand church, Andrew James Smith, the Hastings man who co-ordinated the 'Wake-up call' advertising, and Caleb Hall, a Palmerston North Exclusive Brethren member who helped Andy Smith arrange the printing and distribution of the 'Wake-up call' pamphlets.

43 'National denies involvement in anti-Greens leaflet', Radio New Zealand, 3 September 2005.

44 'Dirty tricks claims traded', Colin Espiner, *Press*, 6 September 2005.

45 Anita Ferguson, email to Bryan Sinclair, Murray McCully and Richard Long, 3 September 2005.

46 Colin Espiner, *Press*, 6 September 2005.

47 Stephen Parker, *TV3 News*, interviewing Don Brash, 5 September 2005.

48 Brash simply received an email from his personal assistant informing him that 'owing to prospective concerns about the [church leaders] meeting... Steven and Murray decided to postpone it'. (Vanessa Rawson, email to Don Brash, 6 September 2005.) Brash replied: 'Ouch.... NOT a good look. How many people will turn up feeling brassed off with National?'

49 Richard Long, email to Anita Ferguson, Don Brash and National Communications Staff, 6 September 2005.

50 Anita Ferguson, email to Richard Long, 6 September 2005, forwarded to Don Brash.

51 Jason Ede, email to National Communications Staff and Steven Joyce, 7 September 2005.

52 'We're doing God's work', *Dominion Post*, 8 September 2005.

53 'Brash says he knew of church pamphlet plans', New Zealand Press Association, 7 September 2005.

54 'Brash mounts desperate campaign to restore credibility', Ruth Berry, *New Zealand Herald*, 9 September 2005.

55 Murray McCully, 'Look left for conspiracies', press release, 8 September 2005.

56 'Key says Exclusive Brethren did not tell him about leaflet', Radio New Zealand Newswire, 8 September 2005.

57 Anita Ferguson, email to Don Brash, National Communications Staff, Steven Joyce and Murray McCully, 7 September 2005, 'Onpassed from Richard'.

58 Noelle McCarthy interviewing Don Brash, 95bFM, 8 September 2005. Transcript on www.scoop.co.nz.

59 *TV3 News*, interviewing Don Brash, 8 September 2005.

60 Stephen Parker, Brash interview.

61 Susan Wood, *Close Up*, interviewing Don Brash, 8 September 2005.

CHAPTER 2

1 Don Brash, 'Why I should be National Party leader', speech to caucus, 28 October 2003. His replies to these points were: 'Yes, I've been in Parliament for less than 18 months, but I've been in and around the political process for more than 20 years, including my 14 years as Governor of the Reserve Bank.... Yes, I'm 63, but in many countries political leaders are just getting started at 70. Reagan first became president of the US at 70, and was re-elected for his second four year term at 74. Chirac was elected president of France for a seven year term at 70. And Alan Greenspan, one of the most powerful people in the world, has just accepted a fifth five year term as Chairman of the Federal Reserve at 77. Yes, I am on the right of the political spectrum, but only in the sense that I fully support the values and vision of the National Party – personal responsibility, limited government, a safety net for those who need help, and all the rest. I've been a National Party supporter for well over 20 years, and remain totally committed to the National Party. Indeed, it is because of that commitment that I decided to challenge for the leadership a few days ago. It is simply not true, as some have suggested, that my strings are being pulled by Ruth Richardson. To the best of my recollection, I have seen her three times this year, and have talked by phone on perhaps two or three other occasions. I respect Ruth Richardson, but nobody pulls my strings.'

2 Ibid.

3 Don Brash, 'Speech Notes for Dr Don Brash, Leader of the New Zealand National Party', 28 October 2003.

4 Ibid.

5 *National Business Review*, 4 April 2003, pp. 1, 4, 10–11, 16, 19.

6 *National Business Review*, 11 April 2003.

7 'Scoring the exchanges', *Dominion Post*, 14 April 2003.

8 'Brash in coup bid', *New Zealand Herald*, 24 October 2003.

9 'Brash's clumsy coup bid puts National in turmoil', *New Zealand Herald*, 25 October 2003.

10 It is not clear who, if anyone, was paying Hooton, but it was presumably Brash himself.

11 Don Brash, 'Speech Notes for Dr Don Brash, Leader of the New Zealand National Party'.

12 Matthew Hooton, email to Bryan Sinclair, 12 December 2003.

13 Hooton's work is an example of the way a PR consultant can find political ammunition for his or her client. He wrote Official Information Act requests on 21 July, 22 July (two requests), 25 July, 31 July, 5 August (five requests), 15 August, 29 August, 21 September (four requests), 25 September and 7 October, probing many different aspects of government anti-smoking funding. Eventually he found information that seemed controversial. Rodney Hide used what appears to be Hooton's research to question Associate Minister of Health Damien O'Connor on 8 October 2003 about Ministry of Health grants to the group Action on Smoking and Health (ASH). See, for instance, 'Government cash backing anti-smoking groups' lobbying says Hide', *New Zealand Herald*, 9 October 2003. A week later, on 15 October 2003, at the opening of debate on the Smoke-free Environments Amendment Bill, MP Peter Dunne moved that 'the Committee stage of the Smoke-free Environments Amendment Bill be discharged and the bill be referred back to the Health Committee'. ACT MPs supported stalling the bill, using as justification the grants to ASH.

14 For instance, Nicola Young wrote the following to Brash about caucus lobbying: 'Chris Finlayson says: You should talk to Georgina [Te Heuheu] and say you know there's a problem with the foreshore policy; if she supports you, you'll address it as a high priority once leader – task force of party members etc etc. Chris happy to ring Georgina if that would help....' (Nicola Young, email to Don Brash, 27 October 2003)

15 http://www.michaelbassett.co.nz.

16 Michael Bassett, 'Time to stand aside, Bill', *Dominion Post*, 28 October 2003.

17 Michael Bassett, email to Don Brash, 28 October 2003 (4.04am).

18 Michael Bassett, strategy advice for Don Brash, 25 October 2003, 5 pp.

19 Michael Bassett, 'Suggested Shadow Cabinet', 25 October 2003.

20 Ibid.

21 Michael Bassett, email to Don Brash, 29 October 2003.

22 Roger Douglas, *Unfinished Business*, Random House, Auckland, 1993.

23 Roger Douglas, 'Why I want to be Prime Minister', 26 October 2003.

24 Roger Douglas, 'Setting objectives for an election-winning National Party strategy', 27 October 2003.

25 Bryan Sinclair, email to Don Brash, 3 November 2003.

26 He came from a political family. One of his relatives, Barry Nicolle, was spokesperson for an anti-environmental front group called Coast Action Network that had been set up by the state-owned enterprise Timberlands West Coast to support its native forest logging. Earlier, another Nicolle relative had been at the forefront of a militant anti-abortion campaign.

27 'Brian Nicolle, New Zealand Political Strategist: Born in Lower Hutt, New Zealand, Brian Nicolle worked in retail banking for twenty years. At the age of 19, he joined the Labour Party as a volunteer.... An enthusiastic supporter of the legendary finance minister, Sir Roger Douglas, when he came to power in 1984, Nicolle worked for him in 1989 and 1990. Since 1993, he has practiced politics and public relations with Awaroa Partners in Wellington, studied campaign management at the American University in Washington, D.C. for a brief period and pursued other interests in philosophy, accounting and marketing.... In 1993, he ran the controversial campaign against proportional representation, and in 1994 helped establish the ACT New Zealand party, which promotes freedom, choice and personal responsibility. No stranger to controversy, Nicolle admits he has managed campaigns where the immediate political gain wasn't apparent. "You sometimes have to lose a few battles to win the war," he explains. "As Winston Churchill once said, you can die only once

in military combat but in politics you can die many times."' (Source: www.fcpp.org, a Canadian think tank where Nicolle was guest speaker in October 2005.)

28 There were two very different lessons able to be taken from the outcome of the 6 November 1993 MMP referendum. The lesson most people took from it was that the anti-MMP campaign lost. A small budget but widely supported pro-MMP campaign won and the electoral system was changed forever. The MMP victory and a strong swing in voting away from the National Party in the accompanying election also decisively signalled the end of public support for free market reforms. The result was a swift realignment of the political landscape, which gave much of the setting of this book a decade later. Three weeks after the election the National Party leader removed Ruth Richardson from her Minister of Finance role. She vowed to continue fighting for 'the goals that [she] entered politics to pursue'. Two days later, the Labour caucus dumped its free market leader, Mike Moore, and replaced him with Helen Clark. But the other lesson, naturally noticed most by the anti-MMP campaigners, was that they *nearly* won the referendum. From MMP's 63% to 23% lead six months before the election, the final result was a tantalisingly close 54% to 46%. Brian Nicolle and the rich backers took heart from that second lesson when they set up the ACT Party shortly after. Since then anonymously funded political campaigns on all sorts of subjects have become a familiar feature of New Zealand politics.

29 Brian Nicolle, fax to Don Brash and Catherine Judd, 25 October 2003.

30 Ibid.

31 Peter Shirtcliffe, email to Don Brash, 26 October 2003.

32 'ACC lobby group may spread wings', *Evening Post*, 14 March 2000.

33 See Chapter 13.

34 'Elaborate money maze hid donors', Geraldine Johns, *Sunday Star-Times*, 22 April 2001.

35 Richard Poole, email to Bryan Sinclair, 30 November 2003. Poole explained that his marketing company had 'current projects focusing on education... with the Maxim Institute at present where we are working with Peter Shirtcliffe, John Graham, Michael Friedlander & Michael Whittaker to create awareness for sensible policies on school choice etc – we are looking after fundraising and some strategy advice.'

36 'PM calls for Kerr's head', *Evening Post*, 6 October 2000. The 'A Generation Lost?' campaign attacked the Labour government over policies that, Poole said, created a 'brain drain' of young people overseas.

37 Diane Foreman, email to Don Brash, 26 October 2003.

38 Diane Foreman, email to Bryan Sinclair, 29 October 2003.

39 'Judd hid knowledge of MP's anguish', Colin Espiner, *Press*, 1 October 2004.

40 http://www.awaroa.com.

41 Peter Keenan, email to Don Brash, 26 October 2003.

42 Don Brash, email to Peter Keenan, 27 October 2003.

43 Peter Keenan, email to Don Brash, 27 October 2003.

44 Peter Keenan, email to Anne Small, 3 November 2003.

45 Audrey Young, 'Brash's inner circle', *New Zealand Herald*, 1 November 2003.

46 Ruth Richardson wrote, complimenting Brash on his 'good call' in hiring Sinclair. Ruth Richardson, email to Don Brash, 1 November 2003.

47 Bryan Sinclair, email to Don Brash, 25 October 2003.

48 Sinclair was one of those, as were Awaroa consultant Rick Marshall, who worked as a PR adviser to the Business Roundtable, and their Auckland University colleague Graham Watson, who worked as an ACT Party official. Marshall was president

of the Waikato University Students' Association in 1997 when Sinclair was vice-president.

49 These courses are another programme for encouraging young people to adopt the CIS beliefs. By 2006 CIS Liberty and Society attendees from New Zealand had numbered about 80–100, including Business Roundtable communications adviser and later journalist David Young, National Party media person and later CIS employee Phil Rennie and education advisers Dave Guerin and Craig Workman.

50 The CIS website – www.cis.org.au – says it is 'Australasia's leading public policy research institute. Founded in Sydney in 1976 by Executive Director Greg Lindsay, it... emphasises the role of the free market in an open society and other voluntary processes in providing many of the goods and services normally supplied by the compulsory methods of government.' It is located at Level 4, 38 Oxley Street, St Leonards, NSW, Australia 2065. The New Zealand address is PO Box 5529, Lambton Quay, Wellington and its New Zealand phone contact is the Awaroa Partners office. Since 2006 it has had a 'New Zealand Policy Unit'. Its board members have included New Zealanders Roderick Deane and Ruth Richardson. New Zealander Denis Dutton has also written for it.

51 The guest list was John Banks, Don Brash, Gavin Cormack, Graeme Douglas, Rob Fisher, Diane Foreman, Stephen Franks, Michael Friedlander, Jenny Gibbs, Rodney Hide, Catherine Judd, Roger Kerr, David Levene, Greg Lindsay, Christopher Mace, Derek McCormack, Rob McLeod, Jenni McManus, Angus McNaughton, Michael Morais, Ruth Richardson, Geoff Ricketts, Brett Shepherd, Bryan Sinclair and Gary Swift.

52 'Brash's inner circle', Audrey Young, *New Zealand Herald*, 1 November 2003.

53 Jane Clifton, 'Beyond Don', *New Zealand Listener*, 27 May 2006.

54 Jim McLay, email to Don Brash, 28 October 2003.

55 Bruce Logan, email to Don Brash, 28 October 2003.

56 Norman LaRocque, email to Don Brash, 28 October 2003.

57 Property developer, emails to Don Brash, 27 October 2003 and 2 November 2003.

58 Property developer, email to Don Brash, 29 October 2003.

59 National Bluegreens member, email to Don Brash, 29 October 2003. He later rejoined the party.

60 Margaret Austin, email to Don Brash, 27 October 2003.

61 David Caygill, email to Don Brash, 28 October 2003.

CHAPTER 3

1 'Payoff for years of economic reform', Peter Keenan, *Dominion*, 14 December 1995.

2 Peter Keenan, email to Don Brash, 11 August 2004.

3 Peter Keenan, Strategy Note, 11 August 2004.

4 Peter Keenan, email to Don Brash, 1 November 2004.

5 Peter Keenan, Strategy Note.

6 Peter Keenan, 'Caucus presentation and speechmaking skills', 12 August 2004. The saying is an adaptation of one by French diplomat and writer Jean Giraudoux (1882–1944).

7 Peter Keenan, 'Strategy Issues: Speech and Policy Releases', 29 October 2004.

8 Ibid.

9 Don Brash, email to Peter Keenan, 31 October 2004.

10 Peter Keenan, email to Don Brash, 1 November 2004.

11 Ibid.

12 'Seven points divide Labour and National in new poll', *New Zealand Herald*, 10 December 2004.

13 David Horowitz, *How to Beat the Democrats and other subversive essays*, Spence Publishing, Dallas, 2002.

14 Ibid.

15 Peter Keenan, 'Strategy Issues: Speech and Policy Releases'.

16 Don Brash, email to Peter Keenan, 31 October 2004.

17 Peter Keenan, email to Don Brash, 1 November 2004.

18 Peter Keenan, 'Strategy Issues: Speech and Policy Releases'.

19 'Political hygiene test' means appearing to show sufficient compassion to underprivileged people, a term Peter Keenan had borrowed from British and American strategists.

20 Peter Keenan, 'Strategy Issues: Speech and Policy Releases'.

21 Don Brash, email to Peter Keenan, 31 October 2004.

22 Peter Keenan, email to Don Brash, 1 November 2004.

23 Ibid.

24 Peter Keenan, 'Strategy Issues: Speech and Policy Releases'.

25 Peter Keenan, email to Anne Small (Brash's personal assistant), 3 November 2003.

26 Peter Keenan, 'Strategy Issues: Speech and Policy Releases'.

27 Peter Keenan, email to Don Brash, 5 March 2005.

28 Ibid.

29 Bryan Sinclair, email to National Party supporter, 3 June 2005.

30 Bryan Sinclair, email to Anne Small, 7 April 2005.

31 Bryan Sinclair, email to Don Brash, 21 September 2004.

32 New Zealand National Party, 'National's Action Plan for New Zealand: The first ten things we will do', brochure, launched 8 September 2005.

33 Don Brash, email to Richard Long, Jason Ede, Peter Keenan and Wayne Mapp, 17 December 2003.

34 This strategy rethink is the subject of Chapter 8.

35 Don Brash, diary, 9 November 2004.

36 Bryan Sinclair, email to Ruth Richardson, 5 November 2004.

37 Ruth Richardson, email to Bryan Sinclair, 5 November 2004.

38 Ruth Richardson, email to Bryan Sinclair, 8 June 2005.

39 Bryan Sinclair, email to Don Brash, 9 June 2005.

40 Don Brash, email to Bryan Sinclair, 9 June 2005.

41 Diane Forman, email to Bryan Sinclair, 7 July 2005.

42 Bryan Sinclair, email to Peter Keenan, 5 November 2004.

43 Bryan Sinclair, email to Don Brash, 24 September 2004.

44 Steven Joyce, 'Who does what, Structure of the campaign, National Party Campaign 2005 Support Sheet', 18 February 2005.

45 As will become apparent, 'influence' does not mean buying influence over specific policies, but rather using their financial contributions to ensure the election of a party with the policies they support.

CHAPTER 4

1 Bryan Sinclair, email to Don Brash, 23 November 2003.

2 Barry Colman, email to Bryan Sinclair, 9 December 2003.

3 Neil Flett, 'Most Confidential', 10 December 2003.

4 Bryan Sinclair, email to Sue Wood, 4 November 2003.

5 'Brash – the right choice?', Colin Espiner, *Press*, 29 October 2003; 'Brash success a long shot', editorial, *Sunday Star-Times*, 2 November 2003; 'A Brash move', Carroll du Chateau, *New Zealand Herald*, 6 July 2002.

6 'Brash success a long shot', *Sunday Star-Times*.

7 'Top economist to visit New Zealand', *Press*, 14 March 1981.

8 Paul Goldsmith, *Brash: A Biography*, Penguin Books, Auckland, 2005, p. 263. Brash's diary, 16 August 2002, p. 134.

9 Paul Goldsmith, *Brash*, p. 112.

10 'Reserve Bank head threatens to resign if act's focus widened', *Press*, 14 February 1996.

11 'Brash urges New Zealand to maintain reforms', *Press*, 5 June 1996.

12 For instance, Don Brash, 'Faster growth? If we want it', address to the Knowledge Wave Conference, 2 August 2001; Don Brash, 'We can do so much better', business address, Albany, 17 May 2002; Don Brash, 'Where to from here?', address to the Orewa Rotary Club, 28 January 2003.

13 'Fundamentally Right', Tracy Watkins, *Dominion Post*, 29 October 2003.

14 Don Brash, email to Peter Keenan, 31 October 2004.

15 Paul Goldsmith, *Brash*, p. 263.

16 'Taxing times for Brash', Nick Venter, *Dominion Post*, 12 November 2003; and 'Questions of leadership at issue', John Armstrong, *New Zealand Herald*, 27 October 2003.

17 Bryan Sinclair, email to Don Brash, Murray McCully and Georgina Te Heuheu, 16 December 2003.

18 Roger Kerr, email to Don Brash, 6 November 2003.

19 Richard Long, email to Anne Small and Don Brash, 1 March 2004.

20 Bryan Sinclair, 'One shot, high stakes, no second place. Rewrite the rule book', 8 November 2004.

21 'Nats talk of selling state broadcasters', Tracy Watkins, *Dominion Post*, 3 May 2004.

22 Peter Keenan, email to Bryan Sinclair, 1 November 2004.

23 Bryan Sinclair, email to Peter Keenan, 17 June 2005.

24 Peter Keenan, email to Bryan Sinclair, 8 November 2004.

25 Nicola Young, 'Plan of Action', 26 October 2003.

26 'Classical liberal with a social conscience', Colin James, *New Zealand Herald*, 29 October 2003.

27 Don Brash, email to Richard Worth, Richard Long, Wayne Mapp, Tony Ryall, Murray McCully and Peter Keenan, 1 October 2004.

28 Richard Long, email to National Communications Staff, Tony Ryall, Wayne Mapp and Murray McCully, 10 October 2004.

29 Don Brash, email to Murray McCully, Gerry Brownlee, Peter Keenan, Richard Long and Bryan Sinclair, 9 February 2004.

30 Don Brash, email to Bryan Sinclair, Murray McCully, Gerry Brownlee, Peter Keenan and Richard Long, 10 February 2004.

31 Jason Ede, email to National Communications Staff, 6 April 2004.

32 Don Brash, email to National MPs, Richard Long, Peter Keenan and Jason Ede, 9 April 2004.

33 Don Brash, standard email on Civil Union Bill, late June 2004.

34 Don Brash, email to Bryan Sinclair, Gerry Brownlee, Judy Kirk, Katherine Rich, Murray McCully, Peter Keenan, Richard Long, Steven Joyce and Tony Ryall, 7 November 2004.

35   'One day soon, "values voters" will decide the election in Britain, too', *Telegraph*, 6 November 2004.

36   Bruce Logan, Maxim Institute, letter to Don Brash, 26 May 2004.

37   Peter Keenan, email to Bryan Sinclair, 6 December 2004.

38   Don Brash, Civil Union Bill second reading speech, 2 December 2004.

39   Paul Goldsmith, *Brash*, manuscript, October 2004.

40   Lindsay Perigo, email to Don Brash, 9 December 2004.

CHAPTER 5

1   Don Brash, 'Nationhood', address to the Orewa Rotary Club, 27 January 2004.

2   Matthew Hooton, 'Internal vs External Audiences', 1 November 2003.

3   Matthew Hooton, email to Bryan Sinclair (for Don Brash), 3 November 2003.

4   Matthew Hooton, email to Bryan Sinclair (for Don Brash), 5 November 2003.

5   Ibid.

6   Matthew Hooton, email to Don Brash, 25 November 2003.

7   Ibid. Hooton also advised that 'in taking initiatives... you should however inform (note, inform not consult) the front bench and others with an interest in the issue'. Brash followed this advice. His caucus colleagues had no say on the policies in the Orewa speech and were informed of it only a few days before.

8   Bryan Sinclair, email to Peter Keenan and Don Brash, 25 November 2003.

9   Peter Keenan, email to Don Brash, 25 November 2003.

10   Don Brash, email to Peter Keenan and Bryan Sinclair, 29 November 2003.

11   Don Brash, email to Peter Keenan, Bryan Sinclair, Wayne Mapp, Pansy Wong, Richard Long, Murray McCully and Gerry Brownlee, 5 December 2003.

12   'Brash lifts National's hopes with strong party-vote poll', Graeme Hunt, *National Business Review*, 14 November 2003.

13   Barry Colman, email to Don Brash, 13 November 2003.

14   'Poll bashes Brash', Nick Smith, *National Business Review*, 12 December 2003.

15   Peter Keenan, 'NBR Poll', 12 December 2003.

16   Ibid.

17   Bryan Sinclair, email to Peter Keenan, 12 December 2003.

18   Peter Keenan, email to Bryan Sinclair, 12 December 2003.

19   Ibid.

20   Peter Keenan, email to Don Brash, 13 December 2003.

21   Ibid.

22   For example: 'I do believe that we need to do some focus groups on what middle NZ (I'm talking United, Don't knows and NZ First) think about Don's strengths and weaknesses.' (Bryan Sinclair, email to Matthew Hooton, 3 November 2003.)

23   Don Brash, email to Peter Keenan, 13 December 2003.

24   Barry Gustafson, interviewed by Simon Pound on 95bFM Radio, 29 September 2005.

25   Peter Keenan, email to Anne Small, 3 November 2003.

26   Matthew Hooton, email to Don Brash and draft press release, 15 December 2003.

27   Don Brash, email to Matthew Hooton, 15 December 2003.

28   Matthew Hooton, email to Bryan Sinclair, 17 December 2003.

29   Peter Keenan, email to Don Brash, 13 December 2003.

30   'I have a nightmare', Gilbert Wong, *Metro*, April 2004.

31   'Brash serves up a portion of politics at business breakfast', Simon O'Rourke, *Daily News*, 20 June 2002.

32 Don Brash, 'A Nation in Peril', address to the ACT Upper South Island Regional Conference, Christchurch, 27 September 2003.

33 Don Brash, address to the New Zealand Chamber of Commerce Annual Conference, Hamilton, 8 November, 2003.

34 Don Brash, 'Nationhood'.

35 'Dog Whistling, a handy tool for aspiring leaders', Richard Harman, Political Update, Busby, Ramshaw Grice, 11 November 2003.

36 'Brash ready to come out swinging', John Armstrong, *New Zealand Herald*, 17 January 2004.

37 Gerry Brownlee, email to Don Brash, 8 November 2004.

38 'Brash's risky Maori strategy', Colin Espiner, *Press*, 28 January 2004.

39 'Readers back Brash speech', *Dominion Post*, 30 January 2004; 'Strong support for Brash's race relations speech', Colin Espiner and Tim Hume, *Press*, 31 January 2004.

40 Two good analyses of the speech are Gilbert Wong, 'I have a nightmare' and Jon Johansson, 'Orewa and the Rhetoric of Illusion', *Political Science*, Vol. 56, No. 2, Victoria University of Wellington, December 2004.

41 Don Brash, 'Nationhood'.

42 Peter Keenan, email to Richard Long, Don Brash and Murray McCully, 5 December 2003.

43 Ruth Richardson, email to Don Brash, 11 November 2003.

44 Don Brash, email to Gerry Brownlee, Simon Power, Murray McCully, John Key, Richard Long, Peter Keenan and Bryan Sinclair, 23 November 2003.

45 'The folly behind Brash's words', Rod Oram, *Sunday Star-Times*, 7 March 2004.

46 Don Brash, 'Nationhood'.

47 Confidential source.

48 Richard Long, email to Peter Keenan and Murray McCully, 16 February 2004.

49 Phil Rennie, email to Richard Long, Peter Keenan and Murray McCully, 16 February 2004. Rennie was a former Young Nationals president and went on to work for the Sydney Centre for Independent Studies.

50 Jason Ede, email to National Communications Staff, 'Subject: This must go to Ruth Berry today, but Murray has sign off on it first', 17 February 2004.

51 Murray McCully, email to Ruth Berry, 19 February 2004.

52 Richard Long, email to National Leader's Office staff and Murray McCully, 19 February 2004.

53 Jason Ede, email to all National Party staff, 20 February 2004.

54 Jason Ede, email to Colin James, 2 March 2004.

55 Colin James, email to Jason Ede, 2 March 2004.

56 Jason Ede, email to Richard Long and Peter Keenan, 2 March 2004.

57 Richard Long, email to Don Brash, National Communications Staff and Murray McCully, 21 February 2004.

58 Don Brash, email to Richard Long, 21 February 2004.

59 For instance: *Carol Archie: You have talked about public perception that Maori who have earned degrees in law or medicine by entering through a quota system, have second-rate degrees. Is that your perception?*
Don Brash: No, it is not. Though having said that, I had an anecdote only yesterday which makes me uncomfortable about that situation.
Carol Archie: The degrees they get, though, you would agree they are the same?
Don Brash: Yes I do. I am talking about perception. Perceptions are quite substantial....

Carol Archie: Some think you are trading on the public's ignorance and their prejudices. Do they have a point?
Don Brash: No, I think the public do have inevitably some prejudices and some biases, and what I am saying is that affirmative action programmes tend to accentuate those prejudices. (Don Brash, interviewed by Carol Archie, *Mana News*, 5 April 2004, recorded by National Party staff media.)

60 Peter Keenan, email to Bryan Sinclair, 27 April 2005.

61 Gilbert Wong, 'I have a nightmare'.

62 Tony Blakely and Bridget Robson, 'Decades of Disparity', University of Otago's Wellington School of Medicine and Health Sciences, 2003–2006. Similar results were available from earlier studies.

63 Television New Zealand, *Hurricane Brash*, broadcast 12 April 2004.

64 Don Brash, interviewed by Carol Archie.

65 'The Rotarian's idol', Anthony Hubbard, *Sunday Star-Times*, 22 February 2004.

66 Don Brash, email to Matthew Hooton, 29 January 2004.

67 Don Brash, email to correspondent, 12 February 2004.

68 Don Brash, email to Matthew Hooton, 30 April 2004.

69 Bryan Sinclair, email to Cameron Brewer, 10 February 2004.

70 Television New Zealand, *Hurricane Brash*, quoted in Johansson, 'Orewa and the Rhetoric of Illusion'.

71 'National members bid to soften race policy', Ruth Berry, *New Zealand Herald*, 26 September 2005.

72 Barry Gustafson, interviewed by Simon Pound on 95bFM Radio.

CHAPTER 6

1 Don Brash, address to the New Zealand Chamber of Commerce Annual Conference, Hamilton, 8 November, 2003.

2 Matthew Hooton, email to Don Brash, 28 January 2004.

3 Ibid.

4 Don Brash, email to Matthew Hooton, 29 January 2004. The hui idea did not gain enough support from others to be carried out.

5 Matthew Hooton, email to Don Brash, 29 February 2004.

6 Ibid.

7 Allen's house is near that of his friend Bob Carr, retired New South Wales Premier ('Carr speculation', *Press*, 29 July 2005).

8 Matthew Hooton, email to Don Brash and Peter Keenan, 19 February 2004.

9 Matthew Hooton, email to Bryan Sinclair, 19 February 2004.

10 'The Powers and Puzzles of Richard Allen', Elizabeth Bumiller, *Washington Post*, 28 June 1981.

11 Dick Allen, interviewed by Kim Hill, *Face to Face*, TV One, 13 March 2003.

12 'Top US adviser attacks UN', Lin Ferguson, *Southland Times*, 22 March 2003.

13 Matthew Hooton, email to Bryan Sinclair, 19 February 2004.

14 'Government review of Maori need', Colin Espiner, *Press*, 24 February 2004.

15 Dick Allen, email to Matthew Hooton, 17 February 2004.

16 Peter Keenan, email to Don Brash, 5 March 2005.

17 Dick Allen, email to Matthew Hooton, 17 February 2004.

18 Don Brash, email to Dick Allen (via Bryan Sinclair), 28 February 2004.

19 Don Brash, email to Bryan Sinclair and Richard Long, 13 June 2004.

20 In response to Trevor Mallard's allegations, Richard Long prepared these lines: 'There will be multiple questions on the following. Do you have Americans working at party

HQ? Do you have American advisors? How much backing does National get from the US? Do you have Americans fund raising for you?' He proposed the following line for the politicians: 'There are bound to be Americans who feel strongly about National's policies and who donate to the party. I simply don't know.' Richard Long, email to Anita Ferguson and Jason Ede, 21 July 2005.

21 'US Admiral raises nuclear strains', Scott McLeod, *New Zealand Herald*, 12 March 2004.

22 Phil Goff, Question for Oral Answer from Luamanuvao Winnie Laban, *Hansard*, 4 May 2004.

23 'Gone by lunchtime?', Chris Trotter, *Independent*, 19 May 2004.

24 Richard Long, email to National Communications Staff, Don Brash, and Murray McCully, 5 May 2004.

25 Don Brash, 'Don Brash welcomes Creech report', media release, 5 May 2004.

26 Don Brash, 'National decision on ship visits issue', New Zealand National Party press statement, 22 June 2004.

27 'Back in the race – now for the real National Party', Colin James, *New Zealand Herald*, 6 July 2004.

28 Chris Trotter, 'Gone by lunchtime?'

29 Dick Gentles, email and attached report to Don Brash, 10 May 2004.

30 Jason Ede, email to National Communications Staff, Don Brash, Murray McCully, Richard Long and Lockwood Smith, 30 July 2004.

31 Don Brash, email to National Communications Staff, Jason Ede, Murray McCully, Richard Long and Lockwood Smith, 31 July 2004.

32 Richard Long, email to Anne Small, Vanessa Rawson, Bryan Sinclair and Murray McCully, 29 July 2005.

33 Jason Ede, email to National Communications Staff, 3 August 2005.

34 Ibid.

35 Richard Long, email to John Carter, National Communications Staff, Phil de Joux, Don Brash, Lockwood Smith, Simon Power and Murray McCully, 27 August 2004.

36 Don Brash, email to Anne Small, Bryan Sinclair, Gerry Brownlee, Katherine Rich, Murray McCully, Peter Keenan, Richard Long, Simon Power and Steven Joyce, 8 September 2004.

37 Peter Keenan, email to Don Brash, 1 November 2004.

38 'Government releases "lunchtime" report', Ruth Berry, *New Zealand Herald*, 15 May 2004; and 'National puts notes regarding nuclear policy in public arena', *Scoop News*, www.scoop.co.nz, 3 August 2005.

39 Dick Allen, email to Peter Keenan, 24 July 2005.

40 'In the 1980s and early 1990s, the Heritage Foundation was a key architect and advocate of the Reagan Doctrine, by which the United States government channelled overt and covert support to anti-Communist resistance movements in such places as Afghanistan, Angola, Cambodia and Nicaragua and generally supported global anti-communism during the Cold War.... The foundation was instrumental in advancing President Ronald Reagan's belief that the former Soviet Union was an "evil empire" and that its defeat, not its mere containment, was a realistic foreign policy objective. Heritage also played a key role in building support for Reagan's plans to build an orbital ballistic missile shield, the "Strategic Defense Initiative".' Wikipedia Encyclopedia, 2006.

41 His meetings there included president Chris DeMuth. 'American Enterprise Institute for Public Policy Research is a conservative think tank founded in 1943 whose

stated mission is to support the "foundations of freedom – limited government, private enterprise, vital cultural and political institutions, and a strong foreign policy and national defense". It has emerged as one of the leading architects of the Bush administration's public policy; more than two dozen AEI alumni have served either in a Bush administration policy post or on one of the government's many panels and commissions.' Wikipedia Encyclopedia, 2006.

42 'The Cato Institute is a large libertarian, non-profit public policy research foundation (think tank) headquartered in Washington, D.C. The Institute advocates policies that advance "individual liberty, limited government, free markets, and peace". Cato scholars are libertarian in their policy positions, typically advocating diminished government intervention in domestic social and economic policies... including such measures as abolishing the minimum wage... diminishing federal government involvement in the marketplace and in local and state issues and enhanced school choice.' It differs from the Heritage Foundation and AEI in that it did not support the Bush administration's invasion of Iraq. Wikipedia Encyclopedia, 2006.

43 Dick Allen, email to Peter Keenan, 24 July 2005.

44 Jason Ede, email to Bryan Sinclair, 4 June 2004.

45 New Zealand National Party, 'Free trade discussed at Don Brash's US meetings', press release, 2 June 2004.

46 Don Brash, Appointment Diary, 16 August 2004.

47 Peter Watson currently serves as President and CEO of the Dwight Group. In 2004, at the time of the Brash trip, he was the Chairman, President and CEO of the United States Overseas Private Investment Corporation. From September 1996 until May 2001, he was Counsel to Pillsbury Winthrop LLP, an American law firm, advising on international business and trade policy matters. He concurrently served as Senior Adviser to Armitage Associates, L.C. From June 1994 until June 1996, Dr Watson served as Chairman of the United States International Trade Commission, and from November 1989 until September 1991, as the Director of Asian Affairs at the National Security Council at the White House.

48 Peter S. Watson, email to Max Bradford and Peter Keenan, 18 May 2004. Bradford also urged Keenan to take up Watson's offer of arranging an informal dinner at his place on one of the free nights in Washington, 'without any MFAT officials!'

49 'Brash considers nuclear ballot', Audrey Young, *New Zealand Herald*, 23 June 2004.

50 'National rethinks its nuclear policy', Colin Espiner, *Press*, 9 February 2006.

CHAPTER 7

1 Peter Keenan, 'NBR Poll', 12 December 2003.

2 Don Brash, Appointment Diary, Friday, 7 May 2004, 7.30am. Breakfast Address to the Property Council of New Zealand at Hyatt Regency Hotel, Auckland.

3 Property Institute of New Zealand website, http://www.propertynz.co.nz.

4 Don Brash, Appointment Diary, Friday, 7 May 2004 9am. Meeting with Private Hospital Assoc (organised by Diane Foreman @ The Regency Boardroom, 12th Floor, Hyatt Regency Hotel, Auckland.

5 Don Brash, Appointment Diary, Wednesday, 10 March 2004, 10am. Meeting with Dr Michael Wooldridge, former Australia Health Minister & Andrew Blair, General Manager, Private Hospitals Association, with Lynda Scott.

6 Don Brash, Appointment Diary, Friday, 7 May 2004, 11am. Meeting with Brian Evans, CEO, Fairfax NZ at new offices, Level 2, Fairfax NZ House, 110 Customs Street West, The Viaduct.

7   Bryan Sinclair, email to Don Brash, 20 May 2004.

8   Don Brash, email to Bryan Sinclair, 20 May 2004. Bryan Sinclair also contributed to the speech. He wrote to Peter Keenan that 'we need a few grab lines that blue collar Joe can relate to... can we not be a bit more populist and say something like "what we need to do is to start building the roads, and stop pussyfooting around the squeaky Green Party, who themselves drive around the countryside in dirty great convoys telling people what is good for them".' (Bryan Sinclair, email to Peter Keenan, 29 March 2005.) Keenan replied that he thought the suggestion was excellent. (Peter Keenan, email to Bryan Sinclair, 30 March 2005.)

9   Tony Garnier, email to Maurice Williamson, 31 March 2004; 'Spotlight on transport', *New Zealand Herald*, 2 April 2005.

10   Maurice Williamson wrote to Tony Garnier on 31 March 2005: 'Tony, I would appreciate your comments. Could you do all you can to organise some positive statement of support from EMA, Chamber of Commerce etc. Maurice.' (Maurice Williamson, email to Tony Garnier, 31 March 2005.) Tony Garnier replied: 'You say at page 14: "What would all that buy? Well, I am not going to get into the business of promising particular roads because it is clearly undesirable for political pressures to become the main driver for the allocation of road investment funds." I suggest you take out reference to what you are NOT going to promise – that will become a headline and potentially lead to negative feed back – and instead focus on what your ARE promising. As I read the speech you could say positively: "Clearly there is a crying need to complete Auckland's long-agreed strategic highway network as fast as possible. The same in Wellington and the rural areas. I promise to focus our efforts on doing that." Say this here (p.14) to replace what you are not promising, and then elaborate as you have with reference to the projects needed for network connectedness to be achieved i.e. western corridor, HBTC etc. I have made some inserts and marked the text in a couple of places to emphasise the case for building a proper "roading network" rather than just building "more roads". Yes, positive media support is being arranged. Regards, Tony Garnier.' (Tony Garnier, email to Maurice Williamson, 31 March 2004).

11   National Party, 'Information for [Don Brash] speech to the New Zealand Property Institute', 7 June 2005.

12   Don Brash, Appointment Diary, Wednesday 30 June 2004 1.45pm. Meeting with British American Tobacco, Level 14, Geni Tower, 66 Wyndham St, contact: Carrick Graham. Hon David Carter accompanying Don Brash. Attending: William Toh, Managing Director, Carrick Graham, Corporate & Regulatory Affairs Director, Andrew O'Regan, Marketing Director, Jonathan Tucker, Finance Director, Belinda Ross, Corporate Solicitor/Company Secretary, Rowan Tonkin, HR Director, Susan Jones, Corporate & Regulatory Affairs Manager.

13   'Tobacco giant to market sweet-flavoured cigarettes', *Press*, 5 June 2004.

14   Don Brash, Appointment Diary, Wednesday, 14 July 2004, 12.30pm. Address to the Wellington Regional Chamber of Commerce Luncheon at the InterContinental Hotel, Featherston St. 'Topic: Don Brash's choice, but would be keen to hear National's views on the SME sector & policies or initiatives which could be applied to promote and stimulate growth (with some Wellington spin!)'
3pm. Meeting with Local Government Forum – Caucus room – Contact: Roger Kerr, NZBRT. Forum (Business New Zealand, Federated Farmers, NZ Business Roundtable etc) – presentation and exchange views on local govt. Attending: John Key, David Carter & Nick Smith.
4pm. Meeting re RMA with Simon Carlaw and others. Venue: Caucus Room. NB:

Roger Kerr has indicated that he is happy to stay on for this meeting. Simon suggests Mr Peter Whitehouse, Business New Zealand, and Mr Ralph Matthes, Executive Director Major Electricity Users Group, be invited to attend.

15 Friday, 13 August 2004, 5pm. Meeting with Rob Mitchell, Managing Director, Roche Pharmaceuticals at 8 Henderson Place, Te Papapa. Tuesday, 17 August 2004, 9.30am. Meeting with Suse Reynolds & Brian Lynch, Trade Liberalisation Network, Don Brash's office. Tuesday, 24 August 2004, 6.30pm. Dinner with Bd Members of the NZ Timber Industry Federation at the Wellesley Club, Wellington. Wednesday, 25 August 2004, 6pm. Dinner with Health Sector CEOs @ the Boulcott Bistro (private rm), 99 Boulcott St. Contact: Faye Pulley, Office Admin, Health Funds Association of New Zealand. Attending: Andrea Pettett, Health Funds Association, Kim Miles, NZ Orthopedic Association, Lesley Clarke, Research Medicines Industry, Cameron McIver, NZ Medical Association, Murray Burns, Pharmacy Guild of New Zealand, Carolyn Cooper, New Zealand Private Hospitals Association, Victor Klap, IPA Council. Thursday, 26 August 2004, 7.30pm. Dinner with Lion Breweries' & DB Breweries' Board Members & Senior Management at Oceania & Eastern, Level 3, 110 Customs St West, Viaduct, Auckland. Contact: Nicky Stewart. Invites to be extended to John Key, David Carter, Tony Ryall. Monday, 6 September 2004, 6.30pm. Host and address Annual Forum Dinner for the Independent Schools of NZ Group – Grand Hall. Contact: Joy Quigley. Approximately 100 delegates & partners, representing Independent Schools in NZ & Aust. (approx 70 from New Zealand & 20 principals from Australia).

16 For example, on 23 July Brash met the Automobile Association on Auckland transport and the managing director of the Canadian natural gas-to-methanol company Methanex, which was lobbying at that time for access to more natural gas reserves as the Maui field ran out. He went from there to give the closing speech to the powerful Employers and Manufacturers Association (Northern) annual conference, before heading out for dinner with the departing Microsoft New Zealand CEO in a private room of the Halo Restaurant.

17 Health Funds Association of New Zealand, *The Long Term Funding of New Zealand Healthcare*, 2004.

18 Beer, Wine and Spirit Council, *BWSC Update*, Spring 2004.

19 Don Brash, Appointment Diary, 4 August 2004. Similarly, he met with the heads of some of New Zealand's biggest businesses for an exclusive private dinner on 27 October 2004 at the offices of investment brokers Goldman Sachs JBWere, 38 floors above downtown Auckland. They were Goldman Sachs CEO Scott Perkins, John Maasland of Carter Holt Harvey, Keith Smith of the Warehouse Group, Neville Darrow of Ports of Auckland and Brian Corban of Genesis Energy. Craig Heatley, one of the major National Party donors discussed later, was also present.

20 The insurance industry links are discussed in Chapter 15.

21 Peter Keenan, email to Don Brash, Tony Ryall, Richard Long and Murray McCully, 25 June 2004.

22 Don Brash, 'Law & Order – A National Priority', 4 July 2004.

23 Peter Keenan, email to Don Brash, Tony Ryall, Richard Long and Murray McCully, 25 June 2004.

24 Police officer and party member, email to Don Brash, 2 July 2004.

25 'Talking Tough', *Marlborough Express*, editorial, 6 July 2004.

26 Peter Keenan, email to Bryan Sinclair, 8 November 2004. He said National needed to stop 'navel gazing about which inevitably low profile policy speech it was doing next'.

27 Don Brash, email to Anne Small, Jason Ede, Richard Long, Peter Keenan and Bryan Sinclair, 15 June 2004.

28 Don Brash, email to Peter Keenan, Murray McCully and Richard Long, 17 August 2004.

29 Richard Long, email to National Communications Staff, Murray McCully, Peter Keenan, Bryan Sinclair and Don Brash, 26 August 2004.

30 Bryan Sinclair, email to Don Brash, 4 September 2004.

31 Ibid.

32 Don Brash, email to Bryan Sinclair, 5 September 2004.

33 Bryan Sinclair, email to Don Brash, 5 September 2004.

34 Don Brash, email to Bryan Sinclair, 5 September 2004.

35 Supporter, email to Don Brash, 7 September 2004.

36 Don Brash, email to Murray McCully, Richard Long, Peter Keenan, Bryan Sinclair, Simon Power, Gerry Brownlee and Steven Joyce.

37 Peter Keenan, email to Bryan Sinclair, 26 August 2004.

38 Peter Keenan, 'Strategy Issues: Speech and Policy Releases', 29 October 2004.

39 Murray McCully, email to Peter Keenan, Steven Joyce and Richard Long, 1 November 2004.

40 In 2002–2003, for instance, one of his main clients was the pro-genetic engineering lobby, Life Sciences Network.

41 Bryan Sinclair, email to Peter Keenan, 5 November 2004.

42 Peter Keenan, email to and from Bryan Sinclair, 5 November 2004.

43 Bryan Sinclair, email to Peter Keenan, 5 November 2004.

44 Peter Keenan, email to Bryan Sinclair, 8 November 2004.

45 Ibid.

46 Party official, email to Don Brash, 8 November 2004.

47 Ibid.

CHAPTER 8

1 Sam Simon and John Swartzwelder, *The Simpsons*, 'Two Cars in Every Garage and Three Eyes on Every Fish' episode, November 1990.

2 Peter Keenan, 'Strategy from here till the election', 8 November 2004.

3 Bryan Sinclair, 'One shot, high stakes, no second place. Re-write the rule book', 8 November 2004.

4 As campaign director, Bryan Sinclair proposed the ACT Party's Australian adviser, Ian Kortlang, or the Australian Liberal Party's New South Wales campaign director and former New Zealand resident, Scott Morrison. (Morrison initially showed interest in the job, but when he changed his mind it went to National Party general manager Steven Joyce.) Ruth Richardson was aware of Morrison being courted and, when he took a different job, she sent details to Don Brash in an email saying, 'Don, I hope he was not two timing you, Ruth'. (Ruth Richardson, email to Don Brash, 8 December 2004.)

5 Peter Keenan, email to Don Brash, 15 February 2005. The email described Keenan's redefined list of functions as: 'Coordinate policy development in line with our political strategy; be a policy gate-keeper.

'Ensure that the Leader keeps in touch with his key caucus colleagues on policy, so that they understand the role their portfolios play in our political strategy; and to arrange a regular cycle of meetings with them.

'Ensure that Leader's time is spent on key issues only.

'Drive the diary in a way that is consistent with our political strategy. Currently, the quality of invitations is dropping alarmingly, and we are not driving the process in any serious way. What happens, is happening virtually by default.

'Ensure the Diary reflects our current key priorities (eg women and the over 60s) or on current issues (Welfare).

'Assist with keeping media opportunities on message: the Leader should be going into all interviews with a clear political agenda and a strong intention to reframe questions in terms of that agenda.

'Assess whether the Leader's public meetings are making an impact and if not, to help craft the message and delivery so that we do make an impact.'

6   Murray McCully, 'Campaign Structure Issues', 9 November 2004.
7   Murray McCully, 'Memo to the Leader', 8 November 2004.
8   Nick Smith, 'Australian election report', 13 October 2004.
9   Ibid. Nick Smith had already raised the need for neutralising issues in caucus a month earlier. Brash had responded at the time: 'At Caucus yesterday, as some of you know, Nick made a comment about the importance of getting potentially contentious issues off the agenda well ahead of the election. I know that most of you have had that very much in mind for some months. But I thought it might be worth just reviewing what those potentially contentious issues might be: a) Nuclear ship visits. I think that that has been dealt with, with our position being that there will be no change in NZ's legislative ban on nuclear-propelled and armed ships unless we obtain an explicit electoral mandate to do that – such as through a referendum. b) Tax cuts for the rich. I don't know that we can ever get that totally off the agenda, but we have got ourselves into a reasonable position I think by indicating that our top priority is a reduced tax burden for low and middle income New Zealanders, a cut in the company tax rate to a rate no higher than that in Australia, and a gradual flattening in the tax scale over time. I don't agree with Wayne's suggestion that we make tax reductions a centre-piece of our policy package (at least, I don't think that is feasible as long as we are talking about reasonably modest changes – he was suggesting only two personal tax rates, 15% and 25%, with an increase in the rate of GST to 15%.) c) Asset sales. Not sure how we best deal with this. I don't think we want to suggest we will never ever sell a government-owned asset, though I think we could agree (1) not to sell Kiwibank (which has clearly become very popular with rural NZers), (2) to sell Landcorp to New Zealand based farmers with the proceeds invested in the environment in some way (Nick's idea, which I think has potentially considerable merit), and (3) to sell any other significant asset through an IPO (rather than through a trade sale auction – in other words, like Auckland International Airport and Contact Energy – although largely irrational (in that an IPO will almost certainly yield less to the taxpayer than a trade sale), NZers seem enthusiastic about AIA but critical of most of the other asset sales). d) Superannuation I think we can deal with this one, though we still need to persuade voters that we can honour our promise to keep the parameters of the scheme unchanged for the next 15 years IF we decide to reduce or eliminate the contribution to the Cullen Fund. What other issues might bite us? Not sure. We are allegedly losing some voters because of my voting for the PRB and CUB, though I am not sure that that holds water. Labour is much more clearly the promoter of those Bills, and they are going up in the polls. United Future, which is the party which most clearly opposed both Bills, is not going anywhere. Comments and suggestions welcome – both about other issues which might bite us and about how we should best deal with the issues I have listed. Don.' (Don Brash, email to Anne Small, Bryan Sinclair, Gerry Brownlee, Katherine Rich, Murray McCully, Peter Keenan, Richard Long, Simon Power and Steven Joyce, 8 September 2004.)

10 'Summary of Current Election Strategy', notes for the Campaign Strategy Meeting, 19 October 2004.

11 Richard Long, 'Strategy views, Response to DB request, Confidential', 8 November 2004.

12 Murray McCully, 'Memo to the Leader'.

13 Ibid.

14 Matthew Hooton wrote: 'Don, You are ultimately going to have to find an economically-acceptable way of backing off on the 4 weeks leave issue, so you should say as little about it as possible in the meantime.

'We will have to look at an "innovative" employment policy that allows us to fudge on this: perhaps it is one with very few, if any, legally-enforceable rules, leaving almost all matters to be negotiated directly between employer and employee, but one which is backed up strongly by "codes" or "guidelines" – anything short of actual legally binding requirements – that "recommend" or "promote" 4 weeks leave, a minimum wage and so forth. We could even say the "codes" or "guidelines" would be developed through tripartite negotiations! Perhaps Ken Douglas or Angela Foulkes could be commissioned to "facilitate" this. There could even be government funding for a brand or logo that businesses could use, including on manufactured products, if their employment arrangements met the code. The more of the latter stuff (which would be emphasised in the politics), the fewer actual legally-enforceable rules we will need politically, so ironically the more fluff the sounder the policy can be in practice. Business people will see through the fluff, understand why you are doing it, and understand.

'Whatever the details – which are a matter for caucus – we are going to need an employment policy that allows us to have a bet each way. As Clark says "Vote National, lose your holidays" is not a good slogan but it is one she will use against us. It will lose us the election and we need to avoid being branded with it at all costs. (In 18 months, we are not going to win the wages/leave trade-off argument with 50% of the population.) So as far as possible without looking like you are running (and risking the "integrity; tell it like it is" theme) keep your head down on it.' (Matthew Hooton, email to Don Brash, 10 November 2003.)

He followed up that email shortly after with a second: 'Don: if you think there is any merit in my previous message, attached is a document that: 1) suggests a story that could be "placed" in the media this week to take the heat out of the issue, and 2) outlines how such a policy could be announced next year. It also occurs to me that the more labour-friendly the details of the code, the fewer businesses that would meet them, which would minimise the market distortion of the brand campaign, but which would also make the policy more politically popular!

'I think this would be a great blend of good economics and good politics: it is not a compromise at the centre, but a classic application of triangulation. Clark would describe the code and commission as window dressing – which they are – but it would sufficiently confuse the issue to take the heat out of it.' (Matthew Hooton, email to Don Brash, 10 November 2003.)

15 National Party, 'National to give workers choice in holidays', press release, 9 December 2004.

16 Peter Keenan, email to Bryan Sinclair, 6 December 2004.

17 Don Brash, email to Anne Small, Bryan Sinclair, Gerry Brownlee, Katherine Rich, Murray McCully, Peter Keenan, Richard Long, Simon Power and Steven Joyce, 8 September 2004.

18 Don Brash, Speech to the Screen Directors Guild AGM, 18 October 2004.

19 'Brash puts TVNZ in picture', Anna Chalmers, *Sunday Star-Times*, 17 October 2004.

20 Richard Long wrote to Don Brash: 'Both TV1 and TV3, as predicted, used brief clips of Don extolling the virtues of asset sales and called it another U turn, but in terms of inoculation it achieved its purpose'. (Richard Long, email to Don Brash, 18 October 2004.)

21 Ibid.

22 'Nats rule out state asset sales', Colin Espiner, *Press*, 4 March 2005.

23 'Nats do U-turn on selling Kiwibank', Tracy Watkins, *Dominion Post*, 4 March 2005.

24 Richard Long, email to John Key, Don Brash, Gerry Brownlee, National Communications Staff, Peter Keenan and Phil de Joux, 4 March 2005.

25 John Key, 'Lifting the performance of the state sector under a future National Government', speech to the Ellerslie Rotary Club, 4 March 2005.

26 Bryan Sinclair, 'One shot, high stakes'.

27 George Chapman, email to Don Brash, 4 December 2004.

28 Richard Long, 'Strategy views, Response to D.B. request'..

29 'Right left behind in polls race', Jonathan Milne, *New Zealand Herald*, 5 December 2004.

30 'They said it', *Waikato Times*, 28 May 2005.

31 Murray McCully, 'Memo to the Leader'.

32 Steven Joyce, 'Key points from Visit to Liberal Party Election Campaign', 10 October 2004.

33 New Zealand National Party, Agenda for Campaign Strategy Meeting, 19 October 2004.

34 New Zealand National Party, Strategy meeting action points, 19 October 2004.

35 New Zealand National Party, Appendix to the Strategy meeting action points, 19 October 2004.

36 'The Guardian profile, Lynton Crosby', Nicholas Watt, *Guardian*, 28 January 2005.

37 Murray McCully, 'Memo to the Leader'.

38 Gerry Brownlee, 'Strategy advice opinion', 8 November 2004.

39 Katherine Rich, 'Memo on campaign', 8 November 2004.

40 Peter Keenan, Strategy Note, 11 August 2004.

41 Peter Keenan, email to Murray McCully, Richard Long, Bryan Sinclair and Steven Joyce, 26 October 2004.

42 Nick Smith, 'Australian election report'.

43 Peter Keenan, 'Strategy from here till the election'.

44 'Summary of Current Election Strategy'.

45 Ibid.

46 Peter Keenan, 'Strategy Issues: speeches and policy releases', 29 October 2004.

47 Peter Keenan, 'Strategy from here till the election'.

48 Bryan Sinclair, 'One shot, high stakes'.

49 Don Brash, email to Steven Joyce, Judy Kirk, Murray McCully, Richard Long, Tony Ryall and Peter Keenan, 24 November 2004.

50 Steven Joyce, email to Don Brash, 24 November 2004.

51 Peter Keenan, 'Strategy from here till the election'.

52 If you have ever wondered why political parties send you those rather inane surveys about your views on various issues, the answer is that they are building up databases to use for direct mail advertising.

53 Katherine Rich, 'Memo on campaign'.
54 'Summary of Current Election Strategy'.
55 Milton Friedman visited Don Brash on 24 January 2005.
56 Peter Keenan, 'Strategy from here till the election'.
57 Ibid.
58 'Brash vs Clark: the Battle for NZ's soul', Helen Bain, *Sunday Star-Times*, 11 September 2005.

CHAPTER 9
1 Richard Long, 'Strategy views, response to DB request, Confidential', 8 November 2004.
2 Ibid.
3 David Farrar, Curia Market Research Limited, New Zealand Poll Update, 7 February 2005.
4 Richard Long, email to National Communications Staff, Don Brash, Murray McCully, Gerry Brownlee and Steven Joyce, 7 July 2004. National's internal polls, conducted by David Farrar's Curia Market Research company, were polling the public every week right through 2004, when Richard Long wrote these lines. The 'probed party vote three week rolling average' for that particular week was about 42% for National and 35% for Labour.
5 Peter Keenan, email to Don Brash, Bryan Sinclair, David Carter, Gerry Brownlee, Judy Kirk, Murray McCully, Richard Long, Steven Joyce and Tony Ryall, 2 May 2005.
6 Peter Keenan, email to Bryan Sinclair, 31 May 2005.
7 'What Women Voters Want', Lance Tarrance and Leslie Sanchez, *New York Times*, 12 September 2004.
8 Peter Keenan, email to Murray McCully and National Communications Staff, 14 September 2004.
9 Peter Keenan, email to Don Brash, 25 September 2004. The article was 'Wooing mom', Kathleen Parker, www.townhall.com, 24 September 2004.
10 Don Brash, Appointment Diary, Tuesday 5 October 2004.
11 Don Brash, email to Peter Keenan, Murray McCully, Richard Long, Gerry Brownlee, Judy Kirk, Steven Joyce and Bryan Sinclair, 31 October 2004.
12 Peter Keenan, 'Next Orewa Speech and Following: What Orewa topic fits the Strategy?', 14 December 2004.
13 Ibid.
14 Don Brash, email to Peter Keenan, Bryan Sinclair, Gerry Brownlee, Judy Kirk, Katherine Rich, Murray McCully, Richard Long, Steven Joyce and Tony Ryall, 20 October 2004.
15 Peter Keenan, 'Strategy Issues, Speech and Policy Releases', 29 November 2004.
16 Ibid.
17 Peter Keenan, email to Don Brash, 14 December 2004.
18 Peter Keenan, 'Next Orewa Speech and Following'.
19 Ibid.
20 Don Brash, email to Bryan Sinclair, 27 December 2004.
21 Don Brash, email to Michael Bassett, 27 December 2004.
22 Michael Bassett, email to Don Brash, 28 December 2004.
23 Don Brash, email to Michael Bassett, 29 December 2004.
24 Don Brash, email to Bryan Sinclair, Gerry Brownlee, Judy Kirk, Katherine Rich,

Murray McCully, Peter Keenan, Richard Long, Steven Joyce, Tony Ryall, Judith Collins, Maurice Williamson and Paul Hutchison, 25 October 2004.

25 Don Brash, first draft of welfare speech, 25 October 2004.

26 Richard Long, 'Strategy views'.

27 Don Brash, first draft of welfare speech. 'What went wrong? In some quarters, the blame is laid at the feet of the economic reforms of the eighties and nineties – the abolition of import controls, the reduction of tariffs, the abolition of farming subsidies, the corporatisation and then the privatisation of previously state-owned companies. And yes, those changes undoubtedly led to much pain and to a great many people losing their jobs. Perhaps the process was not handled as well as might have been ideal. Perhaps more attention should have been given to the need for retraining, or assistance with relocation. Some people with very specific skills relevant to industries which were uncompetitive without protection found themselves unceremoniously tossed on the scrap heap. This undoubtedly was a part of the reason for the sharp increase in those on benefits in the late eighties and early nineties. But no economist that I know of believes that those reforms should have led to a *permanent* increase in the number of those on benefits. Removing protection from inefficient manufacturing industries helped to make export industries more competitive, and increase employment in those industries. Corporatising the 'phone company and the port companies reduced employment in those companies, but again made other industries more competitive, and more willing to hire staff. What about the low inflation policy adopted so enthusiastically by the Labour Government of the eighties and continued by the National Government of the nineties? Surely that is at least partly responsible for the huge increase in the number of those on benefits? Winston believes that. Jim believes that. Jane Kelsey believes that. But Michael Cullen doesn't. And nor do any of the international observers who have studied the New Zealand economy over the last 15 years. I was the person most directly responsible for getting inflation down to a low level in the late eighties and keeping it there throughout the nineties and the early part of this decade. And I have often acknowledged that the process of getting inflation down from high levels to low levels always involves some temporary increase in unemployment. Why? Because after years of high inflation, people come to expect a continuation of high inflation, and gear their decisions around that expectation. So after years of 15% inflation, employees demand wage increases of at least 15%; and after years of 15% inflation, employers readily grant such wage increases. But if monetary policy slows the growth of spending in the economy so that employers find they can only increase prices by, say, 5%, many businesses are forced to lay off staff, or even collapse. Unemployment goes up. Only when wage increases move into line with the rate of inflation targeted by the government – plus some allowance for productivity improvements – will businesses start hiring staff again, and unemployment start to fall. It is now almost universally accepted that, while monetary policy has a temporary effect on the level of unemployment, it does not have any enduring or permanent effect on unemployment. There is certainly no evidence that I know of that tolerating more inflation would lead to a sustainable reduction in unemployment. One of the good things that has happened in New Zealand over the last 15 years is that almost all political parties now accept that.'

28 Michael Bassett, email to Don Brash, 31 December 2004.

29 Michael Bassett, 'Welfare Dependency – what happened to personal responsibility', draft speech, 31 December 2004.

30 Jason Ede (press officer), email to Katherine Rich, 23 December 2004; 'Five draft press releases attached'.

31 Michael Bassett, email to Don Brash, 31 December 2004.

32 Don Brash, email to Bryan Sinclair, 4 January 2005.

33 Don Brash, email to Bryan Sinclair, 16 January 2005.

34 Don Brash, 'Welfare Dependency – what on earth happened to personal responsibility', draft speech, 16 January 2005.

35 These phrases were all added in the last week or so before delivery.

36 Don Brash, 'Welfare Dependency – whatever happened to personal responsibility', Orewa Rotary Club speech, 25 January 2005.

37 Jason Ede, email to National Communications Staff, National MPs and National Research and Advisor Unit, 17 September 2004.

38 Murray McCully, email to Don Brash, 14 January 2005.

39 Don Brash, email to Murray McCully, 14 January 2005.

40 Don Brash, email to Murray McCully, Peter Keenan, Katherine Rich, Richard Long and Tony Ryall, 19 January 2005.

41 Ibid.

42 'Nats set to fight on welfare', Colin Espiner, *Press*, 22 January 2005; and 'Orewa is Brash's bash', Tracy Watkins, *Dominion Post*, 25 January 2005.

43 Anita Ferguson, email to Don Brash, 20 January 2005.

44 Bryan Sinclair, email to Don Brash, 25 January 2005.

45 'Orewa II: a sequel that delivers', Colin Espiner, *Press*, 26 January 2005; and 'War on welfare', Tracy Watkins, *Dominion Post*, 26 January 2005.

46 Jason Ede, email to all National staff, 27 January 2005.

47 'Welfare vision lost in translation', Fran O'Sullivan, *New Zealand Herald*, 1 February 2005.

48 'Brash's sacking of "star" riles MPs', *New Zealand Herald*, 2 February 2005; 'My compassionate conservatism didn't fit', Anna Claridge, *Press*, 2 February 2005; 'No women left on National front line', Tracy Watkins, Press, 2 February 2005; and 'Rich's replacement a welfare hardliner', Haydon Dewes, *Dominion Post*, 2 February 2005.

49 'How Rich fell out of favour with Brash', Sarah Boyd, *Dominion Post*, 2 February 2005.

50 'The Don's hit list', Tracy Watkins, *Dominion Post*, 2 February 2005.

51 Don Brash, 'Faster Growth? If We Want It', address to the Knowledge Wave Conference, 2 August 2001.

52 'Which way Bill?', Anthony Hubbard and Ruth Laugesen, *Sunday Star-Times*, 25 August 2002.

53 Ibid.

54 Bill English, email to Don Brash, 28 January 2005.

55 Don Brash, email to Bill English, 29 January 2005.

56 In March the New Zealand Press Association quoted National sources 'as saying Mr McCully had not been unhappy with the handling of the sacking of Ms Rich, but would have preferred her to have been demoted to the bottom of the party's rankings'. The *Dominion Post* reported 'senior National Party sources' denying suggestions that McCully had resigned from the election campaign committee over the incident. ('Nats deny McCully resignation claims', *Dominion Post*, 10 March 2005.) But he had. At the National Party board meeting on 17 February 2005, party president Judy Kirk 'informed the Board Members about Murray McCully's decision to resign from the Campaign Strategy Committee'. The board backed McCully after Brash 'expressed his hope that the Board would be able to persuade Murray to remain on the team'. Kirk agreed to write to McCully 'expressing the Board's appreciation of

his expertise and hard work' and assuring him that 'the Board had not accepted his resignation and asked him to reconsider'. (New Zealand National Party, minutes of the 17 February 2005 board meeting, p. 4.)

57 Peter Keenan, email to Don Brash, Bryan Sinclair, David Carter, Gerry Brownlee, Judy Kirk, Murray McCully, Richard Long, Steven Joyce and Tony Ryall, 2 May 2005.

58 Bryan Sinclair, email to Don Brash, 5 September 2004.

59 'PR and politics: practitioners share the same principles', Pattrick Smellie, *Independent*, 2 August 1996.

60 'Come in spinner', Stephen Harris, *National Business Review*, 25 June 1993; 'The kingmakers', Ruth Laugesen, *Dominion*, 12 September 1996.

61 Don Brash, email to Richard Long, Peter Keenan, Murray McCully, Steven Joyce, John Ansell and Anne Small, 24 June 2005.

62 Don Brash, email to Phil de Joux, Murray McCully, Anne Small, 17 August 2005.

63 Phil Heatley, email to Don Brash, 15 October 2004.

64 Don Brash, email to Phil Heatley, 15 October 2004.

65 Phil Heatley, email to Don Brash, 15 October 2004.

CHAPTER 10

1 'High pitch, low politics', *Economist*, 23 March 2005.

2 'National hasn't hired the Karl Rove of Oz politics – yet', Kevin List, *Scoop News*, 29 April 2005.

3 'Interview Don Brash', John Armstrong, Audrey Young and Ruth Berry, *New Zealand Herald*, 23 July 2005.

4 'Leaked minutes reveal National's concern about Brash's "flip-flops"', *New Zealand Herald*, 27 July 2005.

5 Richard Long, email to Don Brash, Bryan Sinclair, Steven Joyce, Murray McCully, Jason Ede and Anita Ferguson, 12 August 2005.

6 Steven Joyce, email to Richard Long, 12 August 2005.

7 Richard Long, email to Steven Joyce, Don Brash and Bryan Sinclair, 12 August 2005.

8 Crosby/Textor website, http://www.crosbytextor.com, August 2006.

9 Ibid.

10 'Marginals are the key to victory', David Fickling, *Guardian*, 18 November 2004.

11 'Crosby/Textor appoints new senior consultant', media alert, Crosby/Textor Pty. Ltd., 1 August 2005.

12 Crosby/Textor website.

13 'Tory adviser is tobacco hack', Andy Rowell, *Sourcewatch*, 18 April 2005. The conference agenda included subjects such as 'Youth Smoking' and dealing with the 'Antis', meaning opponents of the tobacco industry. In the Antis section of the conference, a document recorded that 'as Mark Textor showed yesterday, their campaign can certainly claim some success, as the public and opinion leaders appear to believe that we market to kids and we are deceptive or evasive'. However Textor told them it was not all bad news. The document noted that 'while negative perceptions of the tobacco industry are undoubtedly widespread, as Mark Textor pointed out yesterday, they may be more shallow than we imagine'.

14 'Push Your Vote Our Way', Suzanne Smith, *Radio National*, 28 February 1999.

15 David Fickling, 'Marginals are the key to victory'.

16 'The dark wizards of spin', Anthony Hubbard, *Sunday Star-Times*, 14 August 2005.

17 Mark Textor, email to Bryan Sinclair, Lynton Crosby and Jacqui Corbett, 4 June 2004.

18 Steven Joyce, 'Key points from visit to Liberal Party election campaign', 10 October 2004.

19 Mark Textor and Mark Domitrak, 'Strategic Memorandum on National Party Qualitative Benchmark', 10 December 2004.

20 Ibid.

21 Ibid.

22 Peter Keenan, 'Next Orewa Speech and Following: What Orewa topic fits the Strategy?', 14 December 2004.

23 Don Brash, 'A responsible middle course' speech, 9 August 2005.

24 Ibid.

25 'If you listen carefully you'll hear the real message', Claire Harvey, *New Zealand Herald*, 15 August 2005.

26 Ibid.

27 Ibid.

28 New Zealand National Party, minutes of December 2004 board meeting.

29 Steven Joyce, 'Key Messages Over Summer', 14 December 2004. The full wording was: 'Context: National has "cleared the decks" with needed policy changes before the end of the year.

'While the economy is going well currently, it has nothing to do with the Labour Government. They have been lucky.

'Labour has been distracted by its social reform agenda, and is doing nothing to ensure a strong economy going forward.

'We have lost the New Zealand Values of Initiative and Rewards for working hard and "Getting Ahead".

'There is no incentive for individuals to better themselves, be it through the tax system, the education system or the welfare system.

'If we don't put in place plans for a stronger economy now, we will suffer badly in the next economic downturn, our wages gap with Australia will grow, and more and more people and businesses will seek to work from Australia.

'Key Messages: Don Brash and National have plans to ensure a stronger economy by:

'Providing incentives in the tax system for people to be better rewarded for greater effort and hard work.

'Tightening up welfare and ensuring that everybody who can work does work.

'Ensuring an emphasis on standards in education so that students who learn and work hard are recognised.

'Don Brash and National will also:

'Put an end to the treaty grievance industry – Labour is now talking our language but is not making any changes, it is all cosmetic.

'Put an end to race-based privilege. Assistance will be based on need, not race.

'Make our community safer by locking away violent criminals.'

30 National Party Campaign Strategy Meeting, 'Action Points', 22 February 2005.

31 Mark Textor and Mark Domitrak, 'Strategic Memorandum'.

32 Ibid.

33 Mark Textor and Mark Domitrak, 'Qualitative Track Wave II' report, April 2005.

34 Crosby/Textor, 'Moderators Guide for New Zealand April Research', April 2005.

35 Ibid.

36 Mark Textor and Mark Domitrak, 'Qualitative Track Wave II' report.

37 Ibid.
38 New Zealand National Party, 'National's Action Plan for New Zealand', September 2005.
39 Mark Textor and Mark Domitrak, 'Qualitative Track Wave II', report.
40 Peter Keenan, email to Don Brash, 25 April 2005. The wording of the A6 cards was 'Key Message (Long) The key issues facing this country are: improving education standards so that all students can learn to their potential; reducing violent crime so that our streets and homes are safe; reforming welfare so that we don't create a generation who know nothing but dependency; Moving on from Treaty grievance mode to a nation with one standard of citizenship; Stopping NZ incomes falling behind, by reducing the tax burden and reducing pointless and costly regulation. Only National will do these things. Key Message (Short) The key issues facing this country are: improving education standards; reducing violent crime; reforming welfare; Moving on from Treaty grievance model; Stopping NZ incomes falling behind. Only National will do these things'.
41 Ibid.
42 Peter Keenan, email to Bryan Sinclair, 10 March 2005.
43 Steven Joyce, email to Richard Long, Peter Keenan, Murray McCully and Tony Ryall, 17 June 2005.
44 Ibid.
45 Jim Bolger, quoted in Jon Johansson, 'On Treaty and Race', *Scoop News*, 14 September 2005.

CHAPTER 11
1 'Terris attacks welfare state, PC attitudes', *Dominion*, 20 March 1997.
2 New Zealand National Party, *National Notes*, 17 June 2005.
3 'Shot down in the carpark by the PC police', Barry Soper, *Sunday News*, 14 April 1996.
4 Damien Cahill, 'New-Class Discourse and the Construction of Left-Wing Elites', in Marian Sawer and Barry Hindness, *Us and Them – Anti-Elitism in Australia*, API Network, Perth, 2004, p. 81. Various parts of this chapter draw on ideas in his chapter.
5 The Newztext figures for political correctness, which are only indicative owing to changes over the years in what is covered, are: pre-1994 – 46, 1995 – 167, 1996 – 183, 1998 – 234, 1999 – 168, 2000 – 349, 2001 – 379, 2003 – 654, 2004 – 670, 2005 – 749. Note that these totals are not for other variants such as 'politically correct'.
6 'Howard switches election fight to schools', Toby Helm, *Daily Telegraph*, 7 March 2005.
7 Michael Howard, 'Restoring respect – fighting crime', 16 August 2004.
8 Peter Keenan, email to Bryan Sinclair, 23 August 2004.
9 David McKnight, book review of Marian Sawer and Barry Hindness, *Us and Them – Anti-Elitism in Australia*, in *Dialogue*, Australian Academy of Social Sciences, 3/2004.
10 John Wilson, *The Myth of Political Correctness: The Conservative Attack on Higher Education*, Duke University Press, Durham, North Carolina, 1995.
11 Mark Davis, *Gangland: Cultural elites and the New Generationalism*, Allen & Unwin, Sydney, 1997, p71, quoted in Sawer and Hindness, *Us and Them*.
12 Phil de Joux, email to Richard Long, 17 December 2003.
13 Richard Long, email to National Communications Staff and Phil de Joux, 17 December 2003.

14 National Leader's Office, 'Government PC Actions', 17 December 2003. National saw some advantage in targeting smoker voters, as evidenced by them including questions about smoking in the June 2005 Crosby/Textor focus groups (Steven Joyce, email to Don Brash, 30 May 2005) and mentioning the smoking ban in election year speeches.

15 Because it is a political tactic, rather than the pursuit of truth, unrepresentative and even invented examples are used to bolster the claims of 'PC madness'. Political party research staff use large amounts of public resources asking parliamentary questions and official information act requests, discarding most of the information provided, in their search for any actions of the government agency in question that can be used as the PC example to ridicule the whole.

16 Emma Holmes, email to all National staff, 3 December 2004.

17 'Pique Viewing', Diana Wichtel, *New Zealand Listener*, 25–31 December 2004.

18 Don Brash, 'Brash announces National portfolios', 2 November 2003.

19 Don Brash told a National Party regional conference in May 2004 that 'Reforming the RMA, reducing the burden of regulation on business [and] cutting red tape... will be major priorities for the next National Government'. (Don Brash, 'Building a Better Future', Address to National Party Lower North Island Regional Conference, 10 May 2004.)

20 Lindsay Tisch, 'National backs small business', press release, 2 May 2005.

21 John Key, Address to National Party Lower North Island Regional Conference, 10 May 2004.

22 'NZ rated easiest country for business', Vernon Small, *Press*, 10 September 2004.

23 Heritage Foundation, *Index of Economic Freedom*, 2006.

24 'Red-tape claims inflated – survey', Paul Gormer, *Press*, 24 November 2004.

25 Ibid.

26 John Key, 'Too long spent looking in the rear-view mirror', press release, 13 September 2004.

27 Don Brash, 'Fixing the RMA is a top legislative priority', press release, 25 July 2005.

28 Don Brash, 'Achieving Economic Growth', Address to PricewaterhouseCoopers National Tax Conference, 8 May 2003.

29 Don Brash, 'We Are All New Zealanders', An address by Don Brash at Forum North, 29 August 2005.

30 'New Coromandel MP criticises RMA', New Zealand Press Association, 5 September 2002.

31 Ministry for the Environment, 'Key facts about local authorities and resource consents in 2003/2004', March 2005.

32 Ministry for the Environment, 'Streamlining RMA Approvals for Land Transport Projects: A study of delays in major roading projects', February 2003.

33 'John Carter reveals National's defence policies', Radio New Zealand Newswire, 5 August 2005.

34 'Nats demand more money for defence', *Dominion Post*, 2 September 2004.

35 New Zealand National Party, *National Notes*, 26 April 2005.

36 Peter Cozens, 'Funding for Defence', Institute of Strategic Studies, Wellington, 2005.

37 Damien Cahill, 'New Class Discourse', p. 83.

38 Malcolm Fraser, 'The Myth of New Zealand's Miracle Economy', *Australian*, 14 April 1998,

39 Malcolm Fraser, *Common Ground: Issues that Should Bind and Not Divide*, Viking, Melbourne, 2002, pp. 54–5; quoted in David McKnight, *Beyond Left and Right: New politics and culture wars*, Allen & Unwin, Sydney, 2005.

40 Damien Cahill, 'New Class Discourse', p. 88.

41 John Gray, *False Dawn: The Delusions of Global Capitalism*, Granta Books, London, 1998, pp. 17, 38; quoted and paraphrased in David McKnight, *Beyond Left and Right*.

42 Ibid., pp. 70–2, 199.

43 David McKnight, *Beyond Left and Right*, p. 96.

44 Damien Cahill, 'New Class Discourses', p. 90.

45 Ibid., p. 91.

46 Don Brash, 'A new government and a new direction', Address to National Party Northern Region Annual Conference, 17 April 2005.

47 Ibid.

CHAPTER 12

1 John Ansell, email to their mutual friend, 29 October 2003; forwarded to Don Brash 29 October 2003

2 John Ansell, email to Don Brash, 23 November 2003.

3 'In one foul smooch', John Ansell, letter to the editor, *Dominion Post*, 6 May 2003.

4 John Ansell, email to Don Brash.23 November 2003.

5 Don Brash, email to John Ansell, 23 November 2003.

6 John Ansell, email to Don Brash, 27 February 2004.

7 Don Brash, email to John Ansell, 1 March 2004.

8 Richard Long, email to Don Brash, 21 May 2004; and Don Brash, email to Richard Long, 23 May 2004.

9 John Ansell, email to Don Brash, 21 February 2005.

10 'Agency of the year awards', David Gapes, *Admedia*, March 2006.

11 Bryan Sinclair, email to Jo de Joux, 22 February 2005.

12 Brash correspondent, email to Don Brash and Maurice Williamson, 1 March 2005.

13 Bryan Sinclair, email to Don Brash, Maurice Williamson, Peter Keenan and Richard Long, 2 March 2005.

14 Maurice Williamson, email to Don Brash, Peter Keenan and Richard Long, 2 March 2005.

15 Bryan Sinclair, 'One shot, high stakes, no second place. Re-write the rule book', 8 November 2004.

16 Bryan Sinclair, email to Maurice Williamson, 2 March 2005.

17 Maurice Williamson, email to Bryan Sinclair, 2 March 2005.

18 Don Brash, email to Maurice Williamson, John Key, Richard Long, Bryan Sinclair and Brent Webling, 5 August 2005.

19 Steven Joyce, email to Don Brash, 25 May 2005.

20 'Where has Clark's competent Government gone?', Colin James, *New Zealand Herald*, 21 June 2005.

21 'Peters has foot in the door as rivals blacken opponents', Colin James, *New Zealand Herald*, 26 July, 2005.

22 'Parties risk falling flat with guerrilla tactics', Ben Thomas and David W. Young, *National Business Review*, 12 August 2005; 'Caution the watchword for National', Jonathan Milne, *New Zealand Herald*, 19 June 2005; 'Quick wit the way to win, says

creator', *Sunday Star-Times*, 3 July 2005; 'Presenting the anti-politician', Haydon Dewes, *Dominion Post*, 25 August 2005.

23 'Clever election tricks that fit the bill', *New Zealand Herald*, 24 September 2005.

24 Anthony Pratkanis and Elliot Aronson, *Age of Propaganda*, W.H. Freeman, New York, 1992, pp. 12, 138–9. This is the same thing Joseph Goebbels said 50 years earlier. He said that 'the rank and file are usually much more primitive than we imagine' and political messages 'must therefore always be essentially simple and repetitious'. In the long run, he argued, someone can only achieve results in influencing public opinion if they 'reduce problems to the simplest terms' and have 'the courage to keep repeating them in this simplified form despite the objections of intellectuals'.

25 'Peters has foot in the door as rivals blacken opponents', Colin James.

26 Pratkanis and Aronson, *Age of Propaganda*, pp. 139–43.

27 'Presenting the anti-politician', Haydon Dewes.

28 Pratkanis and Aronson, *Age of Propaganda*, pp. 168–72.

29 Richard Long, email to National Leader's Office, 16 August 2005.

30 Richard Long, email to Murray McCully and Gerry Brownlee, 16 August 2005.

31 'Nats' TV ad "all good fun"', Tracy Watkins and Haydon Dewes, *Dominion Post*, 17 August 2005; 'Clever election tricks that fit the bill', *New Zealand Herald*, 24 September 2005.

32 'Taking risks builds brands', *National Business Review*, 10 March 2006.

33 Michael Coote, email to Don Brash, 15 January 2005; forwarded by Brash to Murray McCully, Richard Long and Peter Keenan, saying, 'I think he is making an extremely important point'.

34 Steven Joyce, letter to Helena Catt, Electoral Commission, 10 March 2005.

35 Charles Guggenheim, quoted in Nicholas O'Shaughnessy, *Politics and Propaganda*, Manchester University Press, Manchester, 2004, p. 160.

36 'Political careering', John Ansell, *I think the clouds are cotton wool*, Padded Sell, Porirua, November 2003.

CHAPTER 13

1 'Serenading Don', Steve Braunias, *Sunday Star-Times*, 27 February 2005.

2 'National candidate says Brash bio no hagiography', Danya Levy, New Zealand Press Association, 15 February 2005.

3 Paul Goldsmith, *Brash: A Biography*, Penguin Books, Auckland, 2005.

4 Brian Edwards's biography was declared publicly to have been first proposed by Labour Party president Bob Harvey at a Labour meeting attended by Edwards. There was no suggestion that Edwards had been paid by others to write it. ('A first lady', Bernie Steeds, *Evening Post*, 17 November 2001.)

5 Don Brash, email to Richard Long, 21 May 2004.

6 Richard Long, email to Don Brash, 23 May 2004.

7 Don Brash, email to Richard Long, 23 May 2004.

8 Don Brash, email to Bryan Sinclair, Gerry Brownlee, Judy Kirk, Katherine Rich, Murray McCully, Peter Keenan, Richard Long, Steven Joyce and Tony Ryall, 18 December 2004.

9 Ibid.

10 Don Brash, Appointment Diaries, July 2004.

11 Don Brash, email to Paul Goldsmith, 8 November 2004.

12 Paul Goldsmith, email to Don Brash, 10 November 2004.

13 For instance, he proposed the words 'It amazes me that, as a society, we're quite happy to force people to pay taxes. Why is it that we suddenly become excessively polite

when it comes to someone living off the effort of everyone else for years?' They were used in a slightly modified form.

14 Penguin employee, email to Paul Goldsmith and Bryan Sinclair, 20 December 2004.

15 Don Brash, email to Bryan Sinclair and Steven Joyce, 27 March 2005.

16 Bryan Sinclair, email to Paul Goldsmith and Anne Small, 19 January 2005.

17 Bryan Sinclair, email to Paul Goldsmith, 15 February 2005.

18 Paul Goldsmith, email to Don Brash, 28 November 2004.

19 Bryan Sinclair, email to Richard Long, Peter Keenan and Jason Ede, 23 February 2005.

20 Richard Long, email to Bryan Sinclair, Peter Keenan and Jason Ede, 23 February 2005.

21 Jason Ede, email to Bryan Sinclair and Richard Long, 24 February 2005.

22 Richard Long, email to Bryan Sinclair, Peter Keenan and Jason Ede, 24 February 2005.

23 Steven Joyce, email to Trish Sherson, Richard Long and Bryan Sinclair, 23 February 2005.

24 New Zealand National Party, 'Brash: A Biography – email and website statistics', 10 March 2005.

25 Don Brash, email to Bryan Sinclair, 18 February 2005.

26 Katherine Rich's executive assistant, email to Bryan Sinclair, 23 February 2005.

27 Paul Goldsmith, email to Bryan Sinclair, 15 February 2005.

28 Ibid.

29 Anna Tripp, email to Modus Operandi caterers, 3 March 2005.

30 Confidential source.

31 TVNZ producer, email to Penguin employee, 23 February 2005.

32 Steve Braunias, 'Serenading Don'.

33 'Political Dispatches', *Dominion Post*, 7, 14 and 21 March 2005.

34 Don Brash, email to Richard Long, Bryan Sinclair and Paul Goldsmith.

35 'Speech inspires Brash book', Ursula Hudson, *East and Bays Courier*, 2 March 2005.

36 'Racing cracks whip over "fair tax"', John Jenkins, *Stuff.co.nz News*, 1 June 2005.

37 'Anti-government vote urged by racing industry', New Zealand Press Association, 17 June 2005.

38 Don Brash, email to Lindsay Tisch, Jason Ede and National Communications Staff, 18 June 2004.

39 Richard Long, email to Bryan Sinclair and Lindsay Tisch, 21 June 2005.

40 Bryan Sinclair, email to Anne Smith and Vanessa Rawson, 22 June 2005.

41 Bryan Sinclair, email to Lindsay Tisch and Richard Long, 22 June 2005.

42 Confidential source.

43 Confidential source.

44 Don Brash, Appointment Diary, 13 July 2005.

45 Jeff Drinkwater, email to Bryan Sinclair, 14 July 2005.

46 Bryan Sinclair, email to Jo de Joux and Lindsay Tisch, 3 August 2005.

47 Ibid. The list was: 'Ad copy for fullpage ad in racing book supplied by Nat to FT by Friday 19 August (note, ad placement is being paid for by FT); Red/Blue "Racing" postcard x 10,000 delivered to Hawkes Bay by Monday 22 August (note, designed, paid for and delivered to Hawkes Bay by Nat). Postcard outlines Nat's racing policy summary on the back, with "All Tax" / "Fair Tax" style message on front. This will be distributed by an on-course team paid for by FT; "Vote National For Fair Tax" electronic slide, for use on the on-course big screen, supplied by Nat to FT by Monday

22 August; Party vote logos/correct colours supplied by Nat to FT for winning post signage and miscellaneous signage as soon as possible (for FT to produce); "Message from Don Brash" copy for Friday Flash front page, supplied by Nat to FT by Friday 19 August; Direct mail item, supplied by Nat to FT for mailout to their database (Steven was negotiating arrangements for this, and will know progress, but it will no doubt need to be settled/printed/distributed within the next 2 weeks).'

48 Andrew Slade, email to Brent Webling and Lindsay Tisch, 22 August 2005. (Racing_Booklet_Ad.pdf, 'Here's the ad based on the postcard design. If it's good I'll send it on tomorrow.')

49 The postcard included the House of Representatives logo, showing it was paid from the parliamentary budget.

50 Parliamentary Services, *Members' Handbook of Services*, part 1.3.3 (1)(b).

51 New Zealand National Party, 'National will target taxpayer-funded political ads', press release, 19 July 2005.

52 Andrew Slade, email to Bryan Sinclair, 24 August 2005.

53 Bryan Sinclair, email to National MPs, Lindsay Tisch, Don Brash and National Secretaries, 3 August 2005.

54 *Harness Racing Weekly*, September 2005; and *Pacing and Trotting Guide*, issue no. 44, 2005.

55 Rob McAnulty, email to Bryan Sinclair, 8 September 2005.

56 Jo Davis, email to Lindsay Tisch, 29 August 2005.

57 'Policy makers must listen to what parents want in education', Maxim Institute press release, 1 June 2005.

58 Bryan Sinclair, email to Steven Joyce, Peter Keenan and Richard Long, 30 March 2005.

59 Don Brash, Appointment Diary, 4 March 2005. The meeting occurred in Middleton Road, Riccarton. Brash had also met Bruce Logan a year earlier at a meeting at Maxim's Christchurch office on 8 March 2004.

60 'Social welfare decisions essentially moral judgements', Bruce Logan, *New Zealand Herald*, 3 February 2005.

61 Ibid. The offer was not taken up.

62 Nicki Taylor, email to Bryan Sinclair, 5 May 2005.

63 Ibid.

64 Nicki Taylor, email to Bryan Sinclair, 19 May 2005.

65 Ibid.

66 Richard Poole, email to Bryan Sinclair, 30 November 2003. Poole was in discussion with National at that time about working for it and was describing his existing marketing projects.

67 John Taylor, email to Don Brash, 29 October 2003. 'Congratulations, Don, and be assured of any support I can give, also from John Graham (who has just left my office here) – in educational planning or otherwise. Well handled last night, especially in countering this Labour and Media generated left/right myth!! May the polls leap high soonest! Cheers, John.'

68 Don Brash, National Party televised election campaign opening, August 2005.

69 For instance, New Zealand National Party, 'Schools Policy Launch', 1 July 2005.

70 Anita Ferguson, email to Don Brash, Richard Long, Peter Keenan and Bryan Sinclair, 12 April 2005.

71 Don Brash, email to Anita Ferguson, Richard Long, Peter Keenan and Bryan Sinclair, 12 April 2005.

72 Bryan Sinclair, email to Norman LaRocque, 13 April 2005.

73 Norman LaRocque: 'Have played very softly with Bill [English] and Nicola [Willis]. Was never really sure anything was being taken on board. Seems it has so very pleased. Maybe a lesson for the NZBR – less shaming and more quiet persuasion.'
Bryan Sinclair: 'You've hit the nail on the head. Being a pretty blunt and hardline sort myself, I have certainly had to learn that lesson around this place too. Don Brash said to me en route to Rotorua yesterday that he was very hopeful that you personally would approve of it, and NZBR too. I'm glad you think its a step in the right direction. Many thanks from Don for your own contribution to this – your thinking has had a very direct effect.'
Norman LaRocque: 'Between us, I have always recognised the need to do things differently. Roger has not. Hence, the "sorry" list etc. Glad to have had some impact. Cheers, Norman.' (Emails between Norman LaRocque and Bryan Sinclair, 13 April 2005.)

74 Don Brash, emails to and from Bryan Sinclair, 13 April 2005. LaRocque wrote to National's press staff notifying them that he was 'hoping to organise a series of supportive media releases' from other organisations. He said Brash's speech 'should provide a real point of difference to the socialist horde currently occupying New Zealand!' (Norman LaRocque, email to Anita Ferguson, 12 April 2005.)

75 Maxim Institute, 'No excuse not to cast an informed vote', press release, 16 September 2005.

76 Communicating the Ideal of Liberty Conference, hosted by the Atlas Economic Research Foundation, the Sutherland Institute, and the International Freedom Educational Foundation, Little America Hotel, Salt Lake City, Utah, 14 August 2004.

77 Atlas Economic Research Foundation, http://www.atlasusa.org.

78 Atlas Economic Research Foundation, press release, 9 November 2005.

79 Bryan Sinclair, email to Scott McMurray, 8 March 2005.

80 Scott McMurray, email to Bryan Sinclair, 8 March 2005.

81 Michael Coote, email to Don Brash, 12 March 2005.

82 Bryan Sinclair, email to Scott McMurray and Richard Poole, 17 March 2005.

83 Bryan Sinclair, 'Expatriate Add On', 17 March 2005.

84 Scott McMurray, email to Bryan Sinclair, 17 March 2005.

85 Bryan Sinclair, email to Michael Coote, 17 March 2005.

86 Maxim spokesperson Amanda McGrail, email to Nicky Hager, 4 October 2006.

87 Bryan Sinclair, email to Steven Joyce, Peter Keenan and Richard Long, 30 March 2005.

88 Diana Piggott, NZVotes, standard email to candidates, 26 July 2005.

89 Maxim Institute, 'No excuse not to cast an informed vote'.

90 Ibid.

91 Quoted in 'Right and wrong', Russell Brown, *Hard News*, 1 November 2005.

92 Maxim Institute, 'No excuse not to cast an informed vote'.

93 'Parties object to Maxim's tactics', Karen Goodger, *Nelson Mail*, 28 June 2005.

94 'Group calls for vote splitting', Peter Luke, *Press*, 4 September 1996. VOTE appears to be a typical front group from the ACT Party/Brian Nicolle/corporate funder style of campaigning referred to in Chapter 2.

95 Maxim Institute, 'Major drop in "discarded votes" may show better understanding of MMP', press release, 5 October 2005.

96 Bryan Sinclair, email to Steven Joyce, Peter Keenan and Richard Long, 30 March 2005.

97 Ibid.

98 Amanda McGrail, pers. comm., 10 August 2006.

99 Richard Poole, email to Bryan Sinclair, 8 April 2005.

100 'Thinking of you', Geoff Collett, *Press*, 22 March 2003.

101 Richard Long, email to Vanessa Rawson, Anne Small, National Communications Staff and Murray McCully, 13 July 2005

CHAPTER 14

1   'Big money backed up National's campaign', Martin Kay, *Dominion Post*, 11 January 2006.

2   'Donors give more to Nats', *Dominion Post*, 4 May 2006.

3   Corrupt Practices Prevention Amendment Act, sections 8 and 12; referred to in Andrew Geddis, 'Regulating the Funding of Election Campaigns in New Zealand: A Critical Overview', *Otago Law Review*, Vol. 10, No. 4, 2004. This article is gratefully acknowledged as a major source for this and the following chapter.

4   Royal Commission on the Electoral System, *Towards a Better Democracy*, December 1986, p. 190.

5   Ibid., pp. 188–90.

6   Don Brash, 'Why I should be National Party leader', speech to caucus, 28 October 2003.

7   Steven Joyce, 'Party Funding: The Sharp End', August 2003.

8   Ibid.

9   When the word 'influence' is used in the book, it is not used to suggest buying specific policies. Instead is it means, more generally, influence over the elections through providing funding, having contact with and being taken seriously by the politicians, being consulted and listened to on party business and having the ability to affect the philosophy and direction of the party by supporting or not supporting particular leadership candidates.

10 Peter Keenan, email to Don Brash, 13 December 2003.

11 Don Brash, email to David Broome, 30 May 2004; and David Broome, email to Don Brash, 1 June 2004 (Broome had been a National Party candidate in the Mangere electorate in 1996). They also met with Simon Walker, another of the Centre for Independent Studies grouping and a director of Awaroa Partners.

12 National Party, Return of Party Donations to 31 December 2004 (to Electoral Commission), 27 April 2005. Jennings had moved to Russia in the early 1990s as a consultant helping with the first Russian privatisations. The investment bank Renaissance Capital, which Jennings heads, was estimated to be worth $2.3 billion in 2006 ('The A-Z of Russian oligarchs', *New Zealand Herald*, 3 June 2006).

13 'Ex-pat political givers preoccupied by taxes', Fran O'Sullivan, *New Zealand Herald*, 22 June 2005.

14 Don Brash, Appointment Diary, Thursday 25 November 2004.

15 Party official, email to Don Brash, 18 November 2004. This was the party official who wrote to Brash, saying they had had only two positive responses from 230 invitations.

16 New Zealand National Party, minutes of the 17 February 2005 board meeting, p. 6.

17 Deborah James (National Party Business Development Manager), email to Don Brash and Anne Small, 25 June 2005.

18 Deborah James, email to Don Brash and Anne Small, 211 June 2005.

19 Don Brash's notes for a July 2005 election debate said: 'National has signalled that if elected, it would conduct a "fundamental review" of the practices of Pharmac. This

was in light of Pfizer cancelling a $4 million a year deal with Auckland's Cancer Research Centre over Pharmac's decision not to subsidise certain cholesterol lowering drugs. Dr Hutchison has also put forward the view that Pharmac needs to have greater pharmaco-economic analysis. The review would also assess potential free trade agreement ramifications with the United States and the Commerce Commission's current exemptions to Pharmac regarding reference pricing.' Sarah Boyle, 'Leader's Debate – Points of attack and rebuttal', 4 July 2005.

20 As discussed in Chapter 7.

21 This quote comes from an earlier Private Hospitals Association meeting: Don Brash, Appointment Diary, Wednesday, 10 March 2004, 10am. Meeting with Dr Michael Wooldridge, former Australia Health Minister & Andrew Blair, General Manager, Private Hospitals Association, with Lynda Scott.

22 Don Brash, 'Speech notes for leader's dinners', June 2005.

23 Emma Holmes, email to Bryan Sinclair, John Key and Anne Small, 24 June 2005.

24 Jacqui Dean, email to Bryan Sinclair and Paul Anderson, 20 July 2005.

25 Paul Anderson, email to Jacqui Dean and Bryan Sinclair, 21 July 2005.

26 Don Brash, Appointment Diary, Friday 22 July 2005.

27 'Getting the balance right', *Southland Times*, 14 February 2002.

28 Bryan Sinclair, email to Jemma Montagu, Anthea Graham and Anne Small, 15 March 2005.

29 Robin McKenzie, email to Don Brash, 9 April 2005. Another prospective donor the year before was Vic Wieland, of Accord Engineering in Auckland, who wrote to Brash's office saying 'send someone around – we will definitely help with National Party funding'. Vic Wieland, email to Ben Wilson, 3 June 2004.

30 Rob McLeod, email to Don Brash and John Key, 28 June 2005.

31 John Key, email to Rob McLeod and Don Brash, 28 June 2005.

32 Don Brash, Appointment Diary, Friday 8 July 2005.

33 Deborah James, email to Vanessa Rawson, 1 August 2005.

34 Don Brash, Appointment Diary, Friday 9 August 2005. Party president Judy Kirk also attended this dinner.

35 Don Brash, Appointment Diary, Wednesday 8 December 2004.

36 New Zealand National Party, board minutes, December 2004.

37 Judy Kirk, 'An Invitation' (to the President's Council), October 2004.

38 Deborah James, 'National Party President's Council Fundraising Initiative', October 2004.

39 New Zealand National Party, 'President's Council' brochure, October 2004.

40 Ibid.

41 New Zealand National Party, minutes of the 17 February 2005 board meeting, p. 6.

42 There are probably other names that have been missed and it is always possible that one or two of those listed ended up not giving that year. Thus the word 'appear'. Also, some of the names mentioned earlier in the chapter, such as Peter Talley, may belong on this high value donor list.

43 'Roundtable recipe', Fran O'Sullivan, *New Zealand Times*, 11 May 1986.

44 'Cullen's free trip', *Press*, 9 December 1991. In 1991 Myers paid $16,000 for Labour's new finance spokesperson, Michael Cullen, to travel to the United States to study economics at the Aspen Institute.

45 'Best chance in decades', Robin Munro, *Press*, 2 November 1992; 'Meanwhile, down on the dole', Gordon Campbell, *New Zealand Listener*, 23 July 1994.

46 'Myers flays Govt policy', Matthew Brockett, *Press*, 18 March 2000.

47 'Let the smart Asians in – and stop whingeing', *Otago Daily Times*, 31 October 1988.

48 '"Propaganda wing" label for CIS', Richard Cresswell, *Press*, 22 December 1987.

49 'Entrepreneurs in the realm of ideas', Fran O'Sullivan, *New Zealand Times*, 4 May 1986. PR consultant Simon Walker was appointed executive director the following year.

50 'Our old boy network', David Venables, *New Zealand Listener*, 16 April 1988.

51 'Ducking out for book on Acting up', Jonathan Milne, *Sunday Star-Times*, 16 November 2003.

52 Ibid.

53 'Biggest, best boss', Mary Holm, *New Zealand Listener*, 24 December 1994.

54 The New Zealand participants of the Mont Pelerin meeting include many who became prominent in right politics over the following decades.

55 'Elaborate money maze hid donors', Geraldine Johns, *Sunday Star-Times*, 22 April 2001.

56 'Right wingers getting in on the act', Geraldine Johns, *Sunday Star-Times*, 22 April 2001.

57 Roger Douglas, *Unfinished Business*, Random House, Auckland, 1993.

58 Diane Foreman, email to Bryan Sinclair, 7 July 2005.

59 For instance, Rod Deane, Peter Shirtcliffe and Brash had dinner together on Wednesday, 4 August 2004.

60 This visit is described in the next chapter.

61 Described in earlier chapters.

62 Peter Shirtcliffe, email to Don Brash, Anna Small and Roderick Deane, 19 August 2005: 'I'm delighted that your Wellington Club membership is now finalised.... Meanwhile, best wishes as you head into the heavy stuff, Peter.'

63 Don Brash, Appointment Diary, Tuesday 26 July 2005.

64 Roderick Deane, letter to John Key, 14 March 2005.

65 Ibid.

66 John Key, 'Lifting the performance of the state sector under a future National Government', Speech to the Ellerslie Rotary Club, 4 March 2005.

67 Peter Keenan, email to Don Brash, 1 November 2004.

68 Don Brash, Appointment Diary, 14 March 2005.

69 For instance, in December 2004 Brash asked, concerning a fundraising dinner, 'should we be confining our invitations to the "second rank" of Auckland supporters (in terms of money) [and] specifically NOT invite the Colin Giltraps, the Craig Heatleys, etc?' (Don Brash, email to Bryan Sinclair, Gerry Brownlee, Judy Kirk, Katherine Rich, Murray McCully, Peter Keenan, Richard Long, Steven Joyce and Tony Ryall, 18 December 2004). Giltrap had previously donated $15,000 to National in 1999. Likewise, Horton is listed as a donor in a confidential document and he had assisted National fundraising in earlier elections. ('National candidate shows his true worth in three preposterous ideas', Rodney Hide, *National Business Review*, 30 July 1999.) The article mentions Michael Horton signing a fundraising letter for National's Epsom MP Richard Worth.

70 'Having some big knights out', *New Zealand Herald*, 8 May 1998.

71 'Road to privatisation full of potholes', Brian Gaynor, *New Zealand Herald*, 24 May 1997. When the US companies in the consortium sold out a decade later they took several billion dollars out of New Zealand in clear profit.

72 'Clark slams fat salaries', Matthew Brockett, *Press*, 13 December 1999.

73 '24ct golden handshake for Deane', Adrian Bathgate, *Press*, 7 May 2006.

74 'NZ takeover rules upset Australians', *Press*, 5 May 1998.

75 'Richest Kiwi now much richer with $500', *Press*, 17 July 1998.

76 ' "Persecuted" venture capitalists flee NZ', *Press*, 5 July 1999.

77 'Last Orders?' Carroll du Chateau, *New Zealand Herald*, 15 August 1997.

CHAPTER 15

1   Don Brash, interviewed on Radio New Zealand *Morning Report*, 22 July 2005.

2   Richard Long, email to Anita Ferguson and Jason Ede, 21 July 2005.

3   'Who pays the political pipers?', Nick Venter, *Dominion Post*, 28 October 2006.

4   New Zealand National Party, board minutes, December 2004.

5   'Secret trusts pour cash into National's coffers', *New Zealand Herald*, 4 May 2006.

6   'Campaign finance overhaul planned', *Nelson Mail*, 7 September 2006.

7   'Mallard attacks National use of trusts', Kevin List, *Scoop News*, 23 July 2005.

8   ' "Anonymous" political contributions strain credulity', Graeme Speden, *Independent*, 16 June 1999.

9   For instance, George Chapman, emails to Don Brash, 29 October 2004, 4 December 2004 and 17 January 2005.

10 George Chapman, emails to Don Brash, 4 December 2004.

11 'National's campaign donor unmasked', Irene Chapple, *Sunday Star-Times*, 10 September 2006.

12 Paul Goldsmith, Brash: *A Biography*, Penguin Books, Auckland, 2005.

13 New Zealand National Party, minutes of the 17 February 2005 board meeting, p. 6.

14 Bryan Sinclair, email to Don Brash, 29 September 2004.

15 Don Brash, email to Bryan Sinclair, 29 September 2004.

16 Don Brash, email to Bryan Sinclair, Gerry Brownlee, Judy Kirk, Katherine Rich, Murray McCully, Peter Keenan, Richard Long, Steven Joyce and Tony Ryall, 18 December 2004. Likewise, Horton is listed as a donor in a confidential document.

17 Ibid.

18 Diane Foreman, emails to and from Bryan Sinclair, 7 July 2005.

19 Rob McLeod, email to Don Brash and John Key, 28 June 2005; Don Brash, email to Bryan Sinclair and Steven Joyce, 29 June 2005.

20 Don Brash, email to Gerry Brownlee, Judy Kirk, Steven Joyce, Tony Ryall, Richard Long and Peter Keenan, 21 February 2005.

21 Steven Joyce, email to Don Brash, 22 February 2005.

22 New Zealand National Party, minutes of board meeting, 15 December 2004.

23 Andrew Geddis, 'Regulating the Funding of Election Campaigns in New Zealand: A Critical Overview', *Otago Law Review*, Vol. 10, No. 4, 2004.

24 'Police investigate election pamphlets', Martin Kay, *Taranaki Daily News*, 26 October 2005. He said: 'the [Exclusive Brethren's] leaflet does appear to promote the party vote for National. I have decided to refer the matter to police for investigation as to whether any person has breached section 221 of the Electoral Act 1993, and if so, whether any prosecution in terms of section 221(4) is appropriate.' The police only gave a one sentence explanation of its decision not to lay charges, so their reasoning is not clear.

25 Gerry Brownlee, quoted on *TVNZ News*, 4 May 2006.

26 Following their investigation, the police simply said, without explanation, that no further action was required.

27 National's operations manager Jo de Joux had decided the party could not fund

postcards for the raceday: ' No, we won't be doing a postcard – no budget for this'. (Jo de Joux, email to Lindsay Tisch, Maxine Viggers, Bryan Sinclair and Brent Webling, 4 August 2005. Sinclair then wrote to the National racing spokesperson Lindsay Tisch: 'We [Parliament office] could produce our own flyer outlining our racing policy, seeing as HQ won't fund a postcard. As long as we don't put "vote, donate or support" on it, and we don't use Party Vote logos, it's a valid constituency communication. Andrew Slade could produce 5,000 A5 flyers, or postcards, out of our own Leader's office budget for this, and the Fair Tax people could have them distributed on course as previously planned. If Lindsay wants to do this, he could give Andrew Slade a brief summary of our racing policy in bullet points, and Andrew could design something up that fits the rules?' (Bryan Sinclair, email to Tisch's secretary, 10 August 2005.) Tisch's secretary replied: 'Re flyer – Lindsay thought good idea and he will look at this tonight'. (Tisch's secretary, email to Bryan Sinclair, 10 August 2005.) Designer Slade subsequently designed the postcard, which was distributed by people paid by the Fairtax lobby. The postcard read: 'National's Plan for Fair Tax: The Racing Industry is a unique agribusiness that contributes $1.5 billion each year to the New Zealand economy, provides 18,300 full-time jobs, and exports in excess of $130 million worth of horses annually. It is that important. And, because National realises that, we are prepared to do something about it. The next National Government will put right the tax system that unfairly discriminates against Racing. NATIONAL WILL: Align racing betting duty with that paid by casinos, effectively returning $25 million back into the industry, to enable future development and investment. Allow 100% depreciation writedown of stallions over 2 years. Allow 100% depreciation writedown of broodmares aged 12 or older in the year of purchase. Develop a new consensus on Section 16 of the Racing Act so that no code is disadvantaged. Make it happen. Parliament Buildings, Wellington. www. national.org.nz.'

28 Don Brash, *Don Brash Writes* newsletter, No. 88, 25 August 2006.
29 Alan Towers, email to Judy Kirk, 26 May 2005.
30 Judy Kirk, email to Don Brash, 26 May 2005.
31 Don Brash, email to Judy Kirk, 26 May 2005.
32 Bryan Sinclair, email to Alan Towers and Judy Kirk, 8 June 2005.
33 New Zealand National Party, 'Postcard from New Zealand', June 2005.
34 'Advertising expenditure incurred by the Parliamentary Service in the three months before the 2005 General Election', Controller and Auditor-General, 6 October 2006).
35 Ibid., paragraphs 1.31, 4.43–4.48.
36 Don Brash, email to Bryan Sinclair and Steven Joyce, 27 March 2005.
37 Don Brash, email to Bryan Sinclair, Gerry Brownlee, Judy Kirk, Katherine Rich, Murray McCully, Peter Keenan, Richard Long, Steven Joyce and Tony Ryall, 18 December 2004.
38 Bryan Sinclair, email to Sandra Goudie, 2 December 2003.
39 For instance, American businessman Terry Peabody gave Brash a free journey on his corporate jet on 19 March 2004 and Tim Wallis and Peter Talley gave free helicopter use.
40 Bryan Sinclair, email to Benjamin Wilson, 2 May 2005.
41 Benjamin Wilson, email to Bryan Sinclair, 2 May 2005.
42 Electoral Act 1993, section 214B.
43 Electoral Commission, 'Guide to Election Expenses for Registered Political Parties, 1999'; cited in Andrew Geddis, 'Regulating the Funding', endnote 35.

44 Bryan Sinclair, email to Peter Keenan, 5 November 2004.

45 Bryan Sinclair, email to Don Brash, 4 September 2004.

46 Don Brash, email to Bryan Sinclair, 5 September 2004.

47 Don Brash, email to Bryan Sinclair, 21 September 2004.

48 Don Brash, email to Bryan Sinclair, 21 September 2004.

49 'Talley urges Nats to capitalise on Brash's image', Beth Catley, *Nelson Mail*, 31 May 2004.

50 Don Brash diary, 15 July 2004, 16 July 2004 and 17 July 2004.

51 Nick Davidson, 'Bold and Simple Strategy, National's missing link', 16 September 2004.

52 Bryan Sinclair, email to Don Brash, 24 September 2004.

53 Don Brash, email to Bryan Sinclair, 29 September 2004.

54 Bryan Sinclair, email to Don Brash, 29 September 2004.

55 Nick Davidson, 'Bold and Simple Strategy'.

56 Bryan Sinclair, email to Don Brash, 29 September 2004.

57 Don Brash, email to Bryan Sinclair, 29 September 2004.

58 Nick Davidson, email to Bryan Sinclair, 2 November 2004.

59 Nick Davidson, 'The repackaging of Don Brash', 19 October 2004.

60 Ibid.

61 Confidential source. If the story is correct, the money was not being given to influence the policy, which National already intended, but to help ensure the election of the party.

62 The chain of events with the insurance lobby was as follows. Brash met with Mai Chen (from the law firm Chen, Palmer and Partners) at his office on 17 August 2004 to discuss 'ACC etc' and then attended a Chen, Palmer lunch at Otto's Restaurant in Auckland later that month where Chen's client, Steven Cosgrove of QBE Insurance Limited, was listed as wanting to discuss 'Reprivatisation of ACC'. (Don Brash, appointment diaries, 17 August 2004 and 30 August 2004; guest list for 30 August 2004 dinner.) These meetings led on to Brash and MP Paul Hutchison meeting with Insurance Council CEO Chris Ryan on 13 October 2004, where they had a 'briefing on details of ACC policy meeting with Mai Chen' and to prepare for a 27 October Insurance Council meeting. At 11.30am on 27 October 2004, Brash, Murray McCully and Hutchison attended a meeting of the Insurance Council of New Zealand in Auckland. Discussions between Mai Chen, QBE Insurance and National continued in the 2005 election year, including on 28 July 2005 when Chen and QBE managing director Ross Chapman discussed 'ACC privatisation policy' with Brash and gave him a 26-page aide memoire setting out the details of how QBE believed National's privatisation of ACC should be done. (Don Brash, appointment diary, 28 July 2005; QBE Insurance (International) Ltd, 'Aide Memoire to Dr Don Brash from QBE Insurance (International) Ltd on Greater Competition in Accident Compensation Services', 27 July 2004.)

There is a history to ACC privatisation lobbying in New Zealand. ACC was privatised in 1998–9 by the National-led government following intense lobbying by a group calling itself Choice in Accident Compensation Campaign, made up of the Insurance Council, Business Roundtable and other business groups. National had campaigned on no privatisation in the 1996 election and at first the National ACC Minister dismissed the privatisation proposal as a waste of time. He said 'it would not make workplaces safer and accused the group of acting in self-interest' and that 'a privatised ACC system would... create an environment in which the Government was left to cover the "hard cases" that other companies would not insure, while those companies would reap the rewards of covering the rest' ('ACC lobby bid rejected', Jeremy Kirk, *Press*, 27 February 1996). But the lobbying eventually succeeded. When the Labour-led government reversed National's ACC privatisation in 2000, another business-funded lobby group called One Voice vigorously opposed the change ('ACC lobby group may spread wings', Graeme Peters, *Evening Post*, 14 March 2000). One Voice was co-ordinated by Catherine Judd's PR firm Awaroa Partners and included businessman Peter Shirtcliffe.

63 'Secret deal over ACC claimed', *New Zealand Herald*, 1 September 2005.

64 Richard Long, email to Don Brash, Katherine Rich, Gerry Brownlee, Murray McCully, National Communications Staff, Phil de Joux and Sarah Boyle, 31 August 2005. 'Chris Ryan Insurance Council memo to members, advising on National's ACC announcement, has been leaked to Helen Clark and is in the hands of Kevin Taylor on the *New Zealand Herald*. It will be used to further the conspiracy between National and big business. Chris advises that we should refer queries to him as it was not sent to us, to his knowledge. His letter includes the National announcement, says it is very positive, and goes on to note that "details have been deliberately withheld in agreement with the council". Further details would be negotiated if and when National came to power, he said. Chris has advised Katherine Rich. Katherine agrees with the following lines for her and Don. 'I have no idea what he is talking about. The policy is quite simple. We are allowing competition and businesses can decide whether to enter the market or not. Businesses can decide whether to go with a private insurer or go with ACC. It is a simple policy allowing competition and choice with benefits and cover prescribed by law. To questions about what is meant by deliberately withholding details, we should refer the question to the Insurance Council as it is their statement, not ours.'

65 Royal Commission on the Electoral System, *Towards a Better Democracy*, December 1986, p. 187.

66 Justice and Electoral Committee, 'Inquiry into the 2002 General Election', March 2004.

67 To test this, I contacted the ACT Party Auckland office before the 2002 election and asked how I could make an anonymous donation. A helpful woman called Christine knew the answer immediately and cheerfully explained, 'Well, there are two ways you can do that. If it's under $10,000 it doesn't have to be declared so you can just send in a cheque. If it's over $10,000, the best way to do it is to place the money with your lawyer and they can just send us a cheque saying one of their clients wanted to make a donation.' What she suggested was accurate and legal and shows that 'anonymous' donations are a routine feature of party fundraising. Christine, ACT New Zealand office, pers. comm., 1 November 2002.

68 'Elaborate money maze hid donors', Geraldine Johns, *Sunday Star-Times*, 22 April 2001.

69 Beer, Wine and Spirits Council chair Lindsay Fergusson, letters to Bill Birch, July 1990 and 30 August 1990; quoted in 'Clark renews claims of National deal for funds', Michael Rentoul, *Press*, 18 September 1993.

70 Confidential source.

71 The six-month cut-off for laying charges was chosen to remove uncertainty from election results, but giving time to enforce the laws so they are taken seriously is more important.

72 'Spending blushes are now deep red', Ruth Laugesen, *Sunday Star-Times*, 13 August 2006.

CHAPTER 16

1   This was the 'mainstream' line that Dick Allen had proposed to National eighteen months earlier.

2   'Brash on back foot over Nats' slogan', Colin Espiner, *Press*, 28 June 2005.

3   The attitude of two National advisers to Christians is seen in the following email exchange:

Matthew Hooton to Bryan Sinclair: 'To reach Christians, you go to a New Age Christian conference and "officially open" it. You talk about the importance of vibrancy in contemporary New Zealand life. You say that this means a vibrant economy, a vibrant arts scene, successful sports teams, time for family life etc etc etc and then you say – "all too often in today's busy world, we overlook the spiritual aspects of life. I do not. While I do not have the faith I had in my youth, I welcome the vibrancy of our Christian churches in today's society. Whether traditional denominations which continue to meet spiritual needs today, or the more contemporary groups which have emerged to give new life to the teachings of Christ and the word of God, never doubt my view of your importance to New Zealand life. It is wonderful to share this time with you today." We did this for Mark Blumsky as Mayor of Wellington. Mark's personal life is as unchristian as most of ours, but it worked a treat. It's all about the power of the AND not the tyranny of the OR. You make the church part of today's society rather than in opposition to it.'

Bryan Sinclair to Matthew Hooton: 'Yes, and that's what we did with John Banks. Same sort of messages you note below. Probably weighted a little more Christian in his lifestyle than Blumsky but the same positioning worked. We also had John in about 5 different churches every Sunday for 3 months in the lead up to the election! Just there, saying nothing much. But conspicuous, pressing flesh. Back in the old days of student politics, we also won most of our majorities by organising the Christian vote.'

Matthew Hooton to Bryan Sinclair: 'Fuck we're good.' (Matthew Hooton, emails to and from Bryan Sinclair, 15 December 2003.)

4   Richard Worth, email to Don Brash, 25 February 2004.

5   Ravi Masuku, email to Steven Joyce, 18 August 2005.

6   Confidential source.

7   Richard Long, email to Don Brash and Peter Keenan, 10 June 2005.

8   Don Brash, 'Morality speech', Greenlane Christian Centre, 1 July 2005. 'Bulk Funding: The removal of bulk funding caused the loss of more than $100,000 in operating income for the Elim Christian College. National believes it is school boards and principals who are most closely attuned to the needs of their school communities, and as such they should be afforded the most authority over what happens in their schools. National will move to a single grant for schools covering teacher salaries and operational costs so that school leaders can make the best decisions about the use of those funds.

Funding for Private Training Establishments: Labour has capped the funding available to private tertiary education providers. This cap has restricted the activities of Elim's Ministry Training College and English Academy. National is not concerned with the ownership of tertiary education providers and we believe Labour's caps discriminate against private training providers. We are more concerned to ensure that all providers and courses meet robust quality benchmarks.'

9   Ibid.

10 'Rhema Broadcasting Group History', Radio Rhema, www.rhema.co.nz.

11 'Christians cast into wilderness', Tim Hume, *Sunday Star-Times*, 18 September 2005.

12 Brash spoke to the Getsmart conference at 7.15pm on 14 July 2005.

13 Bryan Sinclair, email to Anne Small and Vanessa Rawson, 14 July 2005.

14 Bryan Sinclair, email to Caleb Standen, 15 July 2005.

15 Ibid.

16 Caleb Standen, email to Bryan Sinclair, 16 July 2005.

17 Bryan Sinclair, email to Don Brash, 16 July 2005.

18 Don Brash, email to Bryan Sinclair, 17 July 2005.

19 Don Brash, interviewed by Jane Patterson, Radio New Zealand *Morning Report*, 13 July 2005.

20 Don Brash, interviewed by Duncan Garner, *TV3 News*, 19 July 2005.

21 Richard Long, email to Anita Ferguson and Jason Ede, 21 July 2005.

22 Brash admitted in 2006 that a father and son team worked at the party headquarters to organise party volunteers to help get the National Party voters to the polling booths on election day. (This 'voter mobilisation' had been identified as an important element in Bush's 2004 presidential victory.)

23 Richard Long, email to Anita Ferguson and Jason Ede, 21 July 2005, ibid.

24 National had been receiving strategy advice from the old Republican adviser, Dick Allen, since February 2004. Also, in November 2004 when National was worrying about its election funding, top US Republican fundraiser and election strategist Jack Oliver visited the party. John (Jack) Oliver III had been invited to work on George W. Bush's presidential campaign by Bush's strategist Karl Rove in 1999 and made his name as the person who broke all previous presidential fundraising records, raising $99 million dollars as national finance director. He raised even more for the Bush–Cheney 2004 campaign, becoming an expert in corporate funding of elections. Three weeks after Bush's 2004 victory he was in Wellington helping the National Party. Some details of his New Zealand visit are recorded in Brash's appointment diary for Thursday 25 November 2004. Brash's 10am meeting with Oliver was held in the Leader's Lounge at Parliament and had been organised by Steven Joyce. Joyce, president Judy Kirk, Richard Long and Peter Keenan were also present at the meeting. The diary entry read:
'Thursday, 25 November 2004 RECESS 10:00 – 11:00 Meeting with Jack Oliver, US Republican Strategist – Leader's Lounge. Contact: Sally Mitchell [US embassy]. Suggested by Craig Heatley; organised by Steven Joyce. Also attending: Steven Joyce, Judy Kirk, Richard Long, Peter Keenan. US Ambassador, Charles Swindells, may attend.'
This shows who had been part of arranging Oliver's visit. The visit had been 'suggested by Craig Heatley' and – strangely for a meeting with a fundraiser/strategist – it says that the American ambassador was possibly attending. It would not be surprising that this was another type of assistance Heatley was giving to the National Party, but it is hard to see how or why it was legitimate for the ambassador to be invited to such a meeting.

25 Don Brash, email to Murray McCully, Gerry Brownlee, Richard Long, Peter Keenan, Bryan Sinclair and Steven Joyce, 20 July 2004. This email was quoted in Parliament by MP Winston Peters.

26 Bryan Sinclair, email to Don Brash, 12 August 2004.

27 Richard Long, email to Steven Joyce, Don Brash, Anita Ferguson and Murray McCully, 22 July 2005. 'Anita; Can you plse onpass to Don. Steven: can you plse call Julian. Diana McCarthy called from the USA and said Julian had been getting

quite a few calls but wanted to keep a low profile unless Don thought he needed to say something. She will talk to Steven Joyce. Her contact details are....'

28 Steven Joyce, email to Don Brash, Gerry Brownlee, Tony Ryall, Bill English, Judith Collins, John Key and Murray McCully, 5 April 2005. 'Hello all, I had prepared some notes for our discussion at the Key Spokespeople meeting last week; and Don agreed I distribute them to you ahead of tonight's meeting, by way of re-cap. They are not minutes; just a note on the campaign strategy (obviously not for wider distribution at this point). It was agreed at the meeting that Bill would do the co-ordination function to ensure a concerted "team" attack on Labour.' The notes read: 'Campaign Strategy 2005: Maximise our vote in a declining economic environment, by attacking Labour aggressively and laying out our own agenda. In doing so, force Labour back as close as possible to a September date, to ensure the best environment for us to achieve best result. Tactics: Lift our attacks on their mis-management. Bring the examples together and sheet them home to Labour and Clark. Key attack themes: Treaty (Seabed and Foreshore, ongoing race-based discrimination, treaty settlement process); Social Welfare (huge increase in numbers on sickness and invalids benefits); Education – (Te Wananga and NCEA); Health – huge increase in spend and declining output, vaccines; Law and Order – Police (111 calls and unassigned cases). Tax: huge tax take squandered, WFF and high effective marginal tax rates; Increased gap in after-tax wages between NZ and Aust ($5000-nearly $9000 from 99 to 04); Real after tax house hold incomes have not grown 99-04. This must be a priority over the next six weeks. Nail them for doing nothing to prolong and enhance good times into the future (also over the next six weeks). Adding costs to businesses. Not removing impediments to growth (RMA, Roading, general infrastructure); Not giving incentives for people to work hard and get ahead (tax, education, welfare); Lay out our own agenda for sustained economic growth. Some of this will be front-loaded to increase momentum and help force Labour back (eg youth justice, roading, education, DOC sites). All three parts of the strategy will be backed up and reinforced by strong advertising – most of it commencing ten days after the budget and starting by reinforcing the image of Labour's squandering and mis-managing.'

29 Steven Joyce, email to Richard Long, Peter Keenan, Murray McCully and Tony Ryall, 16 May 2005.

30 Richard Long, email to National Communications Staff and Peter Keenan, 15 August 2005.

31 Richard Long, email to Kevin Taylor, 16 June 2005.

32 Richard Long, email to Don Brash and National Communications Staff, 17 June 2005.

33 Jason Ede, email to National Communications Staff and Vanessa Rawson, 24 June 2005.

34 Steven Joyce, email to Murray McCully, Richard Long and Don Brash, 10 August 2005; Steven Joyce, 'What this election is All About', 9 August 2005: 'This election is about who has the guts to tackle the issues of mainstream New Zealanders that have been ignored and neglected for too long. After six years of Labour's PC social engineering, its time to restore for ordinary New Zealanders the right incentives to work hard and to get ahead, for the benefit of their families and their country. It is about providing the right incentives in the tax system, in education, and in the welfare system so that our children and grandchildren don't feel the need to move to Australia to have a decent life. Don Brash and National will tackle declining education standards by introducing stricter maths and English standards and holding schools accountable for them. It's about exams not excuses. We will reduce welfare dependency

by requiring work for the dole. It's about providing a safety net, not a drift net. We will reward hard work and initiative by cutting personal taxes for mainstream New Zealanders and their families. Don Brash and National will reverse New Zealand's drift to racial separatism, by ensuring one law for all and basing policy on need not race. It's about Kiwi, not just iwi. We will come down hard on career criminals by abolishing parole for all violent and repeat offending. It's about doing the whole time if you do crime. Don Brash and National will rein in a Labour spending machine that has collected most of the economic growth of the past six years in tax and then wasted your hard-earned tax dollars. These issues are not only important now, but they are important for the long-term future of New Zealand and its people. This election is the last chance for three years for mainstream New Zealanders to say to Clark, Cullen and Labour that's enough – it's our turn. It is the last chance to vote for a Party and a Leader that has the proven ability, the detailed policies, and the guts, to tackle the issues that matter. That Party is National, the Leader is Don Brash. On September 17, give your Party Vote to National.'

35 Richard Long, email to National Communications Staff, Phil de Joux and Sarah Boyle, 10 August 2005.

36 New Zealand National Party, direct mail letter 'It's time for a government that will tackle the issues of mainstream New Zealanders', September 2005.

37 Public discussion of journalism usually revolves around the idea of objectivity, where journalists are supposedly neutral purveyors of news without opinions or biases of their own. In reality, some journalists do appear to be without opinions or biases of their own, but they are not usually the best journalists. A more realistic approach is to accept that there is nothing wrong with journalists having personal political beliefs and biases as long as they are aware of them and still do a professional job, including fairness, accuracy and avoiding conflicts of interest.

38 Richard Long, email to Bryan Sinclair, Peter Keenan, John Key, Murray McCully and Don Brash, 21 July 2005.

39 Bryan Sinclair, email to Richard Long, Peter Keenan, John Key, Murray McCully and Don Brash, 21 July 2005.

40 Richard Long, email to Richard Harman, 25 May 2004.

41 Murray McCully, email to Richard Long, 25 May 2004.

42 Richard Harman, email to Richard Long, 26 May 2004.

43 Richard Long, email to Barrie Saunders, 21 March 2005, forwarded to Murray McCully.

44 Bryan Sinclair, email to Don Brash, 22 March 2005.

45 Bryan Sinclair, email to Anna Tripp, Anne Small and Vanessa Rawson, 10 August 2005.

46 The junior staff member who wrote this, has not been named for privacy reasons. Email, 26 August 2004.

47 Richard Long provided the following analysis of Mark Textor's latest focus group research on 9 August 2005.

'Election State of Play 5 weeks out: Soft and swinging voters are, yes, aware the NZ election campaign has started, but are not yet engaged. They are not engaged because while several entertaining issues and themes of interest have arisen in recent weeks, such as the speeding motorcade, and the nuclear debate, and Iraq, soft voters are still desperately awaiting for the campaign to focus on "the real issues". While they are aware the election, in Don Brash's view, should be about who has the guts to tackle the issues affecting the mainstream, they see BOTH major leaders being distracted. They explicitly expect and desire (and have seen in the past) Brash talk about it being time to restore a focus on the hopes and aspirations of ordinary New Zealanders such as providing the right incentives to work hard and get ahead for the benefit of ordinary families and the nation as a whole. However, they simply do not see Don Brash's advertising on these issues being backed up by consistent day to day policy releases or communications. In other words the Nationals are not meeting the positive expectations their paid advertising has built. While they understand there have been distractions caused by Labour, they figure that if Don Brash wants to run a campaign based on a willingness and, most importantly, an ability to tackle the issues of the mainstream, if he can't do that now, in the heat of the campaign, how can he do it in Government? In other words they are prejudiced against politicians who are unwilling or incapable of putting issues in context and who are unable to cut through with their issues. As one voter said "he's on the defensive the whole time, just because Labour has been attacking them, which is bad. Given the issues we have been discussing it's THEY (the Nationals) who should be on front foot (given the issues I'm concerned about)." Further, the billboards and other advertising, including mail, while generating support, are creating an expectation and a genuine desire for more information? which puts the onus back onto National to follow up on "these issues" and not on others. "We read the message but then there is nothing more substantial behind it." "Brash gets on to something good like that (tax) but then they go off on nuclear." The true "ownable" position is in National communicating that only they have the right incentives in the tax system, the welfare system and in education, so that our children and grand children do not feel the need to move to Australia to have a decent life. In short, again, they wonder if Don Brash can't stick to this message in a campaign, in a credible way, how can he do it in Government? Generally voters expect the "side issue" to be deal with competently (rather than ignored) but for a political leader to then show a willingness and ability to consistently put that answer and position in the broader context of why other issues are even more important.' (Richard Long, email to Murray McCully, Steven Joyce and Mark Textor, 9 August 2005.)

48 'Big and bold but will it be enough?', Tracy Watkins, *Dominion Post*, 23 August 2005.

49 Peter Keenan, email to Don Brash, Murray McCully, Steven Joyce and John Key, 14 August 2005.

50 The rationale for tax cuts had been argued out in the strategy discussions at the end of 2004. Jason Ede had pointed out, as they prepared a speech on tax for Brash, that subjects like 'Vouchers for an increasingly privatised education/healthcare sector' were 'issues for another day'. He reminded his colleagues that there were 'a lot of things we're not telling people'. (Jason Ede, email to Peter Keenan, Murray McCully and Richard Long, 7 December 2004.)

At the end of July 2005 they still had not agreed on a tax policy. When Brash, Keenan, John Key, Murray McCully and Bill English met to discuss the policy at 8pm on 26 July, they were still considering three different tax scale options prepared by National researcher Simon Hay (see below). Three days later, Richard Long sent an urgent email to the strategy team when he heard that Brash had proposed during a radio talkback interview changing the policy further. 'Don said on Leighton Smith 10 mins ago that we may well look at changing our tax policy in the light of Labour's student loan proposals,' he said. He proposed the following lines to 'explain' Brash's suggestion: 'Don was saying that obviously Labour's proposals are being carefully analysed and costed, but by any measurement they are fiscally irresponsible and completely unsustainable and it is highly unlikely that our tax policy, which is fiscally responsible, will be changed in any way.' (Richard Long, email to Murray McCully, Steven Joyce, Peter Keenan, Jason Ede and John Key, 29 July 2005.)

Two weeks after that, on 14 August, the policy had still not been finalised and the campaign strategy team was considering changing it again. Peter Keenan explained the thinking: 'Following the indications that the PREFU [Pre-Election Economic and Fiscal Update] may indicate more fiscal headroom than currently understood, and in light of the horror week or two that we have had, leading to a slip in the polls, the suggestion was that we might consider making the tax cuts even larger.' Keenan said that Key had asked Simon Hay 'to look at dropping the 19% band to 18%: that adds another $1.44 a week by 20k to $7.79/week, another $3.40 by 30k to $13.56/week, another $5.30 by 40k to $23.94'. But Keenan did not agree with the plan. He said 'this all costs about another $360m' and that it would 'push an already heavily massaged fiscal impulse back up to the limits of credibility'. On the political side, 'both John and I feel that we have already got a pretty attractive package, delivering plenty into middle New Zealand'. He explained: 'The most important point is this: as the polls are indicating we are well ahead with male voters (the ones that rate tax cuts the most highly), but once again very weak with female voters (who rate health and education higher, and are more responsive to the softer issues generally, and who are clearly sensitive to Iraq/Washington scare stories).

'Our focus should be on the constituencies that we don't yet have adequate support from – women and the elderly – and not on the tax cut sensitive group, which will be voting National already. I don't think the extra few dollars at the lower end will make much difference to voting patterns, but the scare stories about fiscal stimulus and interest rates might.... If we can take the pressure off our spending cut story, then it is an easier job politically.'

This view was not heeded. The final tax policy did not lower the 19% rate to 18% as had been proposed, but it provided larger tax cuts for middle income people than any of the proposals to date, extending the 19% tax rate to include all people earning up to $50,000.

The Simon Hay 'Tax Package' report of 26 July 2005 explains more of the thinking behind the tax plans: 'This note outlines two alternative tax packages, designed to give greater increases in disposable income in the lower income range than does the current proposition. That package, if you recall, was designed with a family tax element in mind: that, however, was dropped, leaving a tax design that really only took effect from over $40,000. These two alternate packages deliver about $10 per week and rising from around $30,000. Both involve dropping the bottom statutory rate of 19.5%, to 18.0%. The effective rates at the low end (with now smaller LIR, abating at 1%) become 15% and 19% (currently 15% and 21%).

Option 1 focuses on reducing tax rates.

The mid (33% down to 30%) and top (39% to 36%) rates are reduced, with small shifts in thresholds. This package delivers more than option 2 in the 60–75k range, and substantially more (and rising – due to a top 36% rate) above $120k. We would have to deal with the presentational problem of the $1 million dollar income ($30k tax cut).

Option 2 focuses on moving thresholds.

Because rates are not reduced, thresholds can be moved out further. Moving out the lower thresholds further than in Option 1 (to 11K rather than 10K) allows a small $40/year margin of option 2 over 1, between about $15–40k. Because the threshold for the 19% rate is pushed out, this package delivers more between about

$41–55k (up to $450 per year); less between $60–80K; more between $80–120k; then progressively less as income rises, due to the higher top marginal rate.

Tax package (fully rolled out on 1 Apr-08)

Option (1) Rates	Option (2)Thresholds
15% 0–10,000	15% 0–11,000
19% 10,000–40,000	19% 11,000–44,000
30% 40,000–70,000	33% 44–100,000
36% 70,000+	39% 100,000+

Previous option (for comparison)	Labour (for comparison)
15% 0–12,500	15% 0–10,081
21% 12,500–50,000	21% 10,081–40,324
33% 50,000–100,000	33% 40–324-63,672
39% 100,000+	39% 63,672+'

51 Richard Long, email to Don Brash, Anita Ferguson, Murray McCully and Bryan Sinclair, 28 August 2005.
52 'Nats in sense of humour shock', *AdMedia*, September 2005.
53 Don Brash, 'We Are All New Zealanders' speech, 29 August 2005.
54 Dick Allen, email to Don Brash, 15 August 2005; Doug Watt, email to Don Brash, 11 August 2005; Bryan Sinclair, email to Doug Watt, 12 August 2005.
55 Don Brash, 'A new government and a new direction', Address to the National Party 2005 Campaign Opening, Sky City Casino, Auckland, 21 August 2005.
56 Don Brash, Address to the National Party Southern Regional Conference, 14 May 2005.
57 'Remarkable rise of Don Brash', *New Zealand Herald*, 23 July 2005.
58 'How ACT helped Brash take over', Ruth Laugesen, *Sunday Star-Times*, 28 August 2005.
59 Richard Long, email to Don Brash, Anita Ferguson, Murray McCully and Bryan Sinclair, 28 August 2005.
60 Ibid.
61 Brent Webling, email to National MPs, National Secretaries, National Communications Staff and National Research and Advisory Unit, 28 August 2005.
62 Peter Keenan, email to Don Brash, Murray McCully, Anita Ferguson and Bryan Sinclair, 28 August 2005.
63 '7 days to go', *Dominion Post*, 10 September 2005.
64 'National survives Brethren fiasco', Helen Bain, *Sunday Star-Times*, 11 September 2005.
65 'Nats vow to cut petrol prices', Kim Ruscoe, *Dominion Post*, 13 September 2005.
66 'National 6 points in front', Tracy Watkins, *Dominion Post*, 14 September 2005.
67 Don Brash , 'National's First Ten Tasks', speech at the Akarana Yacht Club, Okahu Bay, Auckland, 15 September 2005.
68 Peta Bamber, email to National MPs and National Staff All, 15 September 2005.

EPILOGUE
1   Ruth Richardson, email to Greg Lindsay, Centre for Independent Studies, 1 October 2005.
2   Ruth Richardson, email to Bryan Sinclair, 1 October 2005.

3   'Brash refuses to concede defeat, considers future', Ruth Berry, *New Zealand Herald*, 19 September 2005.

4   'Curtains for Don?', Ruth Laugesen, *Sunday Star-Times*, 16 October 2005.

5   Ibid.

6   Richard Long, email to National Communications Staff, Gerry Brownlee, Simon Power, National MPs and National Secretaries, 19 September 2005.

7   Brash told the National Party staff that 'Richard Long decided not to renew his contract'. Don Brash, email to all National Staff, 1 November 2005.

8   On Sunday 8 January 2006 Rodney Hide posted a photograph on his website www. rodneyhide.com of he and Brash doing dishes together, with the caption 'Holidaying in Greymouth – Who says ACT and National can't work together?'.

9   Confidential sources.

10 'Brash keen to lead Nats into next election', Colin Espiner, *Press*, 19 January 2006.

11 John Ansell presented the plans to National's 22 March 2006 board meeting, where they were well received, and then on 4 March to the weekly National caucus meeting. Steven Joyce's replacement as party general manager, Greg Sheehan, had worked with Ansell on the proposal.

12 Confidential sources.

13 New Zealand National Party, 'Guts' advertisement, *Taupo Times*, 10 August 2006.

14 'Brash ultimately to blame for disaster', Matthew Hooton, *Sunday Star-Times*, 17 September 2006.

15 'Closer to home', Chris Trotter, *Independent*, 29 March 2006.

16 'Wizard's back to stir Right's foul brew', Chris Trotter, *Sunday Star-Times*, 17 September 2006. These personal attack tactics are same in origin and purpose as the anti-political correctness campaigning. Neither require the people on the attack to talk about their own vision and policies, or to debate the benefits of their beliefs over those of their opponents.

17 'Brash calls for core New Zealand values', Haydon Dewes and Rebecca Palmer, *Dominion Post*, 29 July 2006.

18 Remarkably, after all the trouble, Don Brash met Exclusive Brethren representatives again after the election and before Christmas 2005. He finally announced he was severing links with them after the private investigator revelations in September 2006.

19 'Key protagonists deny National leadership tensions', *New Zealand Herald*, 4 February 2006.

20 Ibid. He said, 'There is a 21-year age differential between us and, like all political parties, of course, one day a long time into the future there will be a change. Whether I'm a serious contender those many, many years down the track when it happens, who knows?'

21 'National MPs deny leadership plot against Brash', Tracy Watkins, *Dominion Post*, 3 February 2006.

22 'Key Man', Virginia Larson, *North and South*, March 2006.

23 'Marketing ploy or the real McCoy?', Colin James, *New Zealand Herald*, 23 September 2006.

24 Richard Prebble, *The Letter*, ACT New Zealand, 19 September 2005.

25 Roderick Deane, letter to John Key, 14 March 2005.

26 'Honest Don is beginning to look more like Mr Magoo', Richard Long, *Dominion Post*, 19 September 2006. Key was said elsewhere to have persuaded Brash to soften the party's policies in late 2004/early 2005 on superannuation, annual leave and tax

cuts. These were inoculations and an 'election winning' sloshing around of funds – all 'excruciating' ideological compromises – proposed and decided by the campaign strategy team. But that is how myths are made.

27 John Key, address to the National Party annual conference, Christchurch, 21-23 July 206.

28 'The hidden rifts within the National Party', Chris Trotter, *Independent*, 2 August 2006.

29 'Brash rates himself', Don Brash interview with Peter Luke, *Press*, 22 July 2006.

30 'Brash vents anger over "lousy scum" ', Haydon Dewes, *Dominion Post*, 23 September 2006.

31 'Clark plans new law to block Brethren', Audrey Young, *New Zealand Herald*, 12 September 206.

32 'Oh Brother', Anthony Hubbard, *Sunday Star-Times* , 24 September 2006.

APPENDIX

24 May 2005

URGENT, IMPORTANT & STRICTLY CONFIDENTIAL

Good afternoon Don and John,

Doug Watt and myself enjoyed your presentation this morning at Millennium Hotel. However as backers of the recent 'Wake Up NZ' campaign ($350,000) and as responsible for a very extensive election campaign ($1,000,000) with the sole goal of "Getting Party Votes for National" a meeting following on from our one last week with Steven Joyce is important.

Basically, we believe marketing is the name of the game. Whilst the meeting this morning was excellent it would not have got one extra vote for National. (Everyone there is going to vote National anyway). Getting the message out and to a younger age bracket is paramount.

We believe time is of the essence. Our campaign (a total of seven nationally distributed flyers) is direct and simple:-

It creates and demonstrates MISTRUST in the current Government.
It builds TRUST in a DON BRASH led National Government.

We need a meeting at your earliest convenience anywhere in New Zealand. I'm best contacted at Ph: 03 313 6525 or Fax: 03 313 6064 and am essentially working on our/your election campaign full time.

Regards

Ron Hickmott

Exclusive Brethren 24 May 2005 letter to Don Brash and John Key

A NEW AND RESPONSIBLE GOVERNMENT WILL...

- Make **sustainability** foremost in environmental policy.
- **Link economic and environmental success together** – a great environment can only be enhanced with a strong economy.
- Eliminate **bureaucratic wastage** and the squandering of precious resources within DOC.
- **Save the Kiwi** through effective predator control.
- Establish new **marine reserves**.
- Abandon plans to **land grab** South Island farms.

A true green Government will have a balanced commitment to the environment without the inclusion of the economic, social, health and security policies of the **GREENS** that would **ruin New Zealand**.

USE YOUR PARTY VOTE TO CHANGE THE GOVERNMENT

AUTHORISED BY STEPHEN WIN, FAVONA ROAD, MANGERE.

BEWARE!

The GREEN Delusion

There is nothing wrong with protecting the environment, BUT there is a *whole lot* wrong with the GREENS socialist policies.

The GREENS Policies

TAXES AND THE ECONOMY
- Introduce **capital gains tax** on **family homes**.
- Increase petrol and diesel taxes – diesel prices would go up 30%!
- Introduce carbon tax, putting power prices up by a further 10%.
- Support Kyoto protocol – the one billion dollar bungle.
- Add 4 new Government ministries, 6 agencies and 5 commissions – more **bureaucrats** including a resident artist.

SECURITY / LAW AND ORDER
- Cut defence spending by 50% and disarm our forces.
- Ban the building of new prisons and teach criminals "art".

ROADS
- Spend roading money on uneconomic and novel public transport schemes.
- Block construction of vital new roads with tortuous RMA regulations.

FARMS
- Push high country farmers off their lease-hold land.
- Permit the right-to-roam over private property.

SOCIETY
- Decriminalise illegal drugs like cannabis (marijuana).
- Offer financial assistance to cannabis growers for alternative employment.
- Create "rainbow" communities. Legalise adoption for same-sex couples.

Sources: www.greens.org.nz (July 2005), N.Z.I.E.R. to Treasury (April 2005).

The GREENS Credentials

SELF INTEREST
- Jeanette Fitzsimons is pushing for a coalition with the LABOUR PARTY. Yet LABOUR has culpably neglected our environment.

Consider these facts:
  - Kiwi numbers in serious decline due to ineffective predator control.
  - 77% of native species in decline.
  - 1080 operations have wiped out birdsong in many areas.
  - Millions of hectares of DOC controlled land going to ruin.
  - No possum and stoat control on 85% of South Island estate.

Despite this, the GREENS are posing hand in hand with LABOUR! This confirms the long held suspicion that the GREENS are only *superficially* GREEN.

FAILED IDEOLOGY
- The GREENS have an agenda reminiscent of failed **communist** and **socialist** ideologies. For instance, when Parliament legislated to protect private property rights, the GREENS voted **against** it!
- Tasmania's experiment with a LABOR/GREEN Government was a disaster. They now declare – "never again".

DON'T FORGET ... a failed economy can't afford to spend anything on protecting the environment.

The GREENS dreams are economically unsustainable & socially destructive. The policies of the GREENS are downright dangerous.

Exclusive Brethren 2005 election pamphlet: Beware!

WHAT POLICIES ARE YOU *REALLY* SUPPORTING?

The Howard Government is committed to our Environment.

- $1.1 Billion Dollars allocated to the environment for 2004 - 2005. This is almost triple what the previous Government allocated.
- $400 Million Dollars more than estimates expenditure in 2003 - 2004.
- $300 Million Dollars allocated to the Natural Heritage Trust.
- $463.6 Million Dollars allocated for climate change programmes.

This is a responsible and balanced commitment to the environment without the inclusion of the economic, social, health and security policies of The Greens that would ruin Australia.

Authorised by M. William Mackenzie 11 Baden Powell Place North Rocks NSW 2151
Printed by Woolston Printing, 111 Elizabeth Street, Launceston Tas 7250

BEWARE!

The GREEN Delusion

There is nothing wrong with protecting the environment, BUT there is a *whole lot* wrong with the GREENS socialist policies.

The GREENS Policies
See for yourself on the GREENS web site www.greens.org.au

Taxes & the Economy *
- Introduce gift & inheritance taxes (incl. family home).
- Increase company tax (from 30% to 49%).
- Increase Medicare levy and remove the 30% Private Health Care Rebate.

Drugs *
- Decriminalise illegal drugs like cannabis (marijuana).
- "Pilot programs" to test the effectiveness of controlled availability of heroin.
- "Controlled availability" of cannabis at appropriate venues.
- "Investigations of options" for the regulated supply of social drugs such as ecstasy.

National Security *
- Advocate a non-violent civil defence force to protect us from terrorists.
- Open our borders to all-comers & no asylum seeker to be detained for more than 14 days (even if they're shown not to be refugees):

Society *
- Reduce the population of Australia by 2 million.
- Ban the building of new jails and introduce voting rights for *all* criminals.
- Unconditional dole payments for all.
- Legalise same-sex marriages.

The GREENS Credentials

Self Interest
- Bob Brown says he will support whichever party's policies on the environment are better. However, despite unprecedented funding for the environment by the Howard Government, Bob Brown strikes a preference deal with Labor. This confirms the long held suspicion that the GREENS are only *superficially* GREEN.

Failed Ideology
- The GREENS are a broad-based party with an agenda reminiscent of *failed communist & socialist ideologies.*
- The GREENS have put their own self-interest *well ahead* of any concern for the environment.

DON'T FORGET
A failed economy can't afford to spend anything on protecting the environment.

The GREENS dreams are economically unsustainable & socially destructive.
The policies of the GREENS are downright dangerous.

Exclusive Brethren 2004 Tasmanian election pamphlet: Beware!

Exclusive Brethren 2005 election pamphlet: Beware!
(small version, front)

The GREEN Delusion

BEWARE OF THESE GREEN PARTY POLICIES

- ## Capital gains tax on family homes
  (NZIER to Treasury – April 2005)

- ## Halve defence spending
  (Keith Locke – news release June 1999)

- ## Teach criminals "art"
  (www.greens.org.nz – Justice Policy)

- ## Decriminalise cannabis
  (Misuse of Drugs [Cannabis Infringement] Amendment Bill)

It's time to change the Government

Exclusive Brethren 2005 election pamphlet: Beware!
(small version, back)

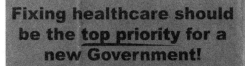

Exclusive Brethren 2005 election pamphlet: Healthcare, who cares?

HEALTHCARE

who cares?

LABOUR'S UNCARING LEGACY

180,672 people now on waiting lists.

119,935 of these can't even get to see a specialist.

1,152 people died in 2004, while waiting for essential treatment.

3,554 people gave up waiting for treatment and went private.

Millions of dollars spent on painkillers for those waiting.

THE GOOD NEWS IS...

 67,000 extra operations could be done next year.

A GOVERNMENT THAT REALLY CARES FOR **YOU** WILL...

- Stop people dying while waiting for surgery.
- Cap waiting times.
- Tap into the huge unused private hospital capacity.
- Stop wasting money on endless paperwork and bureaucracy.
- Lower private insurance costs.
- Eliminate unacceptable waiting lists.

An effective new Government will have the financial management credentials and the ideas to solve the waiting list crisis – and still cut taxes.

CHANGE THE GOVERNMENT TO ONE THAT CARES. USE YOUR PARTY VOTE ✓

Distributed by: N.Z.A.T.H – New Zealand Advocates for Timely Healthcare.
Authorised by: J. Hawkins, 3 Brant Place, Christchurch.

Exclusive Brethren 2005 election pamphlet: Healthcare (Small version)

ARE YOU REALLY SAFE?

How do you feel about Labour's security policies?

Violent crime **is** increasing and we have a serious shortage of frontline police.	**INCREASED CRIME**	**1200 crims out early** Statistics show at least 1200 dangerous criminals will be released **early** over the next 3 years and **most** will re-offend.
$4 million for victims This was the pitiful amount allocated for victim support last year.	**UNFAIR FUNDING**	**$84 million for legal aid** Overall cash spent on legal aid and related schemes now stands at $84 million per year.
395,912 speeding tickets were issued last year. A staggering 188% increase on the year 2000 when there was 137,427.	**WRONG PRIORITIES**	**Up to 100,000 requests** for police help are cancelled each year, including many emergency calls.
Severe reduction of the nation's defence capability has exposed our country to significant risk.	**NEGLECTED DEFENCE**	**Axed airforce** strike wing demonstrates a lack of responsible commitment to regional and national security.

Sources: Government websites including Justice, Corrections, Parole Board and Legal Services Agency. Also Victim Support, Sensible Sentencing Trust and the Police Association websites.

IT'S TIME FOR A CHANGE
Choose a Government that will...

✓ Restore a sense of security to the people
✓ Make violent criminals do the whole time
✓ Increase frontline police numbers
✓ Rebuild confidence in the 111 system
✓ Provide resources for quick response times
✓ Establish a response unit for bio-security emergencies
✓ Take defence issues seriously and re-equip the forces
✓ Boost the morale and protection of our troops

ESTABLISH YOUR RIGHT TO BE SAFE

ELECT A GOVERNMENT THAT TAKES THE SECURITY OF ITS CITIZENS SERIOUSLY.

CHANGE THE GOVERNMENT WITH YOUR PARTY VOTE

Authorised by: M. Powell, 30 Stephen Lysnar Place, MT ROSKILL.

Exclusive Brethren 2005 election pamphlet: Are you really safe?

Exclusive Brethren 2005 election pamphlet: Watch the All Black action (front)

Make your choice!

use your money your way...

...flytoaussieforeverygamebuyanewcaranewkitchen
saveforthekidseducationdineouttwiceaweek
shoutyourselfsomenewclothesnewappliances
payoffthemortgagebuildyourownnesteggtraveltheworld
caribbeancruisemaybedonatetoacharityofyourchoice
flytoaussieforeverygamebuyanewcaranewkitchen
saveforthekidseducationdineouttwiceaweek
shoutyourselfsomenewclothesnewappliances
payoffthemortgagebuildyourownnesteggtraveltheworld
caribbeancruisemaybedonatetoacharityofyourchoice
flytoaussieforeverygamebuyanewcaranewkitchen
saveforthekidseducationdineouttwiceaweek
payoffthemortgagebuildyourownnesteggtraveltheworld
caribbeancruisemaybedonatetoacharityofyourchoice
flytoaussieforeverygamebuyanewcaranewkitchen...

It's your choice – it's your money!

30% of your personal tax money is needlessly swelling the Government coffers.

TAX CUTS – YES!

USE YOUR PARTY VOTE TO CHANGE THE GOVERNMENT

Authorised by: M. Powell, 30 Stephen Lysnar Place, MT ROSKILL.

Exclusive Brethren 2005 election pamphlet: Watch the All Black action (back)

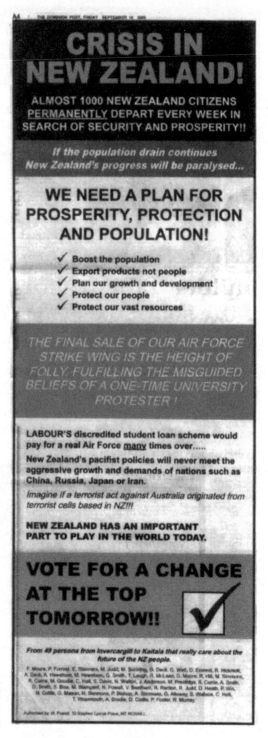

Exclusive Brethren 2005 election pamphlet: Crisis in New Zealand – vote for a change at the top (newspaper ad)

Remember...

Every year thousands of New Zealanders leave for a better life in Australia!

Who can you trust with New Zealands future?

We live in <u>critical</u> times. It is not the time for destroying the family unit and stifling the economy.

What has Labour really done for <u>you</u> in the last 6 years?

It's time for a trustworthy alternative.

USE YOUR PARTY VOTE to CHANGE THE GOVERNMENT!

Authorised by: S.A. Smith, Queens Road, New Plymouth.

Who has the foresight and the credentials to bring prosperity to New Zealand?

...and has the integrity and vision to lead our great country forward?

A NEW LEADER with integrity is <u>urgently</u> needed if New Zealand is to move forward and prosper!

LOW TAX – HIGH GROWTH

- Lower taxes will return money to **hard-working** Kiwi battlers where it belongs.
- Without the restraining shackles of over-taxation, our economy will **boom** – this means more jobs and higher incomes for us all.

CURE THE HEALTH SYSTEM

- A new Government that **really** cares will have a strategy to provide New Zealanders with world-class healthcare.
- **Waiting lists** must be slashed to minimise unnecessary suffering and prevent needless deaths.

EDUCATION

- A new Government must ensure our kids learn to read, write and count before anything else.
- **Excellence** in education will only return when action is taken to fix the NCEA system.
- Social engineering and politically correct nonsense has no place in our classrooms. It has to go!

SECURITY / LAW AND ORDER

- Threats to our nation are **real**. A responsible Government would take terrorism and defence issues seriously.
- Increased Defence Force numbers will provide new **opportunities** and greater discipline for our young people.
- Decent law-abiding citizens will feel safer when violent criminals are locked away for their entire sentence.

ROADING / INFRASTRUCTURE

- Congested roads and an over-loaded infrastructure are strangling our economy and holding us back.
- Choose a new leadership team that has the courage to spend roading money on roads and plan for growth and success.

THE FUTURE

- With gross foreign debt at $152 billion our economy has been placed at serious risk.
- **Only a strong and carefully managed economy will enable families to plan for the future with confidence.**

THE ONLY WAY TO GET AHEAD IS TO CHANGE THE GOVERNMENT.
Lower taxes, no healthcare waiting lists – lets go for it!

Exclusive Brethren 2005 election pamphlet: A new leader with integrity is urgently needed

Racing lobby 2005 election magazine ad

INDEX

ABOUT THE AUTHOR

Nicky Hager began investigative writing in the early 1990s, leading to his 1996 book on New Zealand's part in a US intelligence network called Echelon. One of his articles on that subject won a US journalism award in 1998 and resulted in a year-long European Parliament inquiry. Since then his books, contributions to books and articles have been published in many countries and his work has been reported in hundreds of news stories around the world. In 2002 he was invited to be the New Zealand representative of the Washington-based International Consortium of Investigative Journalists. His 1999 book *Secrets and Lies* exposed an unscrupulous PR campaign run by the state logging company Timberlands West Coast; and his 2002 book *Seeds of Distrust* investigated Labour Govrnment political management of the controversial genetic engineering issue. He has degrees in physics and philosophy and lives in Wellington.